[APPLIED] FOREIGN AFFAIRS

Investigating spatial phenomena in rural and urban Sub-Saharan Africa

edited by Baerbel Mueller

Birkhäuser
Basel

GUABULIGA—WELL BY THE THORN TREE
NORTHERN REGION, GHANA

ON OTHER PLANNING

GUABULIGA — WELL BY THE THORN TREE, NORTHERN REGION, GHANA
ON OTHER PLANNING

AFRICA / GHANA / NORTHERN REGION / GUABULIGA

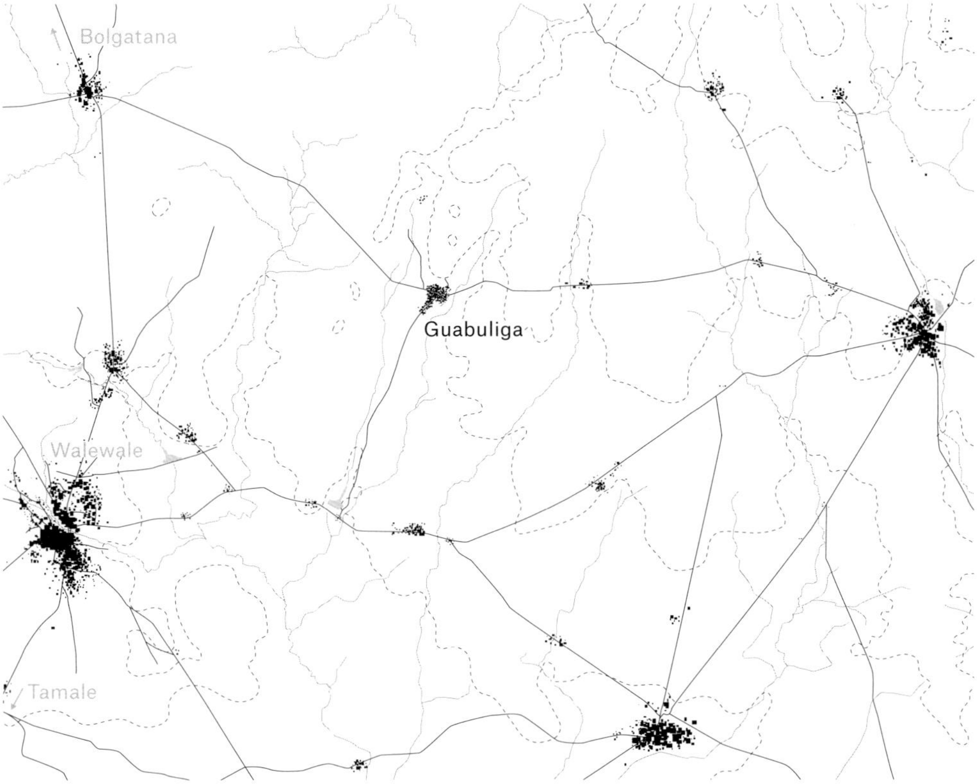

GUABULIGA

Coordinates:	10° 24′ 54.079″ N 00° 41′ 50.899″ W
Population:	2,408 (Census 2010)
Population density:	46.4 inhabitants/km²*
Population growth:	75 %* (1984 – 2001)
Number of compounds:	153
Growth compounds:	+ 4.5 compounds p.a. (2004 – 2012)
Main ethnic groups:	Mamprusi (75 %*)
Temperature:	12°C – 45°C
Average precipitation:	950 – 1,200 mm p.a.
Rainy season:	May – October
Dry season:	November – April
Vegetation type:	Guinea tree savannah
Main livelihood:	Agriculture (96.1 %**)
Main crops:	Maize, millet, soy, beans, rice

* per district
** per district (Census 2010, rural West Mamprusi District)

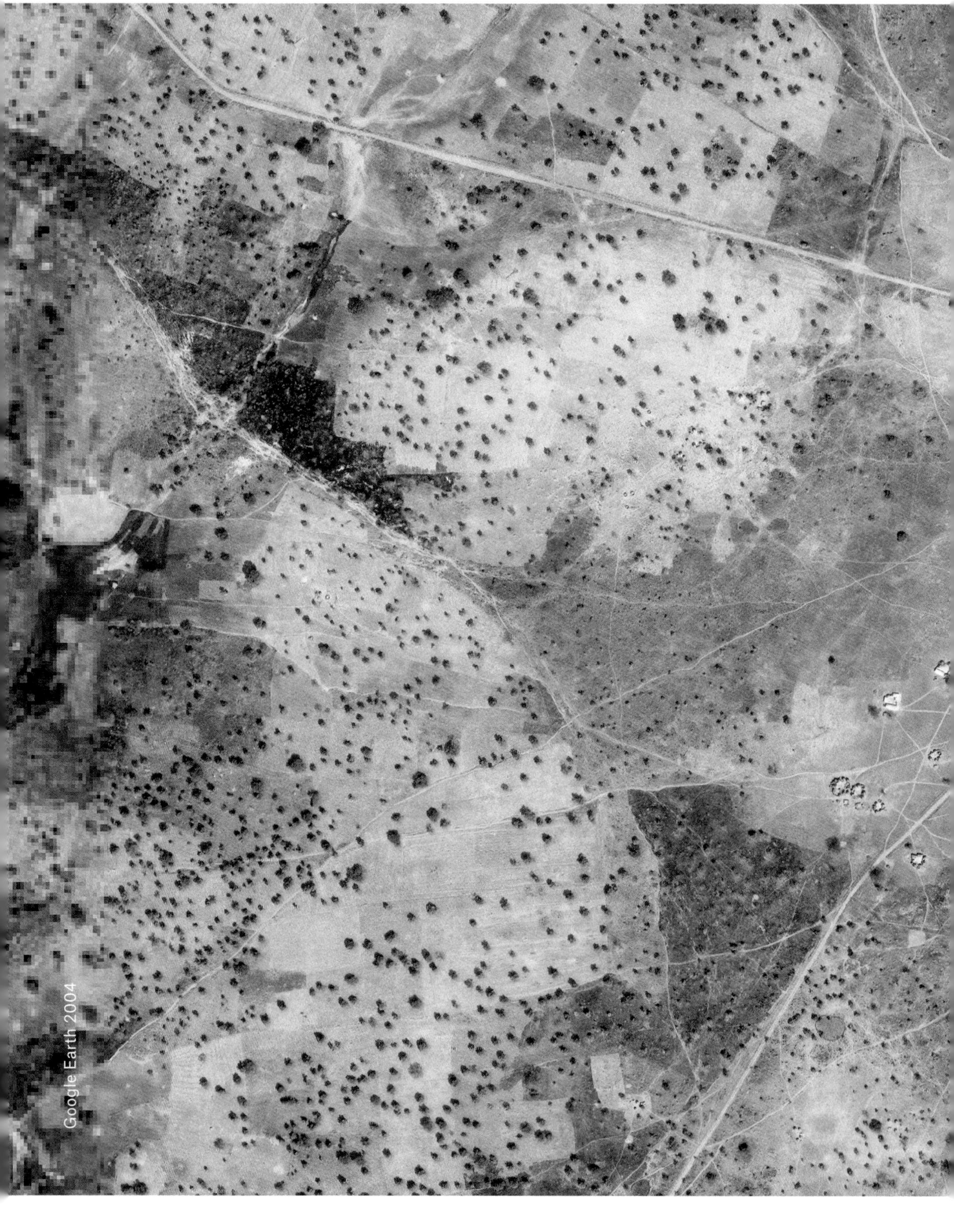

Google Earth 2004

TRADITIONALLY, WE DON'T SELL LAND, BUT THINGS ARE CHANGING OF LATE.

A Conversation between Chief Salifu Mahama Tampurie and Baerbel Mueller
Guabuliga, September 2011

CH: My name is Chief Salifu Mahama Tampurie, with the king title *Zolong-Naa*, the fourth chief of Guabuliga. The Guabuliga community is located in the West Mamprusi district in the northern Region of Ghana. It is predominantly a farming community with a population of about 4,000 people. Most of the people here are farmers. In my estimation, the community is about 120 years old. I am the fourth chief. My grandfather was the first chief, and then the position went to my father and my brother, and now I am the occupant of the skin. My position is a divisional status within the Mamprusi kingdom in northern Ghana. My king is the Nayiri. I was in-skinned chief five years ago. I have two satellite communities, Gaaŋbini and Tunsungu, which are also under me. I rule along with a number of elders, whom I can even call my parents. They are far older than me and they give me good advice as a chief on how the community should be run.

My interest right now is to assist the community in what they do best, which is farming, and to assist the women in what they do best, which is supporting their husbands on their farms, and making the Shea butter extraction. They pick Shea nuts and make a Shea butter extraction and they do a bit of trade. I intend to look into this area and see how best we can perfect the production.

The other area is school education. An infrastructure was built by the Catholic Church who came as missionaries in 1958. The first primary school was named after Saint Michael. As time passed, the community grew in numbers and the infrastructure that was put there was then inadequate for housing all the school pupils. So we called on the government to aid the community by expanding the facility, which now takes care of the lower and upper primary up to the junior high school level. We are lucky to have that facility. Before, the majority of the children were under trees just around the school. We hope that in near future the government will still come and assist with the junior high school. So that is the situation in the school now.

The other challenging issue in this growing community is that the orientation of our buildings is only cultural. You can find families, parents, grandparents, and grandchildren all in one compound. We live with the extended family system. But when a particular house grows to the extent that there is the need to separate, the first son of the house might be given the permission to move out again to start a house. And that is an extension of the first house. So that is the situation, that we are actually living the extended family system.

BM: If the eldest son moves out and starts to build a new compound, how is it regulated in terms of land ownership? Does he have to approach the elders? Or you? Or is it family farming land around the compound, and he can build wherever he wants to?

CH: In the case of the Guabuliga community, the chief is the main landlord of the community. The land is more or less decided over by the community, and the chief is part of the Mamprusi kingdom. I have been selected to occupy the royal skin within that community. I hold that land there in the name of the king, but it is in my hands. We have new settlers who come in and want a place to settle. It's the duty of the chief to give him a portion of the town to settle in. But like I said, if you are a chief and you apportion some part of the land there to a family member or any settler within the community, as time grows, the whole area within his environment becomes part of his compound. So the space just immediately around his environment, if he wants an elderly son to move out and settle there, he only has to to come and ask for the blessing of the chief. "My son is now of age and I intend to move him out, I want him to start in this location. So could you come and give your ancestral blessing to the land for us to start erecting the building?" So when I look at it and if it is the right thing to do, I go there I give my blessings and the first foundation block is given to me and I lay and I bless the foundations and the entire project and tell them to go ahead. That is what happens right now. So before you construct any structure in the community, if I can't go myself as a chief, either a brother or a son will have to

go and do that for them, lay the foundation block for them to start. But as it develops, over time, that portion of the land becomes his because it has been given to him with the blessing of the chief. If you look at it traditionally, the chief is like the landlord and all the natural resources are invested in him, but of course you are also holding it there in the name of the whole community and for the king of the state. That is what happens. Once in a while, a particular family can have issues regarding who should farm where. As a main landlord and a key owner of the land, I then go to the farmland and decide that, well, for peace to prevail, this member of that family should take that part of the land and so and so and then it's settled. Once I see that it's fine, they go ahead and then they start. Before you can acquire any land, there is a need for the chief to collect that land for maybe somebody who wants to do a project there for the entire community. Then it is my duty to resettle the person who is making his livelihood from that land on another piece of land. I have the power to take it from him for the entire good of the community. But of course, knowing very well that that is where his livelihood is, it is my duty to get another portion of land for him or her. Then he continues to do his farming activities or is adequately compensated. If you are in the community as a settler and you decide to leave, naturally the land goes back to the chief who was the person who gave the land to you to settle in in the first place. I can choose to give it to another person who wants the services of that piece of land. Currently, we don't even sell land. Culturally, we don't sell land. We allow you to come to use it for the period of time you want to. When you are finished with whatever, it returns to the owner of the land. Traditionally, we don't sell land. But things are changing of late and anything could happen.

BM: For me it's difficult to understand how it works when there are bigger families, let's say one father has five sons and they all grow up in Guabuliga and then they all go into farming. Then the land is split among the five, or do they get additional land? And is there enough land left for growth?

CH: As you look at the community, currently there is enough land for farming activities, but as we grow, obviously that limitation could come. Right now we don't have any land issues. Sometimes it's human nature that people will want more and more and more. Sometimes you take it and you are not putting it into use. Another member of the family wants to use it, then you block it, just because you want it to be known as yours. When that situation arises, then I intervene. I go in there and say: "My friend, you cannot do this, this person needs the land for his livelihood, so you have to pass it over to him." You cannot challenge that. Usually it is just between families. Every family knows where their ancestors started their farming activities. All that is known in the community. If you are from a different area, you can't crisscross to another family's land to try to do farming there unless it is with their blessing. And even with that, the chief has to be in the know just for future reference. After about ten years, you will be claiming that that is your territory and you even realize that you are the only person farming there, you don't belong to the family that is occupying that piece of land. Once the situation is brought to the palace, we need to actually address the issues as they are and you are told where you are supposed to farm. That is just how we manage the land. For now we don't have any land issues or land pressures. We have problems with the land only when the same family members have problems with the distribution of their family land. If we have to solve big problems, I go to the field myself, I try to listen to them on the field and give them boundaries as to where they should farm and stop. Here we are not practicing that much of a scientific approach to farming. You want to farm, leave the land, move to another piece of land, and allow this one to rest for a year or two. Because of that, you are moving from plot to plot. You acquire a lot of land that is just lying there. Sometimes somebody has the capital to buy fertilizer. So those are the issues that we have. But they are normally being addressed.

BM: What about trees, cutting trees? Is it a topic?

CH: It is a major problem in the community, the felling of trees. In the past, it wasn't an issue because the population wasn't that big. And like I said, the population is made up predominantly of a farming community. We have one farming season in the year, the rainy season, which lasts about four months there and so then we do the farming activities. Afterwards, we use the remaining two months for the harvesting. For the rest of the year, which is six months, there are

no jobs. They have to depend on their harvest over the last season, the past six months, to survive the next six months, to start the season again. If you look at that situation, the off-season, some of them venture—this is a recent development—to fell a few trees for charcoal. Some of them also do their local building and they want to use the branches of trees for rafters, the roof, the building. I have also realized that they are now getting too much into charcoal burning. That is why I have agreed in principle with all my elders that we have put a stop to it. When you are caught by a community member, we set up a committee, you are fined at the palace. We have certain economic tools like the Shea tree, the Dawadawa tree, and a few others. We don't actually mess with those trees because they are the trees from which our women get their livelihood—the Sheanut picking. So we are strict about those. If you fell such a tree you are brought to the palace, you are fined seriously, it serves as a deterrent to others. It might be your family land, it might be your own farm, but if you fell a tree, particularly an economically viable tree from that piece of land, then you'll be disciplined.

BM: I would like to know about the districts of Guabuliga. If you come there as a foreigner you don't have the impression that there are districts. I would like to know what their responsibility is and what makes a neighborhood or a district.

CH: The community of Guabuliga itself has six parts. The first part is called the section of the chief. The royal section. My father was the chief of the community. So he is there in charge of that section. The royal section, I am the leader there. We have another part which is under the leadership of an elder we call Nachinaba. That part we call Gbandana foŋŋu. You have Nouri loabi, you have Samari, who is there as a leader. The orphanage is currently located in Nouri loabi, the leader there is Samari. Samari is junior to Nachinaba, but the two work closely as elders, and they preside over different sections. Then we have another section which is Wudana foŋŋu. If I am not there, Wudana presides over cases with all the elders. Then he has his own section. There is another section in the community known as Kambonaba foŋŋu. Kambonaba is the chief warrior of the community. The community, as we have settled upon, has a defense system, and the commander of the defence system is the Kambonaba. Then we have another area we call Masu foŋŋu, you can also call it Bangola. The Masu is one of my key elders. So you have the Nayiri foŋŋu, which is the royal section, you have Gbandana foŋŋu, you have Nouri loabi, you have Masu foŋŋu, you have Kambonaba foŋŋu, and you have Mossi foŋŋu or Bangola. Those are the six sections. All those people are elders who take care of those sections. If there is a problem that doesn't need to go to the palace, he who sits in his house presides over such minimalities and it's solved within that section.

In addition, we also have women leaders who also address women issues. The most senior person among the women leaders is Mangasia, an elderly person who has lived in the community for a long time, who knows the history of the community, who knows the legal parties of the community, and who knows the problems of the women. So she leads it with the chief and with the other elders. Besides Mangasia, you have Madugi, then you have Saranaba, you have Sarachie, Turinaba, and a few others. They take care of the needs of the community. When we have funerals, the women are more of the moaners there than even we men. So there must be an elderly woman, one of them will be in charge of taking care of them so there is peace and harmony within the funeral ground. If it is a celebration of a wedding, they will be there. Incidentally, there are positions that are respected. When we have major cases that have to do with women, we have to assemble them so they can give their input. As a chief you listen to what happened in the past, how this was solved. The elders are mainly old people. They will guide you and finally you will take an informed decision. When we saw the wisdom of some of you who had been in the community and we felt that now you had become a part of us, we invited you to hold a position as Saranaba, that's exactly what we did with you and you are now a major part of the community. When there are major issues in decision taking concerning the women and the environmental needs of the community and you are within, naturally we have to invite you and hear what you have to say.

BM: For me it is quite interesting that there is the chieftaincy, then there is the government, but there is also religion. It would be interesting if you could talk a little bit about Muslims, Christians, Traditionalists, and the importance of the churches and how they developed.

CH: When the community was started, there were predominantly traditional people and then of course Muslims. I think sometime around 1958, the Catholic Church was the first to come in. The Catholic Church is the oldest in the Guabuliga community. They built the school for us in 1958, but in fact, they were there much earlier. At that time I wasn't even born. Yes, the Catholic Church was the first religious institution in terms of Christianity to come in. Before the advent of the Catholic Church in the community, there were traditional people and Muslims. Now religion is evolving in a way that in addition to the Catholic Church, we have several other churches, up to six or even more. I don't know how many Muslim ones there are, but they have their own attendants. So we are all living together. We are all there and you can have all these religions within one compound. If you choose that this is your faith you go by that slot, it is not compulsory for you to be this or that. Maybe as you are a kid and you are growing, your parents might prevail on you to practice their religion. But as you reach a certain age and you feel that you want to go this way, you go. That is it. As you see in the community, in the big compounds, we are all relatives but you have all these religions being practiced.

BM: But the majority is still Muslim in Guabuliga nowadays?

CH: Well, I would say yes, but if you look at the number of churches as opposed to the number of mosques, you might think that Christianity is now dominating. Some people just come and establish a church within a week and they always have a following anyway. Once they come and they start, they get their following. In terms of mosques, we have one big mosque and a few others like the sections, the six sections that I mentioned. Every section has an area where they pray. Sometimes it is not even a mosque. They just demarcate a certain area where they go to pray. The community started as a traditional community and Islamic community. Most of the naming there is Islamic. All the names that we bear are Islamic names. As you join your church and you grow into it, you begin to name in the Christian way. Yes, Muslims are still in the majority in a way, but if you look at it the churches, they too are growing quite fast.

BM: Could you list communal facilities?

CH: In the community right now, the communal facilities such as schools and marketplaces, we actually have very few. I have told you that the women are predominantly farmers and traders, so we have a very small market where they meet to sell their wares and trade. But it is not an organized place. In the off-season, they try to gather there during the day every three days to sell their trade. When we get to the rainy season, they prefer to meet at the market area after five, after they have gone to the farm, done their work, they come. It is an area that is not organized and I think that we may need to get somebody to plan. In fact, the current location of the market for me is not good. I intend to give them a new site. Or the community looking at this orientation should collectively agree ("Yes, this is a better site for where the market should be"). That is what I intend to do. We will get somebody who can advise us adequately, who knows the community so well that they can say, "Yes, this is where the site should be. I have identified three locations."

Right now, if you look at our culture, we live with our dead. When somebody dies within your family, you bury the person within the compound. I think that this was acceptable when it was a very small community, but now that we have grown and reached this level with a population no less than six thousand, I think there is a need for us to also demarcate a portion of the land and use it as a cemetery, which we don't have yet.

There are communal facilities that I think that we should be thinking about where to locate in the future: to site the market, to site the communal facility, and even a common entertainment ground or playground for our youth. Right now, when there is a social gathering, we have to look for a big house that has a well-floored yard. That is where we meet to do our recreational activities. But I think that in future there is a need for us to have maybe a town hall where we can all meet when there is such social gathering. So when the youth have their entertainment and whatever meetings they have, organizational meetings, they go there. We have a number of NGOs coming to the community. So when you have such a communal facility, their target group can meet them there. When they come, mostly they invite their target groups to shady areas under trees, where they can sit and talk with them.

I think that we could use a town hall, a well-organized market, a cemetery, and our

dying need right now is a clinic, because the closest clinic to the community, as big as it is, is in the district capital Walewale. And we are farmers: around this time, the rainy season, we are faced with reptiles in the bush. When there is a snake bite or scorpions, you have to struggle to get the person to the district hospital on a bicycle, which is ten miles away. So we think that, in planning the community, there is a need for us to identify a site for a clinic which hopefully in my view could even develop into a hospital. So we are looking at all that, but we need somebody with the expertise to come and assist the community to demarcate and actually site all these facilities that I'm talking about. We have challenges in those areas. The way we are building, there is the need to plan the community. So we know, let's leave this site for a clinic, let's leave this site for a market, let's leave this site for a cemetery, let's use this site for a town hall, and sites for many other communal facilities that we envisage in the future. So we need somebody with expertise in development planning to look at it in that direction and advise the community so that we know what these areas have been demarcated for. And even looking at our infrastructure, we realize that we do not really plan the buildings that we put up according to a particular pattern so to speak, so if we are able to map the community and leave settlement plots where you could develop them as designed plots, it's good, rather than telling your first son, "my friend, my compound is big and you are also of age, so you move to this area and settle." It's just like the immediate space in front of your house or to the side of it or to the left of it or even to the back of it. But we think that as we are growing and developing, we should plan the community. So we know that this is the size for houses, these are for communal facilities, and on this side you pass. That is what I think should happen in future.

BM: Do you see Guabuliga growing in all directions?

CH: You know Guabuliga is surrounded by mountains. When I get to the king's palace, they refer to me as *Zolong-Naa*, the chief of the mountainous town. Guabuliga is virtually surrounded by nice mountains, so when I'm approaching the king's palace, they drum that *Zolong-Naa* is arriving. If you look towards the east, the mountain is more pronounced. So for me, progress in that direction might become limited with time. As you develop and you get as far as the mountain, you have to stop. That is why if you look at it towards the north, we have reserved that area for the school. That can now develop up until the mountain and then they have to stop there. So for me the most likely direction would be towards the Walewale main road. So it will be more towards the south, towards Dimia. If you look at the orientation, now I'm thinking in terms of infrastructure, it will be towards Dimia, towards the main road of Walewale and then probably towards Manga for those who want a quiet, peaceful area. People don't even seem to want to develop in that direction now, towards Wulugu, but of course we also want a quiet town. Who knows, maybe in the future we could even climb the mountains and build something with a complete view of the township. Even though you see them as mountains like that, once you get to the top it's flat, very flat and beautiful. I have gone there a number of times. So it's just with time. As we plan, we will know where to put what. That will help.

BM: Could you say something about migration? Are there many people from Guabuliga who have gone somewhere else and are many coming back? How is it related to other cities or to other parts of Ghana, internationally? And could you explain why Guabuliga is named 'Little London'?

CH: If you look at the youth of Guabuliga, a number of them after junior high school—we don't have a secondary school—go to bigger secondary schools in other communities like Tamale, Bolgatanga, they're in a different region. Tamale is the regional capital, the big schools are there. Most of the youth go to bigger schools. From there many go to universities and some are able to leave the country and then when they leave and come back, they see the living patterns of the youth and some are even influenced by them when they come back. So a number of Guabuliga citizens live outside this country. We have a number of them in America, we have a number of them in the UK. As they come and go, it adds to the idea that Guabuliga is their 'Little London'. There are also Guabuliga citizens in London. They are working there, but they come back seasonally. Sometimes after four, five years they come with their families, they visit, and they go back. The same thing with America. My

brother Baba Seidu has been in America for over 30 years. He is even married to a Brit and they are in America. Recently, he came home. So yes, we have people from the community moving out of Guabuliga to settle in other communities within the country because their work has sent them there. Some of them are teachers, some of them are nurses, but as they approach retirement, a few come back. Others settle over there but they still visit. All have funerals, they all come, they perform, then they go back. For instance, we have a number of them in the district capital, Walewale. Some have even come to work and they are staying there. Some went to Accra, struggled for jobs, and eventually realized that they are settling there. When they get there they are farmers. But when they start to work there, they get better and they settle. That is how I think they are making their income. They come home when we have celebrations, funerals, they come. So quite a number of citizens are outside.

BM: So it is not a remote village? It is very connected.

CH: Yes, it is very connected. In fact in the south, a lot of our people who were born there work on cocoa farms and as they eventually establish their own farms and settle, they come home when there is an occasion to. But they belong to certain farms. When the farming is ready to be done, all their citizens come or all the family relations come from the south. Only the ones who are outside Ghana don't come of course, they send some monetary assistance for the performances. So yes, we migrate, but we come back. Others stay, but we are aware of them. When they come and you see there is change in their lives, some have attempted to find opportunities to live in the big towns. Those of us in the royal family have a branch of the family in Nalerigu where the king is. We hold the title of the spokesperson. We call it 'linguist'. That title in Nalerigu is held by my senior brother. A bigger part of the family is there. Anytime we have a problem and it is a royal problem, the family there will naturally have to come to Guabuliga, we all sit down and perform and resolve. We also visit. And besides, our daughters marry men from outside Guabuliga. Some marry within Guabuliga, but some also marry outside Guabuliga. So there is an extension and linkage if you look at all the neighboring villages, our daughters and sisters are married to them. So we share common problems. When there is a problem, they will all come and naturally their husbands will accompany them. Their children who are not part of Guabuliga will come to Uncle Home.

So there is natural migration by way of marriage, by way of searching for jobs for which you have left the community, by way of education for which you have left the community—there are those problems that we have. But they always know that this is where they belong and they come back from time to time.

BAERBEL MUELLER, architect, head of the [applied] Foreign Affairs lab at the Institute of Architecture, University of Applied Arts Vienna, founder of nav_s baerbel mueller (navigations in the field of architecture and urban research within diverse cultural contexts), projects located on the African continent since 2002, recipient of the Ars Docendi State Award for excellence in teaching (2015).

GUABULIG-RANA SALIFU MAHAMA TAMPURIE ("owner of Guabuliga"). *22 April 1962. Zolong-Naa the 4th—the fourth chief, since 2006, BSc in Agriculture, University of Cape Coast, Diploma in Education, studied at the Egypt International Center for Agriculture, 18 years field operation manager of a private cotton company in Ghana, now private farmer.

MIGRATIONS FROM A TO [a]

Hannah le Roux

If August is a month of migration, this August, 2015, when thousands of refugees landed on the beaches otherwise occupied by northerners flown down for the sun, was the month when the very meaning of migration moved. In becoming so moving, so emotively present as part of the human condition, these migrations signaled a shift from a world of discrete and sometimes linked settlements to a world in flux, while the consequences became a public and heartfelt condition. The affairs of foreigners became our affair. The private responses of many Austrians to this heartbreaking situation show great empathy for the condition of people for whom the homeland has become an ephemeral concept. Perhaps this is not surprising, as the historical flux of Central Europe has long engendered an awareness of human movement and the transitory nature of occupation.

How is this consciousness applied in architecture? In the work of [applied] Foreign Affairs, the conditions of global flux create three interlinked conditions for the lab to engage with. The first is the adoption of Africa as a site of ongoing change where migrancy and settlement correspond in unpredictable, non-linear ways. This change has material and immaterial forms, both of which interest [a]FA. The second condition is the one of the mobile lab itself and its particular qualities. The constant reflection, reformation, and looseness of the group, under Baerbel Mueller's direction, raises the question of how architecture holds course across such fluid contextual conditions. The third is the rich and circular relationship between [a]FA's work in Africa, its "home" institution of the Angewandte, and the globalized project of contemporary architecture.

The [a]FA unit stepped into the gap of design for conditions of flux by locating its investigations in Africa around 2011, entering a vast site which it recognizes, above all, as a field of shifting conditions and inspiring energy. Unlike the generic Africa studios that increasingly round off a northern architecture curriculum, there is nothing a priori about the social needs, the nation, the institutions, or even the toolkits of the projects [a]FA undertakes. Instead, the sites and collaborations emerge from connections, seemingly random opportunities inspired by Baerbel's vivid curiosity and enthusiasm for the continent and its innovative capacities. Along the way, the projects manage to discard most of the baggage of generic sites, forms, materials, and climatic rules, those practices of modernism that have constructed a fiction regarding the settlement of Africa.

Rather than bringing an agenda to Africa, [a]FA focuses on reading and reacting to situations. These moments tend to emerge from encounters between the north and south, pauses in

the circulation of practices and people from Africa to Austria and back again. With both partners simultaneously using the projects as ways to escape, settle, consolidate, or experiment, their common ground is the camp: an accommodation between nomadism and settlement that in the process, is shown to be a common global condition.

The specific objects of fascination of this lab are slippery things: the event, the social, the performative, textiles, liquids, wind, propagation, and education. These forces and the shapes they form are orchestrated by youth, but follow the wisdom of the experience of the elders with whom the lab typically seeks out an adoptive relationship. These individuals, whether they are Chief Salifu Mahama Tampurie, Petra Kron, or Faustin Linyekula, are at once deeply committed to the project sites and oriented towards a more distant horizon. Their collaboration with [a]FA hinges on the co-development of a sense of radical localness and absolute openness that lies between the affection for home and the dream of getting beyond its limitations. This apparent tension makes for unique, visionary, and yet entirely appropriate projects at each site.

The operating procedures of the lab seem to be unarticulated, but the presentations that they do convey the distinct self-consciousness and observational precision of migrants, whose skill is to scan the landscape for opportunities. The constant reassembly of student workers creates a band of nomad traders who bring a diverse set of skills, artifacts, amusements, and tales from place to place. As a collaboration between the north and south, there are issues of power at stake, particularly in the encounter between the voluntary and forced migratory paths of [a]FA and its clients. The mobility is, at worst, in one direction, given the significant cost of flights from Europe to Africa and back. But at best—and the chosen collaborators seem very shrewd when it comes to these opportunities—the foreign guests are hosted in exchange for the value that can be generated for their projects through visibility. In between these extremes, the substance of the projects lies in the conversations that serve a mutual end, which is the definition of a shared practice that spans between insider and outside knowledge.

The question of precision is critical to the success or failure of such projects, but it is unhinged from the idea of mechanical technique in favour of a direct, artisanal intelligence. In the context of material poverty within which [a]FA works, the cost of any waste is proportionally huge. At the same time, the potential of radical visions is also extremely valuable, as a way to overcome the inertia of social marginalization.

And so, in the end, [a]FA returns to the material of the modern avant-garde, layered with the contemporary forms of expressionist reading and inscription: theatrical and discursive exchanges, ephemeral constructions and images of the forces at play. In this return, the nomadism of the contemporary condition meets the change of Africa. This is the true route where A meets [a], and back again, forming a path on which the students follow in the footsteps of Baerbel and her mentor, Wolf, and his, and hers, and his, all the way back to that first moment of stepping out from the first place from where we all came and were never truly settled.

HANNAH LE ROUX directs the architecture program at the University of the Witwatersrand in Johannesburg. As a writer, designer and researcher she explores the transformation of architecture through the agency of its users in Africa.

GUABULIGA—WELL BY THE THORN TREE: ON OTHER PLANNING

Baerbel Mueller

Chief Salifu Maham Tampurie approached me in 2011, if I would be interested in working on a master plan for his growing village. I initiated an [a]FA lab with the aim of focusing on alternative, more dynamic, evolutionary strategies instead of a static master plan. After years of working in Guabuliga on an architectural scale[1], another long-term engagement with the village began—a very contextual and bottom-up process.

The lab started in Vienna, with a transdisciplinary group of six students of architecture, landscape design, and water management and environmental engineering. Based on a satellite image of Guabuliga taken in 2004, studies focused on understanding the geometry of the settlement pattern and its environmental context. On-site research was carried out to investigate the status and potential of Guabuliga, with the goals of defining growth parameters, projecting growth patterns, and articulating strategies aimed towards an ecological future for the village. This project phase was based on intense collaboration with the Chief and his elders. Guabuliga's founding myth—the 'Well by the Thorn Tree'—served as a conceptual backbone for contextual yet novel spatial and programmatic scenarios. This environmental and infrastructural approach also seemed to be the right strategy in a (rural) context, in which the design and realization of houses and communal structures naturally lay in the hands of the users themselves.

In planning and architecture, engaging with the (tropical) environmental context is common to a certain extent, but what is too often lacking is the consideration of the socio-cultural context in which a project is located. "It is about climate, light, temperature, and form, but it's also about meaning, ritual, and space" (Lokko, 2013). Contemporary readings of the respective cultural environment and cultural ecology of a project, followed by intelligent abstraction and creative translations are required. The environment and cultural expressions are mutually dependent.[2]

Parallel to the project on the planning scale, each student was asked to work on a narrative mapping in which a specific 'intensity' of Guabuliga was identified. This view from within led to valuable cultural insights, such as the fact that rural values of stability, locality, protection, and control are merging nowadays with (former) outside influences of mobility, urbanity, privacy, and transparency.

In the course of the lab, the potential and challenges of truly contextual, transdisciplinary, transcultural, and participatory work methods have been interrogated: How to deeply read a place and situation? How to enter a space (which is not yours)? How to relate? How to break stereotypes? How to surprise?

1 'my home my bed my mango tree', 2009–2012 nav_s baerbel mueller, commissioned by Braveaurora

2 David Adjaye defines six geographical regions into which the African continent can be divided, based on the idea "that there are underlying qualities that define the cultures of these geographical regions rather than the tribal identities that provide the normal frame of reference" (Adjaye, 2010).

Mapping is particularly instrumental when it comes to the understanding of lived space. Searching for new modes of perception and representation of physical and lived space, narrative mapping is a powerful means to grasp and visualize what unfolds in time and space. Mapping becomes a form of critical visualisation. Parallel to collective investigations on the planning scale, each participant of the Guabuliga lab worked individually on a narrative mapping in which a specific 'intensity' of the village was captured and translated into an artistic, documental, or scientific piece.

Jurgen Strohmayer's 'Do you come back tomorrow?' is a staged photo shoot portraying the self-image of Guabuliga's youth culture. Stefanie Theuretzbacher's 'Living Manifestations' reads the family compound as a spatio-temporal cosmos, presented as an animated drawing. 'The Spatial Cell' by Joseph Hofmarcher became a participatory 1:1 design and realization of three living units built using the local earth technique. Ioana Petkova's video work, 'Rhythms of Production', traces the creation of handmade surfaces. Christian Car's 'Talking Trees' is a collection of narratives on 18 trees and their role in and around Guabuliga and photographs of their physical appearances. Lea Dietiker captures the rhythms and rituals of the production and distribution of cooked food. Antonella Amesberger's 'Market Ground(s)' investigates existing and potential surfaces for the display and sale of market goods. 'Well by the Thorn Tree' shows Theresa Theuretzbacher's research on water sources, water-fetching behaviours, and qualities of water in the village.

Along with the Guabuliga growth plan, the works were first exhibited at the IoA Sliver Gallery in Vienna and then shown at the Guabuliga Gallery to be shared and reflected on with the village.

DO YOU COME BACK TOMORROW?

Juergen Strohmayer
February 2012

Birds fly south, following the riverbed that borders Guabuliga to the east. Embedded in the rolling hills of the Volta River system and Ghana's northern tree savannah, a telecom tower pierces the sky above where two roads meet. Floating, static red lights appear above, to remain for the night as the TV's continuous rumble picks up the fading cries from the football game on the ground.

Through a staged photo shoot portraying Guabuliga's youth culture, I juxtaposed the specificity of the place with the momentary dislocation of the portraitees. A flash illuminates a volume defined by the reflections of whatever is being lit by the travelling light. This volume of light, captured in my portraits, is embedded in its reliance on a light-reflecting context, while the action of emitting a flash remains a dislocating gesture in itself.

The performative aspect of "do you come back tomorrow?" resulted from a disturbance of the evening peace in the village and preconceived ideals of village life.

Vodafone tower, Diptych I–II

A staged photo shoot portraying Guabuliga's youth

RHYTHMS OF PRODUCTION

Ioana Petkova
February 2012

The work documents various people and what lies behind their handmade surfaces. Each pattern emerges from a continuous repetition of movement. This physical act of making demands a certain state of mind.

The still images are taken from a video piece that introduces and compares the different inner rhythms of the makers.

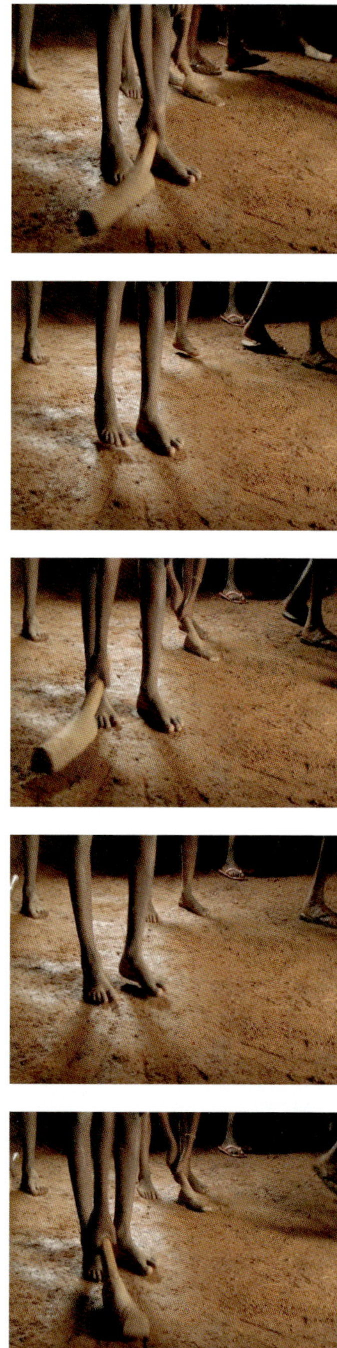

Compound flooring

Basket weaving

Wall building

Wall plastering

Roof making

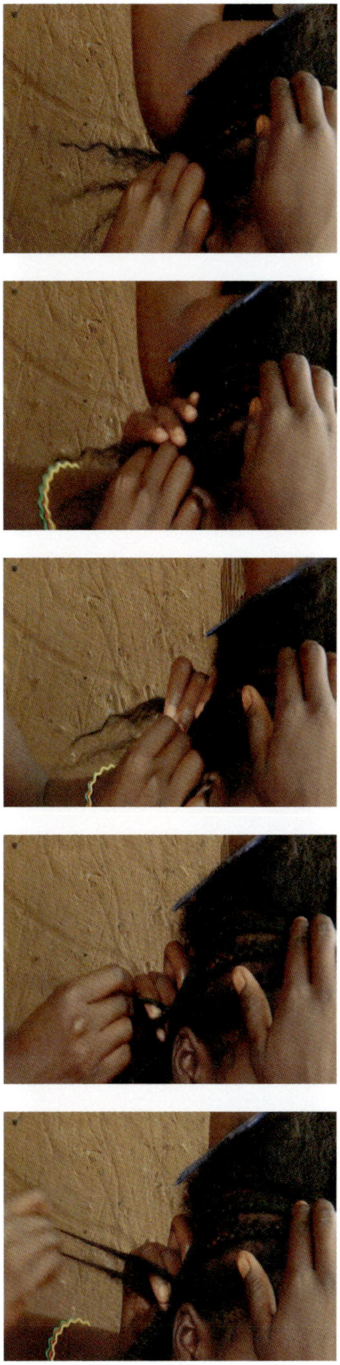

Hair dressing

THE SPATIAL CELL

Joseph Hofmarcher
February 2012

The initial scale of the urban growth pattern of a village like Guabuliga is defined by the individual living cell—the single room. From the room to the house to the neighborhood to the village, each of these elements are like beads on a necklace in relation to similar ones.

Collaborating with local craftsmen, community workers, and four orphans who were being reintegrated into their extended-family compound revealed insights into the tendency towards abandoning traditional spatial setups and building techniques.

Why would the architectural typology of the sequence of single rooms be replaced by L-shaped or rectangular courtyard houses? And why would somebody give up the advantages of the thatched roof just to have a zinc roof? The reasons are practically, economically, and socially driven. The zinc roof is a more permanent material than the thatch, although it is noisy when it rains and a climatic catastrophe when exposed to the sun. Nevertheless, zinc roofs represent a social upgrade. Joining up single rooms into one block is a rational consequence of using the rectangular roofing sheets, as well as the people's desire to introduce orthogonal furniture.

The consequences that arise from this typological transformation are of climatic, spatial, and aesthetic character. The spatial impact manifests itself through the loss of interstitial spaces between the single rooms, which merge together into one vast structure. Furthermore, an extroversion of the interior rooms occurs due to the need for windows. The rectangular blocks have an impact on the urban setup approaching orthogonality.

Abandoning the vernacular spatial setup can result in a loss of intuition for intimate space. These spatial components might also be looked at in relation to questions of identity.

Carpentry: Michael Bayada Sumzimina
Clients: Thomas, Lariba, Isaac and Zilata Dahamani,
supported by Braveaurora

2-10-2012

2-14-2012

2-15-2012

2-23-2012

2-28-2012

3-7-2012

LIVING TOGETHER APART. FORMS OF SOCIALITY IN A KASENA HOUSE

Ann Cassiman

Family life in the compound house of the Kasena of the Upper East Region is organized around modes of being together and living apart, of sharing and dividing, of revealing and concealing. These divergent dynamics are shaped by the material layout of the house, which is not only inspired by a social blueprint that informs the relations between the inhabitants and visitors, kin and allies, and the younger and older generations, but is also embedded in a worldview and ontology that is rephrased in every house's founding story.

The large earthen compound house is called *songo* (in Kasem), which refers to a physical earthen structure consisting of an amalgam of rooms, walls, open spaces, and terraces, as well as to the residential group of families living there. A *songo* carries the name of its founder or an eminent (male) lineage member, and includes an extended family consisting of two to four generations (sometimes up to 60 people): a man and his brothers with their wives, their sons plus wives, unmarried and divorced daughters, and all of the grandchildren still too young to marry. Usually it is the eldest man of the *songo* who is the head of the house. Important decisions are taken in consultation with all of the men of the house, but the *songo* alone carries the final responsibility for all the house matters, for the care of the house ancestors, and for representing the house to the larger clan. He is an authority on important ritual matters and watches over collective possessions such as cattle and land, and he makes sure that the distribution, inheritance, and exchange of these possessions proceeds fairly for everyone in the house. His senior wife is endowed with a comparable authority among the women of the house. She acts as the senior sister to all of the women. In ritual matters, she organizes the women of the house and takes decisions concerning concrete arrangements. When a funeral takes place in the house, when important visitors come, when large amounts of food are to be prepared, when millet beer is to be brewed, and on a thousand other occasions, she oversees and controls the ongoing activities. In more private matters, such as conjugal quarrels and educational troubles, she may interfere as well.

In a living house, there is always someone there to receive the unexpected visitor. Usually it is the head of the house, who stays behind to guard the house when the other members have left for their farming lands or the market. On the hot days of the dry season, the head of the house is sheltered under a shed, a millet-stalk roofed structure pitched in front of the entrance to the house. Lying in this airy place to rest, possibly joined by other men of the house, or by playing children and elderly women, he keeps

an eye on everyone who enters or leaves the house. The shed is erected in the front yard of the house and serves as a public place for gathering and receiving visitors.

Each house consists of a number of rooms and these rooms are ordered in groups of three to four with a kitchen and bathing place, arranged around an open yard. A yard is the smallest unit within the social organization of a kin group, consisting of one household, that is, a woman with her children, sometimes with a (classificatory) sister who stays with them. It is comparable to a nuclear family. The primary concern of a household is the care of children and the catering, including the collecting of firewood and water, and the provision of clothes, school materials, medical help, and so on. Each yard does its own separate cooking, farming, and eating, and a man receives a bowl of food from each of his wives. Children, however, shop around and eat from whichever cooking pot is full. The yards are clearly differentiated from one another by lower walls or narrow openings that connect the rooms around the central cattle kraal.

The whole house is composed of a variety of larger and smaller constructions, as well as round and rectangular rooms, all orchestrated around the open central cattle kraal. As one penetrates the house, the physical outline of the house creates a gradient in regard to the accessibility of the different areas. The voluminous vertical granaries, as well as the various smaller constructions in the cattle kraal and the courtyards, fragment the view one has of the dwelling units. The high walls enclosing the house, and the lower walls surrounding the cattle kraal and the courtyards, protect the inside from exposure to occasional intruders, and shield it from the view of curious neighbors meanwhile imposing a phased access to increasingly intimate spaces.

A senior woman normally owns several kinds of rooms, arranged around the open space of the yard. In one room she keeps her food and cooking utensils (pots, calabashes, baskets, and mats). If she has the respected status of grandmother or senior wife, she might be the proud occupier of a 'twin-room'. This space consists of a double or two-lobed room that can be accessed through a single entrance.

Transitory spaces regulate access to a room. The accessibility of a room is also symbolically indicated by the form and size of its doorway, called 'mouth' (*ni*). The size of the twin-room's doorway indicates its private and intimate nature. Shaped in the form of a keyhole, the door opening is kept very low. Immediately behind the opening, a knee-high, semi-circular wall is erected; this constitutes another barrier to the woman's dimly lit 'sanctum'. The foetal form of the twin-room indicates the extent to which the intimate sphere of the house is associated with the maternal womb. The shape of the door also evokes the twin-room's double meaning: the room symbolises both the belly as well as the womb of the owner. Normally, only the woman's husband, her children, and close intimate friends may enter her rooms. It is only during the chaotic context of a funeral that other people may also enter the female realm, as during a funeral all spatial prescriptions and conventional social rules are momentarily suspended. The first room is the outer room or portal room, where the owner sleeps and stores

her personal belongings. In this dim room, an impressive pile of polished pots is carefully arranged against the wall of the room. The pots and calabashes testify to a never-ending accumulation of belongings by the woman, her mother, and her grandmothers. They bear witness to the women's accomplishments and skills, and represent the core of female power and knowledge. The portal room gives way to the head-room, a round space with a flat roof pierced with holes serving as chimneys. The indoor cooking activities take place in this room. The rooftops of both rooms are used as terraces for nocturnal meetings or for sleeping purposes.

The visual fragmentation, and the play of visible-invisible, of seeing and being seen, is central to the Kasena spatial experience. The more one penetrates the hidden insides of the house and the more one accesses its secrets, the more one is empowered. The differentiation between men's and women's worlds, or between elders and young people, is regulated by (the denial of) visual access. In some clans, for example, in the first days following a child's birth, the newborn child and a specific relative (this can be the father, the grandfather, the maternal grandmother, or the brother and sister) are not allowed to see one another. When the relative and the child (represented by the mother) finally meet, they blow ashes towards one another to lift the taboo, while whispering, "I have disclosed you" (*a piire mo*). The same ritual of disclosure is performed upon the discovery of a young woman's first pregnancy, or at the end of a parturient's period of seclusion, when she 'comes outside' (*o nongi poone*). Leaving the room of seclusion and opening her eyes to face the outside world ritually introduces a parturient to her new status as a mother and the new relation to the world inherent in this status. Whereas female power is constructed through forms of concealment, the power of men reveals itself in the public domain. The public realm is referred to as *poone*, meaning 'outside, open, luminous or illuminated space', 'where the wind blows'. *Nongi poone* (lit. 'to come outside, to appear in the public space') indicates a person's successful transition into a new identity or self.

While seeing is shaped by the house's materiality within an almost sensuous geography, the house's soundscape surpasses this phased spatiality and binds the various yards: the rhythms of pounding muffled by the earthen walls, the rustling sounds of cracking groundnuts, the low voices from nearby yards, the sounds of a neighbor's stirring stick, and the sweeping broom of a co-wife. Some sounds are indicative of special events. For example, when a bride is brought to the settlement of the clan, shrill ululations will penetrate the tranquil night. Similarly, when a funeral starts in the middle of the night, a sad grieving voice, loudly calling out to the deceased, initiates the collective wailing of mourning relatives. Throughout the whole funeral, the horn player's wistful melodies punctuate the silence of the night. Conjugal quarrels may invite house members to intervene, but when money matters are discussed, or rumours are shared, one goes to the intimate interior of the room.

Adult sons and unmarried or divorced daughters are allowed to build a room in their mother's yard. It is becoming more and more common to marry at a later age and consequently,

children live in the mother's yard for a longer time. Nowadays, some sons and daughters engage in higher studies and therefore keep a room in the maternal court, which they occupy when they return home. Often, these rooms, built in a single line and with roofs made from corrugated iron sheets, are constructed as a semi-autonomous appendage. Sometimes the layout of these rooms reproduces the design of the twin-room: first one enters a reception room, where another door gives way to the next, more intimate space. Such rooms usually have a large veranda, which functions as an open transitional space between the yard and the rooms. In today's architecture, the veranda has become a popular attribute of the room. Female rectangular rooms in particular often make use of the transitional space of such a veranda in order to create a deferred access into the intimate realm of the room. On the veranda, women prepare soup for the evening meal, or they peel groundnuts, mould pots, pleat their friends' hair, or feed their children. A visiting close friend or relative will be given a seat on the woman's veranda.

Heavy rains or harsh climatic conditions regularly destroy parts of the rooms and cause cracks in the walls. Each year, this damage is repaired again. The plastering of the rooms adds another mud layer to the house, which the women then meticulously polish with round pebble stones. They are responsible for the cyclical renewal of the house's skin. Some senior women (especially in eastern Kasenaland in Burkina Faso) apply geometrical figures to the plastered surface using white kaolin stones or black and red vegetal paint. These figures show a woman's status and authority, as well as her skilfulness and sense of beauty. At the same time, the drawings also display themes and patterns that symbolize core values in the Kasena lifeworlds.

ANN CASSIMAN is an associate professor of Anthropology (University of Leuven, Belgium). Her research looks at dwelling, sociality, and material culture in rural northern Ghana and the urban setting of Accra, focusing on rural-urban mobility and new modes of urban place-making among women and youth in the *zongo* migrant communities.

LIVING MANIFESTATIONS: SIRIGU

Stefanie Theuretzbacher
February 2012

This work is an attempt to capture and visualize the origins, meanings, and relationships behind a family compound in Sirigu, northern Ghana. It is an attempt to understand how spiritual influences and site specificities shape the family house, and to look at the compound structure as a cosmos, a reflection, and a manifestation of a way of living.

The historical and cultural background of the Mamprusi people in Guabuliga is very different from that of the Kasena people in Sirigu. The Mamprusi originally migrated from Mali (around the turn of the 15th century) and, with time, converted to Christianity and Islam. As a consequence, a lot of traditions and spiritual values were lost. Coming from Burkina Faso, the Kasena are still practicing their animistic traditions and implementing these traditions in their architecture.

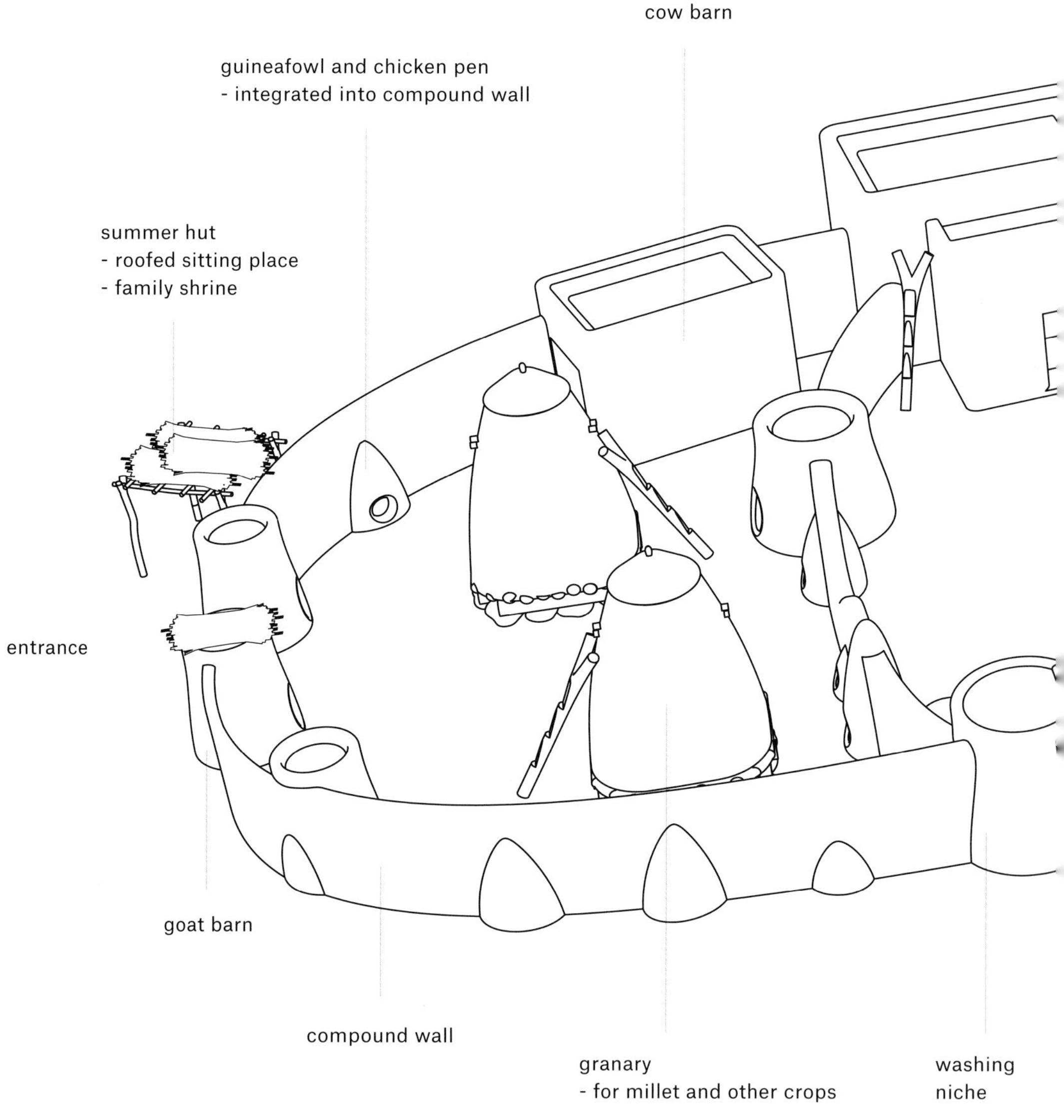
cow barn
guineafowl and chicken pen
- integrated into compound wall
summer hut
- roofed sitting place
- family shrine
entrance
goat barn
compound wall
granary
- for millet and other crops
washing
niche

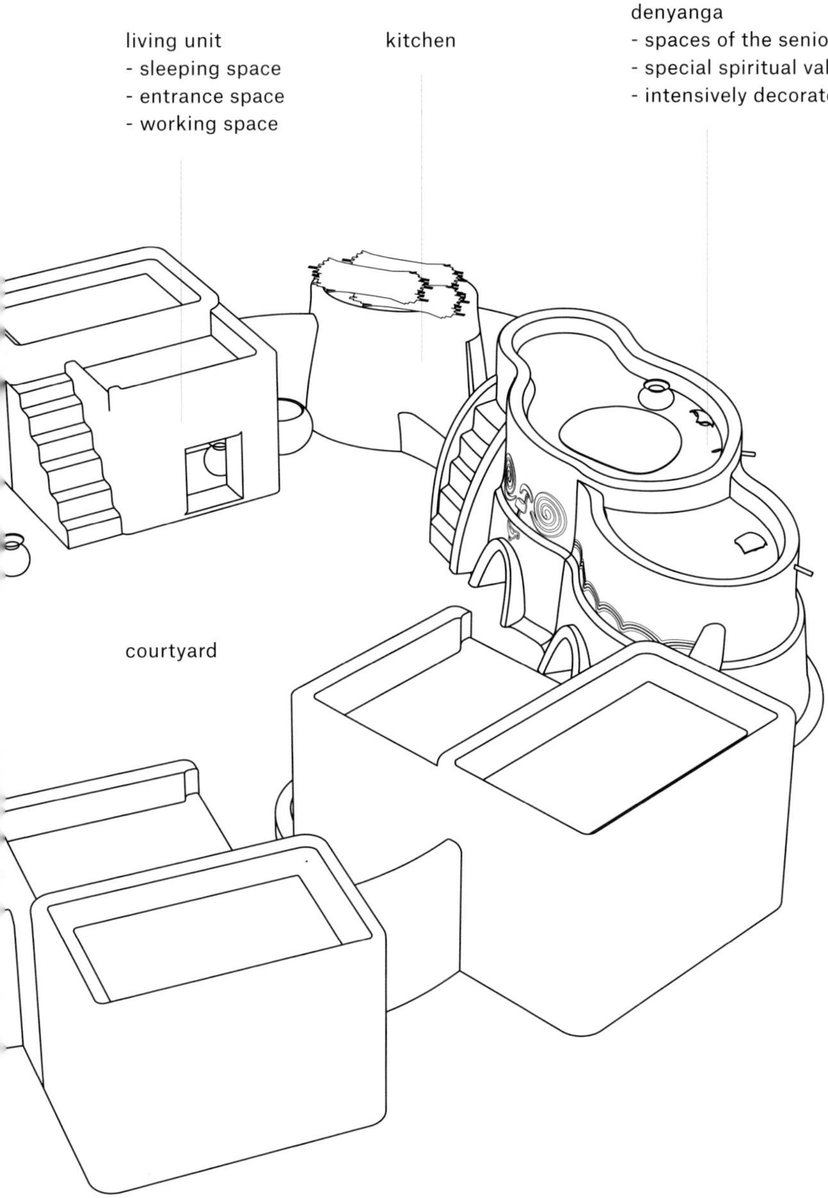

daily/ functional | seasonal/ structural | historic/ spiritual

TALKING TREES

Chrili Car
February 2012

"On this tree, the witches come and meet at night—if you take the bark of mahogany and mix it with Shea nut and dawadawa, you have a medicine for stomach problems—at this Gua tree, there was a pond that never dried out, and that is why the village is called Guabuliga"

In the reality of the village of Guabuliga, trees have a role far beyond just being ornamental objects in open space, they are characters. Everyday life is intimately connected with the tree in front of your house. Trees structure the village with their high and dense crowns; their shade creates places to work and rest, and the children covet their fruits. Trees are individuals as well as resources. One of the mango trees became so big that a family decided to relocate their house in order to avoid cutting down the tree.

In 'Talking Trees', 18 trees of multicultural origin unveil their roles in the village, as well as their botanical significance within various concepts of knowledge transfer. They mirror personal histories of the inhabitants. They are important for the microclimate. Some provide medicine, some are sources of income, and some are even gods.

HISTORIC VALUE
- Thorn tree
- African locust bean
- Teak

SPIRITUAL VALUE
- Kapok
- Baobab

ECONOMICAL VALUE
- Mango
- Shea nut
- Cashew
- Calabash
- Ficus

MEDICAL VALUE
- African mahogany
- Pawpaw
- Moringa
- West African copal
- Neem
- Toronkpaa

NAME UNKNOWN
- Lebbeck
- Cassia tree

Ceiba pentrandra (group) - Kapok - Guŋŋa

Bombacaceae - Origin: Americna tropics, western and central Africa. Properties: Up to 30m tall deciduous tree with horizontal or ascending branches; 40-80cm deep horizontal root system; smooth, pale grey bark; ovoid crown; alternate, digitately compound leaves with 5-9 elliptical leaflets (5-21 x 2-6,5cm); regular, bisexual, 5-merous, pink,creamy, or white flowers; a pendulous oblong-ellipsoid fruit (7,5-30cm x 3-15cm, narrow at both ends; seeds embedded in COPIOUS WHITE FLOSS; creamy-white wood; other varieties up to 60m tall and with spines on young bole.Use: Flowers, young fruits, roasted seeds (although possibly upsetting digestion) are eaten; wood ash as kitchen salt; bee-plant (amber-coloured honey); leaves and shoots as fodder - medicine: root against leprosy, diarrhoea, dysentery; root bark against dysmenorrhoea, hypertension; stem bark against toothache, mouth problems, stomach problems, diarrhoea, hernia, gonorrhoea, heart troubles, oedema, fever, asthma, rickets, swellings, wounds, leprous macules, hypertension, as enema; gum/leaves also against fatigue, lumbago, as alterative, laxative, abortifacient, as eye-bath, dressing on sores, tumours, abscesses, whitlows; leaf sap against skin infections and mental illness, stiffness of the limbs, headaches and bleeding of pregnant women, (veterinary) against trypanosomiasis; flowers agains t constipation;powdered fruit against intestinal parasites, stomach ache; fibre for cleaning wounds; seed oil against rheumatism and wounds

- continued next card -

The witch has killed my brother. He has put medicine in the food and give it to my brother. There are two witches who killed my brother - Like the guŋŋa tree there. In the evening, he jumps up and calls my brother. If you see it, it makes like a fire. And my brother said my stomach is paining. He is go to the hospital, Walewale hospital. He is say, go to Tamale hospital. He is take there my brother. He is die. My brother stomach is the big and he is die. Tamale hospital say that he is buy the grave. He says no. He is pay the man and get my brother and come back to the Guabuliga and put my brother to the ground.

Thorn tree - gua -
Acacia sp.

African locust bean - duwaa -
Parkia biglobosa

Teak - aluura tiiya -
Tectona grandis

Kapok - guŋŋa -
Ceiba pentranda

Baobab - tuwaa -
Adansonia digitata

Mango - manga tiiya -
Mangifera indica

Shea nut - taŋŋa -
Vitellaria paradoxa

Cashew - antiiya -
Anacardium occidentale

Calabash - gmantia -
Crescentia cujete

Ficus – gampiriga –
Ficus sp.

African mahogany – kuka –
Khaya senegalensis

xx – toronkpaa –
xx

Pawpaw – gonna –
Carica papaya

Moringa – arizana tiiya –
Moringa oleifera

African copal – nyoaa –
Daniellia oliveri

Neem – nansaa tiiya –
Azadirachta indica

Lebbeck – xx –
Albizia lebbeck

Cassia tree – xx –
Senna siamea

GUABULIGA FOODSCAPES

Lea Dietiker
September 2013

While we were preparing for Ghana, I already knew that I wanted to do research on the food there and to display my newly gained knowledge of food production and preparation in Guabuliga in a photographic work.

On location, I had the opportunity to plan local dishes with a local lady, go buy the ingredients at the market, and take a series of photos documenting the cooking process. Dishes like Banku with okra stew and the main local dish, TZ (Tuo Zaafi with Alefu soup), were jointly prepared over these days and photographed by myself.

The next series looks at the street vendors in Guabuliga, their strategic positioning in the village, and their settings for specific dishes, necessary containers, and selected furniture. There are different spatial scenarios and types of sales, for example, a table for cooking, or simply a bench in the schoolyard, as well as different types of dishes corresponding to demand and the time of day in which they were sold.

Another series documents the sowing, planting, harvesting, drying, and storage of foods.

Collaborator / cook: Humu Adamu

Banku with okra stew

Yam with cabbage stew

TZ (Tuo Zaafi) with Alefu leaves

Gari beans with yam

MARKET GROUND(S)

Antonella Amesberger
September 2012

Inspired by the functional use of grounds in the northern Region of Ghana, a floorscape proposal was created for Guabuliga's market area. Vernacular modelling of floor surfaces in the region generates workspaces for such diverse purposes as drying, sorting, and presenting food and goods. This was researched alongside market display techniques at the markets of neighboring villages.

As a starting point, a solid volume made out of cement and sand served as the initial prototype. To differentiate areas according to a variety of uses, the proposed platform is divided into surfaces of different dimensions, arranged at different heights. These levels and sizes correspond to specific functional scenarios of market practices as found in the region. Located in the shade of surrounding trees, groups of platforms of this kind would generate a new landscape of the market structure in Guabuliga. Outside of market hours, platforms could be turned into open-air furniture, creating a space of interaction for inhabitants of the village. Proportions were tested by starting with mock-ups made out of wooden sticks and rope. A 1:1 model made out of wooden sticks and canvas was set up on Guabuliga's market location in order to introduce the prototype to the local chief and market women on the village market day.

Prototype

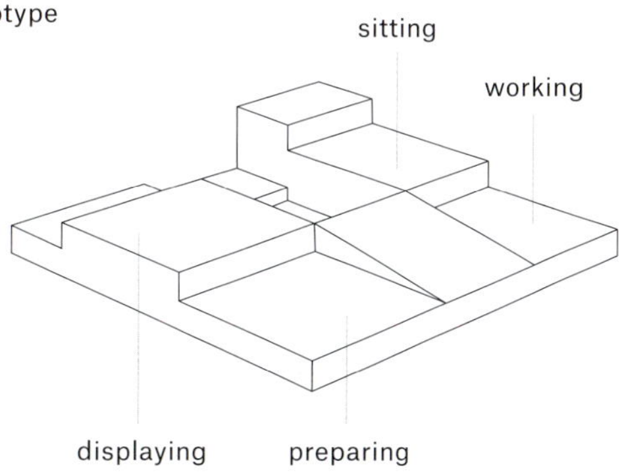

WELL—BY THE THORN TREE

Theresa Theuretzbacher
February 2012

People of Guabuliga suffer from insufficient quantity and quality of water supplies, especially during dry seasons. Most hand-dug wells, which are located in the middle of the village, dry out by the end of the dry season. Boreholes located at the borders of the village, which access deeper water sources, provide water during the whole year.

To get an initial overview of the water quality of certain wells and boreholes, seven water samples were taken to be analyzed by the CSIR Water Research Institute in Tamale. According to the results, six out of the seven water samples were found to be bacteriologically unsafe to be used as drinking water and do not conform with WHO guidelines and Ghana's legal standards.

Women, who are in charge of the water collection, prefer the water from certain hand-dug wells over water from clean boreholes due to its good taste and other benefits. The bag used for fetching the water is made from recycled vehicle tires. These bags contribute to the high level of contamination of the water, as they may carry human and animal pathogens that pollute hand-dug wells during usage.

The 'water movement' plan was the starting point of the project. It traces movement patterns, thereby highlighting information about the most frequented wells and boreholes, as well as underserved areas. Women do not always take the shortest way to get water for several reasons, like the better taste of certain water, or due to social aspects. More people prefer to use the wells on the west side over the boreholes on the east side. Hand-dug wells in the middle of the village are only used by the surrounding residents or the family who constructed the well. This information is important in terms of making decisions concerning the renovation of existing water points or future water supplies.

	E. coli per 100 ml
WHO guidelines	0
Ghana law	0
Guabuliga reality	
W1	363
W5	476
W13	850
HP7	63
HP4	0
W6	684
W12	710

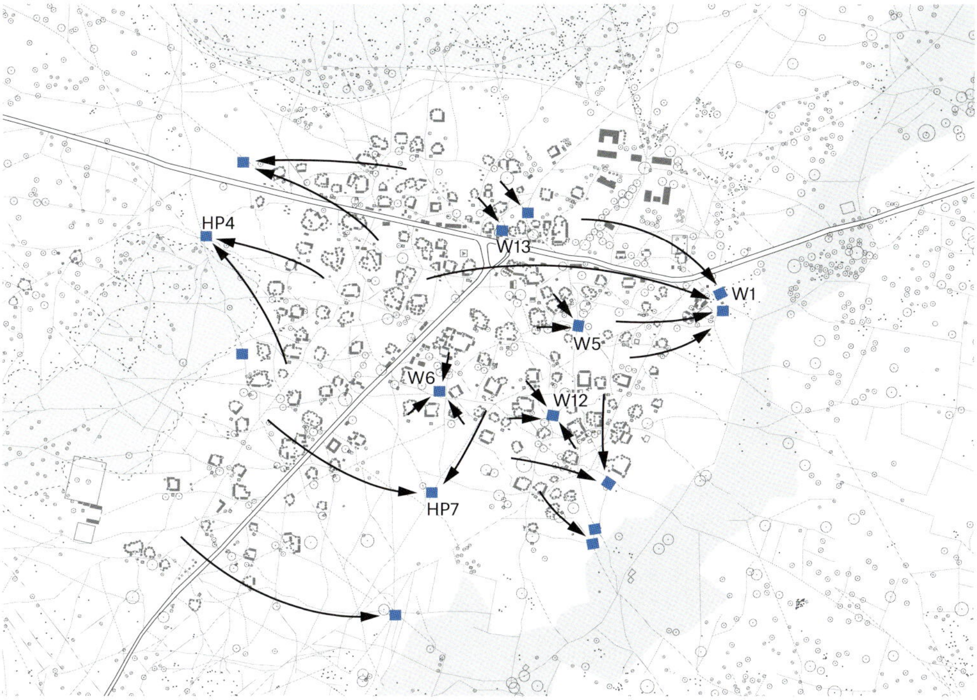

Water fetching and movement map

Well—by the Thorn Tree

Theresa Theuretzbacher
September 2012

E. coli per 100 ml

	Dry season	Rainy season
WHO guidlines	0	0
Ghana law	0	0
Guabuliga reality		
W1	363	1,052
W5	476	42
W13	850	272
HP7	63	732
HP4	0	4
W6	684	55
W12	710	56

A second assessment of the water points that were analyzed in the dry season was done in the rainy season to measure the impact of climatic conditions on the water sources. The results of the bacteriological analysis showed that all drinking water sources from wells were contaminated with coliforms and E. coli, which indicates fecal contamination. The tested wells located in the middle of the village showed better results in the rainy season, while the wells and the boreholes at the borders of the village were less contaminated with E. coli in the dry season. Reasons for contamination could be due to livestock that roam unattended within the village and nearby water sources during the dry season. Water sources could be contaminated through groundwater flow, especially when groundwater levels are high in the rainy season.

A well inspection with Tamale-based water engineer Frank B. Kumah was carried out in addition to the laboratory analysis. A report on the status and an estimate of necessary investments and future costs of the renovation of the wells and boreholes was made. This part of the project highlights that immediate action is necessary in order to reduce the contamination of the drinking water supply.

Consultant: Frank B. Kumah

W1
sealed floor in bad condition,
no hand pump, no drainage,
water fetching with receptacles

W5
sealed floor in bad condition,
no hand pump, no drainage,
water fetching with receptacles

W13
sealed floor in bad condition,
no hand pump, no drainage,
water fetching with receptacles

HP7
sealed floor in bad condition,
hand pump does not work, no drainage,
water fetching with receptacles

HP4
sealed floor in good condition,
hand pump works, drainage

W6
sealed floor in bad condition,
no hand pump, no drainage,
water fetching with receptacles

W12
sealed floor in bad condition,
no hand pump, no drainage,
water fetching with receptacles

Well—by the Thorn Tree

Theresa Theuretzbacher
September 2012

Aside from the necessary infrastructure and maintenance of clean water supply systems, adequate usage is required to improve sanitary, hygiene, and health situations, a factor which is dependent on education. Overcoming habits that are dangerous to the community's health through promoting adapted behavior was the goal of the efforts to improve the situation in Guabuliga. A first training program for children was held to create awareness. The educational material was provided by the Center for Affordable Water and Sanitation Technology (CAWST, 2012), an open online educational source.

Forty children attended the lesson and participated in a drawing competition. The children summarized what they had learned and visually translated these messages into drawings over the course of a workshop. The resulting posters were publicly displayed in the Guabuliga Gallery for several days. One poster was awarded, reproduced, and hung on the walls of public facilities and the school.

Teacher: Rahamatu Dokurugu /
External juror: Bernard Akoi-Jackson

MALOUDA
15

Guabuliga's founding myth—'The Well by the Thorn Tree'—is the conceptual starting point for developing contextual yet novel spatial and programmatic scenarios for the village. A dynamic growth plan articulates strategies for an ecological future for Guabuliga, based on historical, geographical, and climatic parameters. This environmental and infrastructural approach has been identified as a way of avoiding a kind of master planning in a modernistic sense, which is favoured by governmental entities in the region and is generally associated with modernization and development. It turned out to be more relevant to generate an open space policy as opposed to a housing pattern, in a context in which the design and realization of living space naturally lies in the hands of the villagers/users themselves. Dry season gardens, a recreationally/commercially programmed greenbelt that blends into the market place, and connected green arteries that embed culturally activated pockets and sport facilities, all together create a multi-performative carpet that has a spatial, aesthetic, and climatic impact on the rural fabric. Infrastructural nodes serve as initial punctures that allow housing clusters to evolve, while the shape of these clusters responds to external factors and (local) self-generating principles of neighborhood. Only a set of reactive rules on how to dock onto these nodes is spatially defined, so as to secure the desired density of built structures in relation to in-between space. Based on this strategy, variations on potential maps of Guabuliga—with ideal growth forecasts for 2032—have been worked out.

Guabuliga growth directions

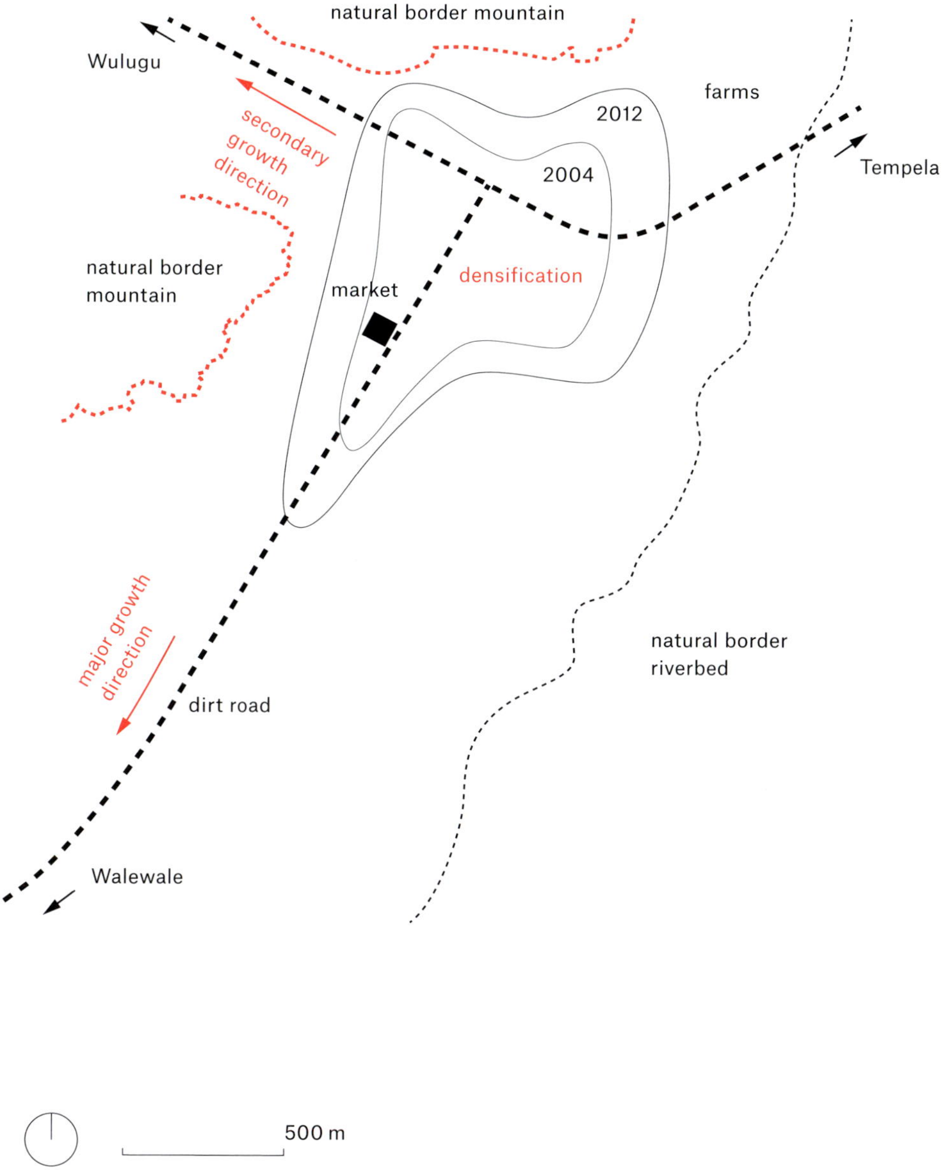

1902

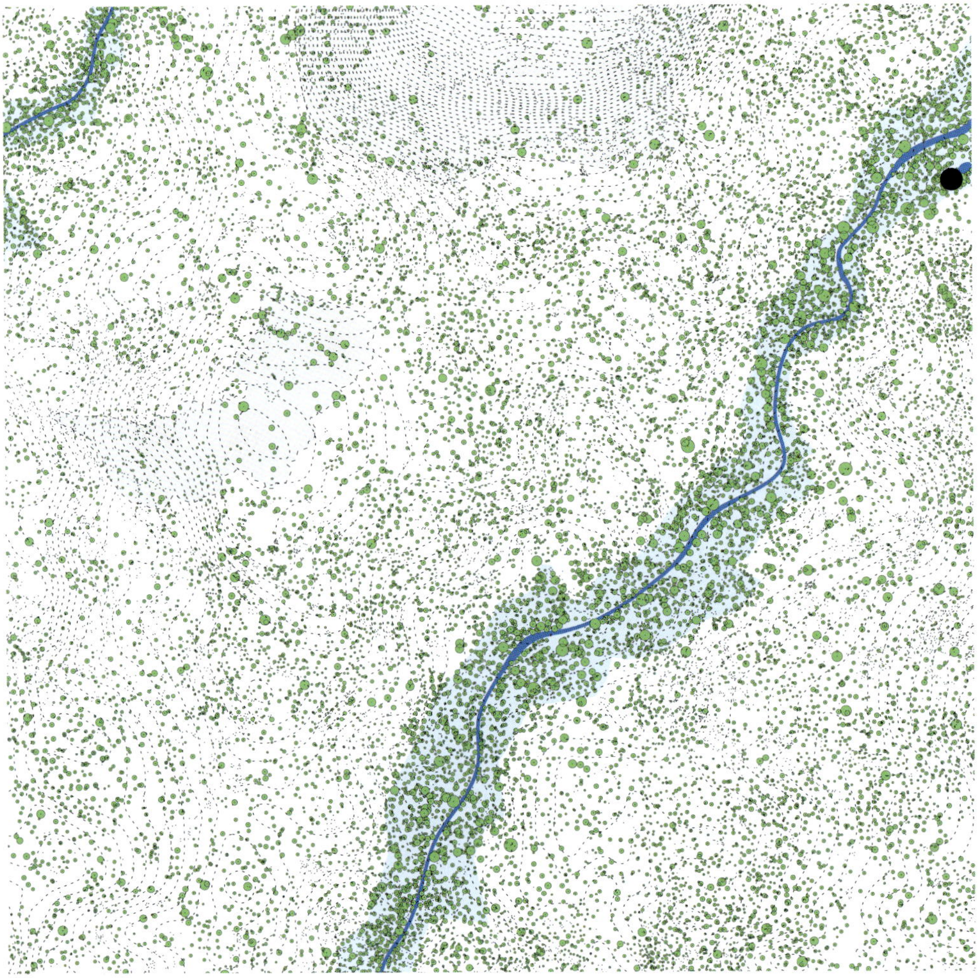

● Well by the Thorn tree

500 m

2004

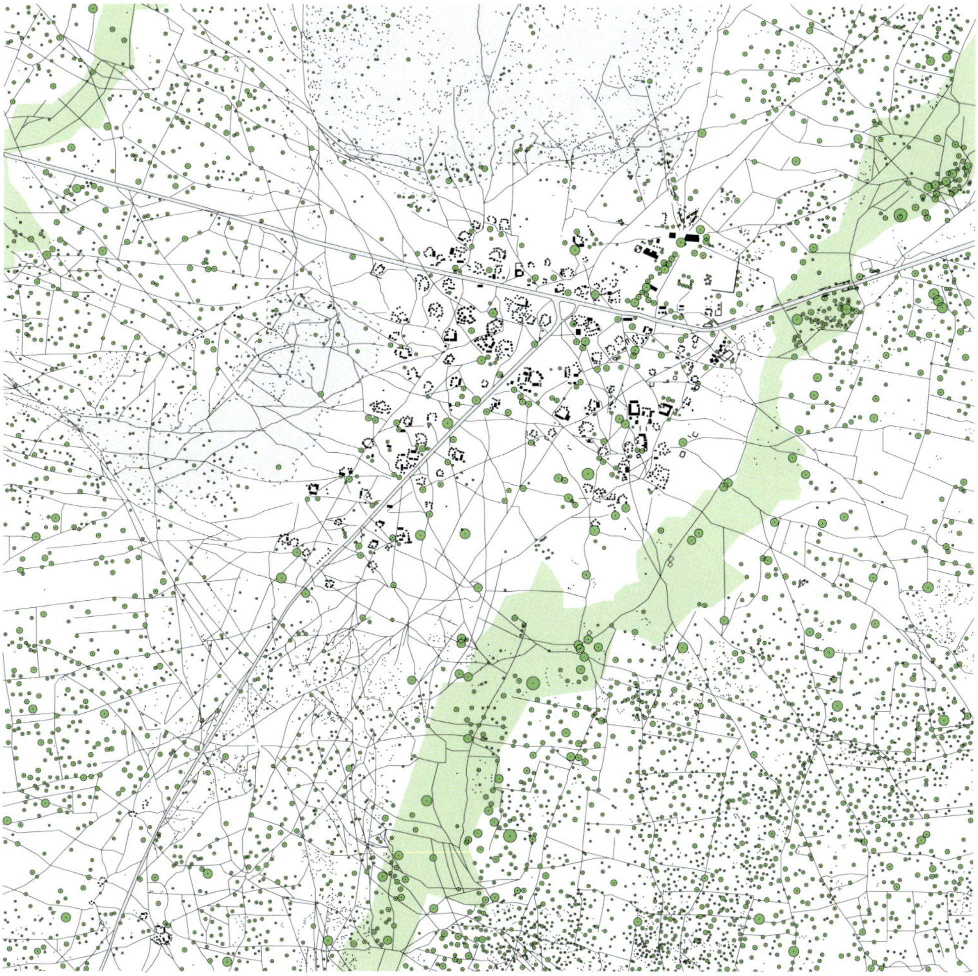

hills
dry riverbed
trees

2012

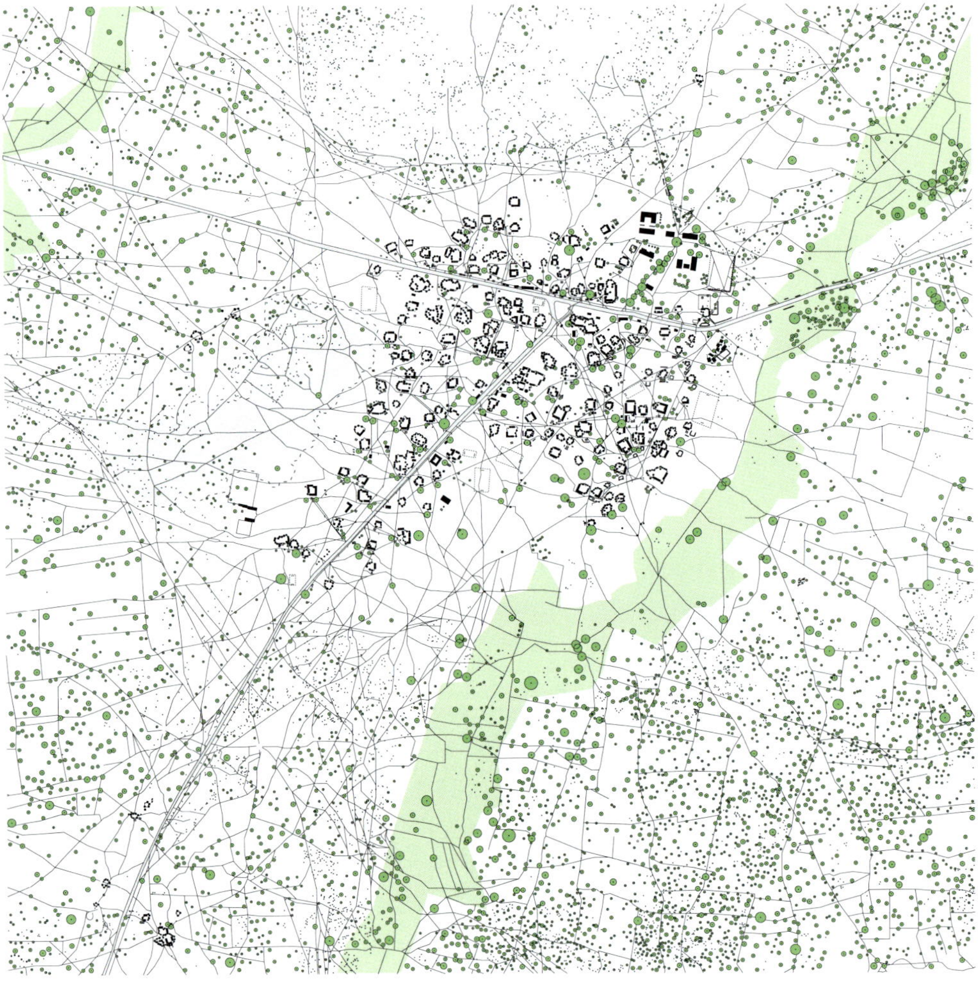

500 m

2032

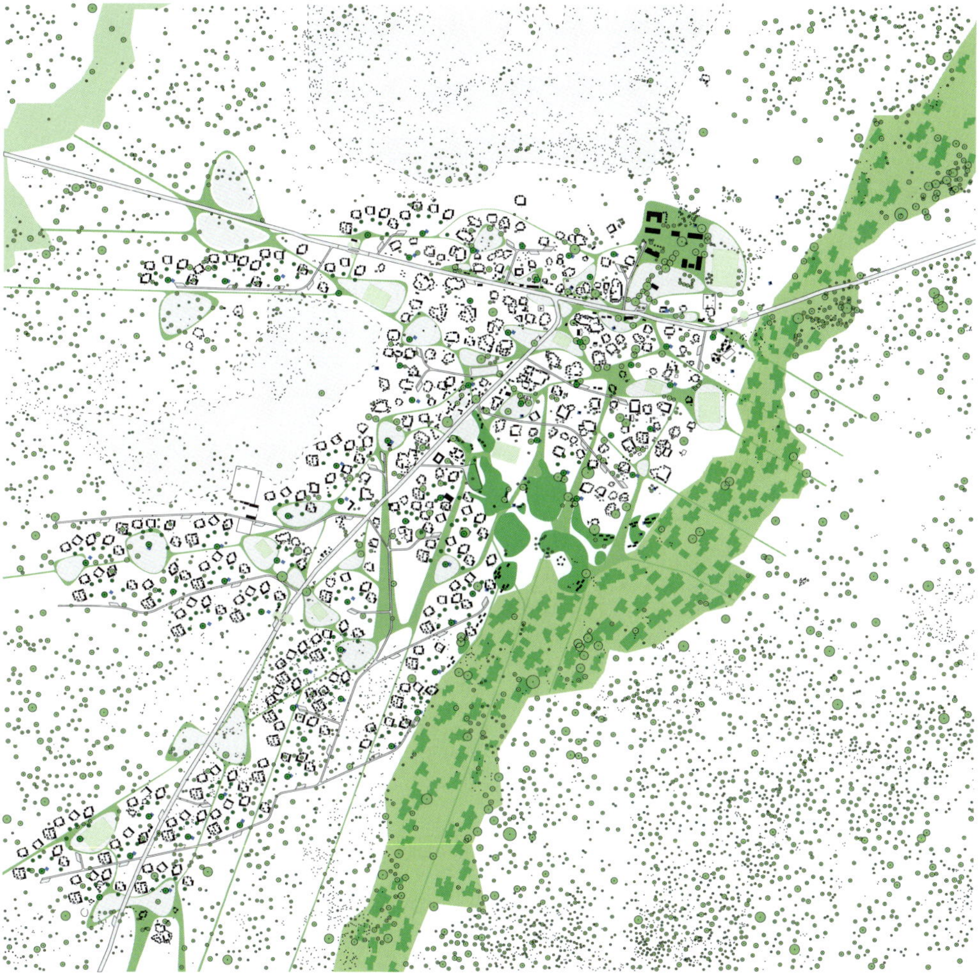

Wind Analysis

Part of the initial mapping process of Guabuliga was an environmental analysis including wind and solar studies. Simulations were done on a village scale to inform the dynamic growth plan of Guabuliga 2032. Vernacular building compounds were grouped in varying arrangements and tested with digital simulation tools, such as computational fluid dynamics (CFD) analysis. Linear, concentric, and radial arrangements of building groups were tested against wind coming from the north and south to simulate the Harmattan wind of the dry season and the more humid wind of the rainy season, respectively. The outcome of these studies informed the generative parameters of future compounds and vegetation zones in the growth plan, as well as the landscape design of the greenbelt. Open space and settlement, trees and houses are arranged in order to channel the wind into the village during the rainy season and protect from the harsh winds during the Harmattan season.

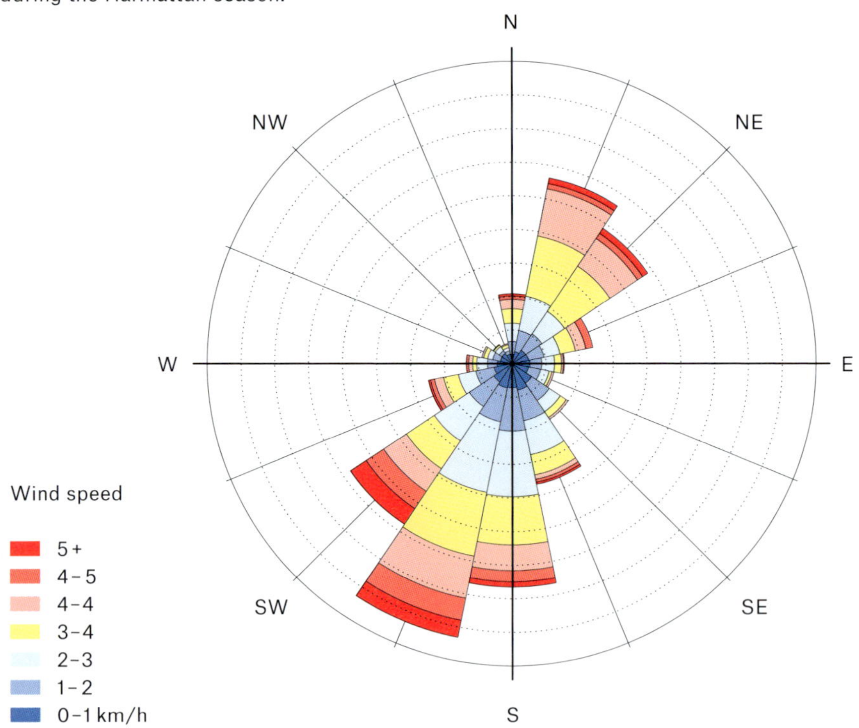

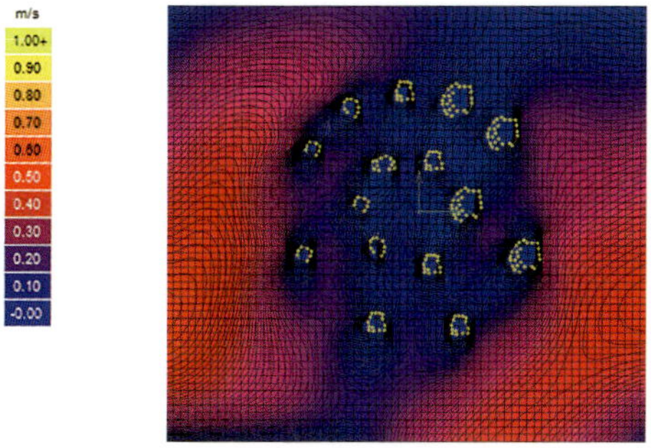

Air flow rate of compound buildings in concentric circular arrangement

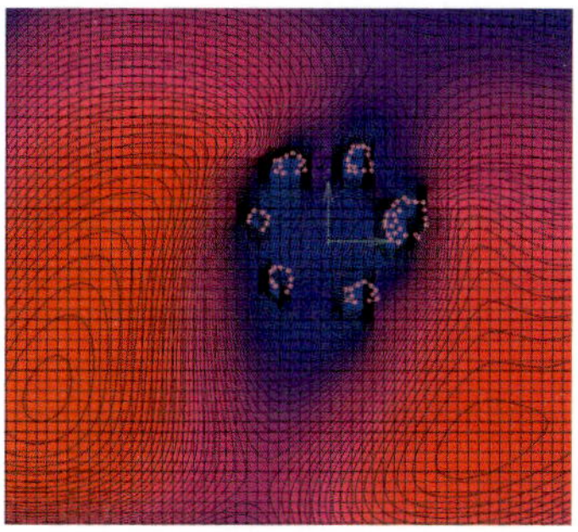

Circular arrangement

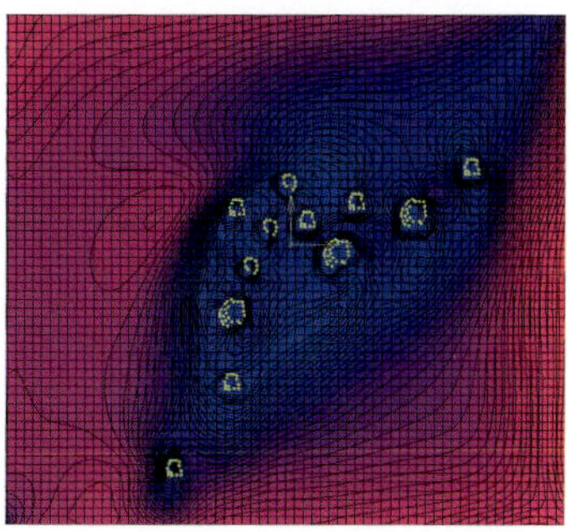

Pocket arrangement

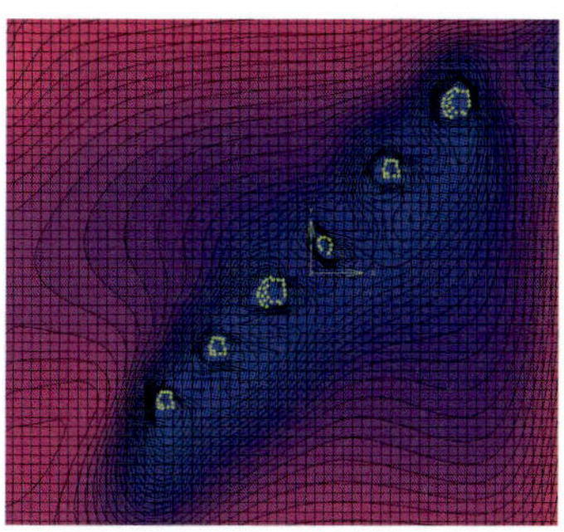

Linear arrangement

2032 Dry Season

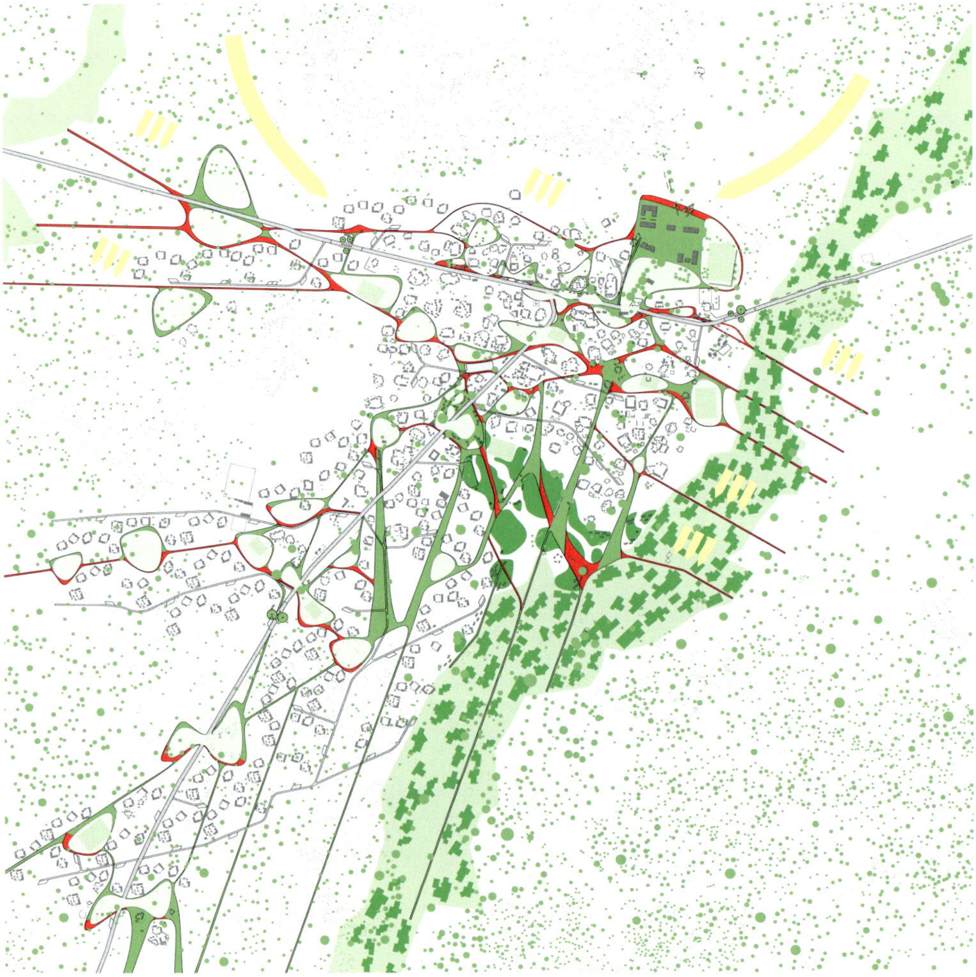

Harmattan, December–March, avg. +32°C

- prevailing Harmattan wind
- pathways with wind-blocking vegetation
- dry riverbed
- pathways with low vegetation
- greenbelt and dry season gardening

500 m

2032 Rainy Season

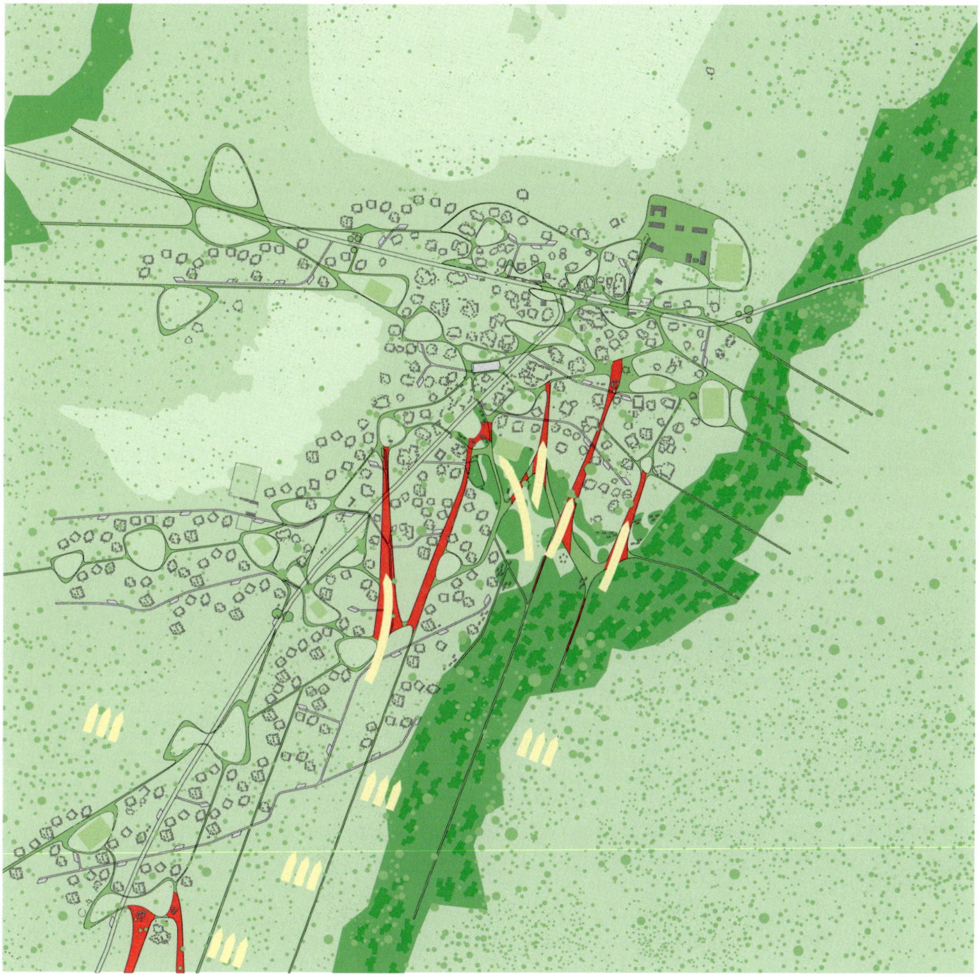

Prevailing wind, April – November, avg. +26°C

- prevailing wind
- wind aisles
- pathways with vegetation
- greenbelt and river bed

FROM RESPONSIVE TO RESPONSIBLE

Bernhard Sommer

When Baerbel Mueller asked me to write on climate responsive planning, I asked myself: Why responsive?

The term is surely derived from the IT field. Yet the projects realized in Baerbel Mueller's [applied] Foreign Affairs program don't apply sophisticated sensor technologies. The projects are not responsive in the way a highly engineered building is. Of course, the planning practice in her lab involves all kinds of simulation software and intelligent, customized scripts. But this is not the only aspect that is fascinating about the [a]FA projects.

The projects always include and incorporate the people who will live with them as an indispensable part of their functionality. I say to live with them to avoid the term use or user, perhaps I should have also avoided the term functionality. This deeply humanistic approach is the universal lesson to learn from [a]FA. Engineers talk about users as much as economists talk about consumers, and Energy Design is usually seen as a consultancy for reducing the demand for resources by increasing efficiency through optimizing shapes, processes, and systems. Yet with all the power and data documentation made possible through computers, it still remains difficult to come up with a convincing answer to the big question of today: the question of energy. By this I mean the fair distribution and clever use of resources, be it any kind of raw materials or the most limited resource in this world: land. Land can not only be polluted like water, it can be cleaned, or exploited and consumed like raw materials that can somehow always be replaced by other materials. Land is devastated and rendered useless for decades—and here I am not (only) referring to (not so) distant wars and rainforests, I am also talking about failures of zoning laws and economic interests that thoughtlessly and unnecessarily consume huge areas of fertile and inhabitable land. A reason for this failure of technocratic administration of natural wealth can be seen in a narrow-minded focus on physical processes and logical cause-and-effect schemes only. It is more than stupid to deny natural forces and logic, it is irresponsible in fact—it would be worthwhile to widen the understanding of what a cause is and what an effect is through cultural concepts. If we treat the people we work with (or for) with respect and dignity—as much for them as for ourselves—we will be able to find new constraints and causes.

When the [a]FA Guabuliga students identified clay and reeds as building materials, as they would be readily available, traditionally in use, and climatically advantageous, they soon found out that, for socio-cultural reasons, these would never be accepted as the basis for a desirable building technology of the future. The fascinating circular base geometries of the compounds were also expected to yield to clear rectangular shapes, as Josef

Hofmarcher describes in his 'The Spatial Cell' project. We are well familiar with disastrous material desires, such as the car. We know that desires can be created, as demand in the economy is being created. So if engineers and architects find out that the use of certain materials and shapes is advantageous, this could be disseminated in a society through advertising from the top down. If this is sustainable, for sure it is costly.

However, the [a]FA team would never have had the resources to change consumer behaviour in such a manner. As people are not perceived as consumers here, nor as users, but as proud people having a social status to defend and knowledge to pass on, they might want to plant a tree and for sure will strive to erect their own compounds. These social forces became part of the project and all considerations regarding climate and sustainability. What the students developed went beyond a responsive design—I would call it a behavioural planning concept. At the Department of Energy Design, we refer to this term as the use of non-linear computational design methodologies that operate through self-organizational processes in order to address a wide range of practical and discursive issues within a designed architectural and urban expression. We are NOT referring to behaviourist psychology by using this term.

Clearly, such a concept is closer to our contemporary understanding of physics, which only applies a deterministic behaviour of the many, rather than the old-fashioned Newtonian actio-reactio. When Rudolf Clausius introduced the term entropy, he could not have been aware of how he had changed the concept of physics from a collection of deterministic laws to a continuum of statistical effects of probability. What now guides us is the consciousness of irreversibility and a more humble approach regarding feasibility.

Life lowers the entropy on earth, or at least in an organism. Consuming solar energy avoids the dissipation of part of the incoming radiation into the nothingness of the infinity of space. Crude oil was generated in this way. If we burn it today, we increase entropy again, eliminating what took thousands of years within seconds.

Future energy concepts should encourage people to behave in a sustainable way, using solar forces, organisms, and geometries to lower or at least not increase entropy. The mastery will come through the development and design of self-organizational processes that shape the urban habitat.

BERNHARD SOMMER, architect, teaches and researches at the IoA's Department of Energy Design at the University of Applied Arts Vienna. He understands energy as a flow that leads time, as a new dimension, into architectural design. Bernhard is a co-founder and principal of exikon, an architectural practice that is strongly influenced by his research.

The dynamic growth plan for Guabuliga includes a responsive strategy that is used to situate and orient new housing clusters. It serves as a tool that generates building arrangements derived from the climatic adaptation and social spaces of the vernacular village pattern.

By defining a series of simple geometric parameters, new compounds are placed according to an *infrastructural node* and a *house tree*. This generates *node neighborhoods* that, in combination, produce an emergent and organic extension of the village. This growth process performs procedurally and is conceived as a step-by-step building guide for the village.

A new neighborhood begins with an *infrastructural node* that is placed 200 m from a water collection point—a sanitary parameter recommended by the IRC International Water and Sanitation Center. This marks the center of the new neighborhood and is equipped with components for a decentralized and exchangeable infrastructure, such as solar energy units, water storage, waste collection points, and a community tree. A *house tree* is then planted according to specified distances and directions from the *infrastructural node* for each new compound. This tree marks the entrance area and front of each compound. All entrances thereby face southwards and are sheltered from the Harmattan winds coming from the north. A *house tree* provides shade and shelter for social spaces, 'summer huts', and work areas, and can be found in the vernacular village growth pattern.

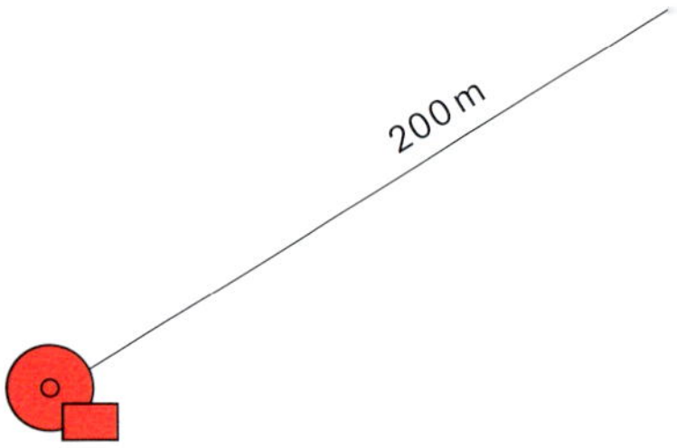

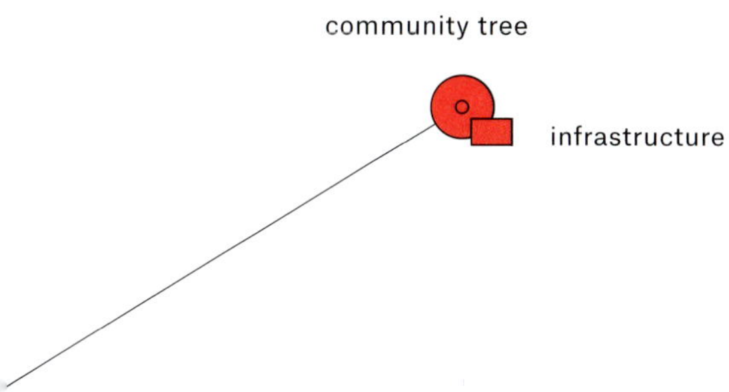

INFRASTRUCTURAL NODE

marks the central location of a neighborhood; includes a decentralized energy unit, a water supply, waste collection points, a community tree.

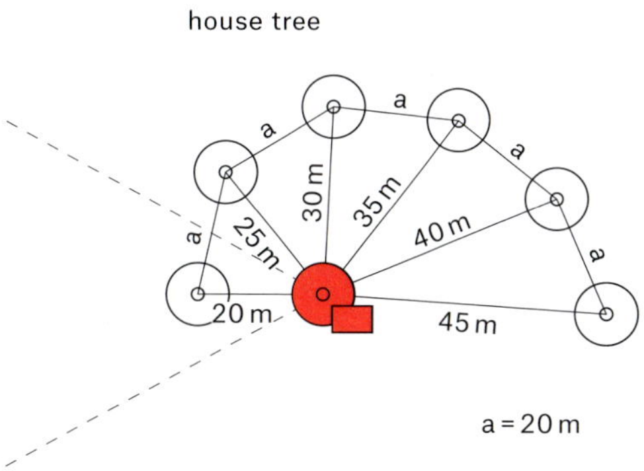

HOUSE TREE

marks the entrance area of a piece of land; houses a summer hut, shaded work areas

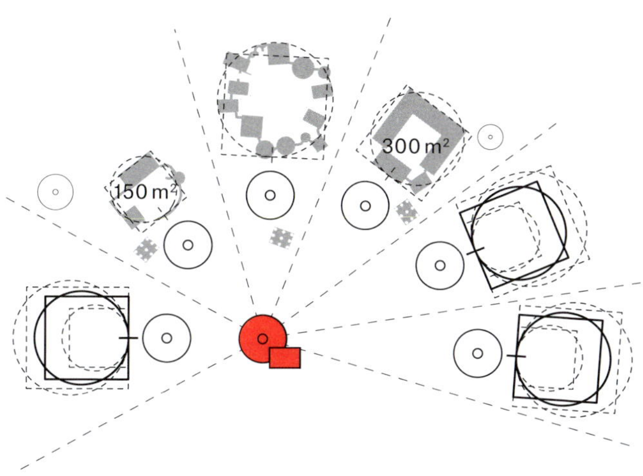

NODE NEIGHBORHOOD

four to six neighbors share an *infrastructural node*, each piece of land provides space for a family compound and a house farm

Family compound areas

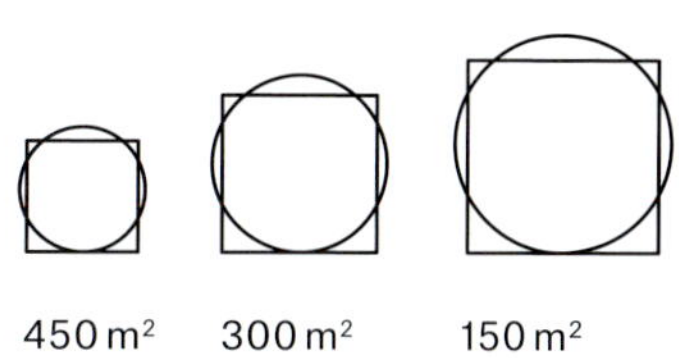

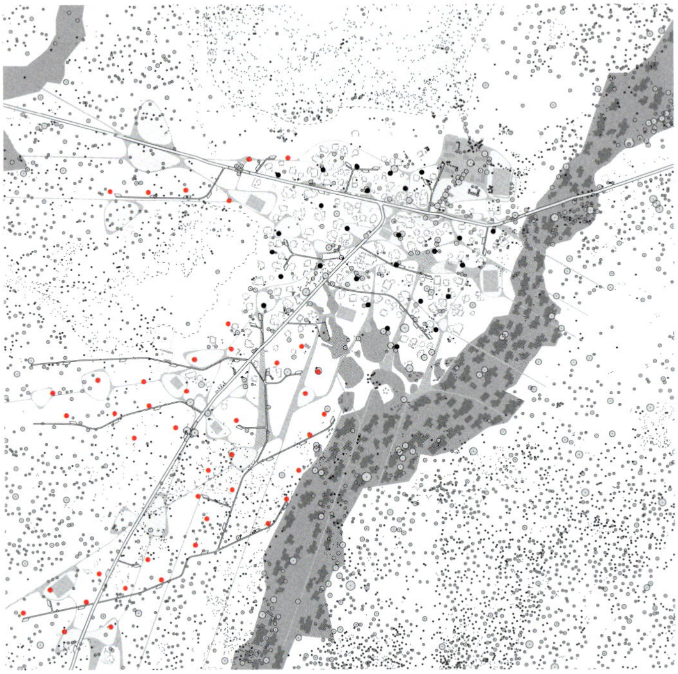

2017

● densification node
● expension node

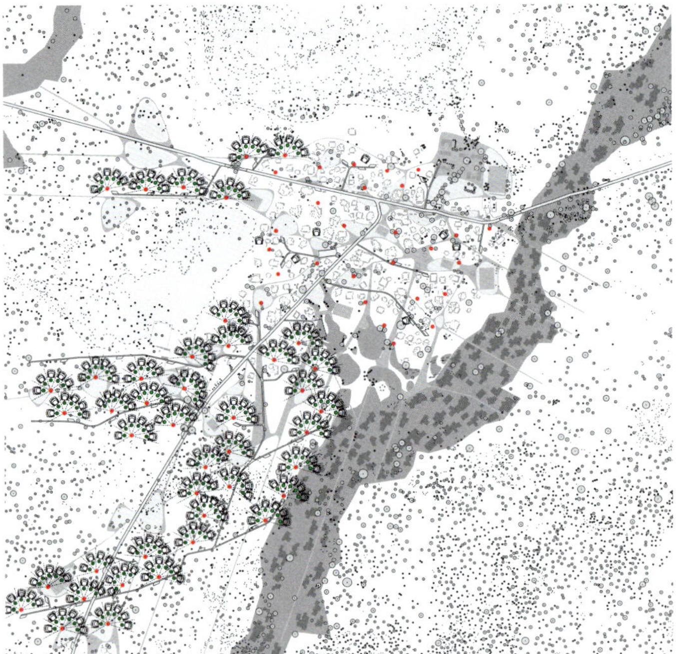

● node

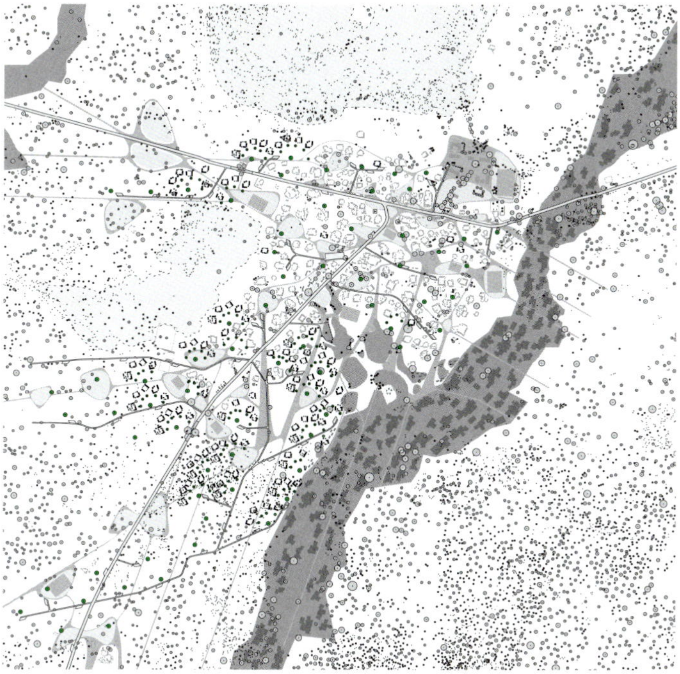

2022

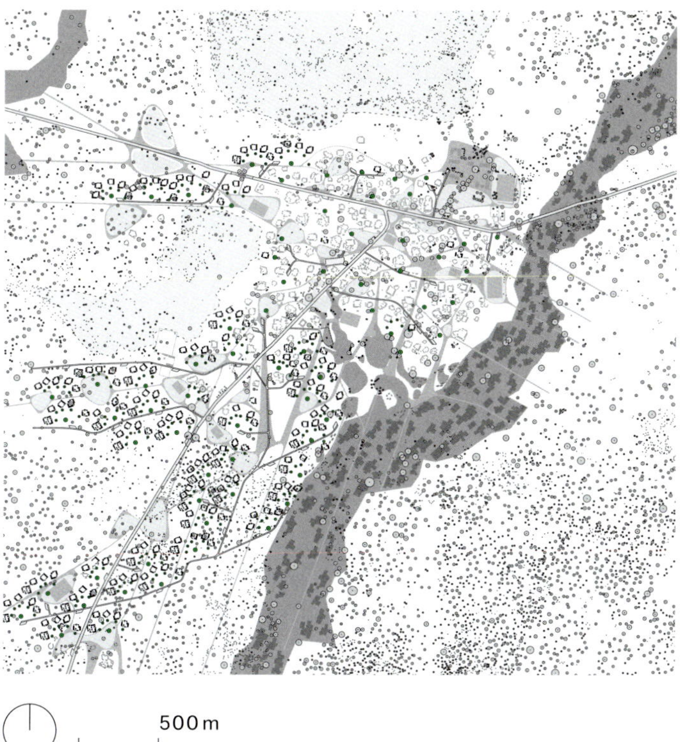

2032

Dry Season Gardens

The dynamic growth plan is based on an open space policy that creates a connective green carpet throughout the village including programmed 'green arteries', a greenbelt that blends into the market place, and 'dry season gardens'.

The Guabuliga greenbelt connects the village to the river bed, which runs from north to south on the eastern side of the village. This river bed has dried out in recent decades but still holds the potential to be used for dry season farming due to its low ground water depths and fertile soil. Currently, a handful of small walled gardens in the riverbed provide their owners with a variety of fruits and vegetables all year round. These gardens were identified as having environmental and economic potential and are prototypical of more extensive dry season farming. They allow for a harvest in a season during which fresh vegetables are scarce or expensive. Gardening during this period of the year not only prevents food shortages, but the rare fruits and vegetables that are grown also improve the attractiveness of the local market. To foster this agricultural scheme, both regional organic farming organisations and Guabuliga's dry season gardening pioneers will mentor other farmers in the practice of dry season farms.

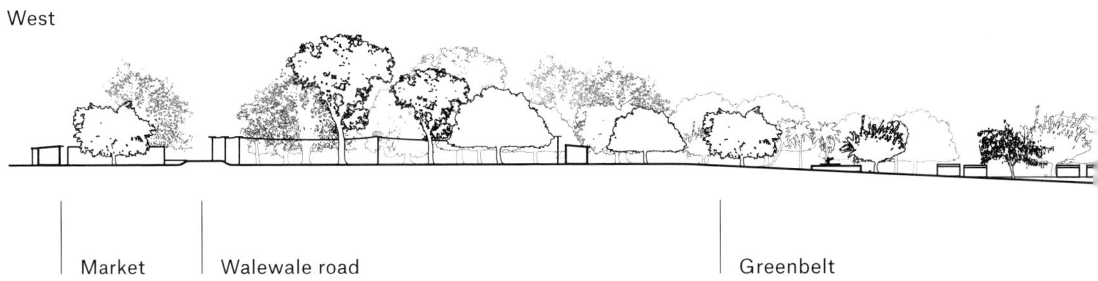

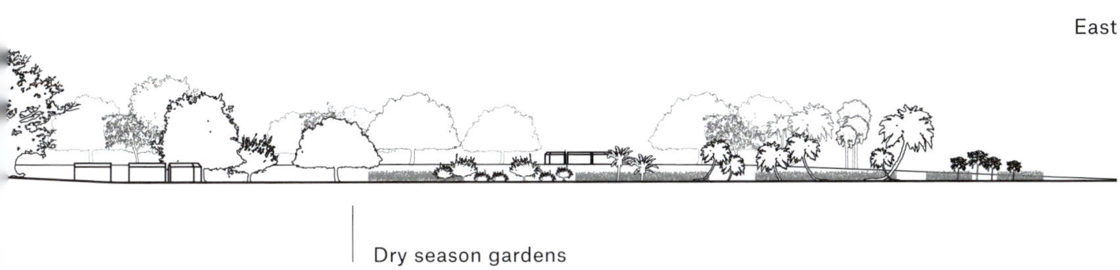
East
Dry season gardens

GUABULIGA GREENBELT

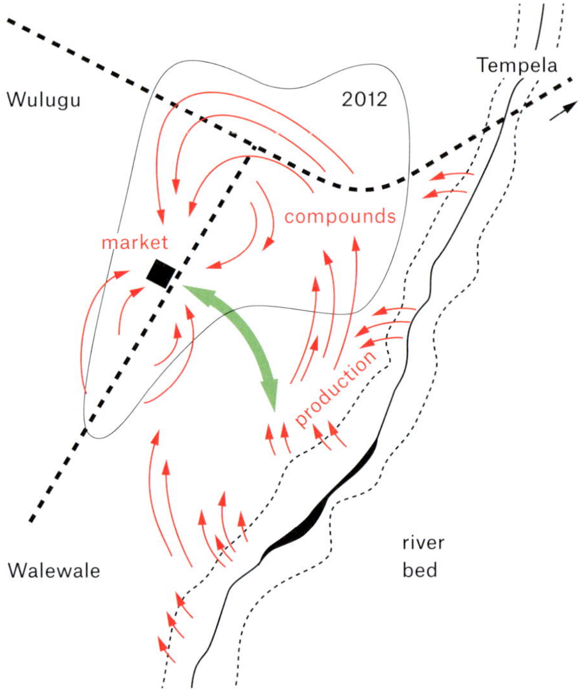

The greenbelt is one of the cornerstones of the Guabuliga growth plan. It is both conceptually and physically at the heart of Guabuliga's sustainable future as a multi-programmed, no-building zone between the central market of Guabuliga and the river bed to the southeast. As part of the ongoing engagement of [a]FA with the village, the greenbelt was identified as a catalyst for the processes described in the growth plan. Efforts towards its implementation began in mid-2012, following the first round of presentations of the Guabuliga project.

In September 2012, Chief Salifu and his council of elders recognized the status of the greenbelt during the second residency of [a]FA in the village. It was formally initiated during a planting day event in which 150 tree seedlings were distributed among the six *foŋŋu** and planted in strategic positions.

The selection of tree species included both indigenous and suitable foreign species and was linked to the future scenarios of the greenbelt. These scenarios promote economic, cultural, and recreational activities situated within the greenbelt area. The variety of tree species covers fruit-bearing trees and ones with other favorable characteristics, such as shading or medicinal uses. The selection of trees and their distribution was supervised by Chrili Car and was based on his mapping project 'Talking Trees' and further research into regional vegetation and planting strategies. The seedlings were acquired with the financial support of the NGO Braveaurora and were bought from several plant nurseries from within the region between Tamale and Bolgatanga, Wulugu and Walewale, and Guabuliga itself, to increase the diversity of trees in the greenbelt.

* *foŋŋu*: family-based, organizational unit that divides the village of Guabuliga and is represented in the council of elders and neighborhoods

Deforestation

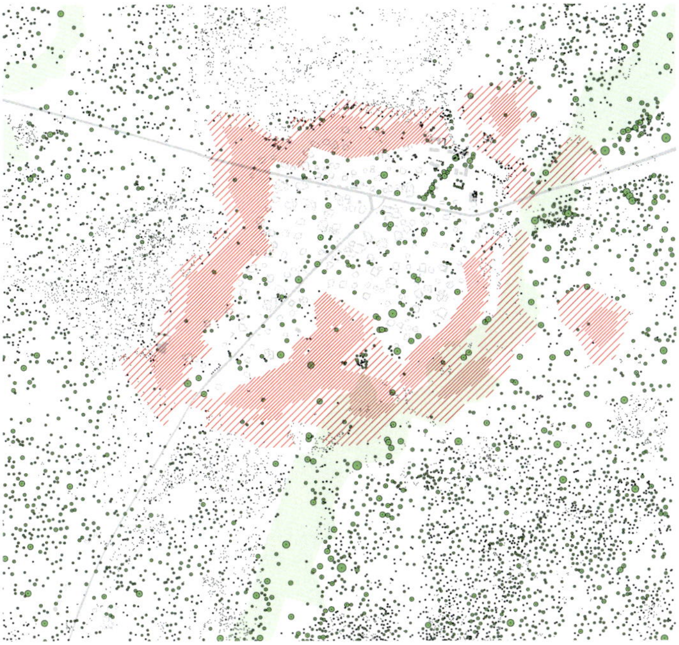

Reforestation, greenbelt and dry season gardens

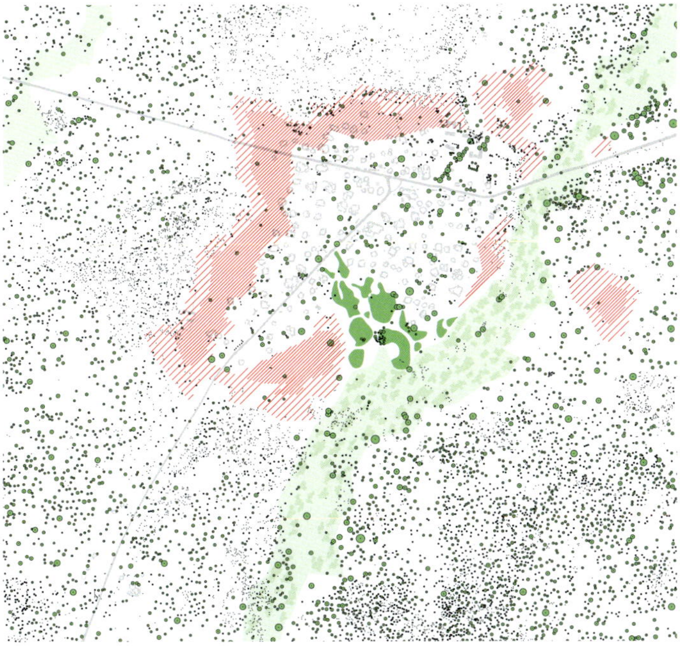

500 m

Sections of Guabuliga

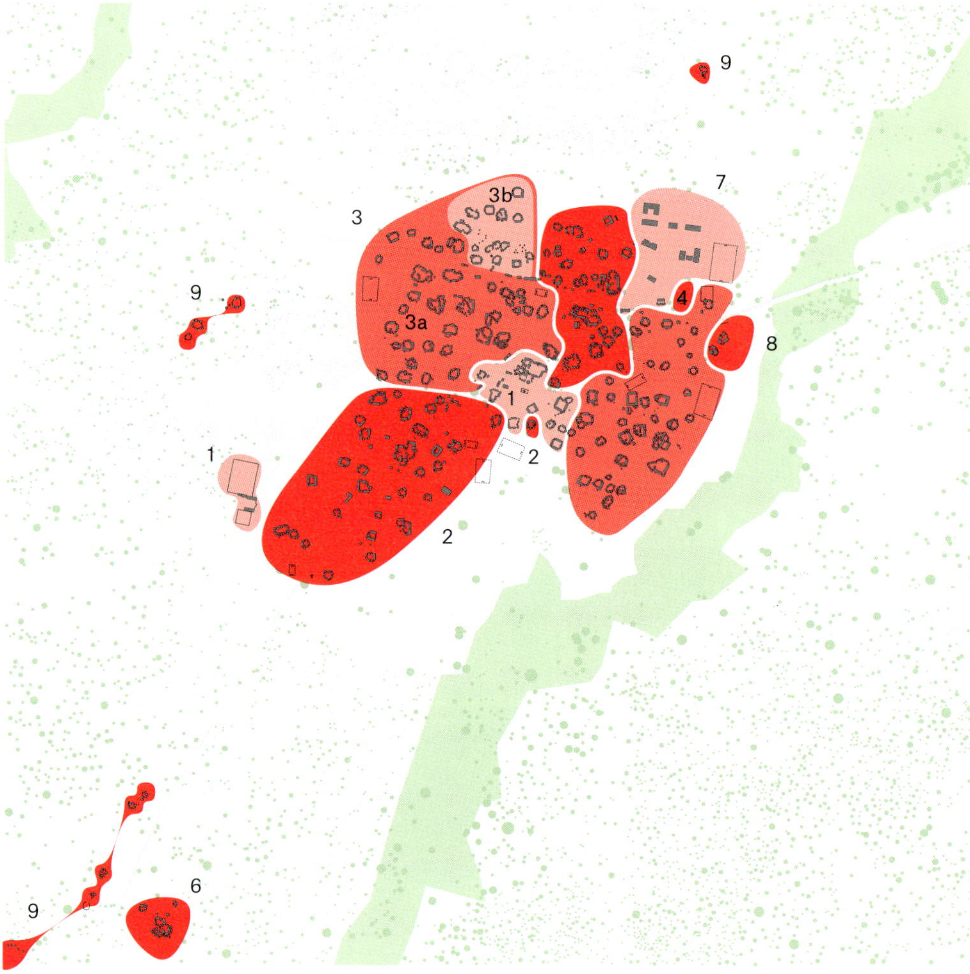

1	Nayiri foŋŋu	6	Mossi foŋŋu
2	Bangola	7	Educational
3	Wulugu foŋŋu	8	Braveaurora
3a	Wudana foŋŋu	9	Fulani compounds
3b	Kambonaba foŋŋu		
4	Gbandana foŋŋu		

500 m

Corresponding Greenbelt Sections

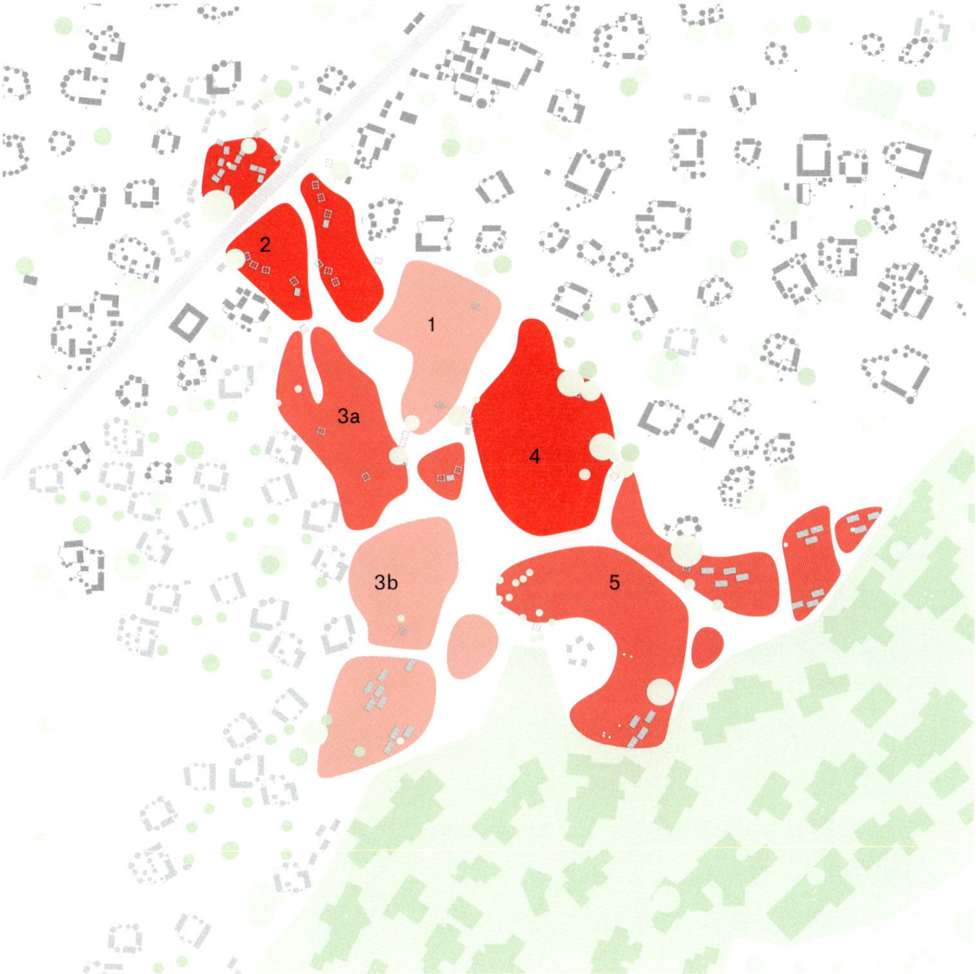

1 Nayiri foŋŋu
2 Bangola
3a Wudana foŋŋu
3b Kambonaba foŋŋu
4 Gbandana foŋŋu
5 Nouri Loabi

Tree Species

- African mahagony
- Kapok
- West African copal
- Neem
- Mango
- Soursop
- Sheanut
- Guava
- African locust bean
- Moringa
- Cashew
- Oilpalm

Greenbelt Planting Plan

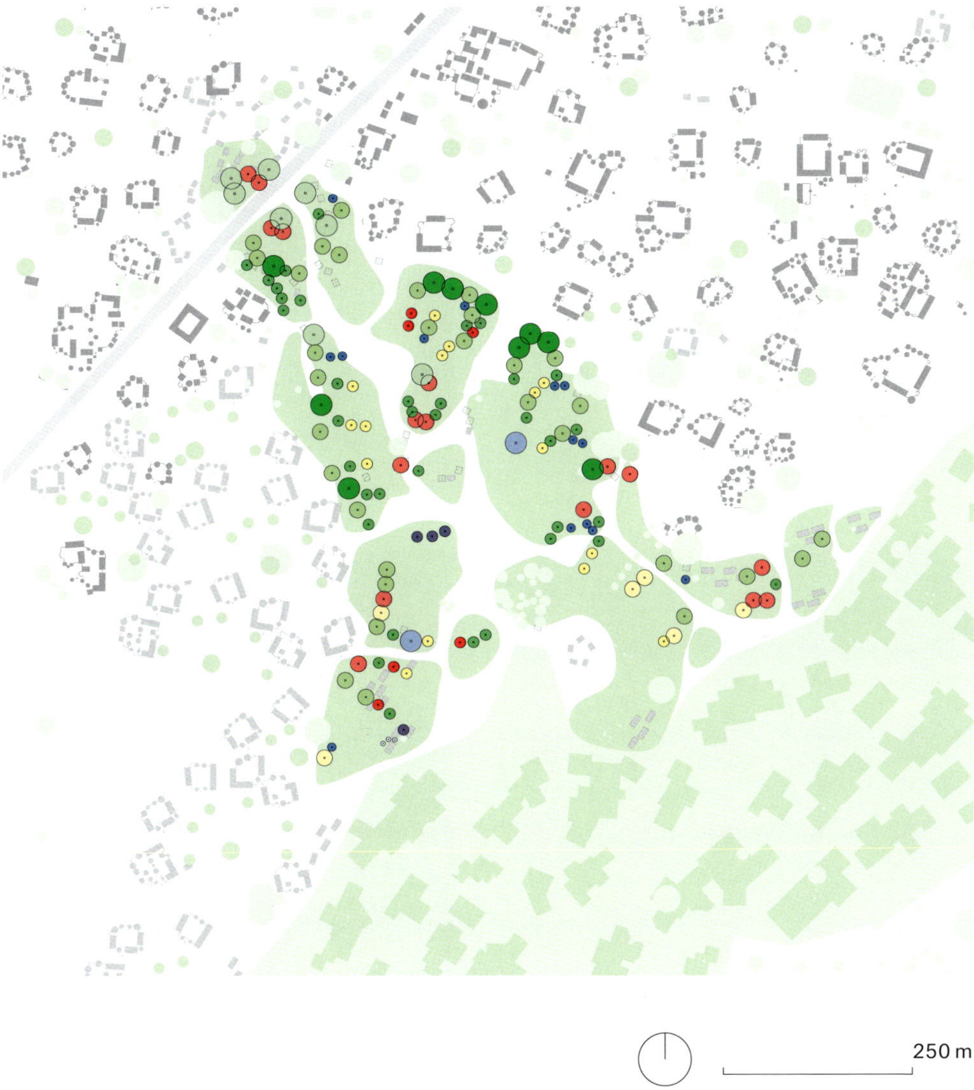

Greenbelt Planting Day
September 16, 2012

First 1:1 encounters with Guabuliga

Drawing Guabuliga 2012

Field work

The team

Evening drawing work

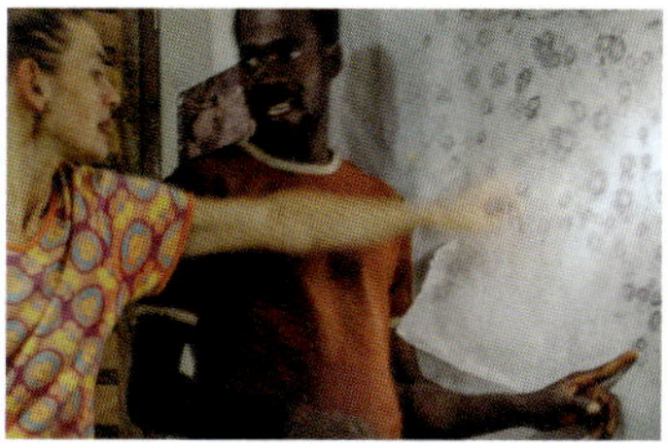

Interviewing Baba Seidu Alhassan

Michael and Joseph designing

Communal house building

Harmattan

At the Chief´s palace

Field inspections

Final presentation with the Chief and his council of elders

Ioana presenting, Baba translating

Meeting Mbatakora, the local doctor

At the edge of the village

Approaching Malam´s garden

Malam showing his plants

[a]FA´s dry season gardening concept is inspired by Malam´s garden

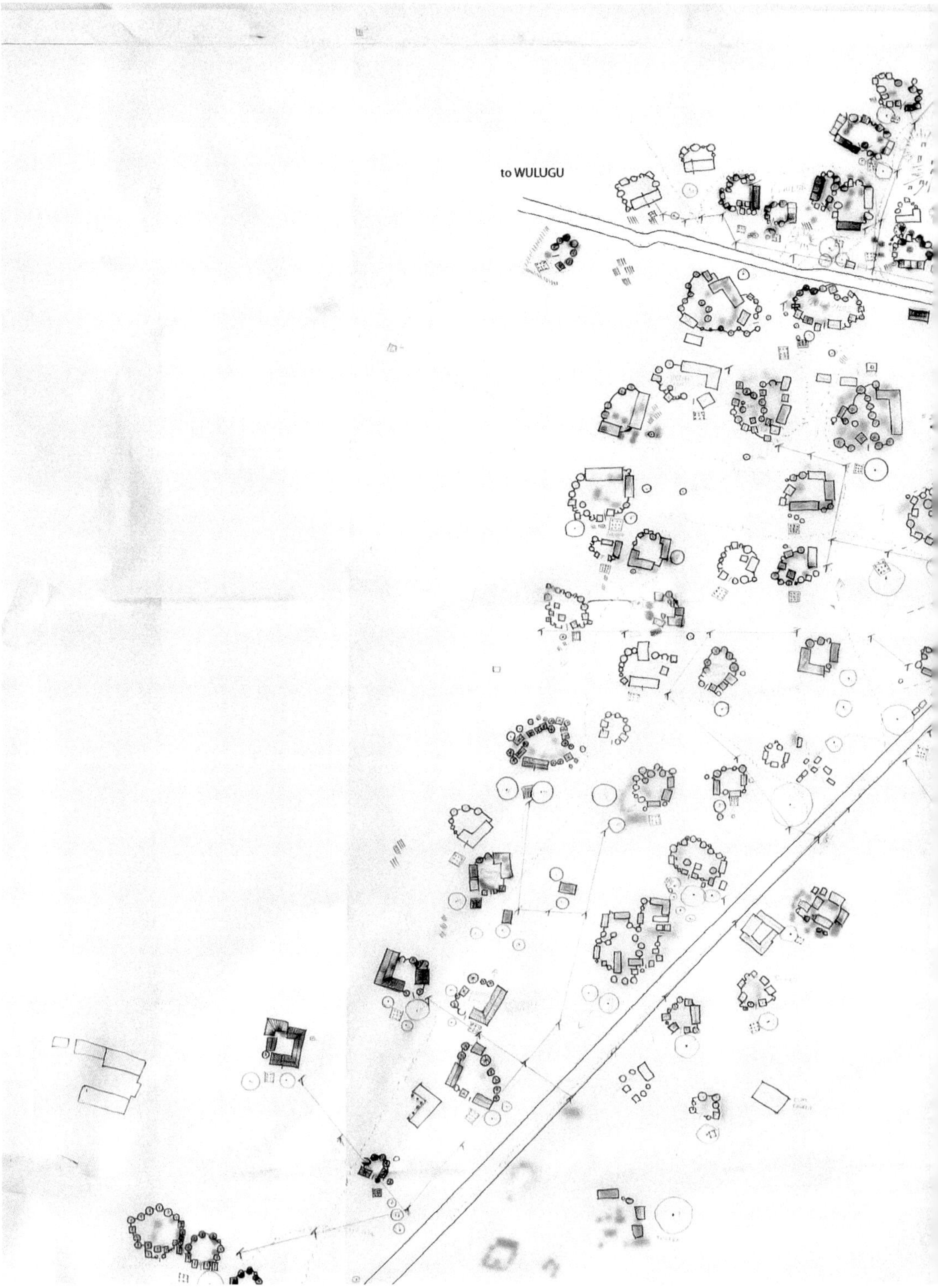
to WULUGU

to NALERIGU

The February 2012 team

Workshop with Nikolaus Gansterer

A break with Peter Strasser

IoA Sliver Gallery exhibition set-up

Peter and his projection set-up

Review with Joe Osae-Addo in Accra

Review with Bernard Akoi-Jackson in Vienna

The September team with Bernard

Exhibition 'DesignBuild Studio-New Ways in Architectural Education' at TU Berlin

[a]FAs exhibition contribution

ENGAGING WITH THE EVERYDAY

A Conversation between
Joe Oase-Addo and Baerbel Mueller
Accra, October 2016

BM: Could you talk a bit about contextual approaches in terms of the African, West African, Ghanaian context?

JOA: Well, I mean that word, 'context', in terms of a postcolonial context in particular, is very tricky. What is our context? It has been redefined in a way by the colonial influence. And so if you talk about a city like Accra, what is it? What kind of construct is it? Is it what you see on Oxford Street with all the Kentucky Fried Chickens? Is that Accra? I think it is. Or is it the old city, which has not been developed for the last hundred years? That is also Accra. Is it the people´s culture that is exemplified by our clothing, which is both people wearing the traditional cloth and people wearing jeans? So I think the context within our geographical boundaries and political arena is a hybrid. And I think, as creative people, we have not been responding to that. If people write about the African context, they talk about the traditional, the historical. But we are a very contemporary continent, a cosmopolitan continent, and we have been influenced by so many things that our context is ever shifting, everchanging. And it is so relevant, more than ever. So I don´t use that word lightly, because it has so many layered meanings—for me!

BM: Nevertheless, your work is based on contextual approaches, and you have always been interested in the cultural contextually. Can you talk a bit about that?

JOA: Yes absolutely! Culture is everchanging, it is dynamic. We are not talking about the drumming and dancing alone. But I think you have to feel culture and live it. It is that intuitive side of understanding what our culture is, that I think is missing. We overintellectualize these notions and explorations of culture. It is you. So you respond to yourself. So what I do is respond to who I am, what I believe. It is my belief system, and it is shaped by many things, especially by the indigenous. That is what I respond to, but clearly, if I look at those things, it needs to be changing; it is not cast in stone. Otherwise it becomes irrelevant as an idea. So you have known me for a long time, starting from my interest in local materials, it is still all there, but now, how do you contextualize all this interest in a more urban setting? The basis is the same, but the results may appear differently. It is that underpinning of culture, economy, which still keeps me going. It may appear different, but it is still the same. It comes from the same place. It is intuitive, deliberately so over the rational: What do we need as a people? Everywhere we go, whether it is the rural or the urban, how can we design to reshape that condition?

BM: Could you briefly talk about the environmentally contextual, or your interest in the environmental approach?

JOA: Good design principles are based on an environmental understanding of place. That´s basic. So, we don t have to reinvent the wheel on this thing. But what I think is missing in our context is our traditional narrative, which says the same things that western approaches do. But we have not taken over that space; we have not appropriated this dialogue to say, we are sustainable as a people. We have narratives, we have stories and approaches that have captured that for a million years. We have great examples that have guided us, we have great stories of protecting our environment, be it the ocean, the land, nature. But we seem to have gotten away from that. So it is important that we reconnect to this origin narrative.

BM: Could you talk about scale?

JOA: I think one of the things that makes it very difficult to push the use of local material, for example, is the lack of scale, the scalability of the production and the scalability of the demand. But I think the onus is on us as creative people, as engineers, as manufacturers, to build the scale, the demand that leads to scalability. Otherwise, all these great creative ideas will never take hold. It has to be market competitive. And that goes not only for products, but for our ideas as well. How do we get the people of Ghana, for example, to buy into a new approach. It has to be economically feasible.

And economy and scalability are two sides of the same coin.

BM: Taking it from a different angle, I have now been interested for years in this notion of urban acupunctures. This, your project here in Jamestown, is small, but it is radiating, it is extremely local, but it is very global at the same time. So you believe in the small-scale.

JOA: I believe in both, the micro and the macro! But often, as designers, we tend to look at the big picture, which is great. So this idea of coming to Jamestown started with my trying to buy a huge building, a warehouse, and converting it into a mixed-used development—and we are still working on it, there is no rush. So I said, why don´t we take fragments of the same idea, and as you said, acupuncture it, fragments of it, and test the idea before we get to the main project. So next will be the guesthouse, Airbnb. This original idea is all about artists´ lofts and creative space, space with retail, with housing, all in one place, and of course with a public square, which is the market. So here you see we have brought the solar kiosk and the market, we have the gallery, which is part of the creative space idea, and we have the cafe, and then the sleeping area. So we are testing these ideas.

BM: And the city is in between everything! I think it is great how it expands with all the in-between spaces.

JOA: That is why it has allowed us to make this wonderful communal garden opposite: before it was a dirt space, all the junk was put there, and now the trees there are growing. So I like your term acupuncture and I would add: it is about engaging with the everyday. What we are doing is not a festival, it is not a one-off thing, it is the everyday. This project may evolve, if you come here in a year it might look very different.

So it is about engaging with the everyday. And it has taught me a great lesson as a creative person, that we have to stop talking like creative people, stop acting like creative people, stop dressing like creative people—all we have to do is engage in a very creative way. That is the best thing, that is where the rubber meets the road. Every day I come here, I have to fight for something. I think architecture has become so relaxed, you can´t have architecture play a big role in development if you don't push the envelope and if you don´t have 'angst', you cannot be comfortable and make change, no, it is not possible. So I encourage people. Acupuncture: once the needle hits, it is painful, but change occurs.

JOE OSAE-ADDO, Ghanaian architect and founder of Constructs LLC, trained at the AA in London, worked and taught in Los Angeles for 26 years, set up his practice in Accra in 2004, and is chairman of ArchiAfrika, a platform for research and projects in Africa and "inno-native (tm)" responses to African architecture.

Presenting the project proposal to the Chief, elders, and villagers

Visiting the Bolgatanga nursery, selecting trees

Selecting trees at a nursery in Gbimsi

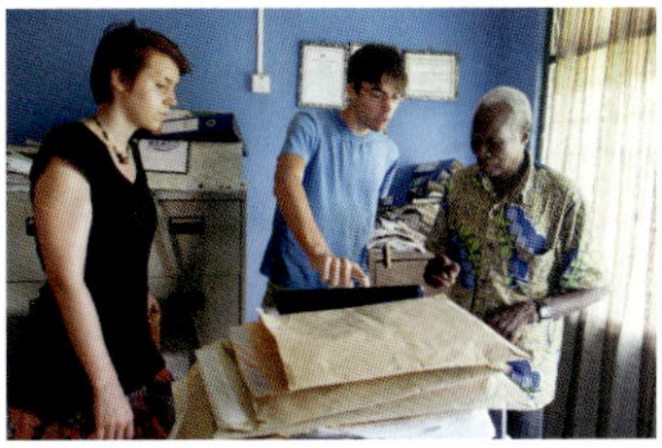

With consultant David Agongo, ZEFP, Walewale

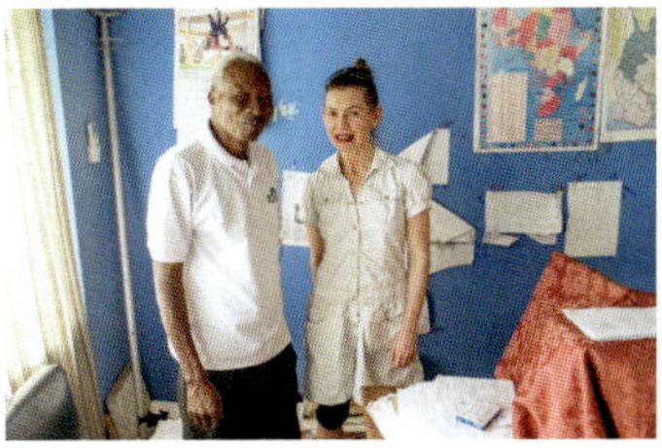

Planting preparations

Flagging tree positions

Joe planting a tree

Tracing water-fetching patterns

At the laboratory in Tamale

Testing water samples

Theresa with Rahamatou

Presenting the drinking water research

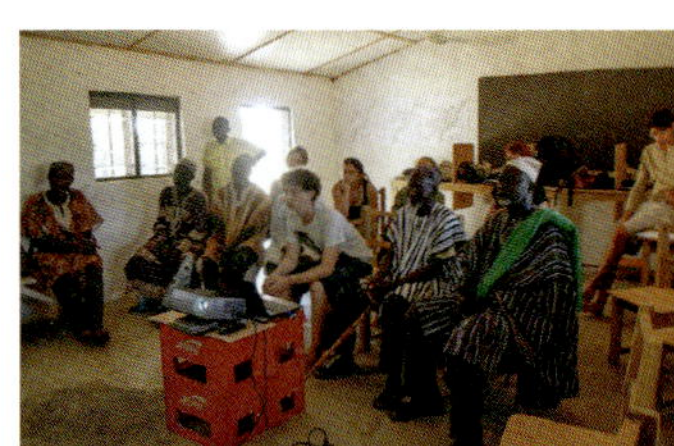

Rainy season

Antonella and her 1:1 mock-up

1:1 tests on the marketplace

Revisiting Joseph´s compound project

Bernard´s land art

Lea´s investigations on cooking and foodscapes

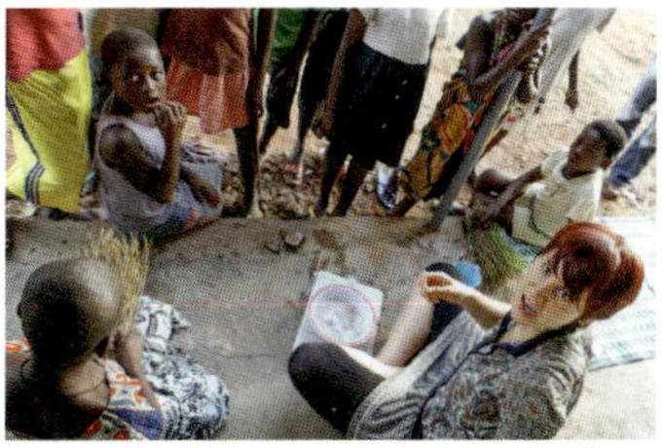

Discussing the future water project with the Chief and the BA board

Solar panels being installed

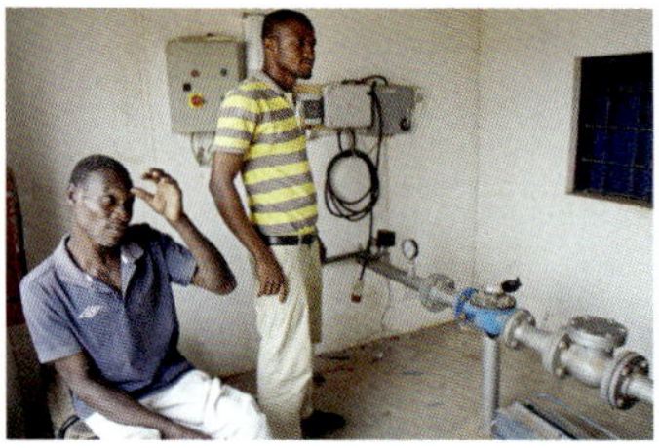

Pumptech Ghana Limited installing the solar-powered pump

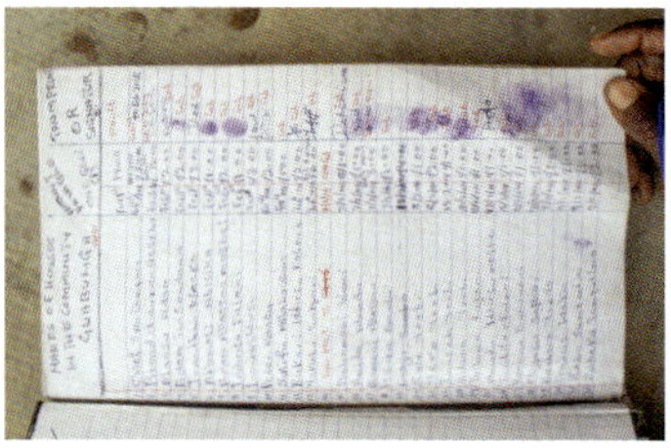

Accounting of the water-fetching fees

Braveaurora's social workers Suzie and Eklimatu

Baba Seidu and Pumptech engineers

Discussing water education with the Youth Harvest Foundation, Bolgatanga

2013 Neptun Wasserpreis nomination ceremony, Vienna

Energy Globe Award Ghana 2014, Ceremony, Linz

The Greenbelt in 2014

Handover of the Energy Globe Award certificate

Chrili Car during his PhD presentation at BOKU Vienna

The Greenbelt school project in 2016

Palm trees on the beach, colourfully dressed women at the market in the tree savannah of the north, with sacred rocks and Baobab trees; unusual impressions, sounds, rhythms, new faces. At the beginning, this was exotic—after some time, just the usual reality—but a reality that remains incredible. A different culture seems to be mostly about different places and practices. It is as much about different concepts of time and the meaning of presence, or existence. For locals, leaving can mean being withdrawn from all existence and one does not enter existence again until one comes back. This fact can be the most critical aspect of projects: when there is a big deadline like a return flight, time becomes a crucial matter. The plan is always to allow for plenty of extra time to get to know the immense natural and cultural diversity. But as the projects increase in complexity, we still always run out of time. Another thing, totally unexpected: sometimes, foreign cultural differences are nothing compared to the various languages we speak in a trans-disciplinary team—even between different universities. So, I try to listen, to learn to see with other eyes and thereby benefit in life, as well as find new modes of togetherness, without which setting out on new quests and visions would hardly be possible.

Chrili Car
born in Mödling in 1988, studied landscape architecture and planning at the University of Natural Resources and Life Sciences (BOKU), Vienna with joint courses at the University of Applied Arts, the University of Vienna, and the University of Klagenfurt; master's thesis on staging place—transition zones of nature and territory in Apam, Ghana and PhD thesis on 'Guabuliga—open spaces of everyday life' external expert for Braveaurora in Guabuliga since 2012; planting concept for HADUWA in Apam in 2013; since 2015, assistance for the [a]FA Immuna labs.

Besides incredible cultural insights and a first-hand experience in sustainability, [a]FA was crucial to my personal design interests—to engage the user in a piece of architecture. Working on the field, getting people involved, and witnessing the immediate social impact of the project has been an extremely valuable pay-off.

The lab also offered me the creative freedom and opportunity to work closely with local artists. This resulted in the video work 'Rhythms of Production' and gave me a different perspective on handmade textures.

Ioana Petkova
born in Sofia in 1988, studied architecture at the University of Applied Arts in Vienna.

I understand my work as an architect as that of a cultural practitioner, which, for me, requires the acknowledgment of a multiplicity of contexts. Working on projects in Ghana and the DR Congo has not only opened thematic directions in my work, but has also compelled me to situate myself within other discourses.

My current research focuses on dynamic urban environments and moving architecture in the context of big data and robotics. For me, this direction of architectural design has a large potential for the rapidly changing cities of sub-Saharan Africa, which assimilate new technologies very quickly. In the [a]FA labs, my work often lingered on the incongruities and paradoxes of spaces confronted with technology. In my work, 'Do you come back tomorrow?', photography and a participatory performance highlight the strangeness of a village evening in northern Ghana, which could have been otherwise easily romanticized. One project I am currently working on is a series of speculative architectural designs in Ghana that suggest alternative futures for the African city. With this work, I am trying to challenge some assumptions about architecture in the African context.

Juergen Strohmayer
has been involved in all the [a]FA labs throughout his studies in architecture at the University of Applied Arts Vienna, where he graduated from Studio Greg Lynn in January 2015. He currently lives in Addis Ababa, Ethiopia, where

he is a Visiting Lecturer at the Ethiopian Institute of Architecture, Building Construction and City Development (EiABC).

Spring 2012. I dropped in on the [a]FA class and was not sure what to expect. Soon, I became fascinated by the thought of going to a totally different country and exploring the life there.

Our group followed the first [a]FA lab, 'Guabuliga—Well by the Thorn Tree', presenting the masterplan/village growth proposal 'Guabuliga 2032'. We implemented the planting concept—the Greenbelt part of the project. Being out in the fields, planting different kinds of trees by hand with the villagers, knowing that those trees would become part of their future, changed my view on life; we were using our knowledge to create life and, at the same time, protect it.

In parallel, each of the group members worked on different, interesting narratives. I had the opportunity to investigate the production, preparation, and consumption of food in Guabuliga. I have experienced that communal cooking and daily life in the courtyards of extended family compounds play an important role in the village and generate a certain lifestyle that I was not used to. It was amazing to see women starting up little businesses and having their own food stands along Guabuliga's red, dusty roads and pathways.

Our team blended different working fields in order to carry out the projects together, to share one another's knowledge, and to learn from each other.

For my own work as an architect, the experience in Ghana raised my awareness of cultural behaviour on the one hand, and on the other hand, made me see how important it is to actually do the research directly in the field where one wants to implant an idea. The trip to Ghana gave me a positive insight into a culture I will never fully understand but will also never forget!

Lea Dietiker
born in Switzerland, 1989. Started to study architecture at the Technical University of Vienna, 2009. Started the Diploma Architecture Program with Wolf D. Prix at the University of Applied Arts Vienna, 2010. Graduated in June 2016 under Hani Rashid at the same institution.

Now I live in Lagos. I'm in love with Lagos. I feel at home in Lagos. Home means moving through a big-city moloch, a waterfront city, a concrete desert, moving within a stagnating, viscous current of vehicles, humans, and goods. Lagos can mean glamour, wealth, champagne, oil, and sailing clubs. Lagos can also mean complete darkness, poverty, fuel scarcity, and slums on water. From a glittering skyline to a police gun barrel pointed at you at the next junction on the street at night.

The beat of drums is what brought me to Mali. The country of desert blues and the earth architecture of the Pays Dogon. Living in adobe buildings appealed to me and roused my interest in how culture and beliefs are manifested in built structures. A year later, [a]FA was founded, so I was able to pursue this interest in Northern Ghana.

The [a]FA collaboration with Studios Kabako and Faustin Linyekula in Kisangani also changed the way I perceive space. The power of water and the power of a drawing in the cityscape. The power of performance and how bodies can define space through movement. The power of an exhibition where the state is powerless. The journey alone is a story on its own.

Lagos: now it's the beat of the city that follows me into my sleep. The deep rattling noise of generators and heat-relieving fans. The muezzin singing, followed by church drums and shouting Nollywood movies from my neighbor's apartment. The polyrhythmic patterns of vehicle horns, Shoki, and Fela Kuti. The sound of tropical rain on tin roofs.

Stefanie Theuretzbacher
born in Vienna, has been working as an architect since graduating from the University of Applied Arts Vienna and has presently shifted her professional focus to the African continent.

Through several [a]FA labs in rural Ghana, the DR Congo, and Alaska, I have gained experience in finding solutions for local water, waste, and sanitation challenges. In all cases, my research was based on a framework that follows the path of the different water sources to and throughout the respective villages/neighborhoods from

the point of source, point of supply, point of consumption, to the point of disposal.

The engagement in Guabuliga, Ghana led to a collaboration with the NGO Braveaurora for the implementation of a solar-powered water supply system on the village scale. During the 9th Vienna Anthropology Days, I participated in developing the workshop, 'Socio-economic Aspects of Maintaining Technical Infrastructure in Architecture and Water Management'.

Together with my Alaskan partners, we are the recipients of the North American Partnership on Environmental Community Action Grant to improve Community-Scale Feces Waste Treatment (CSFWT) in Arctic North America. In 2014 we won the Alaska Water and Sewer Challenge to develop a proposal for innovative and affordable water and sewer systems for homes in rural Alaska. This motivated me to complete my master's thesis 'Concept Design for a Biochar Sanitation System in Kivalina, Alaska', realizing that the challenges for a sustainable water and sanitation supply are similar around the world.

Theresa Theuretzbacher Dipl.-Ing., studied Water Management and Environmental Engineering at the University of Natural Resources and Life Sciences (BOKU), Vienna. She is currently based in Norway and is working for the Climate Foundation as an environmental engineer in the human waste management sector, which is involved in projects in Alaska and India.

GUABULIGA—WELL BY THE THORN TREE

Schedule labs:
December 2011–September 2012

Ongoing implementations:
September 2012–December 2017

Lab head: Baerbel Mueller

[a]FA team: Antonella Amesberger, Chrili Car, Ioana Petkova, Joseph Hofmarcher, Juergen Strohmayer, Lea Dietiker, Stefanie Theuretzbacher, Theresa Theuretzbacher

Guabuliga team: Chief Salifu Mahama Tampurie, Baba Seidu, Baba Seidu Alhassan, and Halidu Abdui Hafiz, Humu Adamu, Michael Bayada Sumzimina, Shahadu Malam Kasim, Rahamatu Dokurugu

Project and implementation partner: Chief Salifu Mahama Tampurie, Braveaurora

Lab reviews, workshops: Andrea Rieger-Jandl, Bernard Akoi-Jackson, Bernhard Sommer, Georg Glaeser, Joe Osae-Addo, Lisa Schmidt-Colinet, Nikolaus Gansterer, Nat Armateifo, Reiner Zettl

Financial support: Institute of Architecture, University of Applied Arts Vienna, Braveaurora, ASAG BOKU

Exhibitions: [applied] Foreign Affairs: Ghana, Nubuke Foundation Accra; The Essence 2012, Künstlerhaus Vienna; [applied] Foreign Affairs: Ghana, Sliver Gallery Angewandte Vienna; Well by the Thorn Tree, Guabuliga Gallery, Guabuliga; design.build.studio, TU Berlin; We Face Forward (towards the city), Whitworth Art Gallery, Manchester; Think Global, Build Social!, AzW Vienna

Conferences: 5th International Congress Bauhaus.Solar 2012; ELLS Scientific Student Conference 2012; Afritecture Symposium, Munich 2013; AZA 2016 Conference, Johannesburg 2016

Awards: Neptun Water Prize 2015 (with Braveaurora); National Energy Globe Award: Ghana 2014; Neptun Water Prize 2013 (nomination); bauhaus.Solar Award 2012 (distinction)

Consultants: David Agongo (ZEFP Walewale), Frank B. Kumah, John Krugu (Youth Harvest Foundation), Osman Sahanoon Kalandi, Saibu Mutaru (BA), Sulemana Fatawu Nantomah (Asiribisi Walewale)

Greenbelt team 2012–2016: Adam Tampulima, Halidu Alhassan, Imoro Baba, Mathiew Bukari, Salifu Alhassan, Yamusah Manlokiya, Wurikamdana Musah

Academic partner PhD Chrili Car: University of Natural Resources and Life Sciences (BOKU), Vienna, ILA; Erwin Frohmann, Karin Raith

Photos:
Antonella Amesberger: 51, 57
Bernard Akoi-Jackson: 83, 95
Baerbel Mueller: 33, 39, 51, 53, 57, 82, 83, 84, 85, 86, 87, 90, 91, 94, 95, 96, 97, 98, 99, 105, 106, 114, 117, 118, 142, 143
Braveaurora: 98, 99
Chrili Car: 43, 44, 45, 86, 90, 126
Christine Widmann: 33
Crable Art: 128, 129, 130, 131,132,133
Elisabeth Schipflinger: 83, 95, 99
Energy Globe Award: 99
Ioana Petkova: 26, 27, 28, 29
Joseph Hofmarcher: 31, 32, 84, 107
Juergen Strohmayer: 16, 22, 23, 24, 25, 84, 85, 87, 94, 106, 118, 119, 120, 121, 139
Lea Dietiker: 47, 48, 49, 82, 97, 118
Martin C. Hess: 115
Neptun Wasserpreis: 98
Nikolaus Gansterer: 90
Sophie Prix: 90
Stefanie Theuretzbacher: 38, 39
Theresa Theuretzbacher: 54, 57

Braveaurora (BA) is an Austrian-Ghanaian NGO that has been operating in Ghana, Guabuliga since 2009, with the goal of offering vulnerable children perspectives for the future. BA also works together with the local authorities and population on a variety of educational, environmental, and economic programs. BA is directed by Dr. Christin ter Braak-Forstinger, Sarah Kotopulos, Julia Obereder, and Baba Seidu.

GUABULIGA—WELL BY THE THORN TREE

Nubuke Foundation Accra,
March 2012

Guabuliga's founding myth—'The Well by the Thorn Tree'—has been the conceptual starting point for developing contextual but novel spatial and programmatic scenarios for the growing village. Directly after an initial intensive field work phase in Guabuliga and a concentrated presentation in the village itself, and right before returning to Vienna to further the work in progress there, the wish was to present and share first concepts and findings in Accra.

There could not be a more powerful exhibition setting than a tree: the free-standing, widely visible Indian Almond tree of Nubuke's garden housed plans, diagrams, drawings, and photos that were pinned on hanging boards. Digital presentations and works were embedded and enclosed in installative structures and objects, hanging from the stronger branches of the tree.

Curators: Baerbel Mueller, Juergen Strohmayer
Works: Chrili Car, Ioana Petkova, Joseph Hofmarcher, Juergen Strohmayer, Stefanie Theuretzbacher, Theresa Theuretzbacher

SLIGHTLY LOST IN TRANSLATION BETWEEN DESIRE, DEVELOPMENT AND DESIGN

(Lines, Shapes, Colours, Dwarf Paintings and Cheerful Smiles)

Bernard Akoi-Jackson

'Meet[ing] me halfway' and coming back again, eventually

Chance acquaintances have ways of mutating into long and sustained collaborative relationships. My initial artistic encounter with Baerbel Mueller began sometime in March 2009. I got a call from Lesley Naa Norley Lokko to participate in an ambitious multidisciplinary project that was to be manifested in the James Fort Prison (now a World Heritage Site), located at Ga Mashie, the local name for old British Accra.

The project's working title was 'Meet me Halfway', and the exhibiting group was to be eventually morphed into a creative collective called 'Hybrid', due to the diversity of its members. This diversity permeated several of the participants' experiences. In these several instances, we were culturally and professionally diverse, differing in aesthetic interests, spatial concerns, and even political positionings. The meetings were held in the Golden Tulip Hotel in Accra. Amongst the prospective participants, I recall meeting Rania Odaymat, Orthner Orthner & Associates, Nii Obodai, Kofi Setordji, and Nat Nunoo Amarteifio. I think Lesley Lokko's interest in my work stemmed from her having seen aspects of my MFA project and the way I was dealing with collective history, memory, and spaces of historical significance. I had staged, in Tema, near the site of the erstwhile Meridian Hotel, a faux-memorial event entitled: 'In Memoriam', in remembrance of the hotel and all it stood for in its prime.

At the 'Hybrid' meetings at the Golden Tulip, Baerbel and I did not really talk much to each other. It was, however, on our onsite visits to James Fort prison that we began talking. Our proposed projects were to have been located in close proximity to each other and we soon realized that we were sort of having similar thoughts about the use of space and possible aspirations of the erstwhile inmates of the prison. Whereas I was seeking to occupy the open drainage systems with excerpt texts from Dr. Kwame Nkrumah's speeches and to create a physical space near Nkrumah's cell from sheer fabric that would have some form of projected images on it, Baerbel wanted to project the ocean onto the wall that barred former prisoners' views of the ocean beyond the wall by installing a huge mirror. The illusory ocean would become a reenactment of the prisoners' desires and aspirations of hope. I think both proposals were about seeking to imagine futures and possibilities beyond the mere physicality of the space. Nkrumah's words of liberation,

rising out of the drains, would intermingle with the dreams of imminent release and freedom for the prisoners, quite like the freedom Nkrumah himself had experienced after having won elections from within prison and thereby emerging out of prison to ascend to the position of prime minister, just before he became president.

When eventually the project was not realized, due largely to bureaucracy and an obvious lack of funding, Baerbel and I promised to still imagine a future of collaboration. I was therefore not entirely surprised when a few years thereafter, I received notice that Baerbel wanted to collaborate with me on a project in the north of Ghana. One of the proposed futures had come. The opportunity to keep our promise of collaborating again had eventually presented itself.

Lines, Shapes, Colours, Dwarf Paintings and Cheerful Smiles: The Guabuliga Mural Project

I came to the Guabuliga project* with previous knowledge of the *Bambolse* wall-painting tradition of the women from Sirigu in the Upper East Region of Ghana. I therefore also had the idea of quoting local practices. I would, however, immediately note that this part of the north was rather 'modest' in terms of wall embellishment traditions in comparison to other places, such as Sirigu. I still managed to develop an aesthetic that dominantly referenced *Bambolse*. This aesthetic was also based on other projects I had already implemented elsewhere in Ghana.

For two weeks, I spent time with the Guabuliga orphans, their caretakers, and the volunteers, sharing my practice and bringing smiles to their faces through the activities developed to realize the murals. The children were put into various groups and these groups were given tasks to perform. The mural design was itself based on lines, shapes, and colours. Since I worked throughout the whole day, the children could go to their specific locations anytime in between their chores and school activities. I also went on periodic 'visits' to the various locations to give advice and help out.

On one particular dawn, I executed a surprise plan that I had been harbouring all along. As my interpretation of the Guabuliga founding myth, I decided to create a painting as a 'gift' to the people of Guabuliga. This painting was, however, not a portable one. I went out under the dawn light, a slight distance from the orphanage in the direction of the next village, and made a painting on a large boulder that was lodged within the roots of a huge tree in a field. I was done by early morning and returned to the orphanage. No one had seen me go or return, so people who saw the painting later started creating myths about who had done it. Some said that it had been painted by dwarves in the woods. Others actually thought the painting was itself a dwarf. It was only a few days later that the townsfolk reconciled the painting in the woods with the murals in the orphanage.

One year after the mural project was completed, Baerbel continued to work in Guabuliga with students, elaborating on various projects. A review visit to Guabuliga in February 2012

* "my home my bed my mango tree", 2009–2012, nav_s baerbel mueller comissioned by Braveaurora

brought me in contact with the steady progress of the projects. At this time, we collaborated with and participated in Juergen's performative piece: 'Do you come back tomorrow?' Later on in the year, I served on the jury of Theresa's children's poster competition in Guabuliga. Eventually all of these projects were shown at the Nubuke Foundation in Accra in the exhibition, Guabuliga: 'Well by the Thorn tree'. The exhibits were positioned around the tall Indian almond tree in the garden compound of the Foundation. As we may now be aware, 'Guabuliga' means 'the well by the Thorn tree'. So it is no wonder that trees or images of trees became prominent features of the entire project. When the exhibition travelled to Vienna, what was most conspicuous about the images I saw at the [applied] Foreign Affairs exhibition at the IoA Sliver Gallery at the University of Applied Arts Vienna, was the enormous silhouette of Chrili Car's mango tree on the wall.

This presented a stimulating parallel to the Indian almond tree that hosted the work-in-progress exhibition at the Nubuke Foundation earlier in the year. The haunting image of the tree's silhouette orchestrated an appropriate context for the Vienna presentation. With the help of technology and a certain amount of ingenuity, the spirit of a local household compound had transgressed borders, been transported through waves, and been transplanted into the context of an exhibition space far away. It was satisfying, even gratifying, to be witness to the eventual realization of an idea—begun some time back through chance meetings between various protagonists—through a truly multidisciplinary collaborative effort.

Indeed, ideas do first begin as a cell of thought, a qualm, an inkling or fluke, seen through a hazy film, of an individual (here, I refer to an initial idea of the chief of Guabuliga). It may grow and become the dream of a group of people, in this case, a team that has taken up the task of conducting architectural, social, developmental, and artistic research, and presenting it in the described manner. Yet what sustains this vision is the commitment and dedication of the holders of the dream. And when this dream has finally seen its manifestation, and so beautifully, too, one is first humbled by the sheer possibility of it and proud, even honored, to have had a certain layer of influence on the celebration, in my case, in the roles of a muralist, guest teacher of the [a]FA project, and reviewer.

The manner in which the collective work of the students—Ioana Petkova, Stefanie Theuretzbacher, Theresa Theuretzbacher, Chrili Car, Joseph Hofmarcher, and Juergen Strohmayer—has been shown is aesthetically, conceptually, and spiritually uplifting: a compound of ideas, images, videos, research material, located in the middle of a well. But this time, it is not just a well of water, which is good for growth, but also a wish for the future, which suggests growth in itself. It is a prospect, a hope, and another dream in the making, another desire perhaps: the projection of what might lie in the future, not only of Guabuliga, but also for all the individuals and groups involved in this project.

Chief Salifu Mahama Tampurie did a great job in his desire for the development of his village and his initiation of this collaboration with Baerbel Mueller, who deserves applause for having

dreamt up this lab in the first place and bringing her students on board. The collaborating lecturers, artists, teachers, and technical personnel have made salient inputs to the success of the entire project, but those most worthy of compliment are the elders and people of Guabuliga, who made their land available for such complex projects.

If there is growth to follow, if sustainability is the intention, then this lab has already begun reaping the fruit. And quite literally, when we consider Chrili Car's eloquent tree silhouette on the wall, as well as his 'Talking Trees' project (which proposed the background for the Guabuliga greenbelt project), growth can be expected for Guabuliga, that little well by the thorn tree.

BERNARD AKOI-JACKSON (b. 1979). (MFA, Kumasi) is an artist-writer whose multi-disciplinary work has become a project in a continual state of metamorphosis. He interrogates hybrid, postcolonial identities through ephemeral, makeshift memorials and performative rituals of the mundane. His work has been seen in spaces all across the world.

[APPLIED] FOREIGN AFFAIRS GHANA

IoA Sliver Gallery, Vienna, June 2012

The IoA Sliver Gallery exhibition took place in one of the interior courtyards of the University of Applied Arts Vienna and presented the dynamic growth plan, 'Guabuliga—Well by the Thorn Tree', surrounded by all the individual mappings that had been done in February 2012. The overarching curatorial strategy was to intersect a Guabuliga compound—a series of round and square rooms arranged around a concentric circle and joined by a compound wall—with the exhibition space. This 1:1 spatial operation resulted in imprints of the Guabuliga compound on the floor and walls of the exhibition courtyard, which were translated into two-dimensional surfaces and abstractions of the compound rooms that were built to create exhibition booths. This exhibition architecture created a unifying concept for the projects in the exhibition and allowed for different exhibition settings for each project. The growth plan was presented horizontally as an animated projection on a 1:1000 topography model of Guabuliga measuring two by two meters.

Curators: Baerbel Mueller, Juergen Strohmayer
Exhibition design: Juergen Strohmayer

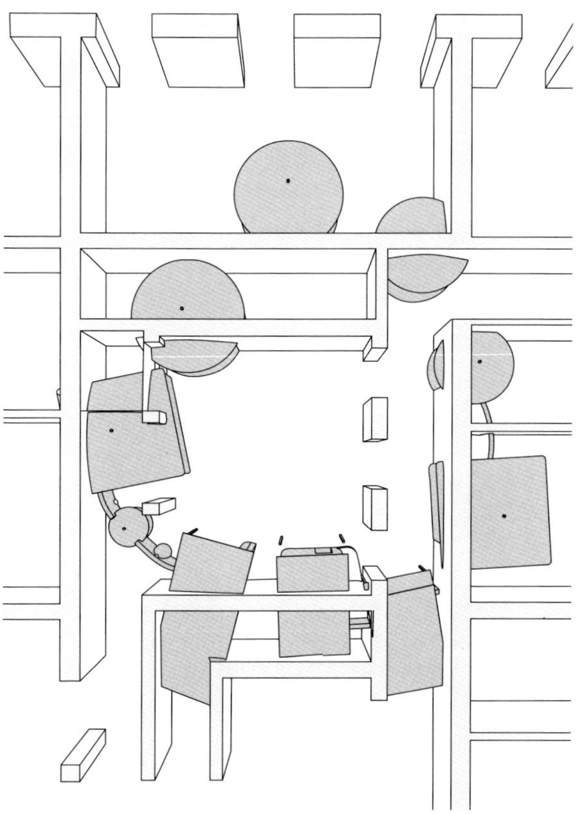

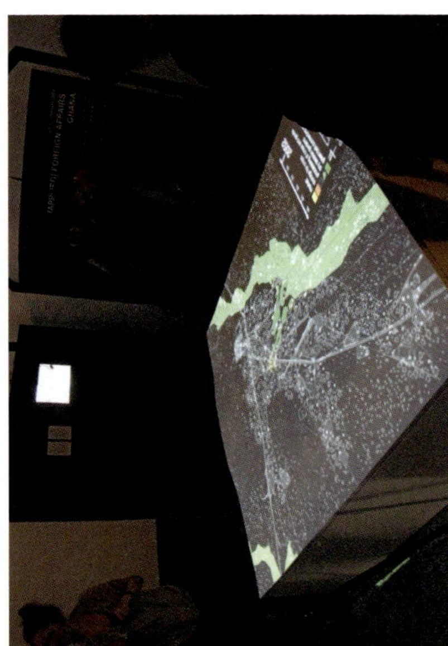

GUABULIGA GALLERY

Guabuliga, September 2013

Coming back to Guabuliga allowed the group to share the work that had been developed with the village between February and September. The work was exhibited in an empty shop located in the village center. The one-room building and the empty space in front of it was re-envisioned as an exhibition and event space with the aim of starting a dialogue with the community.

The Guabuliga Gallery existed for one week and had a different thematic focus each day. The themes included: the Guabuliga Growth Plan, the water situation, and the narrative mappings that were presented in a variety of formats. Drawings by 50 children of Guabuliga—the outcome of a water and sanitation workshop initiated by Theresa Theuretzbacher—filled the walls of the room. Each day, preparations were made in the morning and the Gallery opened in the afternoon, as the people who were coming back from their farms and the village became animated.

During this week, the space in front of the Guabuliga Gallery became a center for people to socialize. Each evening had a different character, as the Gallery transformed throughout the week. A film screening, curated by artist Bernard Akoi-Jackson, gathered a crowd around the porch of the Gallery. A presentation on Guabuliga's water situation accompanied the children's drawing exhibition, and to change focus, the [a]FA group hosted an Austrian-themed evening, presenting food and photos of their home. To close the Gallery, [a]FA gave a party a party by providing music and food sourced in the village.

Through the Guabuliga Gallery, [a]FA engaged with a much larger portion of the village than it had through the more specialized collaborations with individuals or groups such as the village chief and his council of elders. While it was a chance to communicate ideas to the whole village, it also provided a format to engage with people outside of the Growth Plan and Greenbelt project.

Curator: Juergen Strohmayer
Co-curator: Baerbel Mueller

LIVING MANIFESTATIONS SWOPA

Sirigu, September 2012

The [a]FA team travelled to the village of Sirigu to bring back Stefanie Theuretzbacher's 'Living Manifestations' to SWOPA, the Sirigu Women Organization of Pottery and Art in northern Ghana. Sirigu is well known for its traditional architecture, pottery and wall designing. In 1997, more than 150 women of Sirigu have formed an organization for pottery and art. Living Manifestations were presented to one of the SWOPA directors and the drawings were mounted prominently in the showroom of the SWOPA center, to be permanently exhibited.

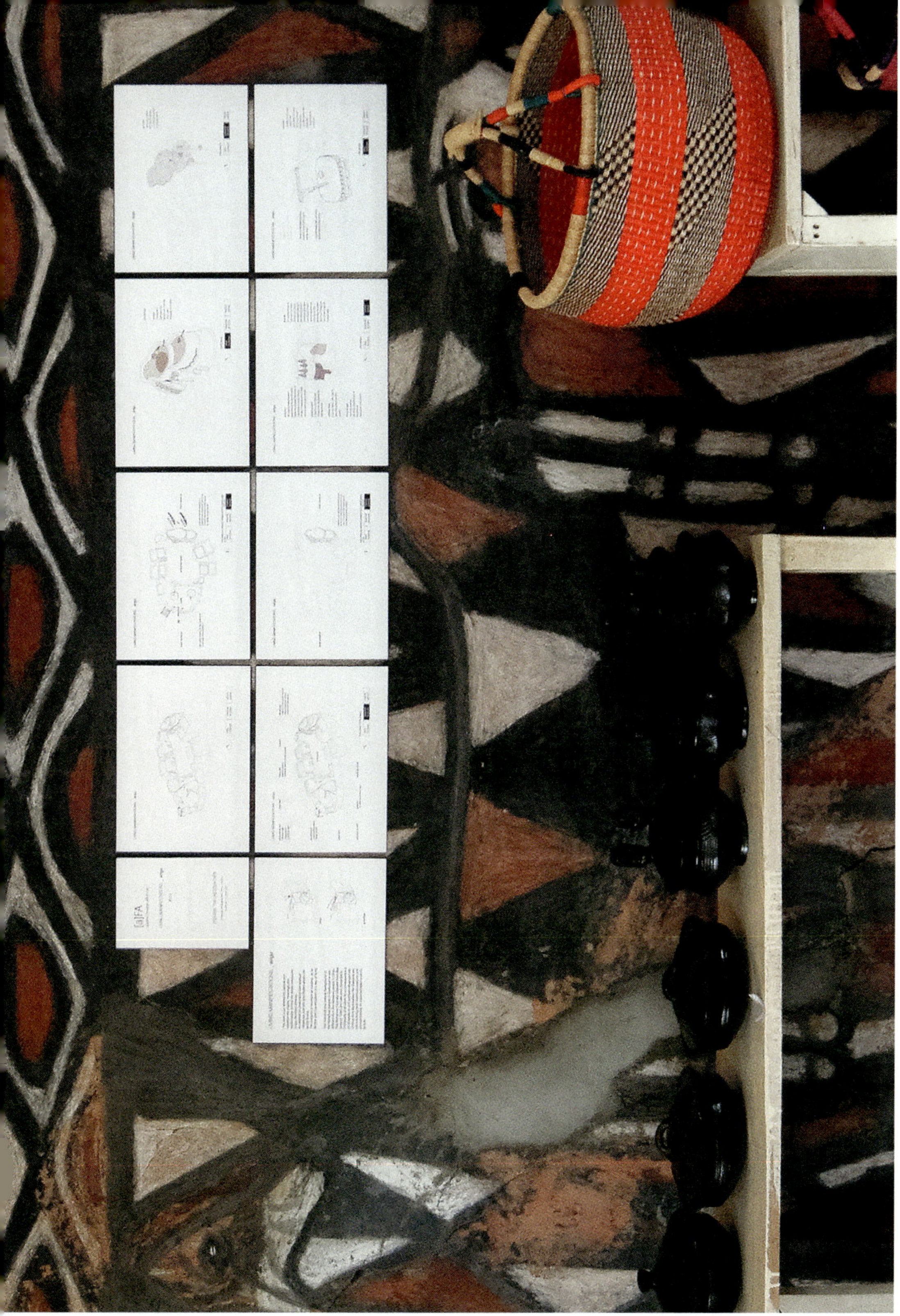

THE SOCIAL TURN IS GAINING MOMENTUM—FINALLY.

Gerald Bast

"Architecture is about giving form to the places where we live. It is not more complicated than that, but also not easier than that. Those places include houses, schools, offices, shops and retail areas in general, museums, palaces and government buildings, bus stops, subway stations, squares, parks, streets, trees along the streets (or not), sidewalks, parking, and the whole range of programs and pieces that constitute our built environment. The form of those places is defined not just by the aesthetic trend of the moment or the talent of a given designer; they are the consequence of regulations, interests, economies, and policies, or perhaps even of the lack of coordination, indifference, and simple chance. The forms these places assume may improve or ruin people's lives."[1]

With this explanation of the architectural concept underlying the 15th Venice Architecture Biennale 2016, artistic director Alejandro Aravena points out a future beyond capital- or power-dominated 'signature architecture', but also roughly echoes a radical claim from Hans Hollein in 1968: "Limited and traditional definitions of architecture and its resources have mostly lost their validity. The environment as a whole is regarded as the effort we put into it and all the media that determines it. The expansion of the human realm and the means of defining the environment goes far beyond a structural determination. Today, everything is architecture, in a way. Architects have to stop thinking only in terms of buildings."[2]

The radical utopian designs and manifests of the 1968 era with which one now differentiates oneself from the mainstream no longer—or perhaps don't yet—exist, but perhaps the strategic placement of feasible counterpoints to the common (building) cultural sector is at least as radical and courageous. "We are interested in architecture as a yearned-for instrument of self-government, as the instrument of a humanistic civilization, not as a result of a formal style but as evidence of the ability of human beings to be the masters of their own destinies. Architecture in action as an instrument of social and political life..."[3] says Paolo Baratta regarding the goals of the 15th Venice Architecture Biennale. This indicates nothing less than a paradigm shift in the understanding of architecture. Even if some who persist in defiant ignorance still argue and explain: "...The problem of urban concentration delivering belts of slums, these are issues, of course they are issues of concern, but they are not the issues that concern architects working in the world. They are working on other things. They are working on the metropolis, on the most advanced arenas. The problem is in this Biennale we have to forget what we all working on, in our real life and suddenly become amateur commentators on social processes which we are unequipped to comment on..."[4]

1 Alejandro Aravena, in: Reporting from the Front, p.23, Catalogue of the 15th Architecture Biennale Venice, Marsilio Editori, Venice 2016

2 Hans Hollein, Alles ist Architektur, "Bau" Schrift für Architektur und Städtebau, 23. Jahrgang, Heft 1/2, Wien 1968, Herausgegeben mit der Zentralvereinigung der Architekten Österreichs

3 Paolo Baratta, in: Reporting from the Front, p. 18, Catalogue of the 15th Architecture Biennale Venice, Marsilio Editori, Venice 2016

4 Patrik Schumacher, June 06 2016: www.vimeo.com/169518191

Indeed, the conjuncture of technological revolutions with social changes that alters large parts of people's private and professional lives on a dramatic scale at historically unprecedented speed, almost provokes uncertainty. We live in a world characterized by extreme complexity and the effects of this complexity are global. Everything somehow depends on everything else, without us always being able to see through the modes of action behind it. Quantum theorists—at least on the theoretical level—can perhaps become more comfortable with this phenomenon. We others, who have been strictly socialized through discipline-oriented education and profession, must painfully acknowledge that specialized expertise only gains power through synergistic coupling with other disciplines. Furthermore, a kind of study of the connection between the disciplines is required.

In the same way in which art and architecture have turned again and again to the latest technological developments and incorporated them into their systems, thereby expanding, transforming, and interconnecting their dimensions, these disciplines must also be applied to the complex social challenges as spheres of activity. 'Signature architecture' will also act as cross-disciplinary support for social processes, as punctuation for social change. Not least due to the interaction between the force fields of digitization, globalization, migration, and urbanization, the political and economic conditions that affect the potential of art and architecture will inevitably be shifted. There is also the question of to whom and what art and architecture has relevance. Ultimately, it is always about interests of artistic, economic, and political natures. What would happen if large parts of the world were heading towards a situation in which it made both economical and political sense to make as much money available for interdisciplinary architectural and artistic contributions to the solutions for social problems in megacities, as that for the construction of shopping malls, conference centers, or grand representative buildings? What if the term innovation is no longer only understood as a technological-economic phenomenon, but also in its socio-cultural dimension, as a part of the process of civilization? What consequences would it have for architecture and art when focusing on the often cited "grand societal challenges" became mainstream? Not because it forces a revolution to happen, but because the societal constellations of power that also have an effect on the cultural sector have political and economic interests in using all the parameters of influence that contribute to the preservation of a positive social process. History has born witness to the fact that art and architecture have the potential to affect social impact.

Claire Bishop's 'social turn'[5], which she first mentioned ten years ago, is gaining momentum—not only under the pressure of economic and political developments, but also through the increasing interest in cross-disciplinary work between the fields of art, architecture, design, technology, humanities, natural sciences, and economics. There is no doubt that this dynamic will serve the development of society just as much as it will the development of art and architecture, if one acknowledges, like Edward Wilson[6], the most famous evolutionary biologist of our time, that art was and is a necessary element of human evolution.

5 Claire Bishop, in: The Social Turn: Collaboration and Its Discontents, Artforum February 2006

6 Edward O. Wilson, in: Die Soziale Eroberung der Welt, C.H. Beck Verlag, München 2013—The Social Conquest of Earth, Liveright Publishing Corporation, New York—London 2012

GERALD BAST is president of the University of Applied Arts Vienna, where he initiated new programs accentuating cross-disciplinary teaching and research and the interrelation between art and society. As author and lecturer he has been focusing on university management, educational and cultural policy, innovation processes and the societal role of art.

FUTURE GUABULIGA GREENBELT

2012–

By its very nature, the Greenbelt is an ongoing project that requires attention and maintenance from the inhabitants of Guabuliga. This is supported by Chief Salifu Mahama Tampurie and the local NGO Braveaurora, who have commissioned Chrili Car to act as an external expert and to coordinate the evolution of the project. Since 2012, he has been visiting Guabuliga regularly to monitor the growth of the Greenbelt and to help create the organizational structures that have led the project towards becoming self-sustainable within the village, to a certain extent.

Following initial setbacks during which trees died due to a lack of maintenance, a Greenbelt team was founded to take responsibility for them and to coordinate between the village, the chief, and his council of elders. The goal of the long-term collaboration between the village, the NGO, and the university is to change behavioural patterns in the community in such a way that they will have far-ranging environmental and spatial impacts in Guabuliga.

Since 2016, the school of Guabuliga is involved on the ground, to ensure that students care for the trees and act as ambassadors for them.

On an academic level, Chrili Car evaluated the Greenbelt project between 2012 and 2015 as part of his PhD 'Guabuliga—Open Spaces of Everyday Life' at the Institute of Landscape Architecture (ILA) of the University of Natural Resources and Life Sciences (BOKU) in Vienna.

THE EVOLUTION OF GREENBELT GUABULIGA

Timeline of Greenbelt evaluation

9-16-2012

Initial planting day, 150 trees are planted.

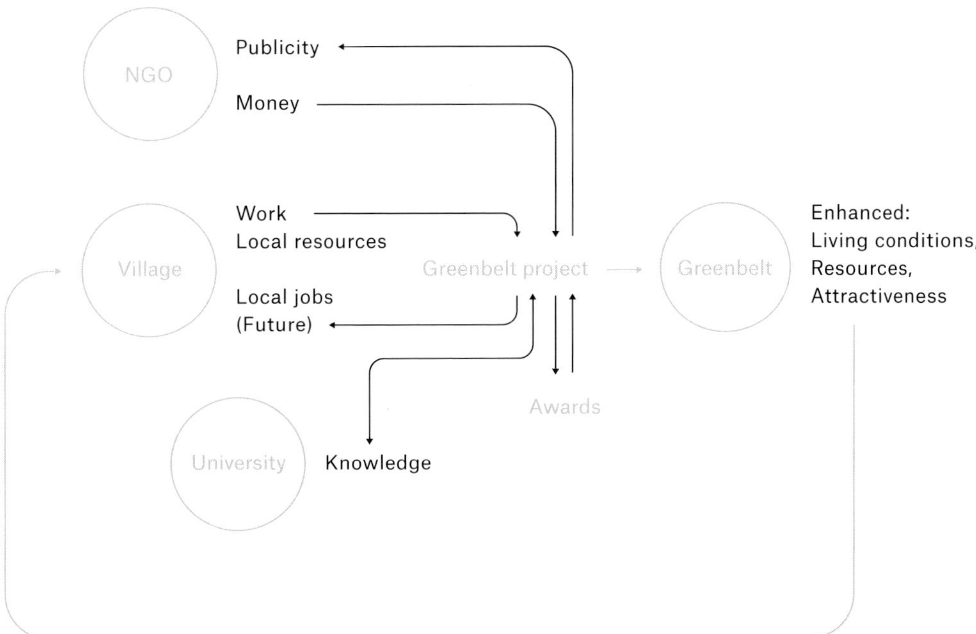

2-6-2013	2-10-2013	2-11-2013
62 % of the Greenbelt trees are found in good condition. 58 trees are in a critical state. Temperatures reach highs of 35°C–39°C	A bag of maize is handed over to the section with the best trees in the Greenbelt.	A Greenbelt team is founded with a young representative per section, as the elders are too old to do regular supervision on site.

Greenbelt February 2013

3-10-2013

The trees are much more vital than they were a month earlier. Maintenance work is carried out regularly.

Temperatures can reach a high of 42°C.

1-25-2014

93 trees are found healthy, farmers have planted an additional 70 trees through their private initiative.

1-30-2014

Greenbelt team meeting: Sometimes team members do not get enough support from their sections. There are difficulties regarding communication with the Chief and the elders.

1-31-2014

Greenbelt village meeting: Greenbelt ID cards with the label 'environmental guardian' are handed out to the young team members, monthly reports to the Chief are scheduled.

3-16-2014

Insufficient watering of the trees. Another 11 trees have died since January and 37 fences are still ruined.

3-20-2014

Greenbelt village meeting: It is decided to distribute the trees among certain families or houses so that responsibilities are clearly defined

Guabuliga Reflecting on the Greenbelt Project

Interviews by Chrili Car
September 2015

SALIFU MAHAMA TAMPURIE
Chief of Guabuliga

I, as the chief of the community, had the privilege to transplant the first tree, which was a Teak tree, and this has been doing well for the past three years now, it is developing so well! The whole Greenbelt project was handed over to us as a community to nurture and foster those plants into full development. But over this period, we have had our own challenges. Some have survived and are doing well, but a lot have died and dried up. Because this project is so dear to us, we—in our own way—are also trying hard to ensure that it is a success.

Baerbel visited this community in 2012 with her students. And they came with so many disciplines: some were studying agriculture, others planning. They came as a team of seven to eight people and surveyed this community. The result of one of those studies was about tackling environmental degradation, something that is also dear to my heart and the heart of the people of Guabuliga. We all realized that our environment was quite a very, very vegetated area. So, over the years, we think we have overexploited the vegetated forest, particularly on top of the mountains. Then we also came to realize that it has had strong effects on our environment, because in the olden days, this community hardly got its roofs ripped off by any form of storm. The vegetated mountain to the east acted as a shield and protected this community against the heavy winds. But overexploitation of the vegetative cover on that mountain rendered it quite useless: now it is virtually bare and our roofs are now being ripped off. So we started feeling it. These days, even when you look at the rain, it comes with anger. The rain comes with some type of energy—a rough, full strength. Earlier it was not like that, it would come smoothly. Because of that missing vegetation to the east, strong winds

9-11-2014

The Greenbelt area is covered with high-standing maize. The first trees have reached a height of 3 m and are mature enough to survive on their own. 62 vital Greenbelt trees are found. No replacement trees have been planted so far and all privately planted trees have died.

9-15-2014

Guabuliga village meeting: the appointed next steps have not been implemented. The Greenbelt team is demotivated. Chief and elders decide to plant replacement trees soon. Monthly monitoring by the elders themselves is scheduled.

9-16-2014

53 replacement trees are organized, the Greenbelt team is asked to come up with another 35 seedlings.

try to destroy even the few trees that are left standing. It is like it is angry, it roars, it comes in with energy. When we were kids, there was a forest there, and each time the storm came, it hit the mountain, but the very high trees acted as a shield—it lifted the wind and in the community you would not even feel the wind, you only hear it going up, flowing, It would just come—'woo o' —and that meant that the wind was flowing past this community.

Now we have started feeling it. That is why the whole community was so happy about this particular project. And when you came and did your studies and it came out that there was a need to improve upon the vegetation, it was a welcome idea in this community, because we have started feeling the effect of it.

So, for now, this is how far we have gone with the Greenbelt and it is not the best we would have wished, but at least some of the trees have survived and they are doing well. This season we will continue to transplant more trees that are acceptable to our soils and the weather, so that in the near future, it is designed. As a community, we will be proud that, together with an NGO, we have been able to produce something that is environmentally friendly, a protectant of our community, as well as beautifying it. I even want to take the further step to announce to this community that regarding that mountain that we all knew was protecting us: henceforth no woman or any other individual for any matter should go there for firewood or to fell any tree for charcoal. In this way, it will rejuvenate itself within the next 5 to 10 years. then we will have our natural shield which will protect this community as it used to some decades back.

DAVID AGONGO
External advisor, ZEFP Walewale

Because people destroy the bush, there is a lot of heat from the sun. The climate is changing: no more rains, no more water. That is why tree planting also supports the earth by protecting it from climate change.

8-28-2015

22 trees have reached the height of 3–4 m and mature. Maintenance has not been improved; only 47 trees are found vital. Conflicts with farmers who farm inside the Greenbelt area are reported. Some farmers seem to fear the loss of farming land as soon as all trees are mature.

9-1-2015

Guabuliga village meeting: Chief and elders direct a strict strategy. Each section is asked to come up with replacement trees on their own within one week.

10-1-2015

The number of trees has nearly doubled to 95. One section (*Nouri loabi*) has set up its own Greenbelt tree nursery: The seedlings are 10 cm high and need to grow more before being planted.

MBATAKORA
Farmer, local doctor

The environment is changing. It was bushy in the olden days. Because of the trees, you couldn't see the mountains, but now they have died. In the olden days, there were a lot of animals. Now they have all gone, they are finished, a lot of animals: buffalos, chimpanzees, these animals with long horns like goats, even lions. Now, if we want to get meat, we have to get domestic animals.

DIGBANDANA
Farmer

In the olden days, when trees were here and then died, they would drop a seed and a new tree would come up. But nowadays, people cut them for firewood. Earlier, there were some trees that bore fruits, like Shea nuts, these blackberries. So when you went there, you could get fruits to eat.

10-2-2015

Guabuliga village meeting: a community meeting is announced at the market. Every section that manages to maintain 20 trees will receive a reward. An extra meeting with the farmers is scheduled. A tight monthly monitoring system is developed.

11-28-2015

The first of the monthly onsite monitorings takes place. Monthly calls between Austria and Guabuliga are scheduled. A collaboration with the school of Guabuliga is set up.

ABDULAI WUDANA
Farmer, elder of Wulugu foŋŋu

We heard about the planting of trees for a long time. But we didn't have someone like you come and educate us about the planting of trees. So we had heard about it and we were doing it, but then you came and opened our eyes even more to the planting of trees. It is very, very important for the community. The reason why it is important to the community is that it controls erosion. It also serves as a wind barrier. And when it is the dry season, people sit under the trees for shade.

NACHINABA MATARI
Farmer, elder of Gbandana Foŋŋu

You educated us that when you cut a tree, you have to replace it. Just cutting down trees without replacing them reduces the environment. All the children were involved—also one of my children: they were planting and they were also looking after the trees. When trees grow up, they provide shade and give us fruits to eat and they also beautify the community. The thing is, our houses are far from the place. So, when we return home, the animals would go and spoil the trees.

SULEMAN FATAWU
External advisor: Asiribisi Walewale

It is the human factor. When you grow something, you include it in your daily activities. But some community members don't devote time and then realise: "Oh, what is happening—my tree is dead". Not that the people don't know. But behaviour change is a gradual process. We need to take it systematically until people start to learn. Some trees have survived; people will start benefitting. Then others will say "Ey! I planted my tree at the same time, now he is enjoying it—I am not enjoying it".

MASU ADAM
Farmer, elder of Bangola

We sent children around to call for a meeting of the area this evening. They will come to the house and tell them how to look after these plants and replace those that have died. So we will have this meeting this evening and maybe Sunday we will plant.

BABA SEIDU ALHASSAN
Electrician

I can start from 2009 up to now—every rainy season there has been a wind storm. So if there is a tree, the wind will not have enough strength to destroy the houses. But because the people are not used to such a project, they have been looking at it as something new. Human nature is that all one's energy is not devoted to protecting the trees—fencing, watering, and other things. There are sticks around everywhere! They can fence them. There is water; but those who are appointed to water only think of payment and other things.

JAHANATU
Farmer

When you plant a Mango tree, this is what you have to do: you put the tree in the earth and if it is the dry season you water it, in the rainy season you don't water it because there is enough rain to water the plants. The reason why trees have died is that when the sun came out, they dried up, when the sun is too hot and you don't know how to properly water, if the water is too hot when you use it, the tree will die. That is why many trees have died, because there was too much sun and some didn't know how to water the plants.

MARTIN ISAAC
Farmer and tailor

I know a lot about and am a part of the Greenbelt. I planted electric pole's trees (Teak). We planted a lot of them and mangos and lots of things. For our area, they gave us 50 of these pole trees and 50 Mango. We always watered them, sharing the duty between houses: one week this house does it, another week that house does. This is how we do it. The whole village came and they gave instructions: you have this site to plant the trees, and you this area—that's how it is.

IMORO BABA
Farmer, Greenbelt team member

I realized I should plant trees, so I planted my own trees. It was my own idea. The benefits are many: it provides fruits, animals rest under them, and when there is heat, the trees are cooling. When you people saw that I was hard-working, you added me to the Greenbelt team. The work was meant to be split between the houses. But some people refused to give support. So I water them. Then some other houses refuse—and I water them again.

ZIVELIN
Farmer, trash recycling expert

Well, I think the problem is that the land there is not for just one person. Many people are farming there. I mean, if someone is farming, like me, and used to plant maize—you cannot control it. We do not stay in the trees overnight. So if the farmers come, if you don't talk to them, they will never understand it unless you talk to them about why the trees bring benefits, then they will understand.

JOSEF
Librarian

The most important thing is: trees are good. When the wind is blowing, it cannot destroy our houses, it cannot destroy any part of our houses. Secondly, you can use the trees: when you are sick, you can use trees for medicine. So I like the trees.

When the trees are dying, because of a lack of care for them, some will say: "White man came with the trees. He went back. So when you go back, I don't care about it. Whether the thing grows or doesn't, I don't care"—that's all.

LUKETO
Food seller

They divided the areas and they gave us the trees to plant. I know somebody related, who was part of it. They serve as wind barriers and also control soil erosion. The challenge is drought because there is not a lot of rain. So, when you go around to water, the trees are dying because of the lack of care. Fetching the water, it's tedious work.

HALIDU ABDUI HAFIZ
Barber

I think the Greenbelt project will help Guabuliga a lot. It will be like a reservation place for people to rest, and a very nice place to view. The only challenge is that the dry season is the time when the trees die so much—there is not enough water for them to grow. Last year there was the big storm, the wind took off a lot of roofs and some of the electric poles collapsed. If you have trees by your house, they protect it so that the wind cannot take off your roof.

Empowering the Base of the Pyramid: Lessons From A Rural Community In Northern Ghana

Christin ter Braak-Fostinger

1. The needs of the base of the pyramid:

The bottom one billion people at the base of the pyramid (BoP) lack it all: basic necessities such as sufficient food, clean water, and adequate shelter. Poor health, lack of nutrition, financial vulnerability, limited education, and a dearth of marketable skills shut them out of the organized market economy.

It is crucial for effective non-profit organizations (NPOs) and non-governmental organizations (NGOs) to understand how their help can create a long-term, positive social impact and foster the important roles that these vulnerable people can play for themselves, for example, through value-creation relationships as local producers, co-producers, or groups in a cooperative. The context in which to start varies of course from country to country, but through investment-ready programs or technical know-how transfer farmers at the BoP can upgrade the quality of their output. With a little training, people at the BoP can also take part in basic production and assembly jobs, or in activities within the service sector, transportation, distribution, and retailing, for example—bridging the "last mile" to the local markets and consumers.

2. The needs of a new generation of philanthropists:

A relatively small group of 'GenXers' and 'Millenials' will inherit over USD 40 trillion in wealth over the next years, much of which is designated to philanthropic giving. Many of those have also created their own wealth, e.g., in Silicon Valley, and understand philanthropy from a strategic angle. These next generation donors desire to be 'hands-on philanthropists' in their approach to giving and social investing with key audiences, including grant recipients, their families, peers, NGOs/NPOs, and other funders such as governments. They are more likely to structure their giving from a standpoint of problems to be solved, rather than institutions to be supported. The new, young philanthropists make up a different crowd: they want to get their hands dirty. 'Giving while living' is their credo.

3. Leveraged philanthropy:

The needs of both the BoP and the next generation of philanthropists can be leveraged in many ways: the help of technology or the building of local value chains for smallholder farmers are just two examples out of many.

(i) Technology makes philanthropy more effective and transparent

It is hard to underestimate the extent to which technology can improve philanthropy. This is true for the on-site work of foundations, NGOs/NPOs, as well as their daily administrative work. Managing donations or project applications electronically and transparently is just the start. Through crowdsourcing, anyone with access to the internet can contribute ideas. On social media, anyone can launch a global advocacy campaign. Digital data makes it affordable for nonprofits of all sizes to assess social problems and track their progress in terms of solving them. At the other end of the giving chain, donors seek better information regarding the social impact that their charitable giving and social investments have. However, assessing the social and environmental impact is much harder than measuring financial returns.

Technology allows individual givers to pool their resources online in virtual giving circles. Collective giving is born. Take, for example, the Giving Tuesday, which unites the US philanthropic community for a day of giving at the start of the holiday season. It is likely that this concept will spill over to Europe's and Asia's giving landscape as well.

Collective giving became famous in 2010, when Bill and Melinda Gates and Warren Buffet founded the Giving Pledge, an effort to encourage their wealthy peers to donate a significant part of their wealth to charity. The number of philanthropists responding to Bill and Melinda Gates and Warren Buffett's appeal for increased generosity has been constantly growing over the years and as of January 2015, 128 billionaire or former billionaire individuals and couples have signed the pledge. A large part of worldwide philanthropic funding still also comes from ordinary people with extraordinary generosity, technology strongly influences philanthropy here as well. To be effective in their giving, these ordinary givers also need access to communities within which they can exchange ideas and sources of innovation. Social networks are beginning to transform the way that individual philanthropists collaborate with one another. The matchmaking power of the Web creates networks of donors who would otherwise have no way of finding one another and sharing opinions. In any case, be it the very 'top of the pyramid' or the 'average giver', a philanthropic dollar can be leveraged in multiple ways beyond classical checkbook charity. Philanthropists today are willing to transfer their skills, networks, know-how, and social services in addition to their money, and in return, expect disclosure of the social impact they create.

(ii) Building value chains for smallholder farmers makes philanthropy more engaged

Smallholder farming accounts for 80 % of all the farms and most of the land that is cultivated in Sub-Saharan Africa (SSA). An assessment has been made that growth generated by agriculture in SSA is more effective towards reducing poverty than gross domestic product (GDP) growth in other sectors. For example, Diao, et al (2012), estimate that the decline in the national poverty rate resulting from agricultural-led growth is up to four times larger than the decline resulting from non-agriculture-led growth.

Rural farm holders often lack the capacity to store or properly transport their commodities. Lacking the infrastructure for roads, water access, irrigation systems, and markets, are further typical constraints. The situation is exacerbated by their lack of information on prices, rendering them vulnerable to intermediaries as there is usually only a minimal or no flow of information. This makes it easy for intermediaries to take advantage of rural producers. Sensitization of smallholder farmers, and building local value chains through producer organizations and their participation, are powerful tools for improving rural farm holders' position.

The involvement of the private as well as the public sector can be very fruitful in that regard. For example, agreements between companies, government agencies, and philanthropic foundations or NPOs can result in funding streams that reduce market risks and free up the business sector to unleash its unique innovative capacities. A new innovative vehicle in that context of cross-sectoral collaboration is the public-private partnership (PPP). Such a partnering between the private and the public sector can take a variety of forms, from direct equity investments by philanthropists to volume guarantees that give companies the assurance of sufficient market demand to investment funds with different risk-return classes. For instance, the Africa Agricultural and Trade Investment Fund (AATIF), which is set up in the form of a PPP, finances projects and companies along the agricultural value chain and develops financial markets across Sub-Saharan Africa.

4. What are the lessons in the context of a remote little village in the most northern part of Ghana—where I am personally the co-founder and president of an international NGO undertaking re-integration and community development work?

As we started our project works in fall 2008, our utmost goal was to initiate a project that enabled the Guabuliga community to help themselves in the long run and to involve the community as closely as possible (through a rigorous bottom-up approach) from the beginning. This sounds nice in theory but was challenged massively in practice. The pitfalls were, just to name a few: cultural barriers (How do we gain the trust of the Chief and the village elders? How do we manage not to be seen as 'the white cash-cow'?), linguistic barriers (How do we effectively communicate with the community, which primarily only speaks the local language, *Mampruli*), technological barriers (In 2008, Guabuliga was located in a kind of 'black hole' where cell phones usually only worked on a random basis and where power was and still can be lacking for days), infrastructural barriers (In the rainy season, the 15 km- long sand road connecting Guabuliga and the main road through northern Ghana is often impassable because of the bad conditions: parts of the road are washed away)—all of these made it difficult for us to get started with our endeavors. But probably the most challenging venture on site in the beginning was finding a trustworthy person who shared our long-term project vision. We were still naive idealist full of ideas and we got screwed. But we learned throughout the process, and immediately started to share our experience with others.

Today, more than five years later, Guabuliga and Braveaurora are partners based on trust and share a common vision: to act as a role-model project in northern Ghana that spread the word on reintegration and family reunification, and actively campaigned against 'fake orphanages' (and the related business with young, unexperienced foreign volunteers) that just pop out of the sand like the little plants after the rain in northern Ghana. As partners that see eye to eye, the Guabuliga community and Braveaurora collaborate and share ideas such as a newly developed training center, a teachers' incentive program, a village microcredit program, a newly installed water board with a money-collecting system, a Young Ambassador Program for re-integration and advocacy, a Greenbelt project, a sustainable waste and upcycling project, etc. A results-measurement framework helps us to measure the social impact for our donors. External partners and experts (like nav_s baerbel mueller and [a]FA, or local cooperation partners and the Ghanaian Department of Social Welfare (DSW), were closely involved as sparring partners since the very beginning.

So what are our key lessons?

A high-impact non-profit organization (NPO) or non-governmental organization (NGO) should:

- work at least as much outside of its four walls as it does managing internal strategies and operations
- collaborate as closely as is possible with—and involve—the local community
- create positive change by leveraging government support and making them accountable whenever possible
- enable and empower communities in order to help them to become self-sufficient, by giving them tools at hand that they have suggested and really need
- make markets work and develop, with the local community, income chains and new income ventures
- remain flexible, learn from pitfalls, and adapt to change and local needs
- share their know-how with other NGOs/NPOs, collaborate on a cross-sectoral basis and nurture nonprofit networks
- hand over projects to the local community as early as it possibly makes sense
- offer new forms of philanthropic engagement for the next younger and more "hands-on" generation of donors
- build strong communities of honorary supporters/donors/experts and involve them as closely as possible
- measure the social impact of their on-site work for their donors
- have a clear exit plan

Dr. CHRISTIN TER BRAAK-FORSTINGER is a financial lawyer and the founder of PVA Advisory, an independent philanthropic advisory firm in Zurich. She is the co-founder and president of an Austrian, Swiss, and Ghana-based NGO that supports vulnerable children in Africa.

THE GUABULIGA SOLAR-POWERED WATER PROJECT

2013 –

During a presentation of the results of Theresa Theuretzbacher's water research in September 2012, Chief Salifu and his council of elders realized how dramatic the drinking water supply situation in the village was. The need for more awareness and education on the topic within the community was discussed. In terms of the physical infrastructure, the most effective solution was the re-activation of the centralized water tank system on a village scale. In 2004, the government provided Guabuliga with a mechanized system for pumping drinking water, together with a distribution network. Four years later, it stopped functioning due to a problem with the electrical transformer. No spare parts were available in Ghana for this type of equipment and the community did not manage to collect the necessary amount of money to acquire another one. A sustainable solution was found by re-activating the water-tank system by means of a solar-powered pump. The NGO Braveaurora realized the urgency of the water issue and included it on their agenda. In cooperation with the authorities of the village, Braveaurora commissioned Baerbel Mueller and Frank B. Kumah to conceptualize and calculate a well-dimensioned project. The NGO went through an intense funding campaign in 2013. In February 2014, the system was installed.

To ensure the long-term success of the project, a lengthy initiation phase was scheduled before the implementation of the solar-power system. The importance of a functioning water board was targeted. A group of elected people formed a water board and were trained to be autonomously in charge of the new infrastructure. The board's most urgent task was to decide on an efficient water tariff collection strategy for Guabuliga. It became clear that women had to be intensely involved and represented in these decision processes, as they are in charge of supplying water to their families. Hence, it was decided that two-thirds of the board members should be women. Moving women into leadership positions of this kind creates the pretext for an improved and gender-sensitive education in Guabuliga.

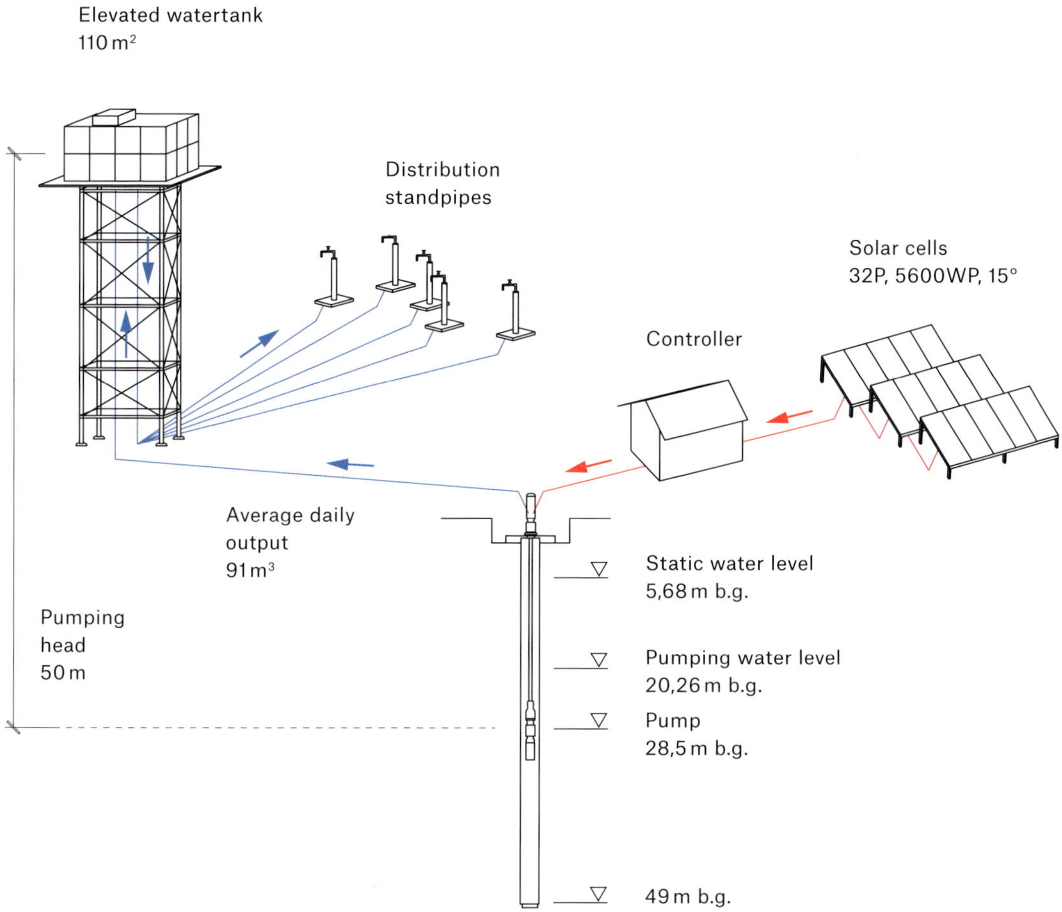
Elevated watertank
110 m²
Distribution
standpipes
Solar cells
32P, 5600WP, 15°
Controller
Average daily
output
91 m³
Static water level
5,68 m b.g.
Pumping
head
50 m
Pumping water level
20,26 m b.g.
Pump
28,5 m b.g.
49 m b.g.

Guabuliga Water Project

Saibu Mutaru
November 2015

Before its reactivation, the Guabuliga water system was not functioning for several years because the power supply for the project was cut due to accumulated debts. As a result, the people had to depend almost solely on contaminated sources of water. In fact, research conducted by [a]FA at the time indicated that the water was highly contaminated with fecal material.

With full financial assistance from Braveaurora, the water project was revived through the acquisition of quality solar-powered panels. The technical consultant for this project was *Pumptech Ghana Limited*. This company facilitated the purchase and installation processes. The project was officially commissioned in February 2014. Since then, the people have had access to a very clean source of water. The water is flowing all the time.

In terms of maintenance, the only technical person in Guabuliga who ensures that the system is maintained is Anass Seidu, who received training for the water project. It is important to mention that Anass Seidu can only do maintenance regarding plumbing work. If there are any electrical problems, the community contacts *Pumptech* to fix the problem.

In order to ensure that the water project is well-maintained, the community decided to form a water committee. This committee consisted of five members who met once a month to discuss how the water system was working and how to improve upon it. The water committee compiled a list of all the active women in Guabuliga and levied each of them to pay a monthly fee of GHC 1. The committee opened a bank account in Walewale into which all contributions were paid.

Currently, there is no water committee because the Chief dissolved the existing one due to complaints that most of the board members were not being effective. The Chief promised to inaugurate a new committee, but this has not happened yet, so there is no regular meeting that can report how much has been contributed or the level of outstanding debts.

SAIBU MUTARU was promoted from Education Coordinator to Project Manager at Braveaurora. He holds a degree in sociology from the University of Ghana, Legon and a masters degree in international development from Edinburgh University (UK). Currently, he is on scholarship at Stellenbosch University (South Africa) pursuing a PhD in social anthropology.

Water Distribution Plan

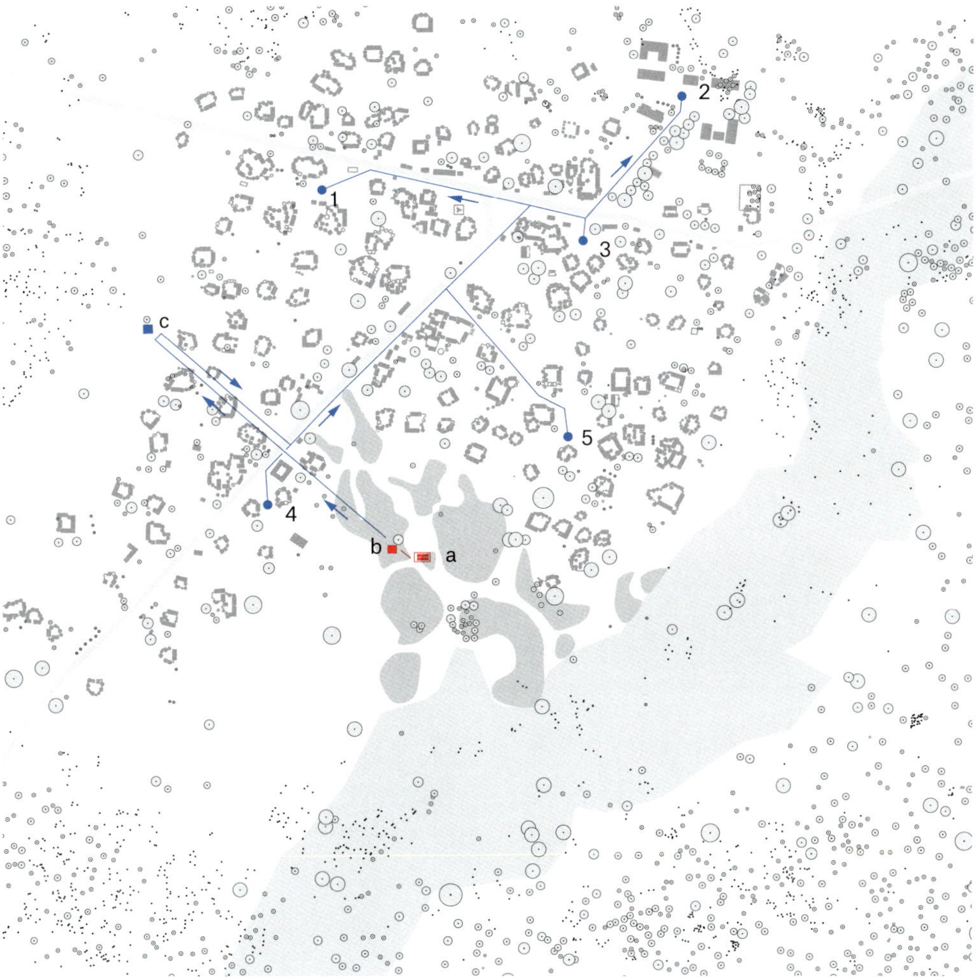

a Solar cells
b Controller
c Water tank
1–5 Hand pump

500 m

Opening Ceremony

February 28, 2014

WHAT WAS, WHAT IS AND NEVER AGAIN

Kojo Benedict Quaye aka Sir Black

Chant...

I don't expect you to forgive me after this oration
And I don't expect you to forget me
I don't expect you to get upset
And I don't expect you to get hurt
I don't expect you to get affected
And I don't expect you to get infected
I don't expect you to get confused
And I don't expect you to get seduced

Somehow we all got to put on some thinking caps now, cause we got to go up
Far up to reach the height, where we can put on some En-light-ten-ment
Because the 666system has destroyed a lot of people so I ask you: What are we doing about it?

The cradle of all humanity
The nest that bred posterity
The land that founded the colours black, brown, pink and white
Which today informs one's identity.
However the filthy prosperity of her 'developed offspring', aka developed nation had been used to justify the persistent indignity of a dying mother.
The craving is inevitable, but to which end?
Greed only desires dividends.
Greed didn't only push you to bite the hand that fed you.
It drove you to stomp the womb that gave birth to you.
Nevertheless there is unlimited evidence, typified by your grand agenda exposed right here in the city of Berlin, some one hundred and thirty years ago

Thievery and exploitation is the order of the day.
When we seek justification, Spencer claimed it was human nature
Henry Barry said, we have as much as possible been able to keep the black man at the level of the beast, if we can extinguish their capacity to see the light our work will be complete.
Others say the black race cannot be civilized and so it must be exterminated completely
Well, you 'developed children' bleed your mother dry in vivid display,
But it's ok, as it helped you keep your profound stature.

Having succeeded, you still continue to enslave the motherland,
You take advantage of her Needs and Ignorance, creating synthetic colonial boarders to put her in shackles, disguised in the forms of Grants and Foreign Aid, Scholarships and Fellowships, Diplomacy and Democracy, Modernization and Liberalization;
not to mention your iron fist of immigration from brainwashing to 'blacksploitation'
this is to say (black exploitation)
Mind you, many empires have risen and fallen, and that norm won't change.
Facts remain though; that those that seemed to persist forever were they that fought the temptation to deviate from man's history and culture.

An everlasting well cannot run dry
Legacies still exist, so that unlike men, truths don't die.
Man conceals in order to control, but God reveals to redeem.
We the roots of this tree we call humanity, can't fold our hand in despair and cry
We won't; we know too well that only the weak seek to find relief in sighs.
A developed offspring who preys on his mother is not a predator, but a pest.
Unfortunately, the cowards and ignorant of today regard this as a conquest

It is absolutely not difficult to tell what the scramble was for, and still is for, is it?
With the insatiable craving for 'gold and control' blindingly visible, even to the optically disabled.
There is difficulty however, and it's in the details, what represents your idea of 'gold' and 'control' or let's say 'go and control'.
Though insufficient, the clear disparity of small haves and a larger have-nots,
The dominance of man lighter colours over darker ones cannot possibly be ignored.

I say to you today 3x Europe!
The 'd-evil' is always in the details.
And don't ask me how?
But if you will, tell me, you will tell them
I told you to tell them ... 3x
Those who took away our drum, they are heavily disappointed and surprised they could not take away our dance.

Chant...

KOJO BENEDICT QUAYE aka SIR BLACK is an African living in Ghana. He is a freestyle spoken-word performance artist and instructor, co-director of Haduwa Arts and Culture Institute and co-founder of the Ehalakasa spoken-word poetry movement. He works with local, international, and cultural institutions around Africa and Europe.

STAGING APAM
CENTRAL REGION, GHANA

ON OTHER ARCHITECTURE

STAGING APAM, CENTRAL REGION, GHANA
ON OTHER ARCHITECTURE

wider discourse

AFRICA / GHANA / CENTRAL REGION / APAM

APAM

Coordinates:	5° 16′ 44″ N 0° 44′ 23″ W
Population:	23,588 (Census 2010)
Main ethnic groups:	Fanti
Average temperature:	29 °C
Average precipitation:	1,500 – 2,000 mm p. a.
Rainy season:	March – July, September
Dry season:	October – March, August
Vegetation type:	Coastal savannah
Main livelihood:	Fishing
Mostly harvested fish:	Herring, Salmon, 'Eban' (*Sardinella aurita*), Tuna
Fishing methods:	Gill net, purse seine, hook and line, Saiko
Facilities:	Secondary school, hospital, Fort Patience Museum, salt industry
Festivities:	Akwambo (for honoring founders), Ntokroko (for making laws), Epa (for settling disputes)

ABREKUM

Coordinates:	5° 18′ 21.5″ N 0° 42′ 46.4″ W
Main livelihoods:	Agriculture, fishing

HADUWA ARTS AND CULTURE INSTITUTE

The Haduwa Arts & Culture Institute is a base for artists and cultural practitioners in Africa and Europe to support excellence and diversity in and through the arts. Haduwa promotes mutual understanding and enhances active local and international collaborations. Over the past few years, Haduwa has collaborated with local organizations that share their art on stage and in workshops. Haduwa works with students and neighborhoods throughout the vicinity of Apam and Abrekum, Central Region, Ghana. This falls in line with the belief in empowering the local community through cultural exchange and collaborations.

Google Earth 2004

WATER IS LIFE: WORLDVIEW, LIVELIHOOD, AND COMMUNITY IN GA MASHIE

Victoria Okoye

The value of water

In many ways, water envelopes and defines community life in Ga Mashie, the historic district of Accra. Perhaps there is no place in the city that has maintained its sea and historical linkages as much as this space has. In addition to the physical coastal location of Ga Mashie, the power of the sea helps shape its community worldview, and livelihoods draw from it. In turn, the community connection to water contributes to a vibrant space for social life, demonstrating the centrality of water to the entire community.

Traditional beliefs run deep in Ga Mashie, and the Ga worldview includes an understanding of and respect for a supreme being (*Ataa Naa Nyongm*), as well as divine beings or spirits of nature (*dzemànwọdzi*). The supreme being is the source of all things: an invisible creator, both omnipotent and immortal. The divine spirits are associated with earthly topographical spaces and features thought to be the natural places of their descent or abode—such as rivers, mountains, and the sea. It is believed that these beings manifest themselves in these topographical features and communicate to the Ga people through traditional priests and priestesses (*wọŋtśɛmɛi*). These traditional priests and priestesses interpret the will of these divine beings, who themselves serve as intermediaries between humans and the supreme being.[1]

Within this Ga worldview, the sea is more than just a physical or topographical feature and source of their livelihood, it is a powerful deity with divine qualities that impacts aspects of their lives.[2] It is the divine will of the sea god to rest on Tuesdays, and on this day each week in Ga Mashie, fishing activities cease.[4] From time to time, some may challenge this belief by going out to sea, but stories prevail of fisherman who have dared to do this and never returned.

Fishing is the oldest livelihood in Ga Mashie, whose origin as a coastal settlement dates back to the late 16th century. Fishing is a livelihood that literally depends on the sea's daily offerings. Even through economic changes—the arrival of European trade and colonial administration, the emergence of Ga Mashie as a global trading and warehouse port, and the relocation of the city's major port and post-independent government administration outside of the area—fishing has remained a central livelihood and identity for Ga Mashie.[4] From the early mornings through to the evenings, teams of fishermen make their way out to sea. It is gritty and physically taxing work and has been indelibly stamped into the human fabric of Jamestown. Seasonal in nature, there are high and low periods: the success of each day's catch has reverberating impacts on households that must work for a seasonal income security. The result: the area is one of the most impoverished pockets within Accra.[5]

1 Sheikh Mustapha Watson-Quartey (2011). "Religion of the Ga People."
2 Interview, Samoa Mark Hansen (2015).
3 The specific day to not go out to sea depends on traditional priests' consultations with the gods. In other settlements of the Ga people (including Labadi or Teshie Nungua), the community may pay their respects to the sea on different days.
4 Nat Nuno Amarteifio (2015). "The Definitive Story of Jamestown British Accra."
5 Global Communities (March 2012).
6 In February 2014, a local news outlet covered the story of a bull that was caught at sea by local fisherman, after it was used as a sacrifice to the gods. From the *Daily Graphic*, February 14, 2014.

The beachside stretches along the coast, and at the harbor, long, lean, and brightly colored wooden boats line the shore, perched along the sand. There are dozens of boats, but each is unique, decorated with colors and intriguing aphorisms. On each boat's long, curved surface, the owner has painted pithy, powerful local sayings and Biblical references in Ga and English. "Fear God," one says, in strong, white block letters. Life, like the sea, may seem unpredictable (despite its cultural heritage, Ga Mashie is one of the city's poorest areas), and although the fishermen are at the mercy of powers stronger than them, their faith instills within them courage, willpower, and inner strength, despite their challenging circumstances, and provides order in an uncertain world.

When the fishermen's catch runs low, traditionalists go deep into the sea and offer a full-grown cow or ram to the sea god, as a means of appeasement or to earn favor. The sacrifice also serves a practical purpose: The sacrifice can serve as bait, attracting fish that can be caught in subsequent fishing rounds. These practices still continue in Ga Mashie and other indigenous settlements of Accra.[6]

Water-based livelihoods are a gendered space: While men go out to sea, women stay on land to sell, preserve, and prepare the catch. Nearly every day of the week, it is women fishmongers who are teeming inside the cramped covered market and along nearby paths to sell varieties of freshly caught fish and seafood. It is also women who prepare fish in various methods, including sun-drying the fish for long-term storage, or smoking it. Near the beach, women find open spaces to spread the silver, finger-sized fish out in the sun to dry; after three to four days, the curled, browned fish are ready for storage and can last for months when properly preserved. These dried fish are a key ingredient in *shito*, a black pepper sauce. Smoked fish is another traditional method of preparation, done in large, multilayered, wood-burning ovens constructed of traditional clay or more modern cement block or metal. Medium- to large-sized fish are laid out on a layered series of trays at the top of the large oven. At the bottom, the women feed special *osha* or *odanta* wood logs into the fire to support the heat that is required for the six-hour-long cooking process.

(Un)Building community

While the water serves as an organizing force and source of worldview and livelihoods, the community has created the beach as a space for informal community life. Previous colonial and post-independent planning policies prevented the building of structures along the beachside. Instead, the planning emphasized a segregation of uses: fishing at the beach, residential and commercial activities taking place in the distanced, elevated space around which the colonial buildings had been laid, and the streets, sidewalks, buildings, offices, and houses packed around them.

Over time, a new community grew up and established itself at the beachside. Wooden shacks served as dwellings for the fishermen, boat repairmen, and security guards and families, enabling proximity to their major economic activities. The community attracted commercial vendors in turn to set up kiosks, popular drinking and small chop bars for eating; their loud music filled the air. Throughout the day, the sound of the waves against the shore is interspersed with the voices of young people at play, especially boys, who start pick-up soccer

Samoa Mark Hansen (August 2015). Interview and beach tour at Jamestown, Ga Mashie.

Sheikh Mustapha Watson-Quartey (2011). "Religion of the Ga People." Online. Accessed November 10, 2015: www.kpakpatseweroyalfamily.wordpress.com/tag/kpodziemo/

CHF International / Global Communities and Accra Metropolitan Assembly (March 2010). Accra Poverty Map: A Guide to Urban Poverty Reduction in Accra.

Nat Nuno Amarteifio (November 2015). "The Definitive Story of Jamestown British Accra." Online. Accessed November 11, 2015: www.modernghana.com/news/655280/1/the-definitive-story-of-james-town-british-accra-b.html

competitions, who challenge each other to diving competitions at the fishing pier, or who simply observe. Open spaces and paths became recreational areas for child's play. Collectively, the community have transformed the beach into an informal multifunctional space through which they actively engage, live, and play with the sea on a daily basis, further emphasizing how the sea serves as the community's greatest resource.

The informal multifunctionality of this place was not part of the city government's plans, and yet it has consistently thrived in the face of government plans for redevelopment. These plans had always been a subtle threat, until recently. In November 2015, the Accra Metropolitan Assembly authorized the demolition of a wide spread of these "illegal structures"—shack houses, restaurants, chop bars, kiosks, and other community-contributed infrastructure—at the beachside. It is part of a long series of demolitions of informal, or "illegal" structures throughout the city, another tangible setback within the constant tug-of-war between government-planned "formality" and community-created "informality."

VICTORIA OKOYE is the creator of African Urbanism and Urban Advocacy Specialist for Women in Informal Employment: Globalizing and Organizing (WIEGO). As an urban development planner and researcher, Victoria engages with informality and bottom-up citizen placemaking, particularly in public spaces, in West Africa.

LET ME LIVE WITH IT AND LET IT MAKE ME CHANGE IN MY OWN TIME

A Conversation between
Kofi Setordji and Baerbel Mueller
Accra, February 2015

BM: What does art mean in this cultural context?

KS: When you ask me as a creative person what art means, I think, when an artist starts to create, the question is: What am I creating, what is it? Art here in Ghana is the everyday, what you see around you. I live in both worlds, I live in the Western world and in the African setting, the Ghanaian setting, and to us, art is everyday. We don't have a time or a place where we go and look for recreation to say "Oh well, let's go to a museum!". We are doing installations and body performances everyday! The way we sell things on the roadside is an art form for us. So we [as artists] try as much as possible to look around and see what we can take from there and create from there. But even this is in a Western context, because art like a painting or sculpture is art for art's sake in a Western sense. Here, art is created for a purpose. When someone dies, we have to wear white. It is a performance, even the way we are buried. There are a lot of costumes that go with it. So art in this context is very general and very broad. It is not only about the artist alone, because every human being is capable of being an artist. And once you can perform one thing or another, then you are in the genre of being an artist. That is why we do not have the word 'artist' in our language, or anywhere here, instead we have "the owner of an idea".

BM: It is a word?

KS: Yes, it is a word: *Adann tor.* A master craftsman is called *Adann tor*. To us, that is the artist, that is the closest word that we have. That is the person who has the idea, which goes back to the concept that ideas rule the world. So the master craftsman is the originator of the idea. That is how we see art, in this context.

BM: What does contemporary art mean in this cultural context?

KS: Well, we use the English language. The source of contemporary means: we are all living in the same time. Contemporary is now. I would say it is ambiguous. To me, it is not necessary to put together art and 'contemporary' because time is time, it is just made up of a series of points. But 'contemporary' does not have a point, because it is just now, now, now. But when you join them, it becomes a line. The Western world always wants to create new things. But if you look at life itself, it has always been the same anyway. Applying a different idea or a different meaning to an old idea, that is what 'contemporary' means, but it is not a particular way of doing things. Time to us is not linear, it is a spiral thing. When I am coming from Europe and leaving Accra and going to my village, I am crossing three different civilizations and ways of doing things. I can do that within 24 hours. And I live in these three places at the same time. So when we are talking about 'contemporary', which one am I talking about? The one where I am sitting in a plane or...? Since I live in these three places, I can always interconnect any point within this parallel thing. So I cannot go back to your past, but we can live the same past day.

BM: What can art do in this (African and Ghanaian) cultural context?

KS: Art is the basis of development; it is the fuel for development. Art is the highest form of human beings at any level. So that's how art brings everybody to a higher place every time. That is the fuel that we should use to change our lives.

BM: And what can art spaces do in this cultural context?

KS: I will start with open spaces. Open spaces are very important. I was amazed when I went to Europe to see open spaces. People who can think 400 years back to the wide center of a town as a space where people can interact. We don't have that. We have what you call 'durbar grounds'. When there is a festival, people use that space. But when you are in a city, there must be open spaces that are designed for neighborhoods so that people can move around. Unfortunately, when we come to the cities, we are not as flexible as we are in our villages, so we tend to move towards the cultural background we come from and don't want

to interact with other people. Public space on the other hand is the road that everybody uses, the pavement. But all these places have their own animated way of life. The pavement, which is supposed to be for pedestrians, is used to sell *Koko*, porridge, in the morning. And then in the afternoon, the person who is selling the rice takes over from the *Koko* seller, so when you want to pass, you have to negotiate to pass on the street. And in the evening, the person who is selling second-hand shoes comes, too. You see, even if it is meant for pedestrians, it is animated in such a way that it has a life of its own.

For artists to reclaim open spaces, they have to act on them. So I see an evolution from open spaces to public spaces, to art spaces... but if this is not happening, it means that the artists in a society are not aware of what they are.

BM: What should art spaces look like in this cultural context? I mean, you have created one and you are about to create another one.

KS: Art spaces are places where people make a statement about 'now' or interrogate what is 'now' a place to which people can come: interdisciplinary people, creative people, musicians, writers, poets. And it is a very important place, because if these are the people who are on the cutting edge, or inform us of what the new norm is, they need to converge at a particular place. And this place can be a cultural center or it can be a space where people create or a place where the creative people and society meet. There are different forms. It could be a studio where it is only the artist's space, or a cultural center like Nubuke Foundation, where a creative person like me interacts with people and then tries to inform other people and nurture young ones.

I am not sure whether the idea of a museum is still valid today. In every age—I am sure—the museum was a matter of curiosity, for people in the Western world to travel abroad and bring back pieces to and to come and show what they have discovered in this New World. So they put it in a place, a curiosity place. But I think a museum in the contemporary sense is a place where you show both the human and the devil: what humans can do with their hands and their brains.

Okay, Ghanaians have existed since 1957. How can we locate the spectrum of how we have thought or how we have developed the environment? It can be retrospective, it can be something which is moving forward, but you have to have a place for it. I think that 21st-century museums must be interactive. The museums today must create that feeling in which you say: "Oh, that was the beginning of it, wow, but this is how it is used now, and in the future, how can it be used..." So you are taking it into the future. Does that make sense?

BM: Yes! But could you also talk about performance spaces?

KS: When we talk about performance in the African sense, we don't have these performance spaces in which there is an art form: culturally, it is built-in for us. Someone dies: they are going to do a performance of rituals of death and it is done, it is there! It is not something that we have to create a space for. It is there. The space comes alive when the performance people come to it. So it is not a space. It is the people who create it who make space for it. It could be in my house, it could be in the garden, it could be in the street. It is already animated, it is not something that we have to create. It is not a space. It is a Western idea that there must be spaces for performance. Like I said before, Africans, or people from here, animate all the time. Have you been to a ceremony of the child? Before they name a child, the newborn is put in a room for eight days; it does not see the sun. On the eighth day, the parents come and then they hand it back and forth to another person through the door eight times—in and out. You see, it is a performance. So I find it very difficult to see an art piece in a white cube, or black box, as a performance. I try to understand it when I look at it compared to the people who do it here everyday. Which one is the art form?

If we, for ourselves, Ghanaians, Africans, living in this continent with a different climate, cannot articulate what art is for us, then there must be something basically wrong. Look at my point: it is up to us to say, okay, we are no longer interested in this form of dance. Think of ballet for example: I have seen people doing real ballet, which is impressive. And I see the people here who work so hard in muscle training and exercise and flexibility. Why are they doing this when it does not have a meaning for them? Some people from Canada came to study the dance in the Voodoo cult and created a dance from it; that is fine! But for me, to have the meaning of what contemporary dance is pushed down my throat, I have a problem with that. I am not living the life of a Western person: I live here with this dance that is my contemporary. Let me live with it and let it make me change in my own time.

BM: Are there other examples? I mean in this courtyard here, in this space here (Nubuke), you have a stage, and you are about to build a bigger stage. And there is a spoken-word culture, a contemporary spoken-word art scene here in Accra. They need spaces, no?

KS: Yes, I am creating this space—I may not agree with everything—but I am still creating it. The premise is that I have a linguist who can receive words, who can receive the history of 500 hundred years in a day. See, our history is a spoken word one. So if it is a spoken-word culture, why am I looking for new spoken word when it is already with us?

BM: But you see it differently in terms of the fine arts than you do in terms of the performing arts. Doesn't the performer need the stage as much as you as a painter need the museum?

KS: What I don't like is the 'fashion' side of it. I don´t want people to tell me what is contemporary. If we look at the history of painting, it came from the cavemen. It is not European or African, it is human. The 'in' thing is to be contemporary, that is my problem!

BM: My point is not so much about the contemporary, but the space. You said that what fuels development and our societies and life is art. I have looked at the impact of art institutions, such as Nubuke, the Raw Material Company, and Studios Kabako. They have had an impact on the respective cities they are located in, and that is also because they are physical spaces.

KS: I can agree with that. Nubuke is an animated place. It is a place where we can imagine that people are trying to redefine the space. That is okay. Yes, the space is important.

KOFI SETORDJI is a Ghanaian sculptor and painter. His practice expands into the designing of fabric, furniture, houses, and the mentoring of young artists. He is the founder of the Arthaus Artists residency and the Nubuke Foundation, a cultural art space in Accra, Ghana.

"A new place cries out for a new ceremony, but of course it is the new ceremony that should have come first—it is the ceremony of all meanings that should have dictated the shape of the place, as it did when all the great mosques and cathedrals and temples were built. Goodwill, sincerity, reference, belief in culture are not quite enough: the outer form can only take on real authority if the ceremony has equal authority—and who today can possibly call the tune? Of course, today as at all times, we need to stage true rituals, but for rituals that could make theatre—going to an experience that feeds our lives—true forms are needed. These are not at our disposal, and conferences and resolutions will not bring them our way.

In other forms of architecture there is a relationship between conscious, articulate design and good functioning: a well-designed hospital may be more efficacious than a higgledy-piggledy one: but as for theatres, the problem of design cannot start logically. It is not a matter of saying analytically what are the requirements, how best they can be organized—this will usually bring into existence a tame, conventional, often cold hall. The science of theatre-building must come from studying what it is that brings about the most vivid relationship between people—and is this best served by asymmetry, even by disorder? An architect is better off if he works like a scene designer, moving scraps of cardboard by intuition, than if he builds his model from a plan, prepared with a compass and a ruler.

If the theater seems to need a certain crude element, this must be accepted as part of its natural soil. Most architects remain blind to this principle—and era after era the most vital theatrical experiences occur outside the legitimate places constructed for the purpose."

Peter Brook,
The Empty Space, A Book About the Theatre: Deadly, Holy, Rough, Immediate;
Touchstone, 1995

REFLECTIONS ON BUILDINGS FOR PERFORMANCE

A Conversation between
Dr. Awo Mana Asiedu and Petra Kron

PK: For me, the most important sentence in Peter Brook's text is that an architect should be "studying what it is that brings about the most vivid relationship between people." This leads directly to the Haduwa *Apata**, the performance building we constructed in Apam. We started with a workshop for students of the performing arts and architecture on "staging space and staging stage". The architectural students observed the performing arts students and their behaviour. Dancers were dancing blindfolded and the architectural students evaluated their movements: "How did they react to the sunlight? How did the wind influence them?" This was active research on performance specifics. To work in this crossdisciplinary way is important when it comes to spaces for the arts or the performing arts.

AMA: We are saying that the performer's body or the performer's movements should suggest the kind of space s/he could perform in, which for me is really new. If you think of the fact that often performances take place within a space and the performers make use of that space, this thinking is rather the other way round. The architecture should consider the shape of the performance and then create a space to fit the performance. In a lot of senses I guess there is truth in that, in the sense that if you look at traditional African performance for example, which engenders a lot of performer-audience interaction. Therefore it can never be on a proscenium stage. You want the audiences around the performance so the actors can interact freely with them. In a certain sense, that is why traditionally a lot of performances take place in the round. If you have drummers and dancers in any community in Ghana, traditional drumming and dancing is always in the round. So I think it makes a lot of sense that the performance should determine the space. But somehow for a long time we have worked in the opposite way. I wonder if that affects the kind of performances that are created, because then the performers are not free to move out of the space.

PK: This is Peter Brook's opinion—he is demanding it and it is also my opinion. If you look at new buildings or structures that are going to be built in the future, it is crucial. But on the other hand, disregarding buildings and architecture, no matter where you perform, it is always about the interaction between the audience and the performers. So wherever you are as a performer, you have to take this into account, be it the sound, the light, or the weather conditions if you are outside, or where the audience is seated. When you talked about traditional African theater, this was actually what Peter Brook did.

AMA: It is about performance as ritual. He is looking at performance as ritual. He refers to temples, cathedrals, and mosques.

PK: If we talk about the contemporary performing arts, what does it need?

AMA: Who was it that said, "All you need for performance is the performer and the audience."? Was it Grotowsky? Where we are now, there could be a performance here. We have had a performance here before in this space. So in a certain sense performance could happen practically anywhere.

PK: So it should be a people's place, suitable for people and performers.

AMA: This also introduces the whole notion of flexibility. It can change. It should be a space that can adapt to different kinds of performances. But having said that, performances should also be able to adapt to different kinds of spaces.

PK: I do think if you build a theater or a stage, performers have to be involved. It should be an interaction, a dialogue, a continuous communication about this future performance space. And a theater should always be placed in or near an existing community, not an opera house in an artificially created opera village in the middle of nowhere. If you implement or build a new theater, think of where you are, look around yourself. What kinds of people are living there? How do you actually get them involved? How can the building already help to establish a relationship with the outside, with the landscape as well as the going and coming and sharing? The building has this as an assignment. Whenever I refer to Apam, to the *Haduwa* Apata, it is about how to get the local community involved. One way is of course making our work as artists relevant to the community. In Apam we give workshops to the schools. The *Haduwa* Apata is situated on the coast, there are fishermen. Instead of shutting it off—the Apata—we want them to use it. Use it for shade...

AMA: That is a very broad view on performance. Because in a certain sense you are asking that the community should perform there, even thinking of the fishermen using it as shade. You are saying the space should be so connected with the community that the performance is not a sacred-once-in-a-while something, but an everyday something? Is that what you mean?

PK: Personally, I would be so happy if performance was a part of everyday life. Performing arts help us to reflect on our lives, our societies, our politics. So why shouldn't it be part of our everyday?

AMA: But in a certain sense you are asking that it is not only artists who should perform there and then you are bringing it down to the very lowest level, that every action that takes place within that space then becomes performance.

PK: Actually that's what I'm saying. For me a performance space is a space where voices can emerge and be heard. Of course it is different if fishermen sit there.

AMA: Then there is no audience.

PK: Exactly, performers go there and perform for an audience. I already conducted or directed performances without an audience and it still was a performance. The performers were totally in sync with the environment. It was really magical. So not every performance necessarily needs to be in front of a zillion people. Coming back to the question, what is necessary for a performance space and does it work with the *Haduwa* Apata?

AMA: It certainly has a sense of flexibility and multi-dimensional performance, performing towards the ocean, towards what I would call the main front. The larger opening. It certainly has a sense of flexibility, and therefore a certain sense of differences of audiences, audiences from different angles as well.

PK: You see, for me, what is so special about this place is that it's a unique structure and that it

really melts into the landscape. There are different possibilities and directions you can perform in. It is also in a rural or fishermen's community. During the workshop 'staging space and staging stage', we had a performance in front of the main church in Apam. We wanted to see how the audience reacted as an audience. Where do they place themselves? Our backdrop was the church wall. What I observed, being in Ghana and having taught at the School of Performing Arts at Legon, is that there is a real interaction with the audience. There is always a co-performance in the audience. They comment, they react, they join in, they shout, they start dancing.

AMA: Yes! Some European group got angry because of that. "Let us perform for you!" they seemed to be saying! They did not like the audience joining in on the performance.

PK: It of course also depends on the performance.

AMA: Sometimes the intrusion doesn't help the performance.

PK: In Apam the local performers have a percussion group, they have some traditional dancers. They perform when they have a local festival or event.

AMA: Would that space—the Apata—speak to people like that also? Would that space be useful? Say if the local troop or cultural dancers or even a festival wanted to shift venue and go to the Apata, would it work for them?

PK: I totally think so. The Apata, what I like so much about it, is flexible. It looks like a shell that is evolving but also protecting. It protects from sun, from rain, from wind, really suitable for a theater in this climate zone, also in this cultural environment. The local performers wouldn't have difficulties performing there.

AMA: But do they have the sense that they can use the space?

PK: Not yet, because it's not theirs and they haven't been introduced to each other. Last week we had a workshop with schoolchildren and they loved it. They lived in it. We put carpets on the floor and they were working on the carpets. In the drama classes at the School of Performing Arts, if there is nothing going on, students sit there in the shade to study, to talk, to relax. The people are using the space, it's not just used for performances. It is used for lectures. This is what we would like to achieve as well.

AMA: I think it's interesting. I am reflecting on how the architects would have designed this place at the School of Performing Arts at Legon, if they had started by observing performers in the space. The struggles we have had with this huge building they are building for us at the School is that the architects worked in total isolation from the people who are going to be using the space. It is taking so long to build it because there is no dialogue between the designers of the space and the people who are going to use it. It is frustrating. For me, the space is almost useless even before it is finished because there was no consultation between the designer of the space and the performers. I think this is what Peter Brook is talking about.

PK: Right. Even if it is a hospital that is being designed, it won't be as healing.

AMA: I guess that's true. I think it's a very deep, useful thought for building a theater space that we unfortunately haven't made much use of in this country. I am sorry to take it back to that. Even the National Theater, this place is so sad; I don't even want to go there. I am working with somebody else on a paper about the involvement of the Chinese in the Ghanaian arts and culture. They came and gave us this space; did they consider the Ghanaian context?

PK: They might not even know the Ghanaian context I'm afraid. For me, a house or a building or a structure is something like a theater play or a piece of dance. It is about the communication between the people. The architects in this case are the artists and the performers, and the users of the place are the audience. If they don't come together it is like dead theater, using Peter Brook's terminology. I think architects are artists.

AMA: A lot of architects have artistic backgrounds. They are artists in their own rights. There is a working group of the International Federation of Theater Research called Theater and Architecture. It's a theater and architecture group and they consider spaces. They are really concerned with the architecture of theater as art. Performance spaces

are artistic spaces. I was serving on the University's Building Committee once and there was an architect who was always concerned with the newer buildings coming up being out of sync with the older buildings. He was thinking of the artistic nature of the older buildings. He did not understand how they give permits for certain buildings to be built in certain places.

PK: There are so many different architects, but the ones who are designing buildings should take this into account. The designers alone might also not be able to take in all the needed information without the others.

When I look at the Apam workshop "staging space and staging stage" again, there were seven to ten young architects and each one was researching a different field. One was researching shade, one was researching the wind, the other one the sun, the next one the vegetation, again others the sound. Stage performance buildings must always take care of the acoustics. Some were just watching the audience behavior. So all these factors came into the design. It is a group design not only of the architects, but also of the performers involved. This is why for me it is such a unique place.

AMA: To summarize, one of the key things we were saying is that performance spaces shouldn't just happen without considering what kind of performances would take place there or even who the performers would be. That's one thing. Another thing we talked about is the flexibility of a performance space; that it shouldn't be there just for occasional performances. It should be a useful space for other kinds of performances that don't necessarily have audiences. The need for collaboration when building the space, the need for the architect to work together with the performers—the ideas should come from both. They shouldn't be in isolation from each other.

PK: Also, it should be in sync with the local community, so that they are somehow involved and value the space and relate to it as well.

AMA: So that's something that we need to work on for Haduwa, for the community to fuel the building.

PK: We also talked about establishing outdoor performance spaces and that in the future some kind of markets could be held there with many ways of drawing people there and using the space—isn't it about energy and that that energy fills the atmosphere for future performances?

*"Apata" is an Akan word which alludes to "shed" or "shelter" or "hut". It speaks to a space (communal or home) whose meaning is deepened by the relations inherent within it. It could also be a space intended for rest.

AWO MANA ASIEDU, BA, MPhil, Ph.D., is a senior lecturer in the Department of Theatre Arts and the last former acting director of the School of Performing Arts at the University of Ghana.

PETRA KRON, Ph.D. (ABD), is a cultural anthropologist, performing artist, and production manager for plays. She creates art platforms in cross-cultural and cross-disciplinary contexts.

STAGING APAM: ON OTHER ARCHITECTURE

Baerbel Mueller

The evolution of art spaces on the African continent and their effects on the contexts in which they are located has been a most thrilling development over the last decade. New forms of connecting art and society, and of engaging local and international audiences have emerged. Artists, cultural producers, and curators have either been leaving behind a given institutional framework or creating a new one where there has been no place for contemporary art forms thus far. They have found platforms on their own according to their own needs and visions.

In Ghana, more and more young artists are moving from product-focused to dialogical forms of art. In the course of this movement, new working modes and new networks are evolving, and alternative spaces of artistic production and (re)presentation are being requested. How can these forms of cultural practice be housed? How can these claims be translated into a territorial setting or spatial envelope?

When [a]FA was invited to work on a master plan for the overall program of the Haduwa Arts and Culture Institute, the first critical question was: How could a future institution for performing arts stay alive and best promote itself in its first phase? It was assumed that in the specific situation of Haduwa's remote location, the conception, design, and construction of a stage as attractor would be the answer for a first, innocent, and at the same time, fully prominent gesture.

I was interested in starting the project from the scale of the (performing) body, not from an architectural scale. This was not only appealing on a programmatic level, but also because the Haduwa board consists of artists and cultural workers: Bernhard Akoi-Jackson, Kojo Benedict Quaye aka Sir Black, and Petra Kron. Against this backdrop, an [a]FA team of students of architecture, landscaping, and social design collaborated with students of the performing arts who had formed the Lab DC at the University of Ghana in Legon, Accra, under the guidance of Petra Kron. The idea was that intensely experiencing the site and its context with one's own body and with all one's senses—in a transdisciplinary manner—would allow for a deeper understanding of its ecology: a set of environmental and cultural parameters could be catalogued based on body space and framing interventions.

The challenge became the generation of a culturally, ecologically, and economically new typological model of an open institutional space, which mingles the diverse temporalities of architecture, art, and the everyday.

"How do we make emerge beauty that does not lie and truth that is kind?" Lemi Ponifasio

The design process evolved from the insights gained through the body space experiences and started with a diagrammatic series of potential spatial organizations of staging(s) which encompasses different relationships between the performing artists and their audiences. A multifunctional staging ground has been designed in which each performance and gathering can be positioned in a unique way. The resulting project is a floorscape and roofscape located at the seafront borderline of the Haduwa site. In dialogue with the floorscape, the roofscape also adapts to the given topography, rather than being shut off from its surroundings. The *Apata*[1] is a giant bamboo dome with three open arches facing in different directions—a grid-shell consisting solely of bamboo.

The design has mainly been developed through physical models on different scales, which were digitally optimized. A series of workshops were organized in order to understand the pure scale of the project, to test the material properties and behaviour of bamboo, to invent details for a roofing skin, and to get prepared for constructing in Ghana. On site, the bamboo builder Jörg Stamm was invited to lead an initial bamboo workshop, for both the [a]FA team and a group of local workers. The textiles department of the Angewandte was also involved, with the aim of translating local textile and roofing techniques into designs for the bamboo dome. To engage with the social context, artistic interventions were already taking place at this point.

From August 2014 onward, the *Apata* was built by the [a]FA group, with a steady team of local workers. Over weeks, 41 bamboo arches were produced, raised, and joined. Membrane sheets were cut, welded, and mounted on the roof by means of a specific lacing and welding technique and the concrete base points of the structure were finished. By the end of December 2014, the construction was completed.

The type of reactive space that was created epitomizes an alternative to total social and aesthetic control: an unfamiliar piece of bamboo architecture, which is difficult to categorize, as it is not a "proper" building, but is also not just a secondary landscape.

The evolutionary process from body space, to bamboo building, to the textile arts has been the subject of navigation between artistic fields and scales. At best, the resulting architecture speaks for itself and to its users, and the process of becoming is therein inscribed.

1 'Apata' is an Akan word which alludes to "shed" or "shelter" or "hut". It speaks to a space (communal or home) whose meaning is deepened by the relations inherent within it. It could also be a space intended for rest.

In order for the site to be truly read, the appropriation of the terrain was conceptualized in a slowed-down manner. It was identified that the piece of land needed to be intensely interrogated previous to any intervening, both in and of itself and in its environmental and cultural context. Equipped with their previous research, the team of architecture and landscape design students, together with 14 performing arts students, worked on site in order to explore it first with their own body space and all their own senses. The transdisciplinary approach allowed the group to test real site conditions and to simulate spatial outlines through a system of feedback between the professions. A set of parameters could then be catalogued based on these body spaces and 1:1 framing interventions, which later influenced the size and location of the stage.

The dimensions of the stage of the E.T.S. Drama Studio at the University of Ghana in Legon, Accra thereby served as a reference. The theater is a multifunctional space, which can be used as a proscenium stage, arena, or theater-in-the-round, with an open-air auditorium. It was visited and analyzed by the group before the footprint of its stage was inscribed on site.

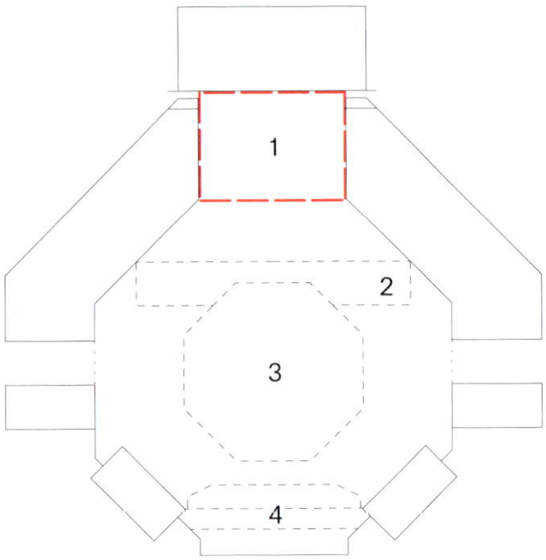

1 Stage (8 x 5 m)
2 Apron and wings
3 Arena
4 Endstage

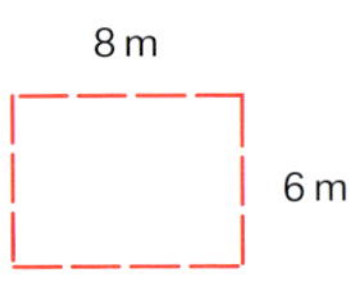

1:1 Stage Outlines

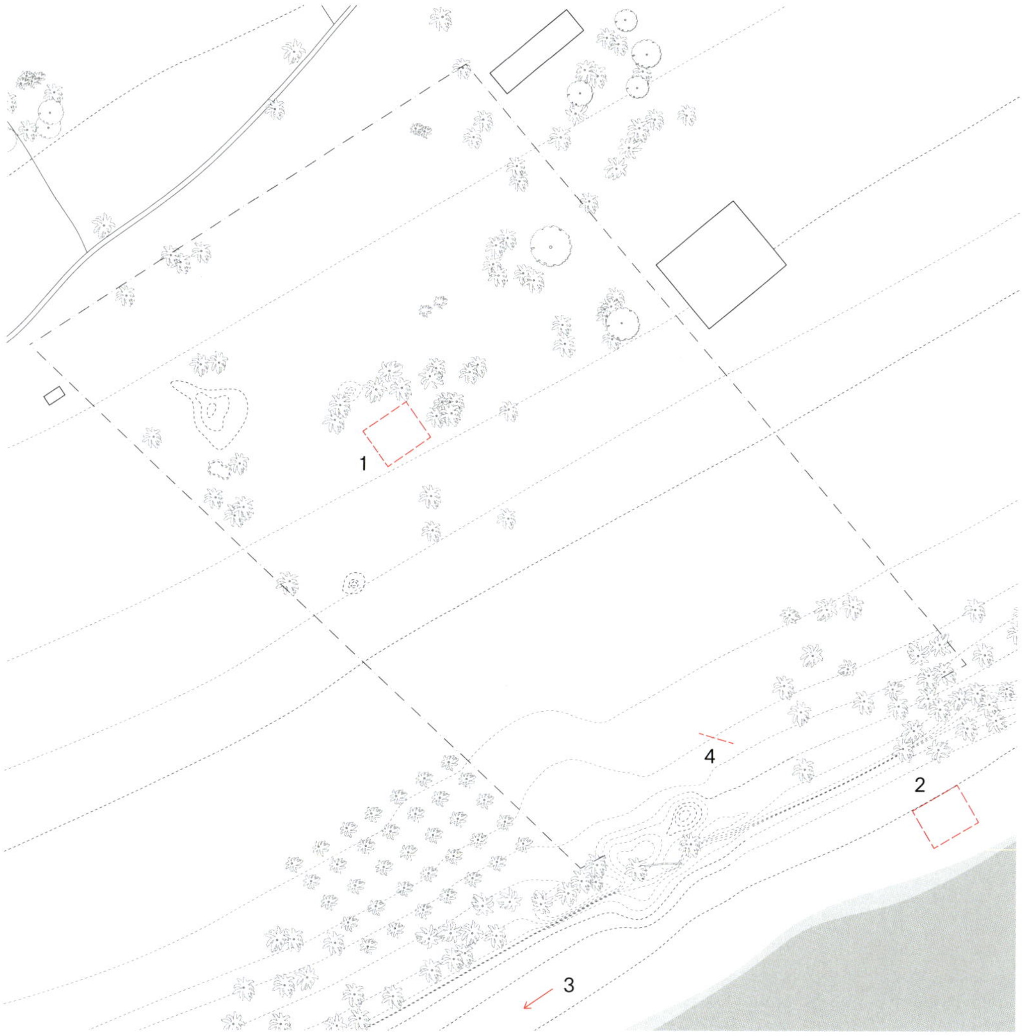

1 Terrain
2 Beach
3 Apam town
4 Framing mock-up

Body Space: Staging Apam

A five-day experiment was conceptualized in the form of a transdisciplinary workshop on staging in the broadest sense: being on stage and working on stage, staging a space and designing a stage. Three different spatial scenarios were thereby set up and tested. The outline of the footprint of the Legon stage was inscribed onto the inland area of the site (Terrain), the beach in front of it (Beach), and in Apam town (Apam). Visual experiments (Burning Field), acoustic exercises (Soundscapes), and encounters with a real audience (Apam) deepened the staging experience on a sensorial and socio-cultural level.

Participants: [a]FA and Lab DC
Concept: Baerbel Mueller, Daniel Aschwanden, Petra Kron
Guest teachers: Abiodun Odukoya, Othello Johns

Framing 1:1

'Framing' is a term that refers to the conceiving, composing, and forming of space, and acts as a point of departure for examining the state and flux of the relationship between architecture and the environment into which it is placed.

After framing the site from the point of view of several versions of horizontal stage formats, the team built a huge frame out of bamboo and erected it as a vertical landmark on the spot that had been identified as ideal for the future stage, based on the previous performative experiences and experiments.

First, the land had to be cleared of its vegetation, followed by an intense one-day construction process: the team built a 6 x 4.5-meter bamboo frame on the beach, carried the frame onto the land, positioned it, and hoisted it up. Once erected, the frame changed how the topographical relations could be perceived, thereby giving a new sense of scale to, and opening up new perspectives on, the site itself, as well as on the city of Apam.

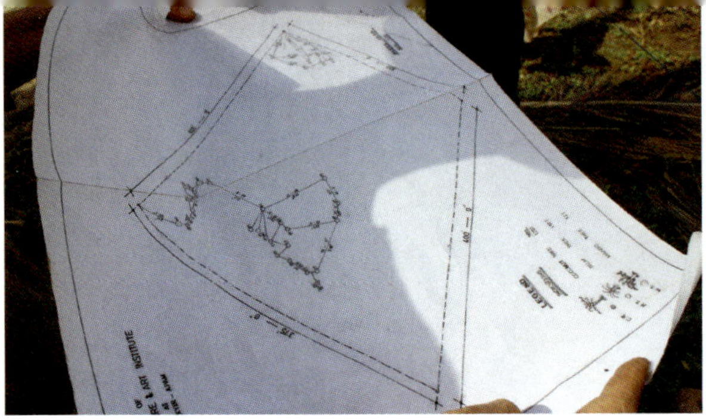

STORIES FROM THE BAY

Frida Robles

When I first came to Apam, I was void, I had done no research, I wanted to be blank, open, alert. As part of my research, I decided not to take any photographs, thinking they could be too intrusive, too objectifying, too colonialist. Instead, I dedicated my time to catching stories, to searching for the stories that narrated Apam and its neighboring village, Abrekum. Stories and names usually fit tightly together, there is a name behind a story and a story behind a name: I am always searching for the ghost that lives between these two. I walked around the bay and up the hills to search for these stories, I was hesitant of my role not only as an artist, but especially as a foreigner. What is the purpose of art? What is the purpose of travelling? Could I contribute to these towns with my research? I didn't know, till this moment I was questioning my practice. But what I can say is that I learned. These teachings were not evident, they were disguised in the midst of a foreign language and a foreign culture. The stories had a meaning that I could not fully understand. Stories are not transparent. For this collection of memories and stories, I talked to about 20 inhabitants of the bay, one of them, a taxi driver, became a friend. He drove me to his house and talked to me about his notions of life, this conversation was not recorded, but it spoke to my heart. That is the value I find in talking to people, to be able to witness their experiences, what they have learned from life, and maybe to communicate these teachings. Here, I have selected only a few passages, a few stories that were gathered in the bay next to a nameless sea. The collages positioned next to them are my graphic interpretation.

This work was done thanks to the kindness and translations of Jude Kurankyi and Isabella Narh.

1. I am exhausted, you can kill me.

Narrated by Kobina Essandoh Baidoo

It all started this way: about 500 years ago, there was a civil war close to Cape Coast. At that time, all Fanti people were together living in the same place, but the violence spread them out. The Fanti tribe was no longer together. They were fighting against each other for the possession of the land.

In one village, there was a fetish priest, she was a woman. She was married and was pregnant, but her husband was killed on one day of battle during the civil war. She was left alone and she had to protect her unborn child. Since she was a fetish priest, she had the ability to be invisible from time to time. So, anytime they tried to shoot her, she would disappear into the environment, she would be part of the trees and the soil around her.

She continued disappearing, every time someone would attack her, she would melt into the landscape only to appear in another town. On one of these days, she ended up in one town close to the sea, in a small bay surveilled by the *Nanapassa* rock. When she arrived in this town, she was really tired. She had decided to rest under the shade of a palm tree when suddenly, a man, a hunter, showed up. The fetish priest saw that the hunter was holding a gun and she thought that the hunter was one of the enemies. She didn't have enough energy left to disappear and move to another town. She was exhausted. The only sentence that she could articulate was, "I am exhausted, you can kill me". *Abre-kum*.

The hunter was not there to kill her and, as he could see her tiredness and her condition, he took her home, where the new baby and the new town was born. The town of Abrekum.

2. I will take care of myself

Narrated by Adwoa Nyiamful

The day I gave birth to my son was the very same day that they overthrew the first Ghanaian president. And there was no water in the city, people were bringing water from outside. I had a newborn baby and there was no water, so we had to use sea water to clean the baby. And when my little girl mentioned that that day was the day that the first president Nkruma was overthrown and this baby was born, they came to arrest me and sent me to prison. When I see these little girls just jumping around, playing around, it's funny for me because they have not seen anything yet. Because of the experiences that I have gone through, if a man comes and marries me and then starts playing around, I will immediately tell him: just pick up your things and go away. I will take care of myself. That is how I have been living my life.

3. Where money is kept

Narrated by Emmanuel

Our ancestors tell us that if you go to the forest, the one located at the end of the bay in Abrekum, you can see gold being guarded by a ghost. The ghost is a crocodile and it will come for you and will give you some gold if you dare to come back. The crocodile is no longer there, if you go there, you cannot see it anymore. The crocodile dried up.

4. Love and enemies

Conversation in a salt mine

Q: Do you work here?
A: Yes, this place belongs to me.

Q: Since when has it belonged to you?
A: I bought it in 1965.

Q: From whom did you buy it?
A: I bought it from the government.

Q: How big is it?
A: 80 acres.

Q: Does it have a name?
A: Yes, Love and Enemies.

Q: Is there a story behind the name?
A: I heard that there was a misunderstanding concerning this particular plot, so when I got it, I named it "Love and Enemies".

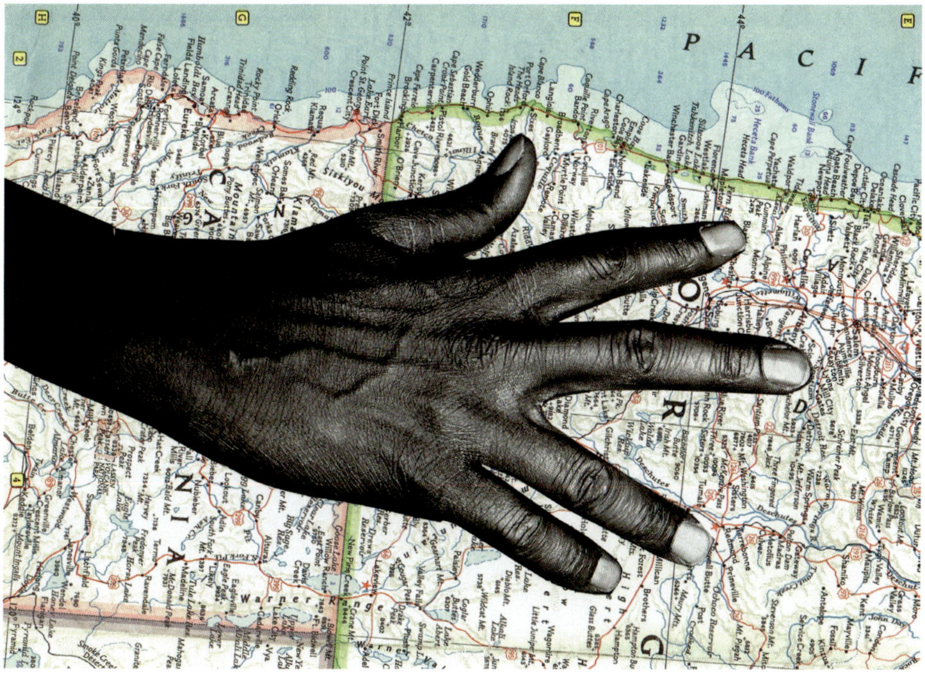

PERFORMING THE BAY

Serge Attukwei Clottey and GoLokal,
Daniel Aschwanden, Conny Zenk

In a series of interventions in Apam town on the Haduwa site itself, and through provocative processions in between both, the context of the town and the bay were reflected on and highlighted. Frida Robles´s collection of stories from the bay were shared with an audience, artistically translated, and performed in the framework of the artists´ collaboration.

the year
themselves

rituals
Living

Performers: Serge Attukwei Clottey and GoLokal

BEYOND TERRITORIES—TRANSVERSAL PRACTICES

Barbara Putz-Plecko

We didn't cross the border, the border crossed us.*

It is incumbent on academic institutions and art schools to recognize their social mission, to make themselves aware of current and future issues and challenges that have social relevance, to address these actively and, accordingly, to develop appropriate formats for the conduct of study and research. This requires both a critical practice (one that also reflects the conditions surrounding one's endeavors, the interests that motivate them, and their consequences) and a general framework that favors new movements and encounters and permits the creation of open, experimental spaces. As a consequence, attention is also focused on (institutional) infrastructures, which must constantly be reconsidered, called into question, adapted, or renewed.

It has long since become clear—and not only as a result of the dramatic developments in the Near East and last year's mass movements of refugees—that we must not only realize that we are living in a world for which we all bear responsibility, but also that this realization must be followed, on the large scale and the small, by adequate actions.

In his book *Together: The Rituals, Pleasures and Politics of Cooperation*, the American sociologist Richard Sennett describes cooperation as one of the most essential and necessary abilities one can possess, virtually as a 'craft' that will determine our future. For how, he asks, can people who differ fundamentally with regard to their experience of the world, their relation to the world, and their idea of what is self-evident live together and cooperate with each other—in a world that is characterized by competition and inequality more than ever—in order to accomplish something, to preserve something, to alter or to renew something? How else but in a collective spirit can we sensibly meet the challenges of the present and the future? The ability to act together appropriately, however, entails certain prerequisites: taking an interest in each other, learning to communicate with each other, relating to each other both in thought and in deed, sharing knowledge, being able to correlate different perspectives constructively, collective decision-making through negotiation, acknowledging multiple meanings, contraries and differences, measuring one's actions according to criteria other than mere personal interest, and, not least, the ability to reflect critically on the ways in which one goes about one's work.

* Slogan read on a T-shirt, Los Angeles, 2011

Aside from dialectical forms of communication—the ultimate aim of which is to open the way towards finding a synthesis and, especially, to develop the practice of communicative dialogue—Sennett sees an open-ended exchange of intentions and experience as essential, which eventually makes deeper mutual understanding possible.

Providing cooperative impetus, writes Sennett, must be the order of the day. Changes of perspective, flexibility of points of view, constructive ways of dealing with ambiguousness—all of this absolutely must be encouraged and supported so that our ability to cooperate is neither further repressed by institutional structures (and here Sennett refers to—among other things—analyses done by Amartya Sen and Martha Nussbaum in *The Quality of Life*, 1993) nor further undermined by the existing social order (cf. Sennett, 2012, p. 374).

His plea for dialogue-based, collaborative practices—which harbors an expectation that such practices will allow new ways to coexist to emerge—is very much in line with current processes of transformation in the arts and sciences in regard to disciplines being opened up and boundaries being crossed. It has long since become clear that the unrelenting specialization of the sciences and their fragmentation into increasingly narrow areas of concentration is a development that frustrates efforts to deal constructively with the major, urgent problems of daily life. The boundaries between science, art, and society must become more permeable, and research processes must be geared toward addressing issues that have relevance to our everyday lives and incorporating non-scientific forms of knowledge. Complex problems can in most cases be better understood and more effectively dealt with in cross-disciplinary processes, that is, in integrative research processes: boundaries between disciplines are crossed, heterogeneous research practices and forms of knowledge become closely intertwined; problems are defined from a cross-disciplinary perspective and solved independently of disciplinary bounds (cf. Mittelstraß, 1998, 44f.). In order for this to take place, interaction through open and transparent dialogue among all persons involved is essential. The resultant process of mutual learning—a shared learning of the arts, the sciences and forms of practice - shapes cross-disciplinary collaboration and renders it fruitful. However, such collaboration also demands considerable presence on the part of everyone involved. What grows out of this—and what proves effectual—is knowledge that reflects social awareness, knowledge that has a particular potential to initiate development and innovation and to generate strategies for grappling with social issues.

In view of these observations, the university must set itself the task of opening up its institutional structures, breaking its institutional routines, and—by transcending institutional boundaries and boundaries between disciplines—enabling new synergies to be tapped. In concrete terms, this also requires—through modification of familiar frameworks, rules and habits—making room for the unforeseeable and creating the conditions necessary for experimentation in cooperative and collaborative processes, and conditions for learning and investigation, in order to make it possible to redefine the space in which we act and coexist.

In the course of the last century, the cult of the artist as genius, that is, the dominance of the individual author as well as conventional aesthetic autonomy, were repeatedly called into question by various avant-garde movements and countered by the creation of production collectives. By the same token, one of the most significant accomplishments of the modern art movements was to blur the boundaries between disciplines. Forms of cooperation between the arts and the sciences (which gave rise to various kinds of knowledge that are of equal importance) have been both a logical and a fruitful consequence of this evolution. Crossover projects involving different art forms, different artistic and scientific disciplines and a concern for practical relevance to our daily lives have become an obvious and important part of a contemporary practice of art and design. Even such a major exhibition as the 15th Architecture Biennale in Venice highlights their significance when, under the catchphrase launched by architect and curator Alejandro Aravena, "Reporting from the Front", it approaches—from the most diverse angles—the question of how social responsibility, in a constant struggle against economic pressures, together with the design of more humane living spaces are to shape the environments in which we live, both now and in the future.

Due to the way in which the world is currently constituted, the position of the artist is being more radically redefined and is being considered more in its relation to social, economic and political structures and dynamics.

At a time of great uncertainty, in an unresolved contest of forces, collective practices could be a possible artistic response to the situation and could open up a space for forms of knowledge that could break the mold of conventions—cognitive, political and social (cf. Kester, 2011, p. 11).

However, this also means constantly subjecting the group and the collective's modus operandi to self-criticism—and also developing a mode of thought characterized by 'intersection', a transversal practice—one that transects existing axes and definitions.

Current political, social and economic developments make it perfectly clear: deconstructive thinking is needed in order for us to be able to break up the binary forms of logic and the binary structures that legitimate inequality and social exclusion. A kind of network thinking is also needed, a way of thinking in terms of difference that recognizes ambivalence, contradiction and contraries without immediately seeking to iron them out, a mode of thinking that does not require forced disambiguation of the multilayered and the complex. Both of these—deconstruction and thinking in terms of difference—and their interplay constitute an essential element of a transversal practice that can lead to new forms and concepts of our ability to act politically possible.

In the projects carried out by Baerbel Mueller in the form of [a]FA Labs, I was able to recognize all the above-mentioned fundamental characteristics of a contemporary practice that self-critically demands accountability and is able to consider, from different

Grant H. Kester, *The One and The Many: Contemporary Collaborative Art in a Global Context* (Durham and London: Duke University Press, 2011)

Jürgen Mittelstraß, "Interdisziplinarität und Transdisziplinarität," in *Die Häuser des Wissens: Wissenschaftstheoretische Studien* (Frankfurt am Main: Suhrkamp, 1998)

perspectives, the conditions, the network of interrelationships in such a practice it is embedded, as well as the consequences that these imply. These characteristics are inscribed in the projects themselves. They constitute their foundation. They remain a reliable frame of reference—even in working conditions that are sometimes difficult due to exterior factors.

Thus, both multifariously and consistently, these projects give life to an aspiration—and to developmental dimensions that derive from that aspiration—of an art university today that sees contributing to social developments and to the identification of problems to be addressed as its mission—a mission that it takes seriously. Everyone involved in the projects deserves thanks for this.

BARBARA PUTZ-PLECKO, artist, professor, and Deputy Rector of the University of Applied Arts Vienna. She is also Head of the Institute of Art Sciences and Art Education, the Department of Art and Communication Practices, and the Textile Department. A focus of the last two is developing contextual, transdisciplinary, and transcultural art practices.

Richard Sennett, *Together: The Rituals, Pleasures and Politics of Cooperation* (Yale University Press, 2012)

Amartya Sen and Martha Nussbaum, *The Quality of Life* (Oxford University Press, 1993)

STAGE EVOLUTION DIAGRAMS

As a starting point in the design process, the architecture of theater spaces and concert halls—from Greek amphitheatres, to Hans Scharoun's philharmonic hall in Berlin, to Friedrich Kiesler's Raumbühne—were investigated. Contemporary and experimental practices in the performing arts field were discussed, all in regards to spatial relations between performer and audience, stage and auditorium. Bodies in public space and public gatherings were looked at as performances, both in Austria and in Ghana.

For the design of the Haduwa stage, it was of interest to come up with a spatial concept that does not determine specific positions of performers and audiences, but rather allows for unpredictable appropriations.

At the same time, it was intended to create specific spatial scenarios which would offer a diversity of uses, functioning on different scales, and orientations and degrees of publicity/intimacy.

Both cultural and environmental parameters were thereby considered. The land was read in its topographical context, with its specific vegetation and direct access to the ocean. Cultural aspects of all types were incorporated into the search for an ideal spatial configuration. The spatial characteristics of traditional cultural events were interpreted as non-directional and participatory, visual relations to cultural landmarks in Apam were considered. Besides responding to the given cultural and environmental context, the goal was to design a new kind of performance space, beyond a conventional spatial organization, and based on new ideas of openness, accessibility, and low-threshold boundaries.

Inspired by the stage of the E.T.S. Drama Studio, Legon

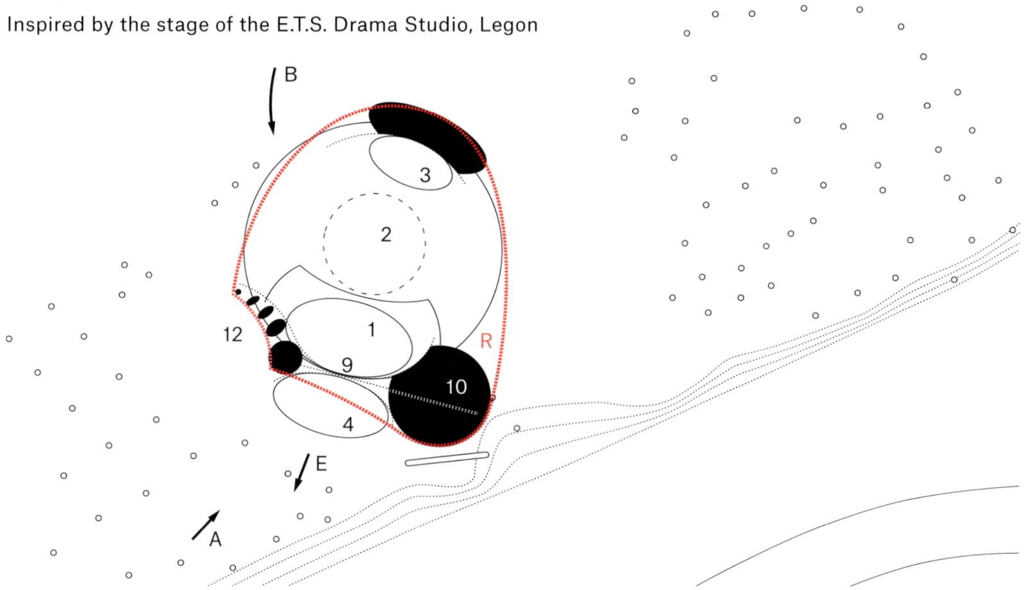

A series of stages

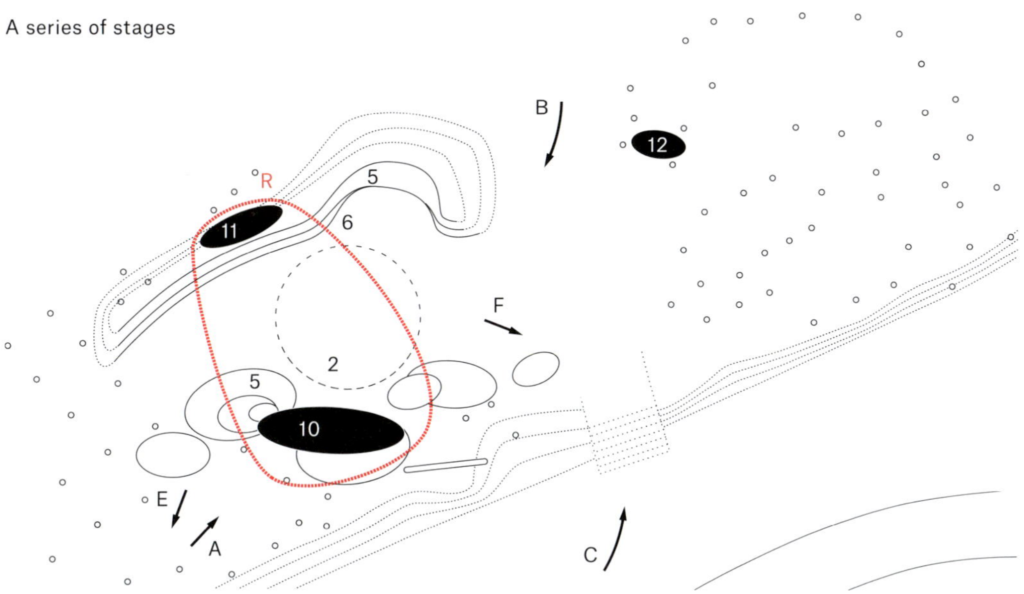

1	Stage	7	Ramp / slope	R	Roof
2	Arena	8	Bridge	A	Wind
3	Endstage	9	Windscreen	B	Approach land
4	Sea Stage	10	Backstage	C	Approach beach
5	Platform	11	Studio	E	Apam view
6	Sitting steps	12	Lounge / bar	F	Sea view

Open arena

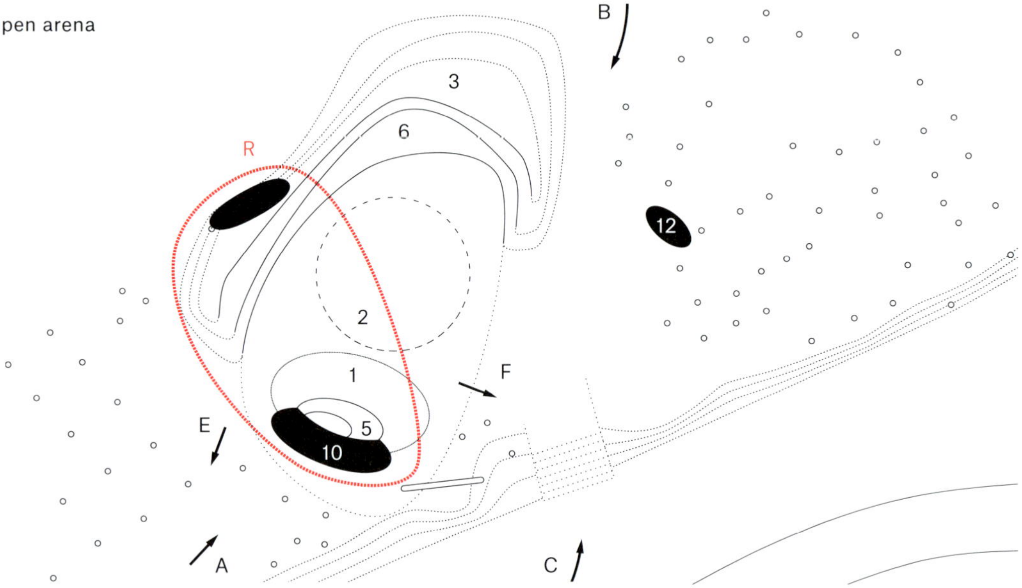

Inversion of Kiesler's Raumbühne

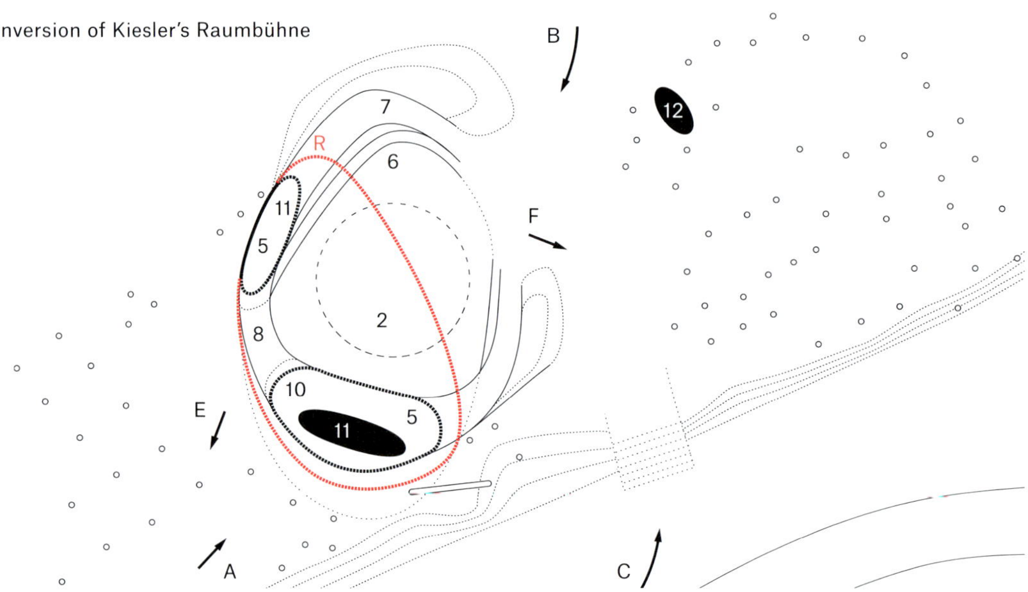

Stage ribbon along the shoreline (design 2014)

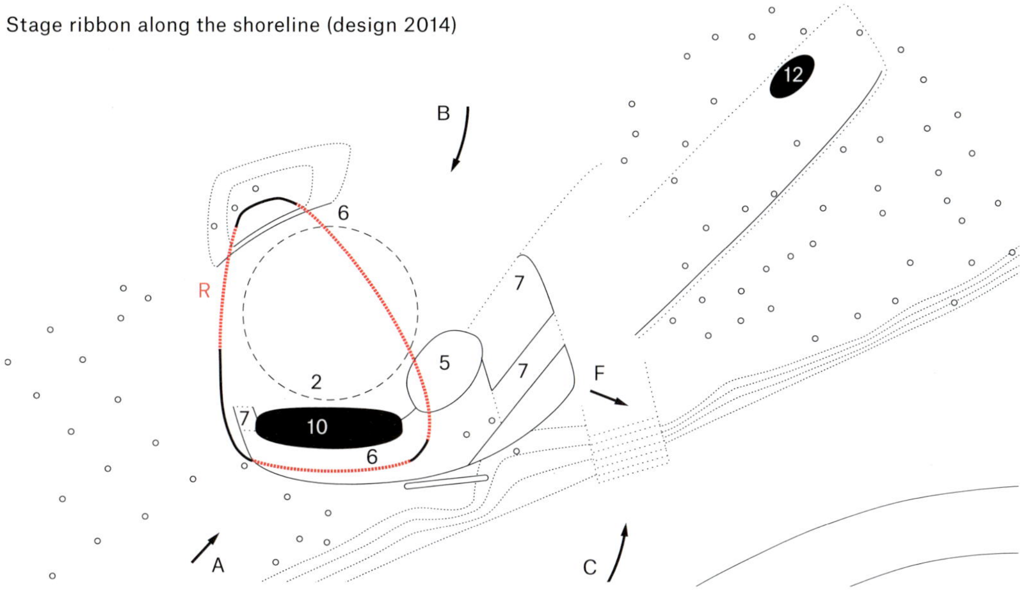

Dispersed stages (design 2015)

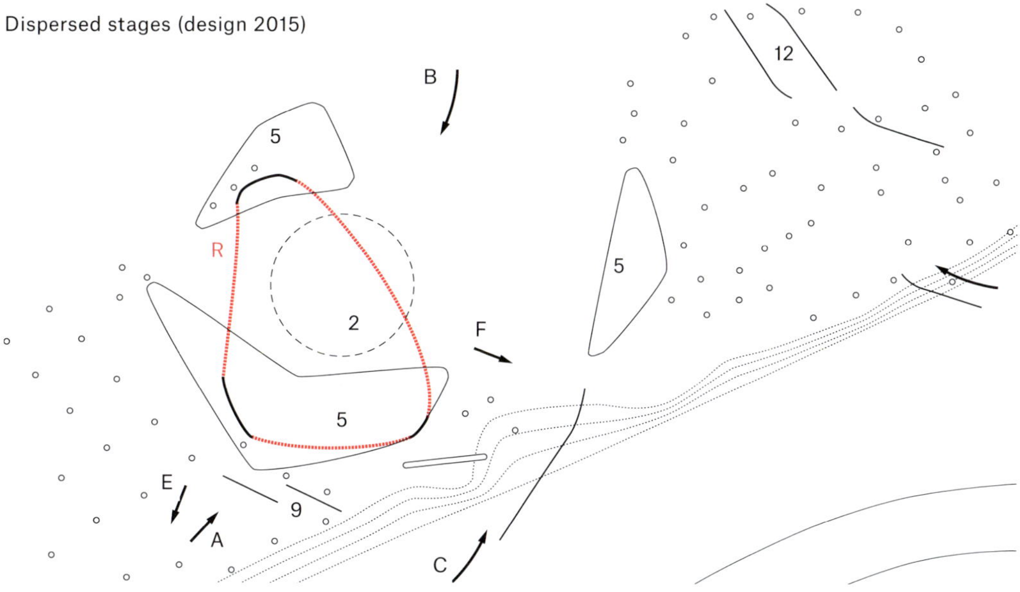

1	Stage	7	Ramp / Slope	R	Roof
2	Arena	8	Bridge	A	Wind
3	Endstage	9	Windscreen	B	Approach Land
4	Sea Stage	10	Backstage	C	Approach Beach
5	Platform	11	Studio	E	Apam view
6	Sitting Steps	12	Lounge / Bar	F	Sea view

a
3
1
2
a
5
7

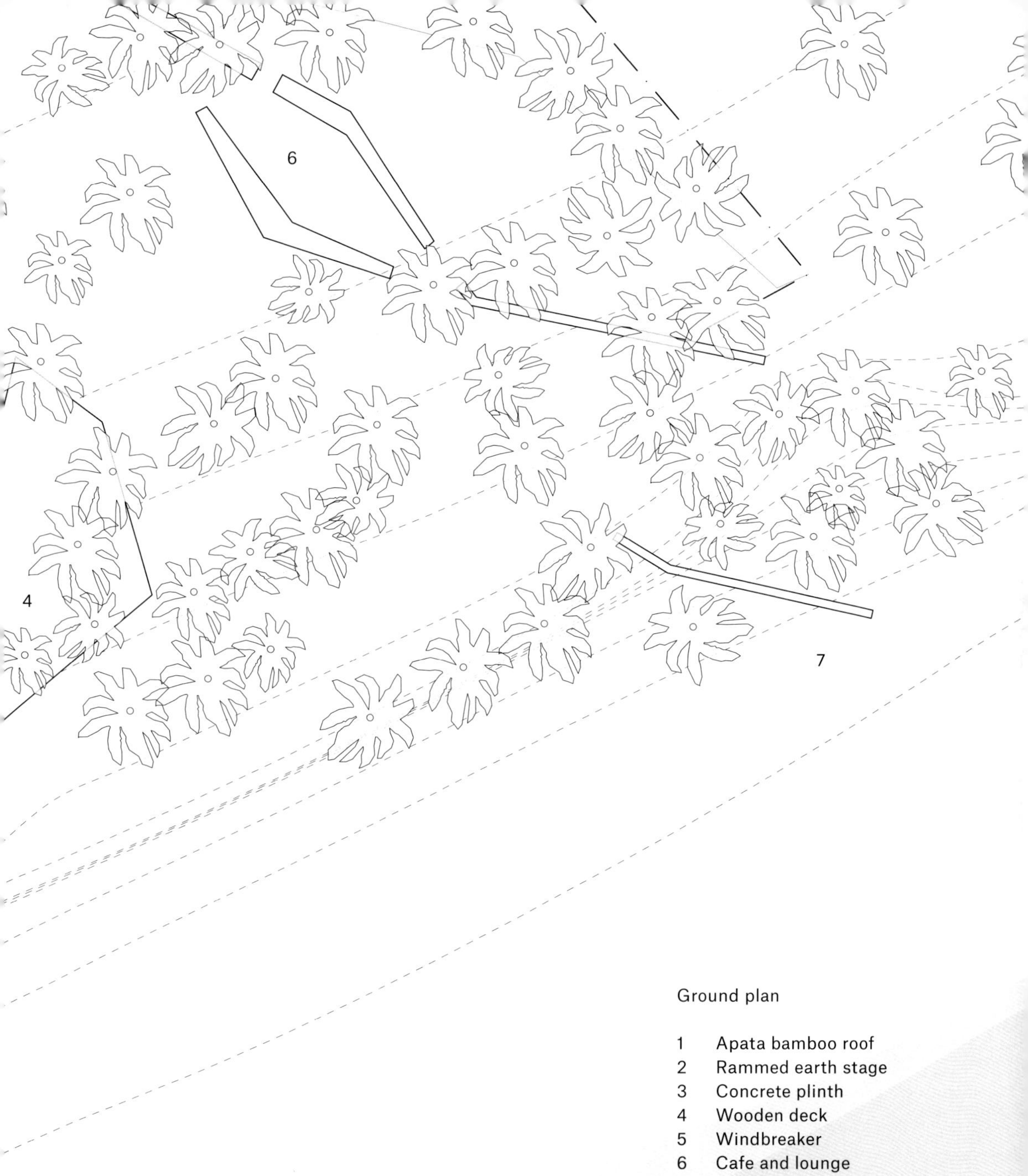

Ground plan

1 Apata bamboo roof
2 Rammed earth stage
3 Concrete plinth
4 Wooden deck
5 Windbreaker
6 Cafe and lounge
7 Beach entrances
a Section

10 m

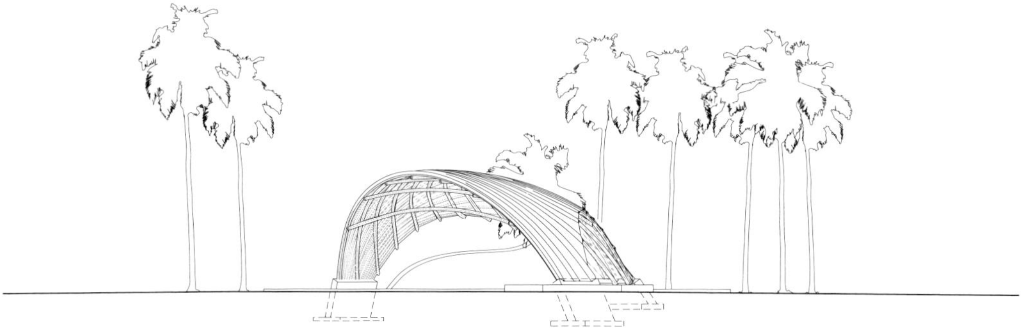

North Elevation

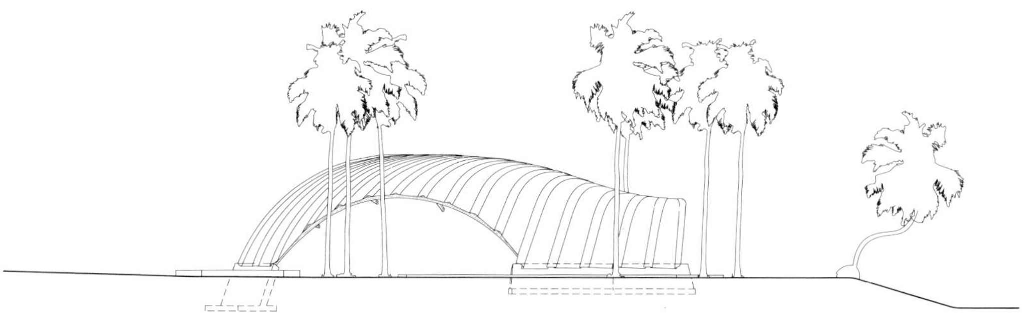

West Elevation

South Elevation

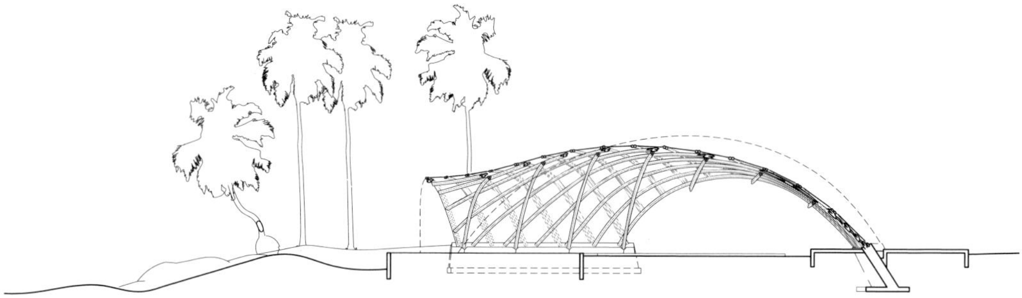

Section a-a

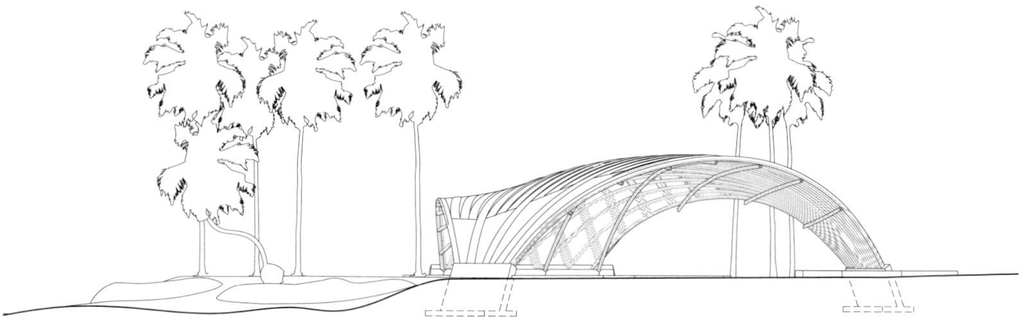

East Elevation

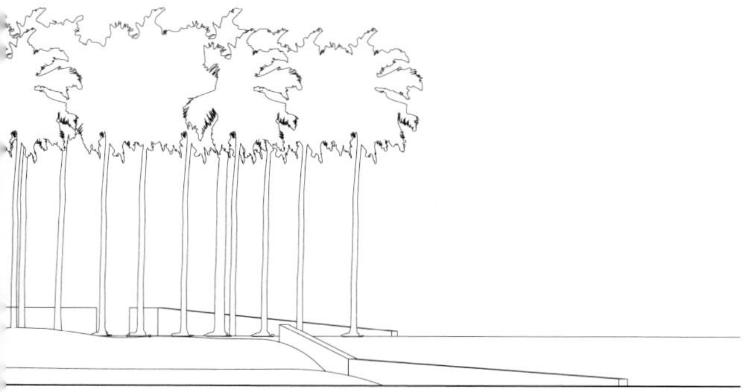

Zoning Plan

1 Performance
2 Communal kitchen / cafe
3 Infrastructure
4 Artist residencies
5 Kindergarten and women's center
7 Office / entrance
8 Caretaker

Site Plan

1 Apata with stage landscape
2 Cafe and lounge
3 Backstage and storage
4 Artist residencies
5 Kindergarten and women's center
6 Sanitary block
7 Parking area
8 Caretaker
9 Beach entrances

Western Panorama

Northeastern Panorama

Wind Analysis

Observations and measurements on site show that wind appears periodically, with constant speeds. While it is nearly windless on site in the morning, by noon, permanently strong winds occur and remain until the late afternoon.

The particular challenge of creating useable spaces for performances of arts, theatre, and music, while coping with the high wind intensities on site, became a driving design parameter for the bamboo Apata. Wind studies using fluid dynamic software suggested a positive effect from the designed roof geometry. The wind, which comes from the ocean, is directed over the roof by its shell shape and its orientation. By sliding along the top of the roof surface, the wind is split into micro-vortexes that slow down the wind speed. Further inland, the wind comes back to the ground 10 meters behind the roof, creating a wind-free area there, carrying breezes to the very back of the terrain, where air flow is missing.

The structural requirements of the occurring wind loads are dealt with by fracturing and subdividing the loads over multiple structural members and the membrane. Unlike with a sail, where heavy loads meet a minimum of joints, in the case of the Apata design, many connection points such as the bamboo joints and membrane welding seams subdivide the wind loads across the whole structure. This allows the connecting members to be smaller in dimension.

In terms of acoustics, the design team had to take the constant white noise created by permanent winds and crashing coastal waves into account. One approach towards dealing with this acoustic issue in a performance venue would have been through massive volumes at building scale to direct the acoustics and the wind strain. The strategy that was chosen in the end was the use of perforated, woven structures, which slow down wind and diffracts and absorbs sound at multiple frequencies.

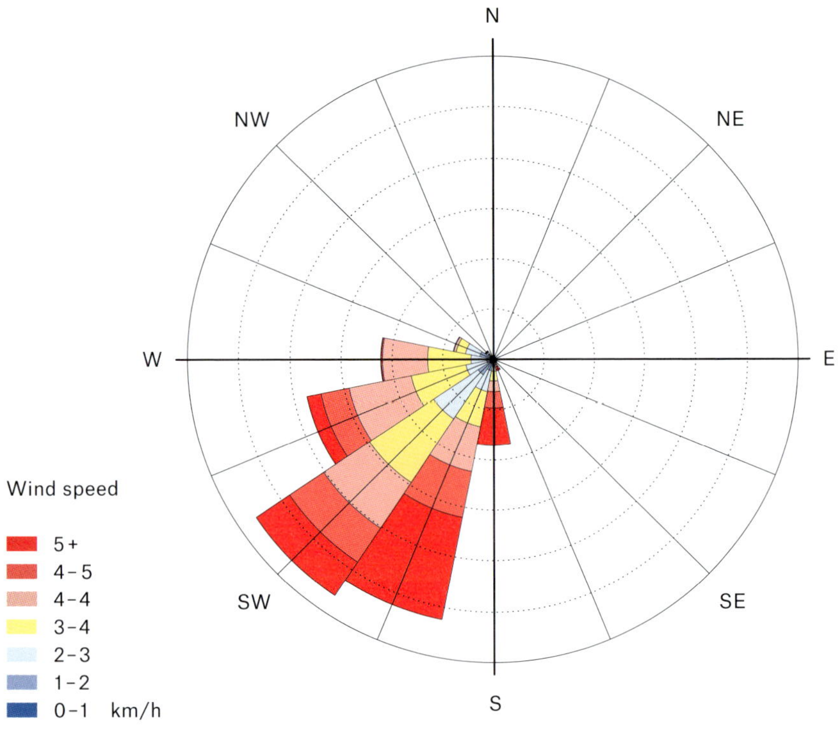

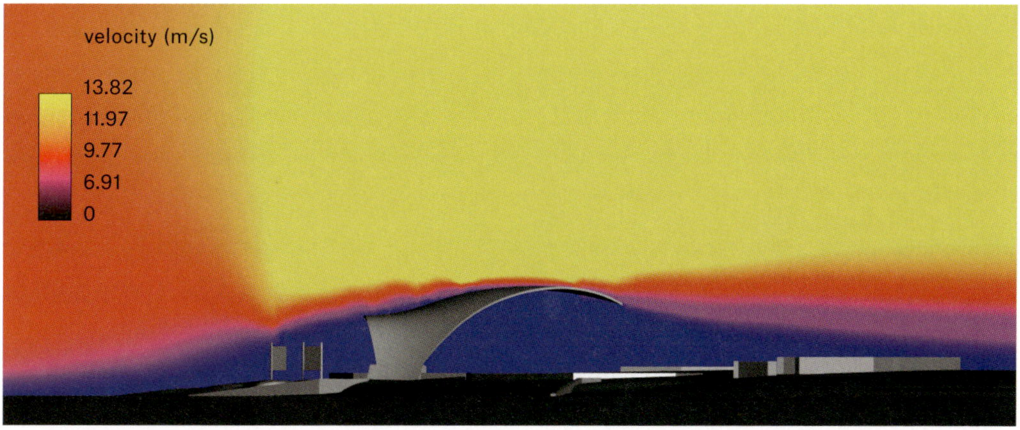

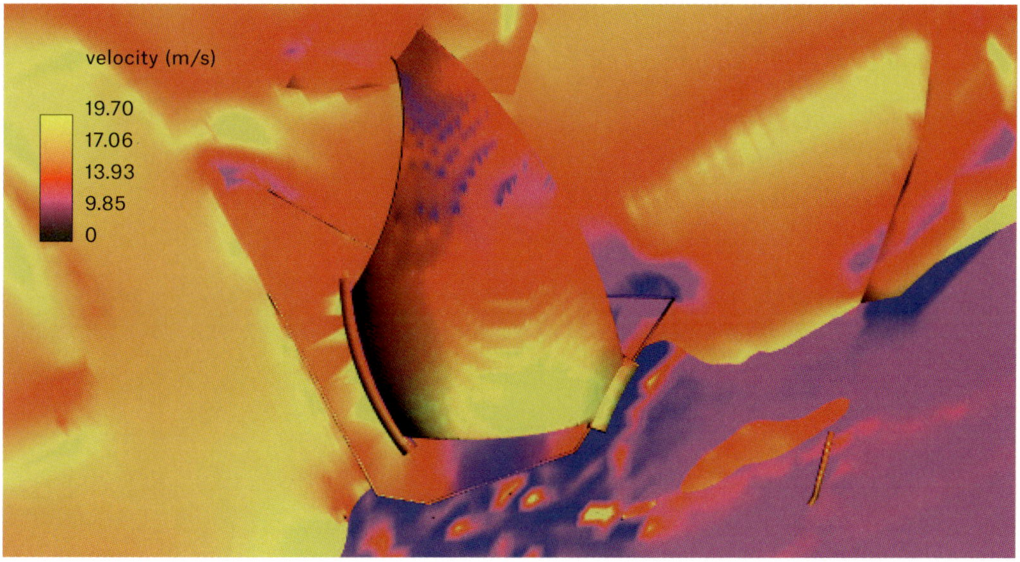

Wind simulations

Sun Positions and Shading

The Apata is designed to offer shaded performance spaces throughout the whole day. Different areas of the sheltered space underneath the bamboo roof are protected from the sun at different moments of the day. Both the positioning of the roof on site and the design of its shape have the effect that the roof casts a large shadow in the late afternoon that extends eastward across the site. This space that is shielded from the sun can be used for performances with larger audiences. The main stage oriented towards the ocean is shaded throughout the day, every day of the year.

June 21, 09:00 a.m.

December 21, 09:00 a.m.

June 21, 12:00 p.m.

December 21, 12:00 p.m.

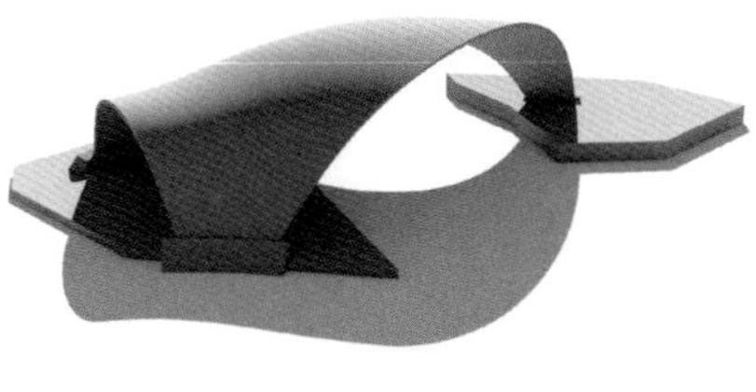

June 21, 04:00 p.m.

December 21, 04:00 p.m.

Construction Logistics: Arches

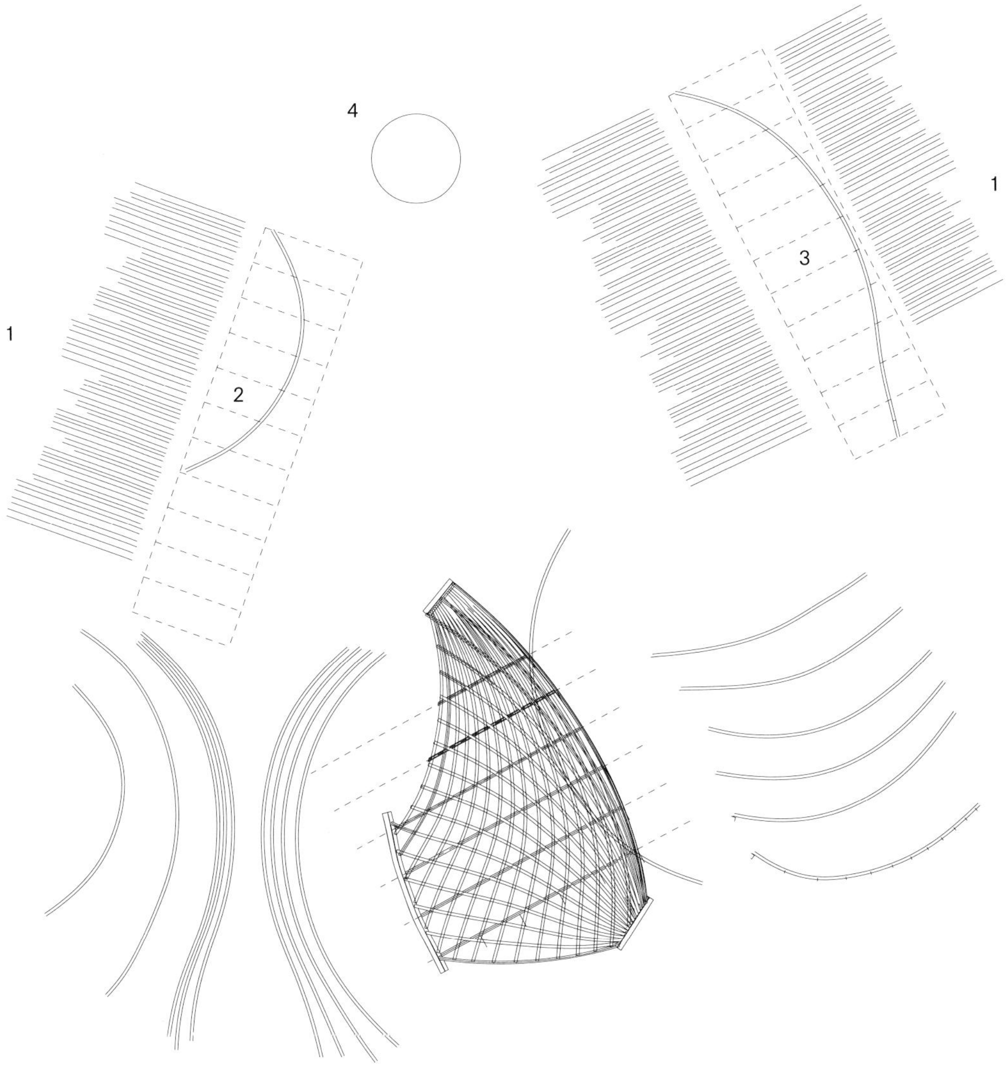

1 Bamboo grading
2 Matrix west
3 Matrix east
4 Concrete mixing

Gridshell

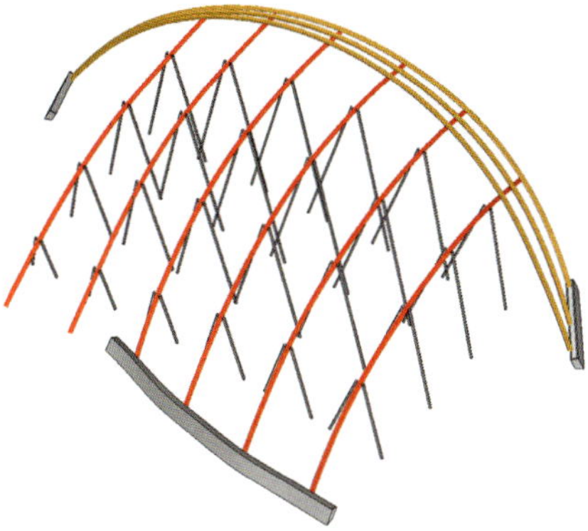

Double bamboo arches
on temporary support
(inner layer)

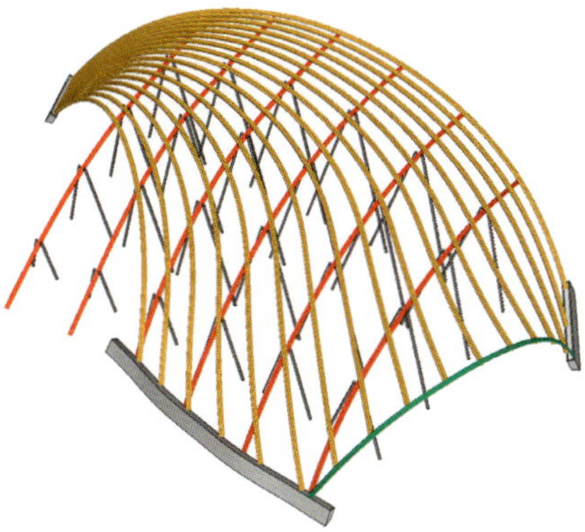

Triple bamboo arches
(middle layer)

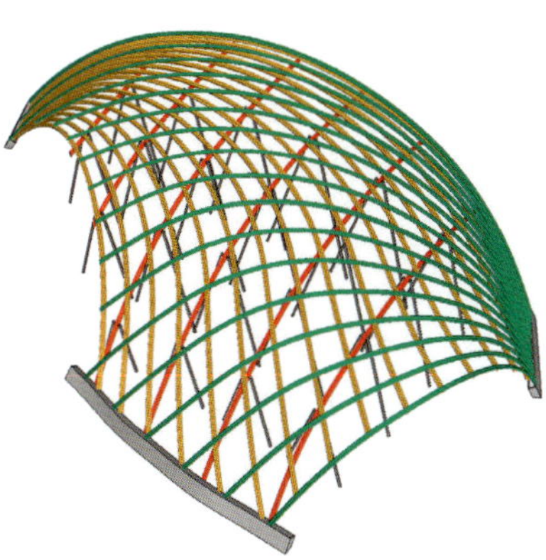

Double bamboo arches
(top layer)

Details of Bamboo Construction

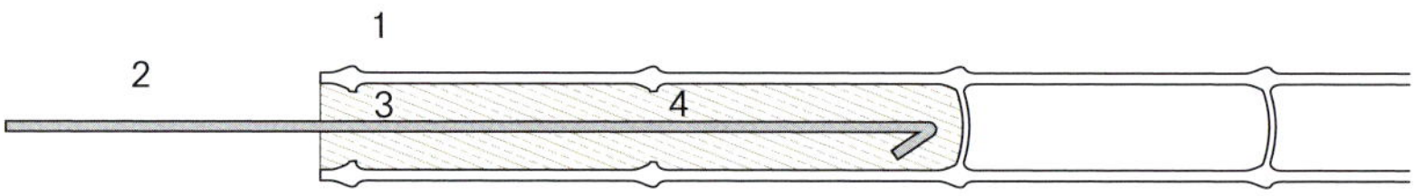

Bamboo beam grouting

1 Bamboo culm
2 Steel rebar
3 Mortar
4 Punctured bamboo node

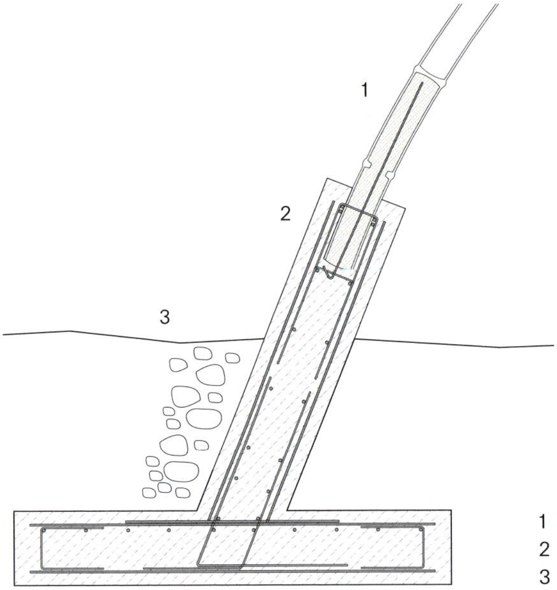

1 Bamboo arch
2 Grouted foot with reinforced hook
3 Erosion protection

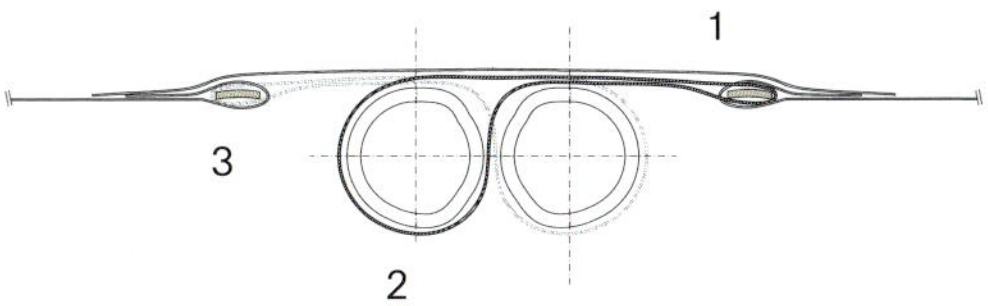

1 Welded tarpaulin cap
2 Rope on bamboo arch
3 Welded tarpaulin hemstitch with split bamboo piping

Tarpaulin on bamboo arch

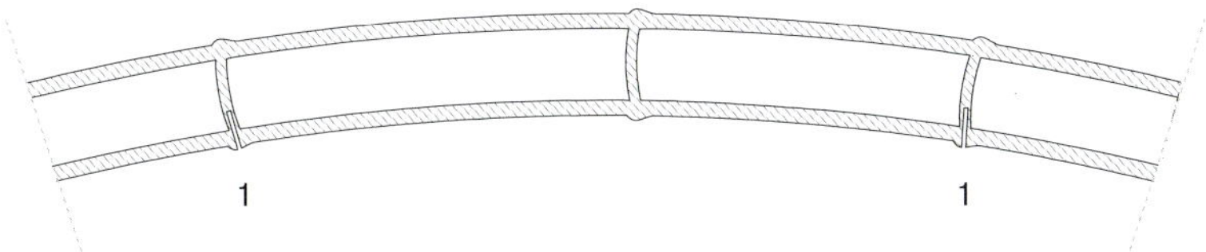

Cross section beam

1 Chainsaw cuts at nodes for bending

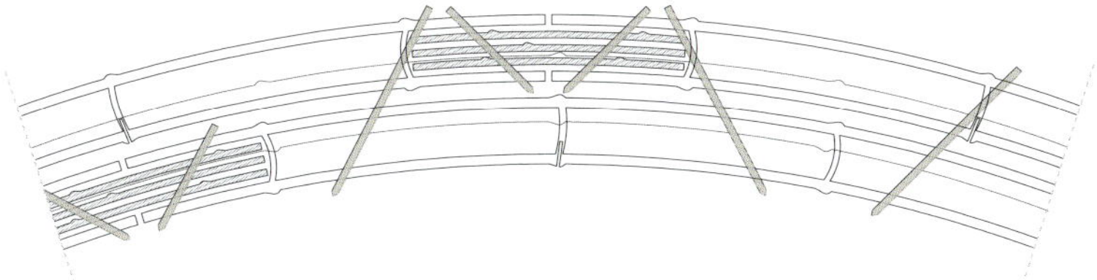

Beam assembly

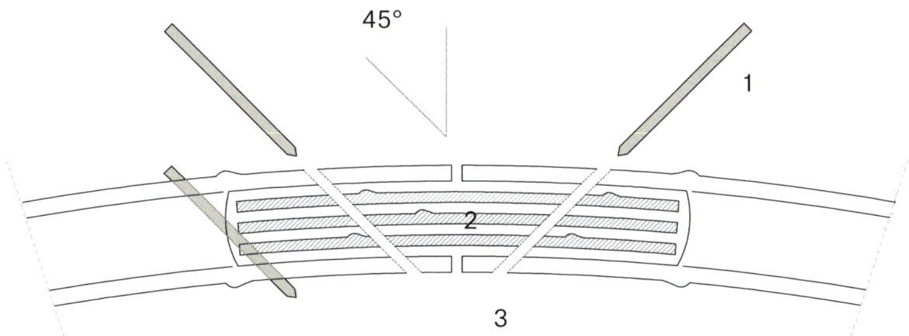

Elongation of a single bamboo beam

1 Bamboo nail
2 Split bamboo batch
3 Drilled nail pocket

Single bamboo joint

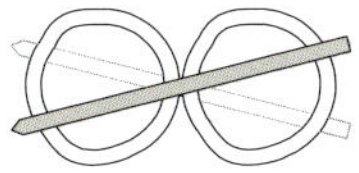

Double bamboo joint

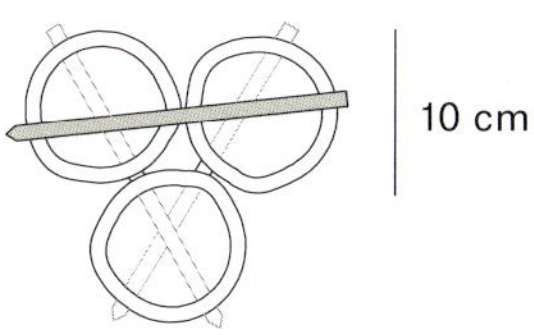

Triple bamboo joint

Membrane

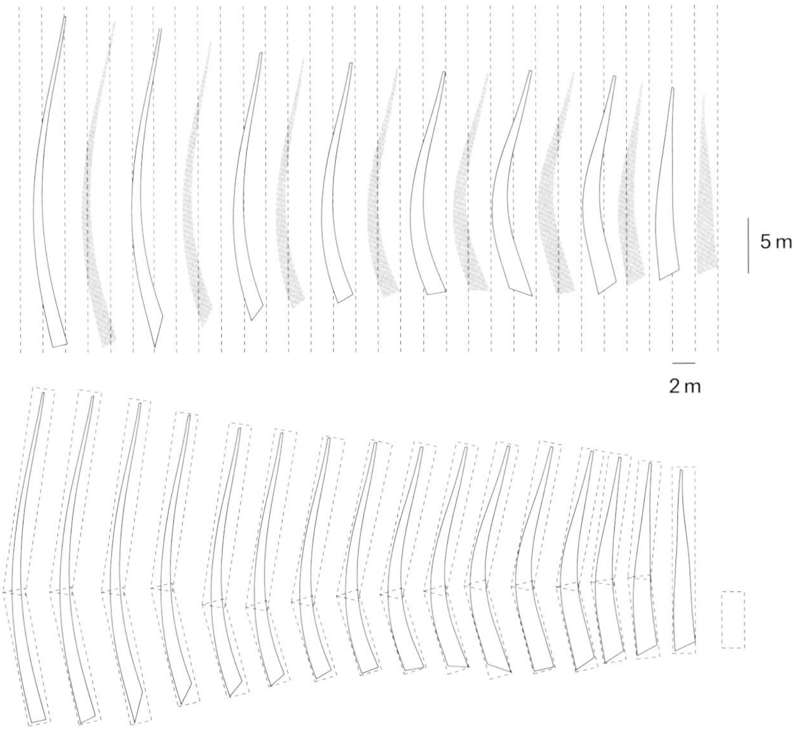

Unrolled tarpaulin
on 2 m matrix

Cutting pattern
on 2 m wide
tarpaulin roll

Estimated roll length:
370 m

Tarpaulin roof cutting pattern

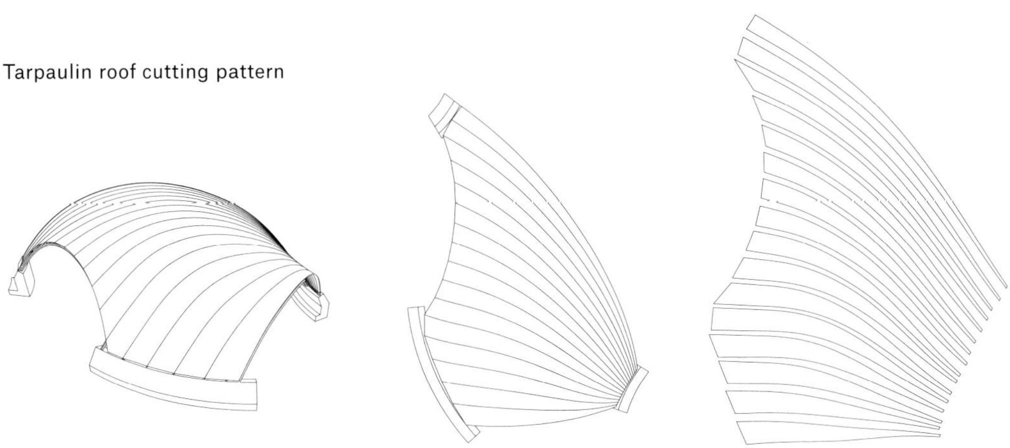

1 Perspective
2 Top view
3 Unrolled tarpaulin

Bamboo gridshell

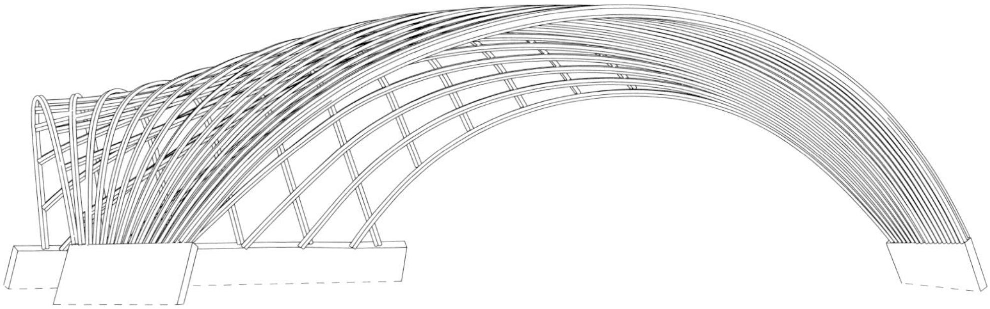

Gridshell layer a and b

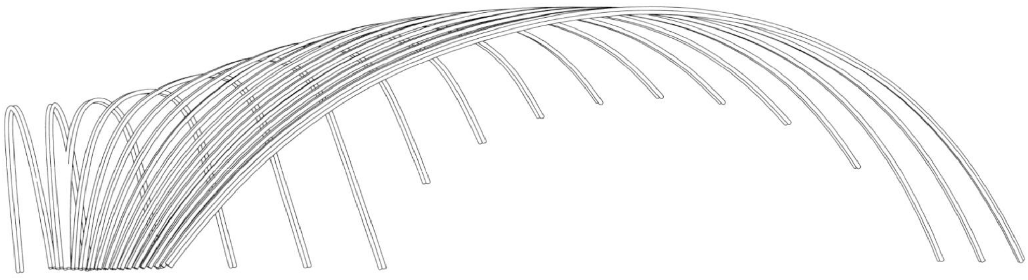

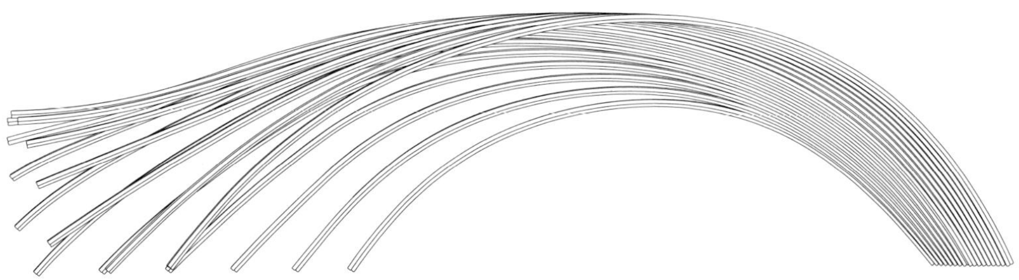

THE ANALOGUE BECAME DIGITAL— AND WANTS TO BECOME ANALOGUE AGAIN

Klaus Bollinger, Robert Vierlinger

Working on this project is asking us to put our awareness of creating the environment into perspective. Low-tech organic building materials are giving rise to new possibilities for ecological local architecture, but are presenting both challenges and opportunities for new means of design and planning in the form of a peculiar rural high-tech project.

Frei Otto was one of the greatest innovators in terms of using materials for their intrinsic properties, re-configuring them for large and light structures with a minimal footprint through a synthesis of form and function. Following these pioneering paradigms of shaped-material intelligence, the digital revolution provided methods of high-end form-finding to the design mainstream. The analogue became digital—and wants to become analogue again, by way of a physical manifestation of the simulated, of course, but first of all by a collaboration of crafts—in the sense that high-precision computational design needs to display a certain degree of sensitivity to analogue conditions and processes. As the workflow within digital interfaces requires preparation of the artefact, it also needs preparation that fits the workflow of crafts. Bridging the gap between the ideal and the real, the translations to building culture, and the reintroduction of locality, is now posing challenges to a synthesis of different technologic levels in design and fabrication phases: the designer-builder is shifting from architectural to structural to constructive to socially competent with the said intersections requiring negotiation and integration. The meaningful interplay between human and machine designer must be determined.

Bamboo and its high flexure actively define the form of the shell, and thereby set up new drivers of design. The idealized digital model in this project is aimed at helping the designer to find a high-performing shape and patterning, by first of all lacking many of the constraints of the real world. The bending of the bamboo rods happens in a distinct manner, approximating the elastic curve and not just a designed shape. Fabrication needs the rods to be bent in one direction only, the rods come tapered and in different diameters. The erection process is limited to what can be done by just a few women and men as only limited professional service is available. Extraordinary loads introduce disturbances to the mechanism; imperfection and fabrication tolerance alter the entire system such that the critical spot eventually wanders haphazardly. One after the other, these conditions have to be considered in order to maintain the central role the model plays in predicting possible forms. Digital tools and contemporary methods in non-linear simulation, evolutionary form-finding, and multi-objective optimization allow for an integrated approach towards negotiating architectural, structural, and economic targets that are in conflict with

each other. They produce options, in a setting of manifold goals and constraints, for exploring possible configurations and guiding the human user towards an informed design. Still, modern tooling only serves as an aid for identifying ideals, for which coherence with building conditions always remains a matter of skilled modelmaking and human design decisions. High-end tools like Karamba and Octopus can be used to include the entirety of a project's aims, but the prototypic character of architectural projects still reclaims resolution and requires abstraction.

The challenge of augmenting human skills with digital ones involves the interface that is necessary in order to ask the right questions regarding usability and applicability. In contrast, the use of high-tech methods in a low-tech setting can be seen as an ultimate test of relevance. The term 'new hybrid' for this project can no longer only be understood in terms of the physical manifestation of an artefact, but now also in terms of the way it is designed, planned, built, and reused to ultimately promote the holistic quality of the built environment.

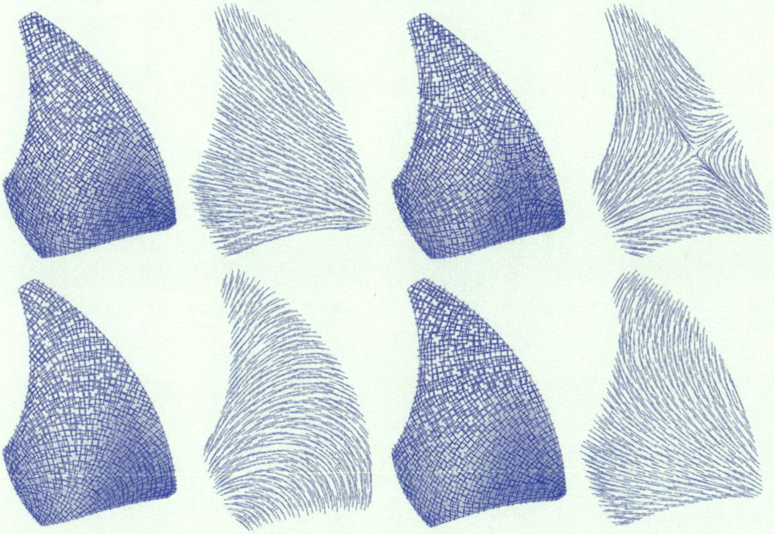

A multi-goal environment generates a variety of patterning proposals; each solution has different qualities, the final decision is left up to the designer

KLAUS BOLLINGER is head of the Institute of Architecture at the University of Applied Arts in Vienna. His interests lie in technologic developments that lead to an advancement of design strategies and formal vocabulary. He is the founder of Bollinger+Grohmann.

ROBERT VIERLINGER is an interdisciplinary consultant and researcher. At the University of Applied Arts Vienna he co-initiated architectural-technological research projects while investigating digital design representation for his PhD. He acts as a consultant for Bollinger+Grohmann engineers.

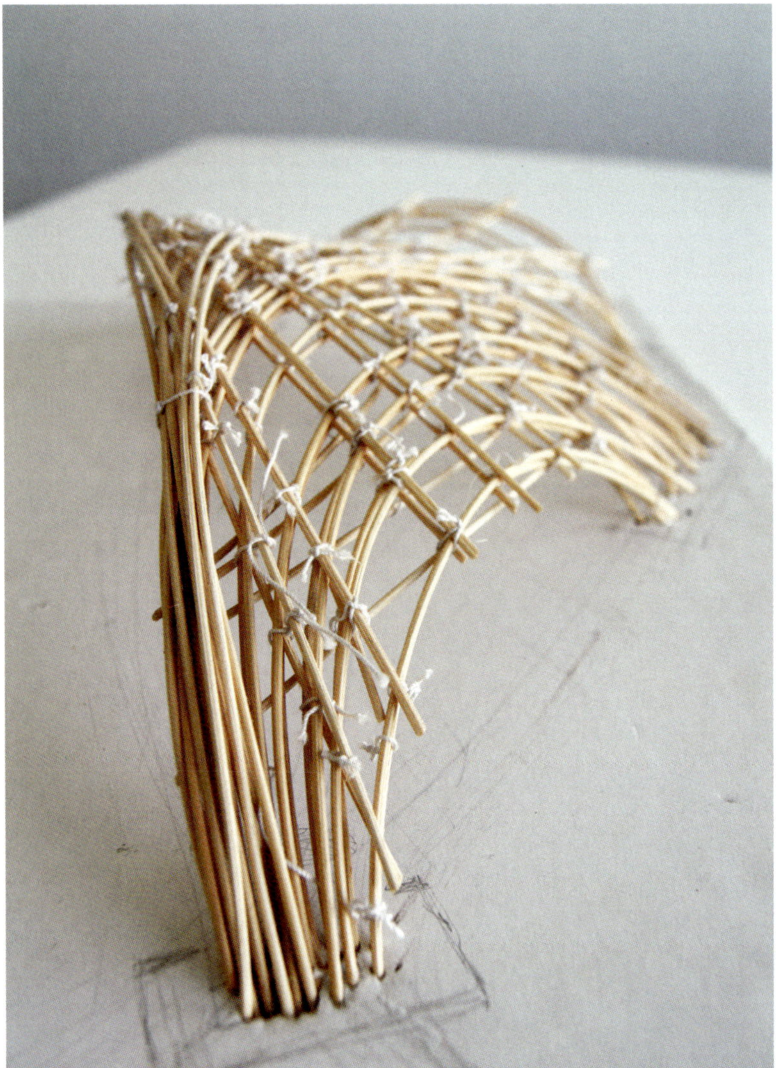

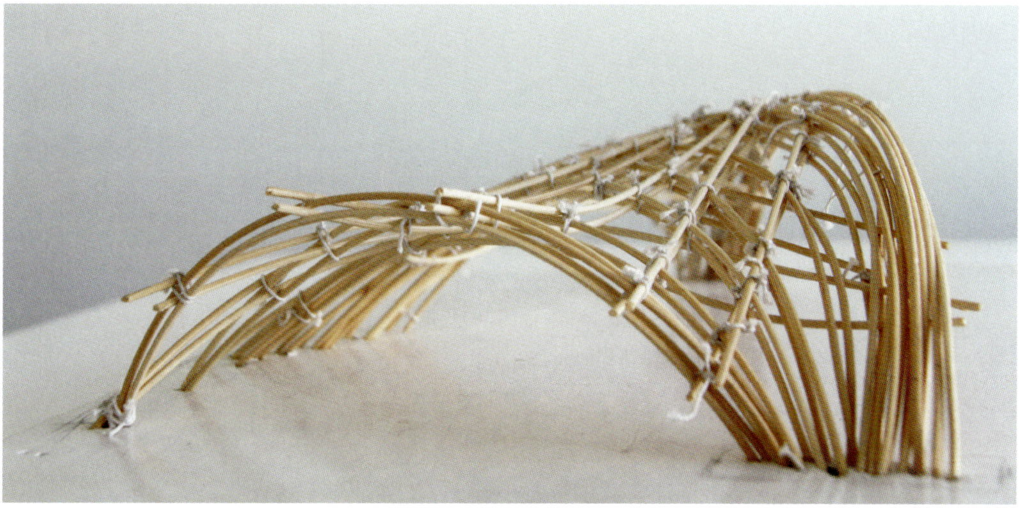

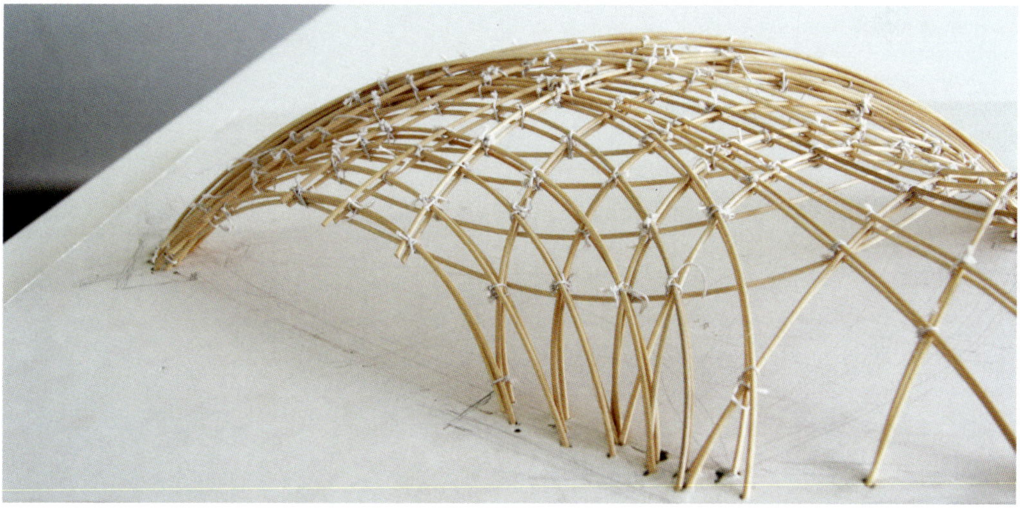

Scale 1:100

Physical Models

While the design of the plan and floorscape of the project has been driven by programmatic and cultural parameters, the orientation and shape of its roofscape have been generated by its environmental context and its materiality: bamboo. Building physical models has thereby helped in understanding the sculptural potential and material qualities of bamboo. The Apata was mainly developed with physical models of various scales, from 1:100 to 1:200, to 1:10, which were digitalized and structurally optimized as 3D models. The need to grasp the entire space, as well as to develop the structure of the bamboo gridshell and its layering, resulted in a back and forth between the computer and the physical models.

In particular, the model at a scale of 1:10 allowed for a discussion about and test of the density of the grid, the layering of bamboo arches, and potential membrane roofing, all in regards to aesthetic, constructive, and structural decisions. In order to understand the pure scale of the project and to test material properties, such as the structural behaviour of bamboo, two 1:1 workshops took place in Austria in a subsequent step, before leaving for Ghana to build.

Franz Sam

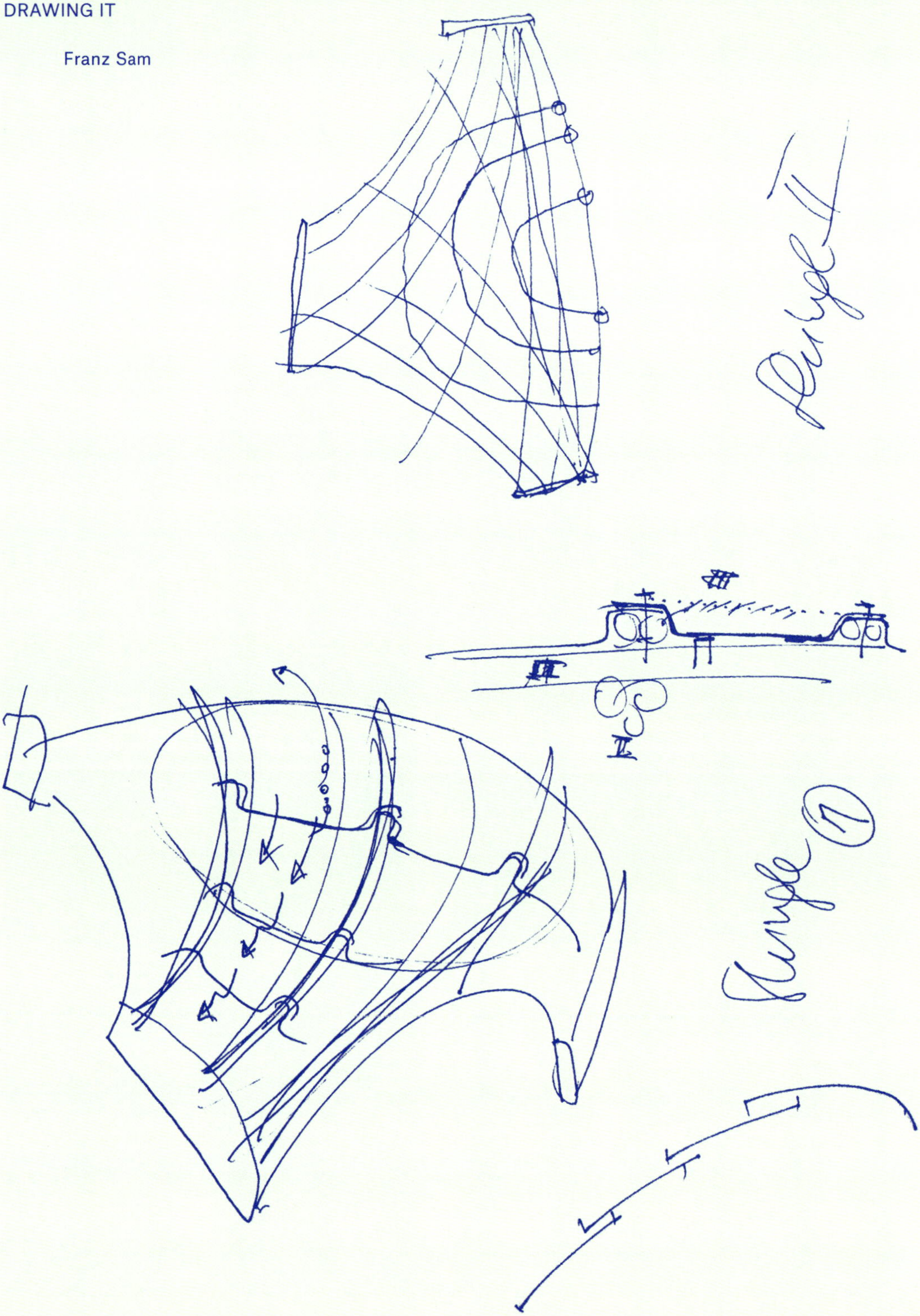

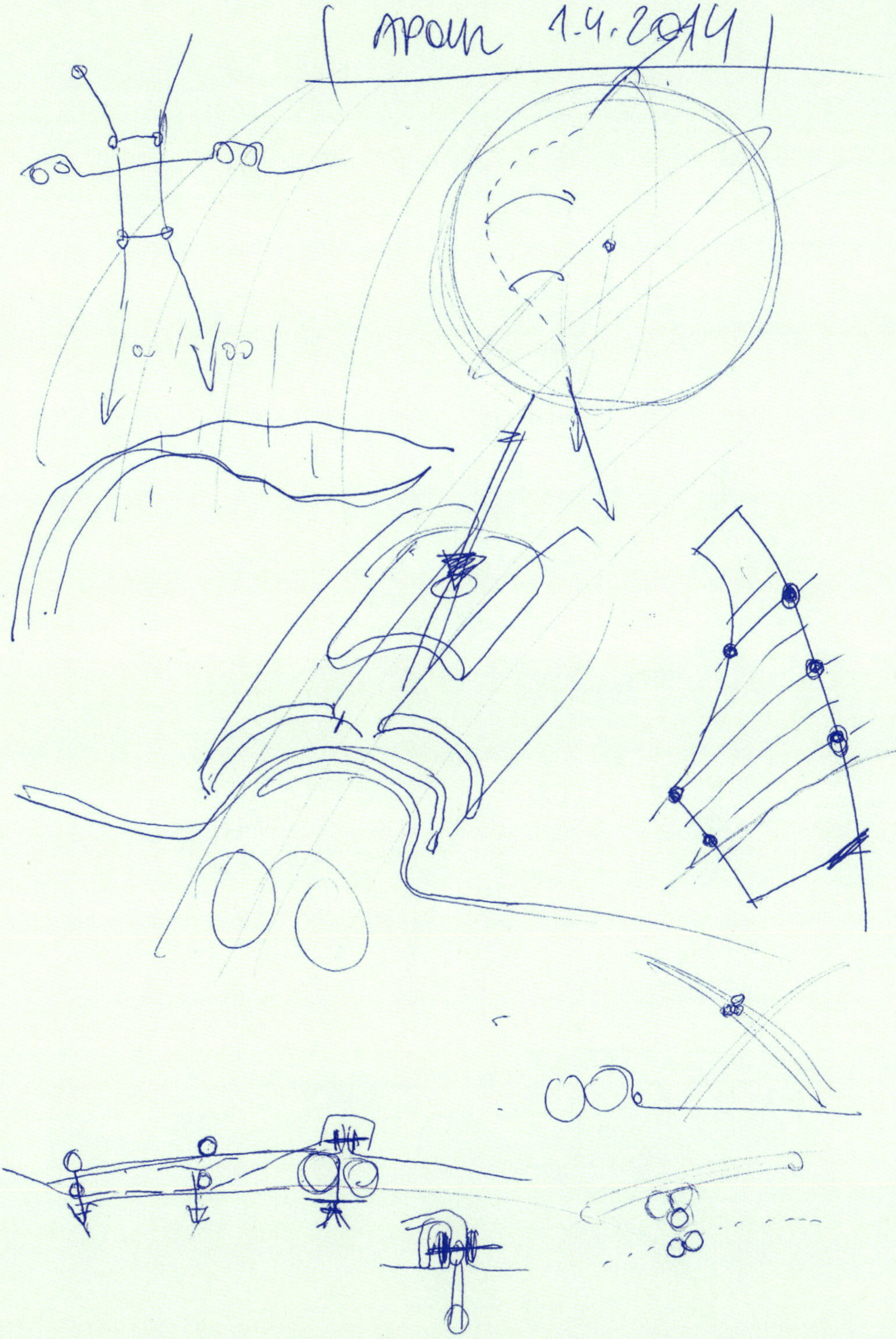

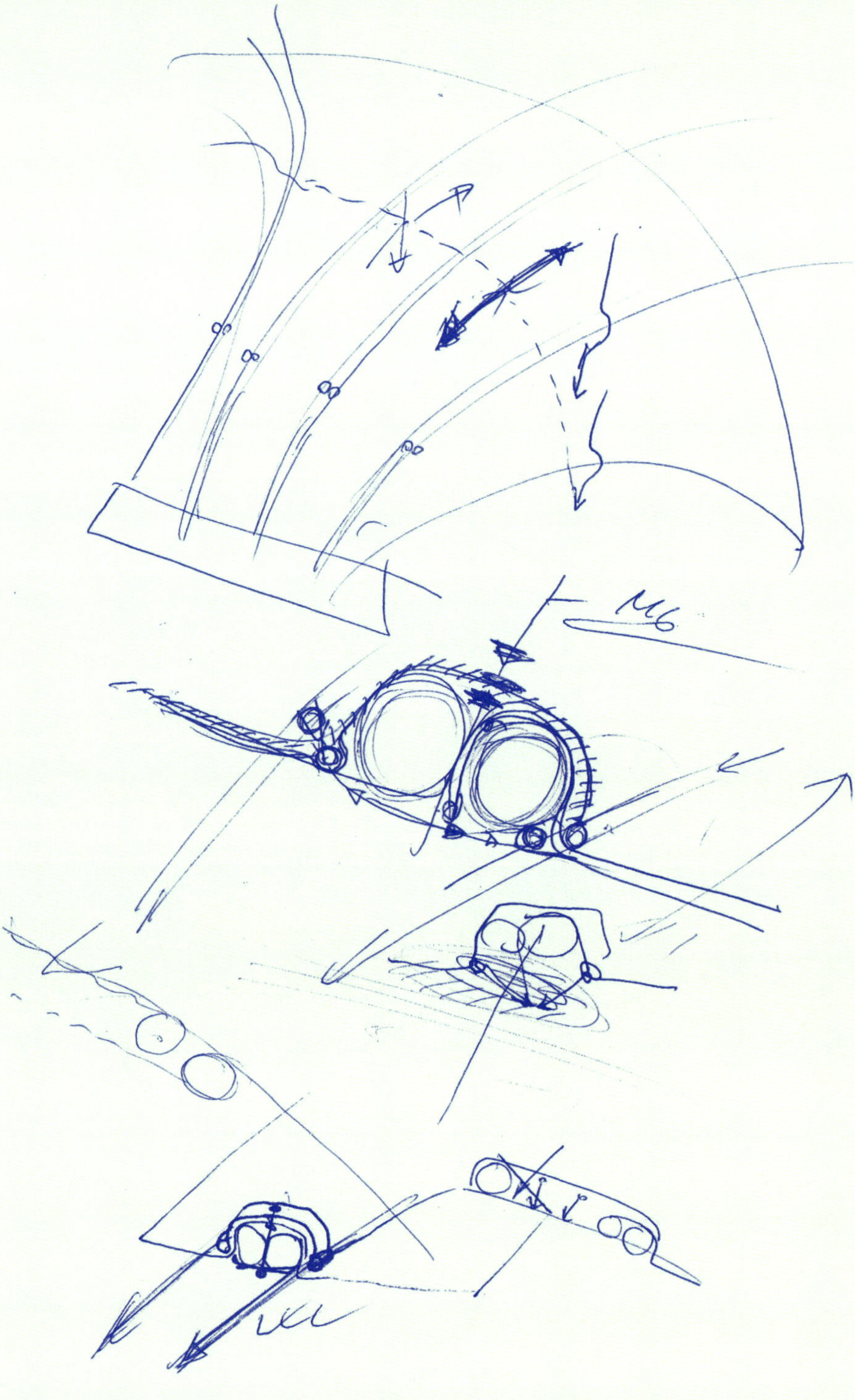

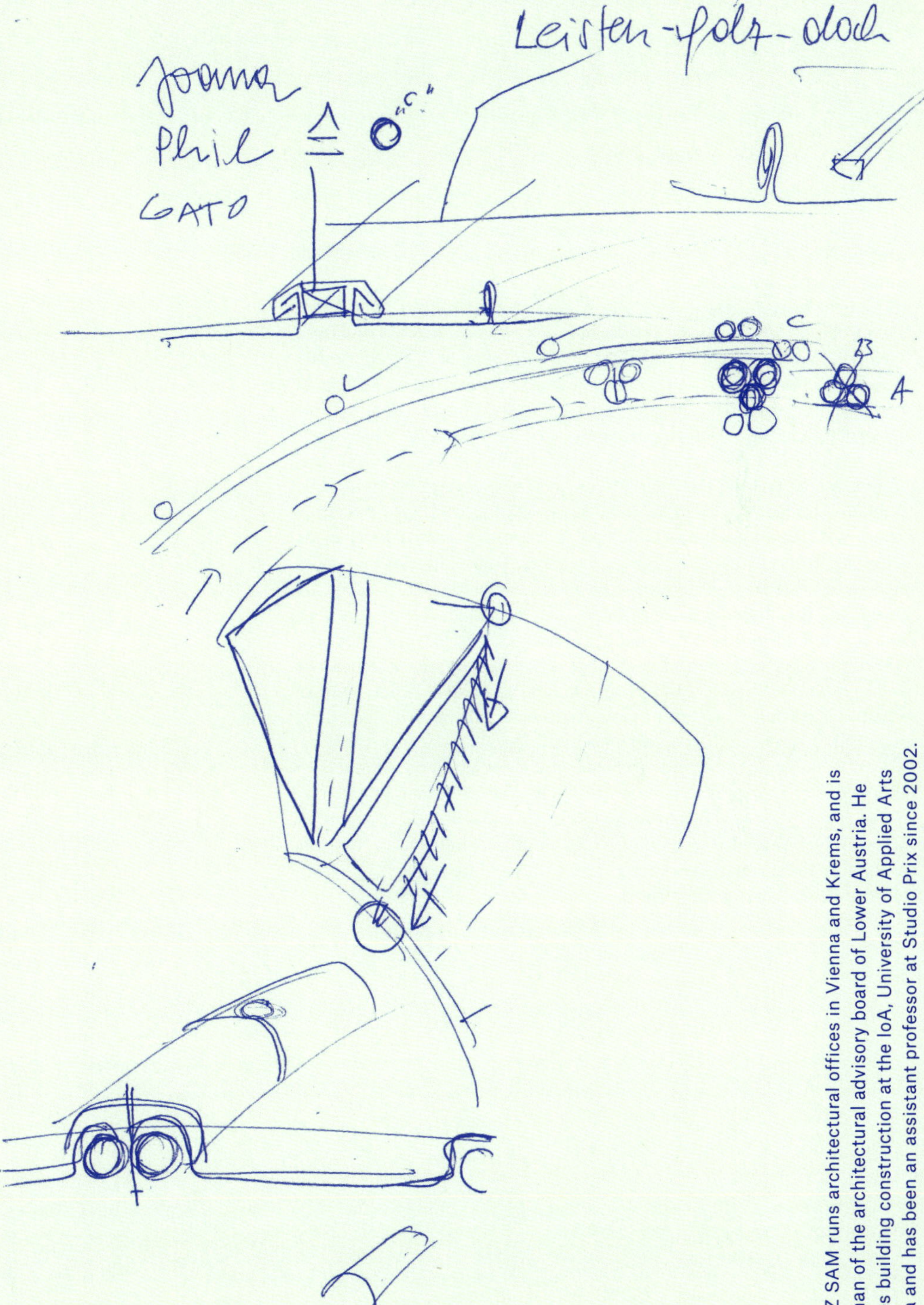

FRANZ SAM runs architectural offices in Vienna and Krems, and is chairman of the architectural advisory board of Lower Austria. He teaches building construction at the IoA, University of Applied Arts Vienna and has been an assistant professor at Studio Prix since 2002. Sam was a project architect at COOP Himmelb(l)au from 1985–1992.

PUTTING GHANA ON THE WORLD MAP OF BAMBOO

Jörg Stamm

Building with culms of *Bambusa vulgaris* is a biological and structural challenge. The most mature bamboo poles have to be selected according to diameter and curve, wall thickness, and then treated against beetle attacks with boron salts. A cleverly designed bamboo structure will be well-protected against rain and ground moisture as air-dried poles will not be affected by fungi, even in the most humid climate. As the *Haduwa* project has shown, a proper grading system of curves and diameters is the only way to find the poles best-suited for the prefabrication of the bamboo arches on the matrix on the ground. It's a dangerous yet very emotional moment when these huge bamboo arches are raised onto the foundations and composed to form the final shell. The project is a fine example of engineering and craftsmanship, which will enhance art performances in a country that usually gives little thought to such outstanding endeavors. Hopefully, the structural performance of the rather neglected *Bambusa vulgaris* will not let us down, and this building will become a long-term example of an excellent bamboo structure protected by a high-tech membrane. Not only will the local artists enjoy the shell as a durable shelter against sun and rain for their training and performances, its unique design and unusual raw material may well stimulate their creativity. This inspiring example of architecture, made with sustainably harvested bamboo, will spur the local tourist industry into looking at a neglected resource as a viable construction material. It took a year of intense work to go through the planning, fundraising, harvesting, preservation, laying of foundations, assembly, membrane design, and construction. Let this project be the ignition spark for a motor that will drive bamboo architecture in Ghana and West Africa.

JÖRG STAMM, born in 1963 in Germany, lives in Columbia. He is a trained carpenter who started working with bamboo in 1992. He is the creator of large-scale bamboo projects all over the world, and one of the most renowned bamboo experts of our time. He has worked for UNIDO, GIZ, GTZ.

INTERWEAVING

Starting from the design phase of the project, the potentials of textile techniques were explored in order to research, conceptualize, and design a skin for the primary structure of the bamboo dome.

Interweaving has been conceptualized as an interdisciplinary and experimental course, together with the Textile Department of the Angewandte. After an initial workshop in Vienna in December 2013, a textile team also got involved on the ground in February 2014, researching local textile techniques, materials, and vernacular roofing.

Back in Vienna, the aim was to come up with artistic translations of the local findings. Driven to nourish the design process of the roofing of the bamboo dome from an artistic perspective rather than an engineering one, parameters were defined, and textile students worked on a variety of samples of similar materiality, but in hybrid techniques.

Inspired by local techniques that were found in different forms of shelter in Ghana, students developed textile structures that were meant to be components, adaptable to the specific requirements of the building and its context. The students focused on netting, braiding, and sewing, corresponding to materials, production infrastructure, and handicraft skills found in the field research. The fishing net acted as a conceptual starting point for adjoining materials that form a surface, ranging from 'feathering' (similar to local grass-roofing) to shingle-roof systems. The traditional way of braiding palm leaves was used to join different materials and build structures with varying characters. This practical research led to design questions relating to the pattern that was reflected in the final roof skin.

Roofing Samples: Clelia Baumgartner (top), Sandra Bamminger (bottom and next pages)

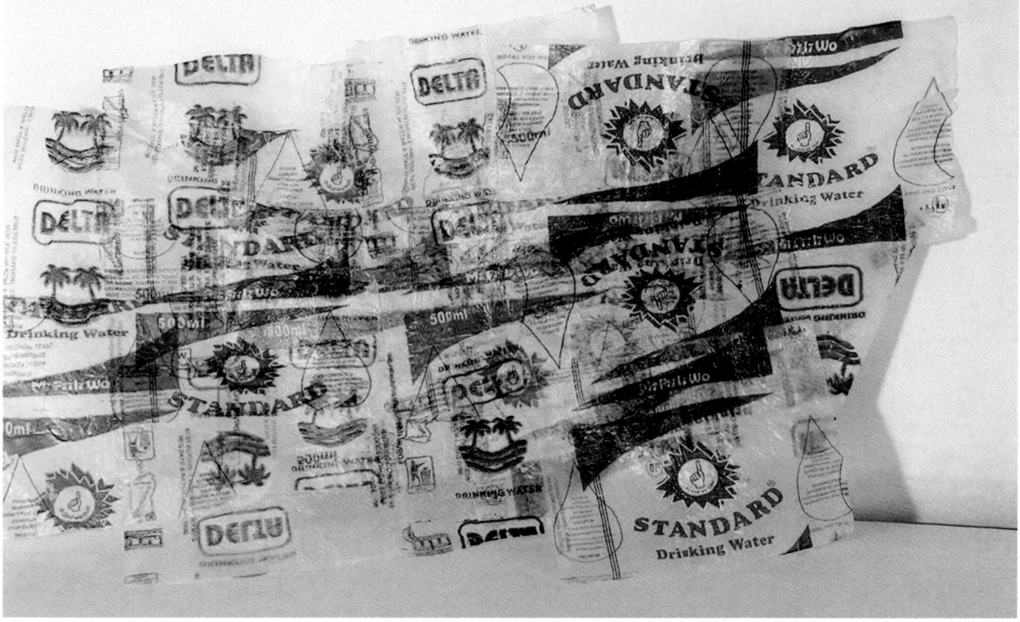
DELTA
STANDARD
Drinking Water
DRINKING WATER
500ml
STANDARD
Drisking Water

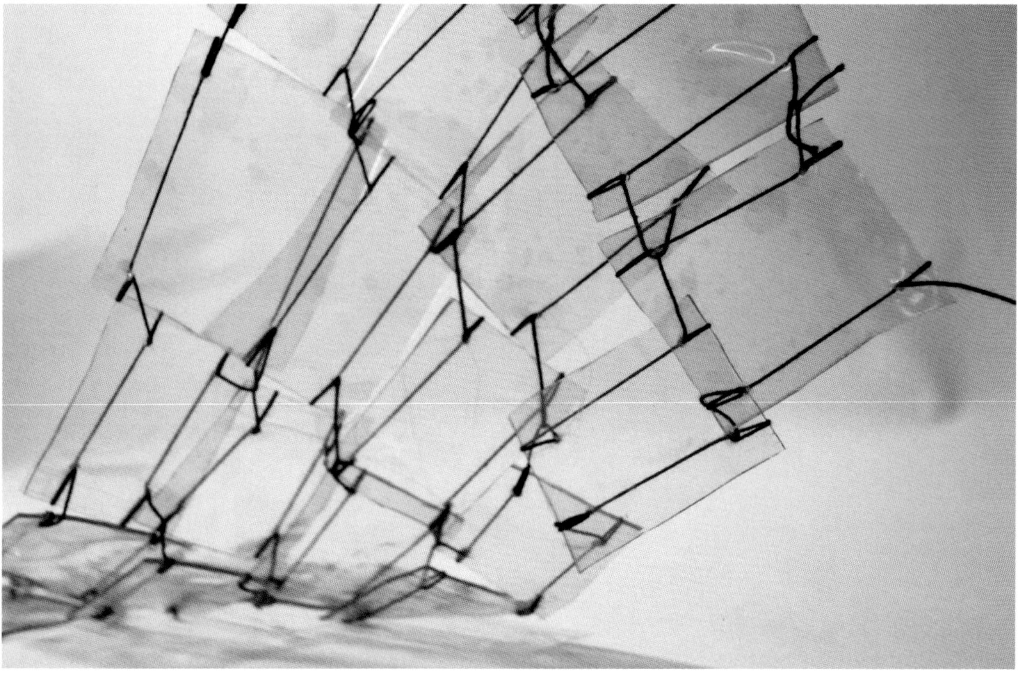

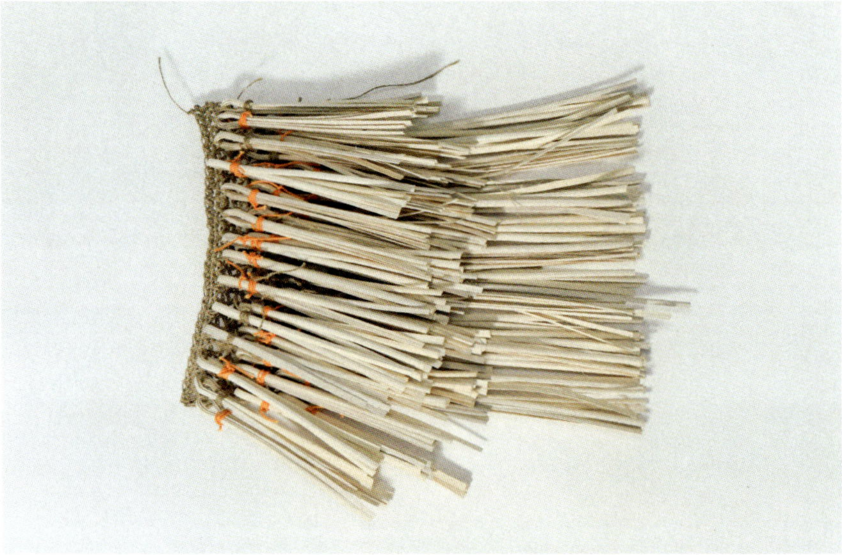

WINDBREAKER DESIGN

The collaboration between [a]FA and TEX was continued after the completion of the Apata, focusing on interventions in and around the bamboo structure that enhanced the functionality of the stage areas. As part of this research, windbreakers were designed to protect the sheltered space underneath the Apata from the effects of coastal winds. The intention was to make the stage attractive for more intimate and smaller-scale performances and events. The interdisciplinary group developed a series of material samples and the hanging system for these wind barriers. The resulting design is a series of porous surfaces that slow down and break up wind coming from the Atlantic Ocean, as well as muffle noise coming from the surf of the beach. This strategy mimics the way wind behaves when hitting coastal vegetation. The large textiles are hung on metal pylons that are scattered between the Apata and the beach and fit in visually with the vertical palm tree trunks in the vicinity. The pylons are plugged into cast foundations and can be erected in multiple configurations. Both the pylons and the textiles are deployable elements that can be mixed and matched in terms of arrangement and height according to the needs of the performer and event.

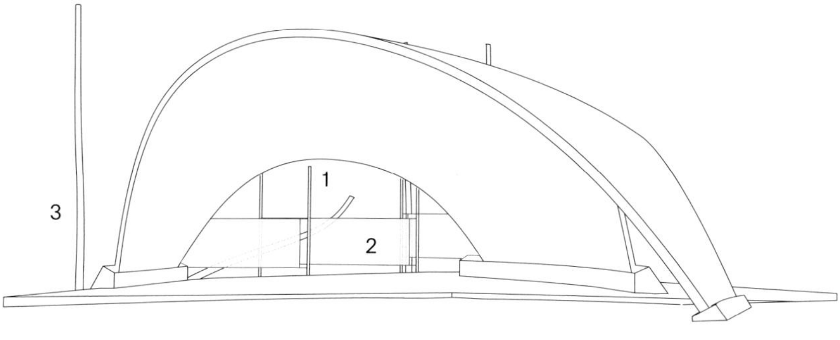

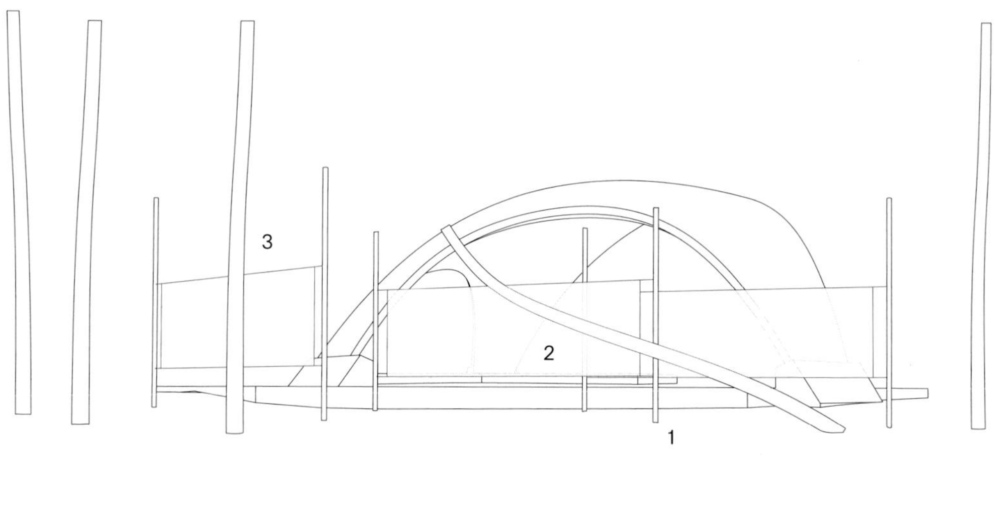

1 Pylon
2 Windbreaker textile
3 Palm tree stem

Windbreaking Textile Design

The textile design consists of several layers that are arranged in varying orders.

Layer 1: Net
White fabric strips are knotted into a close-meshed fishing net, also used by local fishermen. This layer diffuses the wind and decreases its force. Material: water-resistant synthetic fibre

Layer 2 : Grain bags
Locally available bags for grains are cut and sewn together in a new way that catches wind in rhombus-shaped pockets while also allowing it to partially pass through. The pockets self-inflate when the wind hits the surface. Material: plastic

Layer 3: Cut into stretch
This layer is modelled after a fishing net and is itself used in two layers. Cuts in the fabric are directed vertically and can be adjusted by tensioning. This increases the wind flow through the material while releasing the tension decreases it. Material: car protector fabric

Layer 4: Drapery
This layer has staggered holes that diffuse the wind. The curtain can be gathered by pulling ropes, creating more or less attack surface.

Samples were produced that were 70 cm high and 200 cm long.

Cut into stretch

Drapery

Designs: Tanja Happel, Afra Kirchberger, exhibited at Galerie Göttlicher, Krems-Stein, Austria, July 2015 as part of the exhibition "Interweaving: Body, Space, and the Gesture of Interweaving", curated by Manora Auersperg.

INTERWEAVING TEXTURE

Memories of a first encounter with Ghana—for me, an encounter with the unknown. A fusion of colors, sounds, smells, accompanied by a feeling of being overwhelmed. Bodies draped in an endless variety of colorful, patterned fabrics; interspersed among them, the lackluster silver of capacious metal basins and fish. Ropes in the sand—stacked up meticulously, waiting. Nets—spilling over the edges of boats, beached like monstrous bodies.

XXXXXXYYYYYYZZZZZZZZZYYYYYYXXXXXX
XXXXXXYYYYYYZZZZZZZZZYYYYYYXXXXXX
XXXXXXYYYYYYZZZZZZZZZYYYYYYXXXXXX
XXXXXXYYYYYYZZZZZZZZZYYYYYYXXXXXX
XXXXXXYYYYYYZZZZZZZZZYYYYYYXXXXXX
XXXXXXYYYYYYZZZZZZZZZYYYYYYXXXXXX
XXXXXXYYYYYYZZZZZZZZZYYYYYYXXXXXX

Experiencing myself as the foreigner as we make our way through the crowds. Inherent in every encounter is a question... How can we relate to the other, to what makes him, her or it different—from us? In an effort to make sense of the unknown, I become part of it—drawing on personal experience. I make the world that surrounds me my own—I find... myself. But just where is that different he, she or it? Just where—and how—do we meet each other?

XXXXXXYYYYYYZZZZZZZZZYYYYYYXXXXXX
XXXXXXYYYYYYZZZZZZZZZYYYYYYXXXXXX
XXXXXXYYYYYYZZZZZZZZZYYYYYYXXXXXX
XXXXXXYYYYYYZZZZZZZZZYYYYYYXXXXXX
XXXXXXYYYYYYZZZZZZZZZYYYYYYXXXXXX
XXXXXXYYYYYYZZZZZZZZZYYYYYYXXXXXX
XXXXXXYYYYYYZZZZZZZZZYYYYYYXXXXXX
XXXXXXYYYYYYZZZZZZZZZYYYYYYXXXXXX

Locating myself—within the spatial framework that stretches itself out between memory and actuality.

XXXXXXYYYYYYZZZZZZZZZYYYYYYXXXXXX
XXXXXXYYYYYYZZZZZZZZZYYYYYYXXXXXX
XXXXXXYYYYYYZZZZZZZZZYYYYYYXXXXXX
XXXXXXYYYYYYZZZZZZZZZYYYYYYXXXXXX
XXXXXXYYYYYYZZZZZZZZZYYYYYYXXXXXX
XXXXXXYYYYYYZZZZZZZZZYYYYYYXXXXXX
XXXXXXYYYYYYZZZZZZZZZYYYYYYXXXXXX
XXXXXXYYYYYYZZZZZZZZZYYYYYYXXXXXX

Red silk—in exchange for slaves and gold, unraveled from cloth and rewoven—transformed.

XXXXXXYYYYYYZZZZZZZZZYYYYYYXXXXXX
XXXXXXYYYYYYZZZZZZZZZYYYYYYXXXXXX
XXXXXXYYYYYYZZZZZZZZZYYYYYYXXXXXX
XXXXXXYYYYYYZZZZZZZZZYYYYYYXXXXXX
XXXXXXYYYYYYZZZZZZZZZYYYYYYXXXXXX
XXXXXXYYYYYYZZZZZZZZZYYYYYYXXXXXX
XXXXXXYYYYYYZZZZZZZZZYYYYYYXXXXXX
XXXXXXYYYYYYZZZZZZZZZYYYYYYXXXXXX
XXXXXXYYYYYYZZZZZZZZZYYYYYYXXXXXX
XXXXXXYYYYYYZZZZZZZZZYYYYYYXXXXXX
XXXXXXYYYYYYZZZZZZZZZYYYYYYXXXXXX
XXXXXXYYYYYYZZZZZZZZZYYYYYYXXXXXX
XXXXXXYYYYYYZZZZZZZZZYYYYYYXXXXXX
XXXXXXYYYYYYZZZZZZZZZYYYYYYXXXXXX
XXXXXXYYYYYYZZZZZZZZZYYYYYYXXXXXX
XXXXXXYYYYYYZZZZZZZZZYYYYYYXXXXXX

...the memory takes shape, develops an identity of its own as its density gradually increases...

XXXXXXYYYYYYZZZZZZZZZYYYYYYXXXXXX
XXXXXXYYYYYYZZZZZZZZZYYYYYYXXXXXX
XXXXXXYYYYYYZZZZZZZZZYYYYYYXXXXXX
XXXXXXYYYYYYZZZZZZZZZYYYYYYXXXXXX
XXXXXXYYYYYYZZZZZZZZZYYYYYYXXXXXX
XXXXXXYYYYYYZZZZZZZZZYYYYYYXXXXXX
XXXXXXYYYYYYZZZZZZZZZYYYYYYXXXXXX

A translation attempt is woven into a frame of references—a double-relatedness, between contexts.

XXXXXXYYYYYYZZZZZZZZZYYYYYYXXXXXX
XXXXXXYYYYYYZZZZZZZZZYYYYYYXXXXXX
XXXXXXYYYYYYZZZZZZZZZYYYYYYXXXXXX
XXXXXXYYYYYYZZZZZZZZZYYYYYYXXXXXX
XXXXXXYYYYYYZZZZZZZZZYYYYYYXXXXXX
XXXXXXYYYYYYZZZZZZZZZYYYYYYXXXXXX
XXXXXXYYYYYYZZZZZZZZZYYYYYYXXXXXX

Entering into a relationship with the world—a nascent movement with a character of its own. A process in which perception and thought evolve... And slowly, a possible order becomes apparent—multiple constellations of interpenetration. Interweaving. Sensory perception stretches itself out to span the world that becomes its object—like the warp in the loom. And throughout, in a back-and-forth movement like that of the shuttle—the mind's pathfinding, conceptualization.

XXXXXXYYYYYYZZZZZZZZZYYYYYYXXXXXX
XXXXXXYYYYYYZZZZZZZZZYYYYYYXXXXXX
XXXXXXYYYYYYZZZZZZZZZYYYYYYXXXXXX
XXXXXXYYYYYYZZZZZZZZZYYYYYYXXXXXX
XXXXXXYYYYYYZZZZZZZZZYYYYYYXXXXXX
XXXXXXYYYYYYZZZZZZZZZYYYYYYXXXXXX
XXXXXXYYYYYYZZZZZZZZZYYYYYYXXXXXX
XXXXXXYYYYYYZZZZZZZZZYYYYYYXXXXXX

Kente cloth—narrow strips woven by hand, joined together to form larger surfaces, made to fit and to be fitting for the body they are to enrobe—a symbol of cultural identity. Handed down from generation to generation, the formal variations of the woven patterns tell a story—a story that writes itself. Adding elements of other local cultures to the technique and patterns used, weavers have constantly inscribed historical and social contexts in the continuum of what is thus transmitted.

Texture. Within each continuous kente strip, clearly defined areas of varying structure assert themselves. An alternation of weaves. Plain weave—weft-face… Plain weave—interface, a space of encounter, an impregnable place. A dynamic space of interlaced effectiveness—at first, an X-Y-Z performance, then orientation. Blocks of patterns in the weft-face—a concentration of meanings. Structure of total communication engages the space—and develops a sense of its own.
XXXXXXYYYYYYZZZZZZZZZYYYYYYXXXXXX
XXXXXXYYYYYYZZZZZZZZZYYYYYYXXXXXX
XXXXXXYYYYYYZZZZZZZZZYYYYYYXXXXXX
XXXXXXYYYYYYZZZZZZZZZYYYYYYXXXXXX
XXXXXXYYYYYYZZZZZZZZZYYYYYYXXXXXX
XXXXXXYYYYYYZZZZZZZZZYYYYYYXXXXXX
XXXXXXYYYYYYZZZZZZZZZYYYYYYXXXXXX
Text. From Latin *texere*, "to weave", "to braid"—appropriately: a coherent statement. Close to the very essence of all that is textile in the making, acquiring cohesion in the process of construction, acquiring form, giving rise to a close-knit constellation of forces—feeling, wanting and thinking—in the accumulation of references made… In the arrangement of the basic structure, a fabric takes shape; a materialization of human references.
XXXXXXYYYYYYZZZZZZZZZYYYYYYXXXXXX
XXXXXXYYYYYYZZZZZZZZZYYYYYYXXXXXX
XXXXXXYYYYYYZZZZZZZZZYYYYYYXXXXXX
XXXXXXYYYYYYZZZZZZZZZYYYYYYXXXXXX
XXXXXXYYYYYYZZZZZZZZZYYYYYYXXXXXX
XXXXXXYYYYYYZZZZZZZZZYYYYYYXXXXXX
XXXXXXYYYYYYZZZZZZZZZYYYYYYXXXXXX
XXXXXXYYYYYYZZZZZZZZZYYYYYYXXXXXX
The associative thread passes through a fabric of references, incorporating motifs along the way.
XXXXXXYYYYYYZZZZZZZZZYYYYYYXXXXXX
XXXXXXYYYYYYZZZZZZZZZYYYYYYXXXXXX
XXXXXXYYYYYYZZZZZZZZZYYYYYYXXXXXX
XXXXXXYYYYYYZZZZZZZZZYYYYYYXXXXXX
XXXXXXYYYYYYZZZZZZZZZYYYYYYXXXXXX
XXXXXXYYYYYYZZZZZZZZZYYYYYYXXXXXX
XXXXXXYYYYYYZZZZZZZZZYYYYYYXXXXXX
XXXXXXYYYYYYZZZZZZZZZYYYYYYXXXXXX
A sign interwoven, *Abusua ye dom*—the extended family is a force—speaks of cohesion.
XXXXXXYYYYYYZZZZZZZZZYYYYYYXXXXXX
XXXXXXYYYYYYZZZZZZZZZYYYYYYXXXXXX
XXXXXXYYYYYYZZZZZZZZZYYYYYYXXXXXX
XXXXXXYYYYYYZZZZZZZZZYYYYYYXXXXXX
XXXXXXYYYYYYZZZZZZZZZYYYYYYXXXXXX
XXXXXXYYYYYYZZZZZZZZZYYYYYYXXXXXX
XXXXXXYYYYYYZZZZZZZZZYYYYYYXXXXXX
XXXXXXYYYYYYZZZZZZZZZYYYYYYXXXXXX
XXXXXXYYYYYYZZZZZZZZZYYYYYYXXXXXX
XXXXXXYYYYYYZZZZZZZZZYYYYYYXXXXXX
XXXXXXYYYYYYZZZZZZZZZYYYYYYXXXXXX
XXXXXXYYYYYYZZZZZZZZZYYYYYYXXXXXX
XXXXXXYYYYYYZZZZZZZZZYYYYYYXXXXXX
XXXXXXYYYYYYZZZZZZZZZYYYYYYXXXXXX
XXXXXXYYYYYYZZZZZZZZZYYYYYYXXXXXX
XXXXXXYYYYYYZZZZZZZZZYYYYYYXXXXXX
…slowly, a possible order becomes apparent—multiple constellations of interpenetration.
XXXXXXYYYYYYZZZZZZZZZYYYYYYXXXXXX
XXXXXXYYYYYYZZZZZZZZZYYYYYYXXXXXX
XXXXXXYYYYYYZZZZZZZZZYYYYYYXXXXXX
XXXXXXYYYYYYZZZZZZZZZYYYYYYXXXXXX
XXXXXXYYYYYYZZZZZZZZZYYYYYYXXXXXX
XXXXXXYYYYYYZZZZZZZZZYYYYYYXXXXXX
XXXXXXYYYYYYZZZZZZZZZYYYYYYXXXXXX
As the text is being written, thoughts, gradually defining themselves, begin to fall into place.
XXXXXXYYYYYYZZZZZZZZZYYYYYYXXXXXX
XXXXXXYYYYYYZZZZZZZZZYYYYYYXXXXXX
XXXXXXYYYYYYZZZZZZZZZYYYYYYXXXXXX
XXXXXXYYYYYYZZZZZZZZZYYYYYYXXXXXX
XXXXXXYYYYYYZZZZZZZZZYYYYYYXXXXXX
XXXXXXYYYYYYZZZZZZZZZYYYYYYXXXXXX
XXXXXXYYYYYYZZZZZZZZZYYYYYYXXXXXX
The thread—following the trace of a memory—is the continuation of the event, metamorphosing, wandering, changing directions. It refers to everything that lies along the way, carrying with it the familiar. Following in succession are moments of appearance and moments of apparent absence; the obscure is followed by an emergence, a thought, a brief pause perhaps—only for the thread to take another deep plunge—capable of combining dissimilar things without distinction.
XXXXXXYYYYYYZZZZZZZZZYYYYYYXXXXXX
XXXXXXYYYYYYZZZZZZZZZYYYYYYXXXXXX
XXXXXXYYYYYYZZZZZZZZZYYYYYYXXXXXX
XXXXXXYYYYYYZZZZZZZZZYYYYYYXXXXXX
XXXXXXYYYYYYZZZZZZZZZYYYYYYXXXXXX
XXXXXXYYYYYYZZZZZZZZZYYYYYYXXXXXX
XXXXXXYYYYYYZZZZZZZZZYYYYYYXXXXXX
XXXXXXYYYYYYZZZZZZZZZYYYYYYXXXXXX
Apam Apata. A space—not yet there—that contains within itself a fundamental notion, in my mind closely entwined with impressions of Ghana. A stage, situated on the Atlantic shore, called Haduwa. The meaning of the word—connectivity—is architecturally manifest in a bamboo structure suggestive of things textile. A space—an attempt at responding to the dialogue-based practices of a young Ghanaian art scene, a space that welcomes context and, incorporating it, gives it form.

One day, within this extroverted, multifunctional space, an area is defined; here we join a group of young people from the neighboring fishing village. Each one has brought with him or her a personal sign to use. Inscribed on kites that these young people built themselves, each of the signs ascends into the air, one at a time, each in its own peculiar way. We establish a relationship with the place itself, a place where we can dabble; we want to comprehend its fundamental constitution.

XXXXXXYYYYYYZZZZZZZZZYYYYYYXXXXXX
XXXXXXYYYYYYZZZZZZZZZYYYYYYXXXXXX
XXXXXXYYYYYYZZZZZZZZZYYYYYYXXXXXX
XXXXXXYYYYYYZZZZZZZZZYYYYYYXXXXXX
XXXXXXYYYYYYZZZZZZZZZYYYYYYXXXXXX
XXXXXXYYYYYYZZZZZZZZZYYYYYYXXXXXX
XXXXXXYYYYYYZZZZZZZZZYYYYYYXXXXXX
XXXXXXYYYYYYZZZZZZZZZYYYYYYXXXXXX

Flags became a space of encounter, with individual symbols joining to form a collective story. Flags require wind to unfurl and to tell the story they have to tell. The signs become detached from the background, they become objects that enter into a mutual relationship. Each person can be both one and every one of these objects. Moving, combining, forming a group. Telling a new story each time.

XXXXXXYYYYYYZZZZZZZZZYYYYYYXXXXXX
XXXXXXYYYYYYZZZZZZZZZYYYYYYXXXXXX
XXXXXXYYYYYYZZZZZZZZZYYYYYYXXXXXX
XXXXXXYYYYYYZZZZZZZZZYYYYYYXXXXXX
XXXXXXYYYYYYZZZZZZZZZYYYYYYXXXXXX
XXXXXXYYYYYYZZZZZZZZZYYYYYYXXXXXX
XXXXXXYYYYYYZZZZZZZZZYYYYYYXXXXXX
XXXXXXYYYYYYZZZZZZZZZYYYYYYXXXXXX

How can we communicate, interpret signs—without sharing the same kinds of experience?

XXXXXXYYYYYYZZZZZZZZZYYYYYYXXXXXX
XXXXXXYYYYYYZZZZZZZZZYYYYYYXXXXXX
XXXXXXYYYYYYZZZZZZZZZYYYYYYXXXXXX
XXXXXXYYYYYYZZZZZZZZZYYYYYYXXXXXX
XXXXXXYYYYYYZZZZZZZZZYYYYYYXXXXXX
XXXXXXYYYYYYZZZZZZZZZYYYYYYXXXXXX
XXXXXXYYYYYYZZZZZZZZZYYYYYYXXXXXX
XXXXXXYYYYYYZZZZZZZZZYYYYYYXXXXXX

The unfamiliar place occurs in the familiar place. The unfamiliar space in the familiar space.

XXXXXXYYYYYYZZZZZZZZZYYYYYYXXXXXX
XXXXXXYYYYYYZZZZZZZZZYYYYYYXXXXXX
XXXXXXYYYYYYZZZZZZZZZYYYYYYXXXXXX
XXXXXXYYYYYYZZZZZZZZZYYYYYYXXXXXX
XXXXXXYYYYYYZZZZZZZZZYYYYYYXXXXXX
XXXXXXYYYYYYZZZZZZZZZYYYYYYXXXXXX
XXXXXXYYYYYYZZZZZZZZZYYYYYYXXXXXX
XXXXXXYYYYYYZZZZZZZZZYYYYYYXXXXXX

XXXXXXYYYYYYZZZZZZZZZYYYYYYXXXXXX
XXXXXXYYYYYYZZZZZZZZZYYYYYYXXXXXX
XXXXXXYYYYYYZZZZZZZZZYYYYYYXXXXXX
XXXXXXYYYYYYZZZZZZZZZYYYYYYXXXXXX
XXXXXXYYYYYYZZZZZZZZZYYYYYYXXXXXX
XXXXXXYYYYYYZZZZZZZZZYYYYYYXXXXXX
XXXXXXYYYYYYZZZZZZZZZYYYYYYXXXXXX
XXXXXXYYYYYYZZZZZZZZZYYYYYYXXXXXX

Sign—brings to mind a conception previously formed, imitating perceptions; is in a state of expectation.

XXXXXXYYYYYYZZZZZZZZZYYYYYYXXXXXX
XXXXXXYYYYYYZZZZZZZZZYYYYYYXXXXXX
XXXXXXYYYYYYZZZZZZZZZYYYYYYXXXXXX
XXXXXXYYYYYYZZZZZZZZZYYYYYYXXXXXX
XXXXXXYYYYYYZZZZZZZZZYYYYYYXXXXXX
XXXXXXYYYYYYZZZZZZZZZYYYYYYXXXXXX
XXXXXXYYYYYYZZZZZZZZZYYYYYYXXXXXX
XXXXXXYYYYYYZZZZZZZZZYYYYYYXXXXXX

When does dialogue emerge from multiple positions—or a collective gesture from individual?

XXXXXXYYYYYYZZZZZZZZZYYYYYYXXXXXX
XXXXXXYYYYYYZZZZZZZZZYYYYYYXXXXXX
XXXXXXYYYYYYZZZZZZZZZYYYYYYXXXXXX
XXXXXXYYYYYYZZZZZZZZZYYYYYYXXXXXX
XXXXXXYYYYYYZZZZZZZZZYYYYYYXXXXXX
XXXXXXYYYYYYZZZZZZZZZYYYYYYXXXXXX

Experiences and personal inferences resurface in a different place, and there they form a structure, they give direction to the way a group goes about its work. The scope of interest and analysis finds itself being extended from one place to another. An intervention in a gallery in Krems, Austria, provides us with an opportunity to invoke that distant place, Ghana—mentally, we bring functional, social, cultural aspects of all that is susceptible of change into what is happening here.

XXXXXXYYYYYYZZZZZZZZZYYYYYYXXXXXX
XXXXXXYYYYYYZZZZZZZZZYYYYYYXXXXXX
XXXXXXYYYYYYZZZZZZZZZYYYYYYXXXXXX
XXXXXXYYYYYYZZZZZZZZZYYYYYYXXXXXX
XXXXXXYYYYYYZZZZZZZZZYYYYYYXXXXXX
XXXXXXYYYYYYZZZZZZZZZYYYYYYXXXXXX
XXXXXXYYYYYYZZZZZZZZZYYYYYYXXXXXX
XXXXXXYYYYYYZZZZZZZZZYYYYYYXXXXXX

Work content, local references and the personal interests of each—interlinked by work that takes place through dialogue—all become more closely connected in collective action. Probing the place as a social space, we experiment with ways in which it can be occupied and inhabited, we dabble in forms of collective investigation and action. Stretching the material, finding our bearings, searching, giving order to things. Interweaving—body, space, and the gesture of weaving.

The configuration of references, which derives its strength from a multiplicity of interlacements, is expressed in a network of interventions of a material nature. It is far more than the sum of its single components. The movement in space amounts to an attempt to move among the various artistic works, contexts, positions—from one to the next, and at the same time throughout. The framework, the content, the text, the fabric. The loom is in a state of expectation, the warp threads are in place.
XXXXXXYYYYYYZZZZZZZZZYYYYYYXXXXXX
XXXXXXYYYYYYZZZZZZZZZYYYYYYXXXXXX
XXXXXXYYYYYYZZZZZZZZZYYYYYYXXXXXX
XXXXXXYYYYYYZZZZZZZZZYYYYYYXXXXXX
XXXXXXYYYYYYZZZZZZZZZYYYYYYXXXXXX
XXXXXXYYYYYYZZZZZZZZZYYYYYYXXXXXX
XXXXXXYYYYYYZZZZZZZZZYYYYYYXXXXXX
XXXXXXYYYYYYZZZZZZZZZYYYYYYXXXXXX
Clothing, doffed and deconstructed, will be brought in, threads and strips will be joined together, a surface will emerge.

The cot on which one cannot yet lie will tell us something about the body.

The body will be rediscovered in the surface.

A fabric in the making.

from "Teil 8 bezieht sich auf Teil 1–5..." exhibition text of *Interweaving_Körper, Raum und die Gest des Verwebens* (2015, Galerie Göttlicher, Krems) by Laura Egger-Karlegger/ Manora Auersperg

MANORA AUERSPERG lives and works in Vienna. In her artistic work she investigates the relationship between the human body and space, which is also central in her teaching practice at the University of Applied Arts Vienna, Textiles—Free, Applied and Experimental Artistic Design, Institute of Art Sciences and Art Education.

KITES AND FLAGS WORKSHOP

February 2015

Kites – Individual work

The students are asked to create their own kite with an emblem on it. This emblem is a character/sign/symbol they can identify with and invent individually. This emblem expresses the student's vision of a "creature" that can support, guard, protect, and/or be empowered by.

Flags – Teamwork

The students are asked to form groups of four or five to work on their "flag". They bring together their emblems as a source of inspiration and starting point for a story they want to tell.

What happens if their characters/signs/symbols meet in the flag's space? The aim is to develop a picture through teamwork. The flag is a symbolic space for encounter, action, adventure, wishes, and dreams.

Program:

8:00 a.m. – 12:30 p.m.
Welcome and introduction
Kite workshop
Presentation of the kites
Flag workshop: introduction and conception

12:30 p.m. – 13:30 p.m.
Lunch break

13:30 p.m. – 16:30 p.m.
Flag workshop in groups: design and realization

Partners: [a]FA (for Haduwa Ghana) and the Textile Department of the University of Applied Arts Vienna, with the School of Abrekum / Kobina Esandooh
Workshop instructors: Barbara Putz-Plecko, Manora Auersperg, Tanja Happel, with Baerbel Mueller and Isabella Narh

Listening to an interview on Haduwa´s mission

Discussing Friedrich Kiesler´s "Raumbühne" and other stage design concepts

Outdoor body space scores

Daniel Aschwanden introducing performative techniques

A one-day workshop, run by Daniel Aschwanden

Body space exercises 1:1

Staging one's own body

Investigating the E.T.S. Drama Studio at the University of Ghana in Legon, Accra

The Lab DC performing for the [a]FA team

Petra, Baerbel and Daniel leading the transdisciplinary lab together

Andrea presenting her research on West African patterns

[a]FA showing preliminary work done in Vienna

At Nubuke Foundation in Accra

Kofi Setordji speaking about the arts in Ghana

Daniel and Kofi

[a]FA and the Lab DC arriving in the Central Region

Kojo Benedict Quaye aka Mr Black, organizing

Evening lecture by Mae Ling-Lokko

First day on site

[a]FA and the Lab DC team creating shelter

Framing exercises 1:10 and 1:1

The [a]FA team presenting first findings to the Haduwa board

Organizing material for the exhibition installation at Nubuke Foundation Accra

Ilias installing his woven piece

Joseph building a model with a basket weaver at his workshop

Ewa mounting her individual mapping

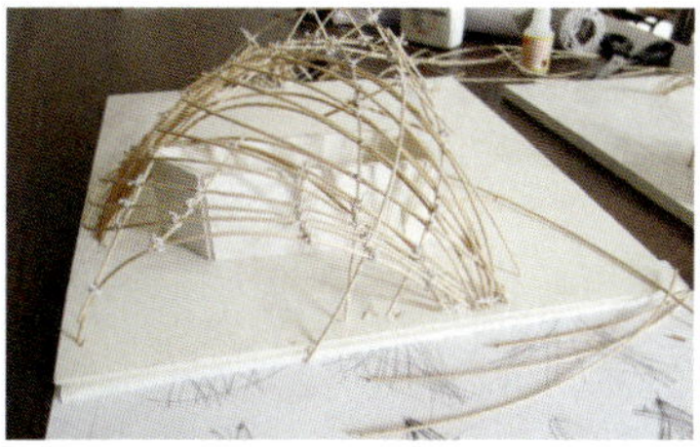

Working on the initial 1:100 model

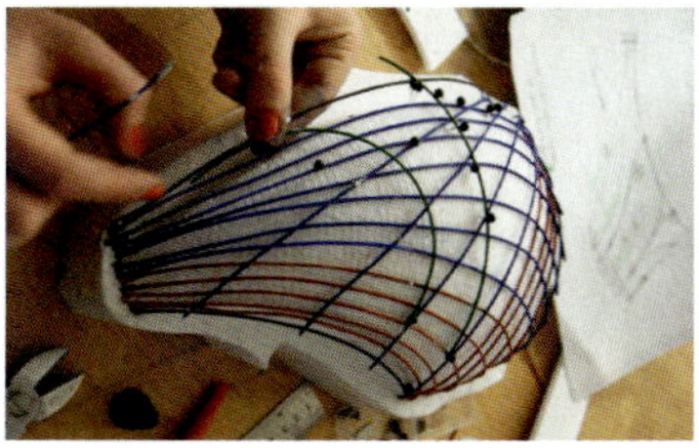

Specifying the structural members and layers

Building the 1:10 model

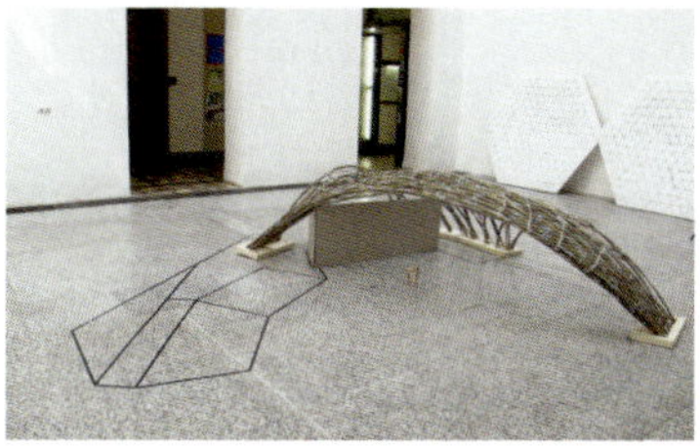

Presentation for Petra Kron, Reiner Zettl, Daniel Aschwanden and Mr Black

A 1:1 workshop led by Franz Sam

Building an arch with roof battens

Simulating the largest bamboo arch in full scale

Lifting the arch

Firma Stelzer in Herzogenburg hosting [a]FA

Set-up for a load test with roof battens

Load test with single bamboo beam: 200 kg load makes 70 cm displacement

Triple bamboo beam set-up

Breaking point at 600 kg

A two-day workshop on textile techniques led by Manora Auersperg

Transdisciplinary work between students of architecture and the textile arts

Afra braiding

A guest lecture by artist Serge Attukwei Clottey

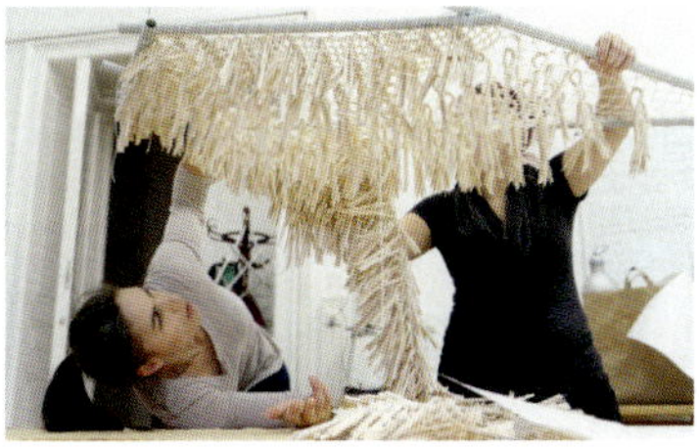

Design by Sandra

Interweaving: an interdisciplinary semester

Philipp, Ilias, Ioana, Franz, and Manora searching for solutions

Designs and samples for potential roofings; Sarah Steiner

Applying first findings to the primary structure of the bamboo dome

Water sachet recycling by Clelia Baumgartner

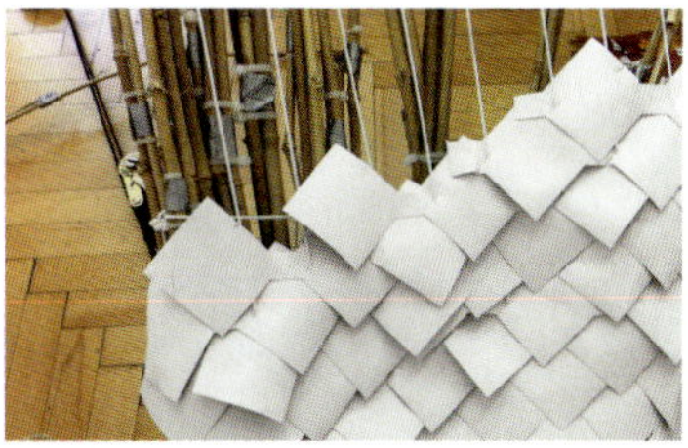

Shingle tests on a 1:10 scale

Meeting with Nana Edu Effrim X, Chief of Apam

Joseph, Petra, and Bernard presenting the project

Chief Nana, his elders, [a]FA, and the Haduwa Board

Joseph and the foundation team of workers, with Clelia

Joseph and Baerbel outlining on site

Clearing the land

The foundation located towards the beachfront needs depth due to the less stable ground

Building reinforcement cages from single iron rods

Formwork work

Work on the longest and curved foundation

BAMBOO HARVEST AND TREATMENT

Our bamboo growing 110 km away from our site

Identification of the Right Age

Young bamboo is fresh, green, smooth, and shiny. As it grows quickly, it has a narrow wall thickness and nodes that are set far apart. Bamboo culms that can be used for construction are at least four years old and thus have aging marks: dirt, spots, and lichens. They are no longer light green. If the bamboo is harvested too early, the cells are not lignified enough, so they mainly contain water—this causes the cells to contract and the culms to become brittle when the bamboo dries. After about seven years, a bamboo culm turns from dark green to a sand colour. It dies naturally and the cells start to degrade. This bamboo is then no longer suitable for construction.

Meeting with the bamboo expert Balumba

Bamboo Harvest

Bambusa vulgaris is a clumping species. Only one third of a bamboo clump is harvested so that it can regenerate. The most mature bamboo grows on the inside of the bamboo clumps. The bamboo is harvested in a horseshoe manner, leaving the younger bamboo culms on the outside intact, while the older culms inside are removed. They are cut as low to the ground as possible, as the lower parts are the strongest and therefore the most suitable for building. The natural curvature is already taken into account at the time the harvest according to the building purpose.

Borax Treatment

All the nodes are punched with an iron rod, the last node is left intact. The length of the bamboo is designated on the iron rod with chalk. The culms are put in a vertical position with the intact node on the bottom. It is filled with borax solution from the top. 3 l borax per 100 l water are brought to a boil and then cooled until lukewarm. The punched culms are filled with the water. After 5–7 days, the last node is punched and most of the borax solution is emptied, which can be reused again. The bamboo is treated, then should be dried for about one month, but protected from sun and rain. This treatment doesn't harm the environment as borax is basically a salt, it only changes the smell and taste so that the bamboo does not attract insects.

Acquisition of *Bambusa vulgaris*

Nodes being punched

Borax and water being mixed and boiled

Being filled in with Borax solution from the top

The last node being punched to empty the culm

Treated bamboo being stored, protected from sun and rain

Jörg Stamm inspecting the quality of our bamboo

The production of hundreds of bamboo nails starts

A 10-day workshop led by renowned bamboo builder Jörg Stamm

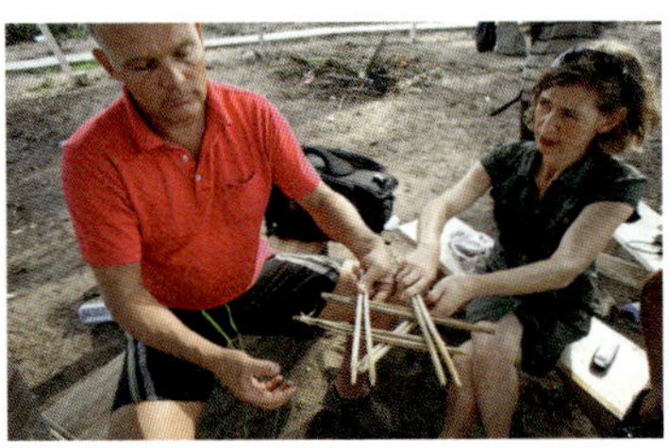

Bamboo nail bundles are treated with Borax

Evening lectures by Jörg

Set-up of the matrix for the construction of bamboo arches on ground

Selection according to diameter and curve

Learning how to build single, double, and triple arches

Preparing to move the first and biggest bamboo arch

Grouting of footpoints of arches

The arch-lifting team

FRAMEWALK EXPERIENCE

Alfred Elikem Kunutsor
Apam, May 2014

The framework within which this year's Framewalk was put was one that opens up several opportunities and rooted selves—in terms of geography, genre, and cultural and societal dynamics. This journey, as is characteristic of every Framewalk, began with very little knowledge of what would be. The ability to not know the details of what is ahead of me allows space for wonderful things to happen through the accidents, and living within, through, around, and with the moments that presents themselves. These moments are the driving force for me.

Not knowing how the indigenes of Apam would respond to us at the beach gave me something to look forward to and an experience to cherish for a long time. I engaged with sound, rhythm, and movement in ways that dramatized the core of our existence. The ocean was a wonderful backdrop against which this epic drama unfolded. It sang songs that I had never heard before. It made us move in ways that seemed common yet uncommon. The sun smiled down on us with beauty and elegance.

The interconnectivity of space and place rooted the end product of what this intercultural experience was aimed at attaining for all participants. We used different spaces for generating and creating materials for the video shoot. Translating what was created in these different spaces to a place (Apam) resulted in a new experience altogether. Within this place were historically rich spaces that had their own story to tell. We went there with ideas of our story and, together with the opportunities made available by these spaces, we told a joint story of what we are, who we are, and where we are. I believe these stories will linger on in our minds and will forge ahead with the prospects that exist in the future. I believe these prospects are bright, as was evident in my experience on the Haduwa site during the performance for the shoot. Seeing the product we managed to come up within the space gives me a voice to say *"ba ni ba ni wohw3."*[1]

1 Sheikh Mustapha Watson-Quartey (2011). "Religion of the Ga People."

ALFRED ELIKEM KUNUTSOR has a BA and MA in Dramatic Arts from the University of the Witwatersrand South Africa. Working across many disciplines, he has lectured, run workshops, and performed in a wide range of projects. He has taught Performance Studies at the University of Ghara Legon, Accra and currently teaches Creative Arts at the Tema International School.

Founded in 2009, FRAMEWALK – THE CROSSCULTURAL WEEK is based on relational, cross-cultural works in the performing arts and in the arts in general, and explores the embodiment and transformation across cultures and traditions through participation. Framewalk Apam was hosted by the Haduwa Arts and Culture Institute.

Frida, Daniel, Serge, and the GoLokals performing the bay

Clelia and Gifty creating a textile piece made from flotsam on site

Frida collecting stories in Apam

The Framewalk Apam team

Filmmaker Arne Flegstad documenting

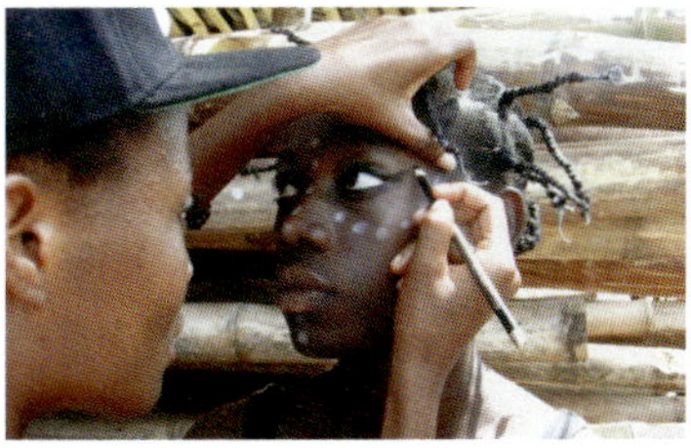

Bella and Angelica preparing to perform

Abiodun Odukoya and the Framewalk musicians

Performing the Apata under construction

The February 2014 team of students and workers

Clelia netting with a fisherman

Manora and Clelia investigating shingle techniques

Discussing the outline of the Apata and next steps

Physical models on site

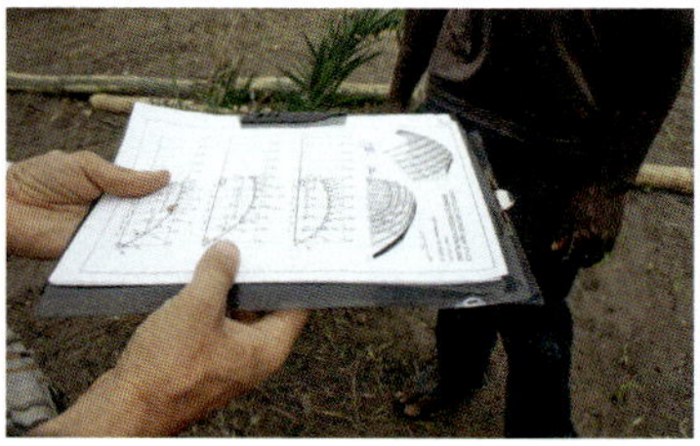

Construction drawings for 41 arches

Starting to build an arch on the matrix

Lifting the first arch in August 2014

Selecting bamboo culms with the required diameter and curvature

Connecting arch to foundation reinforcement

Elisha, Joseph, and Ilias building a triple arch

Antonella and Chrili connecting single arches together

Carrying the arch from the matrix to the structure

The inner layer of the bamboo arches is erected

Intersecting arches are joined with bamboo nails and rope

The ends of an arch are forced into position

Arches are connected with the reinforcement of the foundation

The next layer of triple arches is pulled over

Lifting up the last triple arch

Applying a third layer of arches on top

Precisely positioning a joining

Removing the supporting poles

The bamboo dome without scaffolding

Drawing the tarpaulin roof-cutting pattern

Projecting the pattern 1:1 onto the material

Drawing cutting lines

Packing the marked tarpaulin rolls

Discussing roofing details

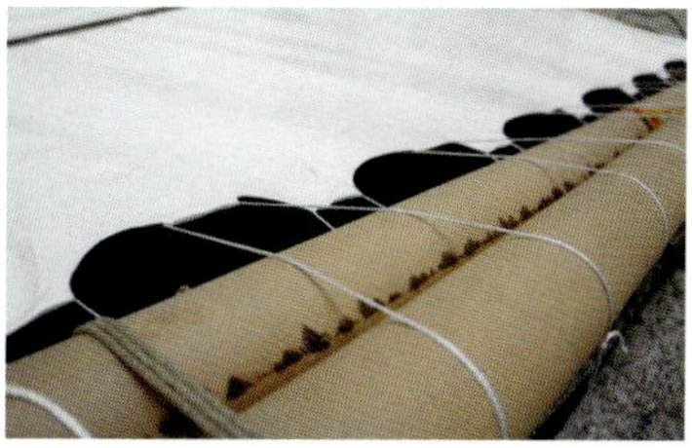

A 1:1 roofing workshop led by Christoph Kaltenbrunner

Welding tarpaulin pieces together

Franz, Baerbel, and Christoph discussing the prototype

Testing the prototype in the summer rain

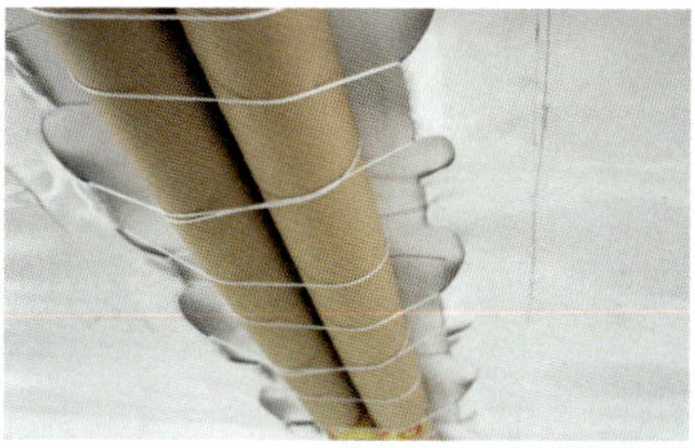

Heavy box packed with tarpaulin arrives from Austria

Unpacking

Chrili and Antonella welding pieces together

The first banners are put on the roof

On the ground, the piping is filled with split bamboo

The banners are fixed onto the primary bamboo structure with rope

Howard tightening the rope using a special knotting technique

Caps to cover the bamboo beams

Welding the caps on top of the roof

Elisha fixing the generator—almost on a daily basis

September 2012:	Start of collaboration between Haduwa and [a]FA
October 2012:	[a]FA Staging Apam starts in Vienna
November 2012:	On Body Space, workshop led by Daniel Aschwanden
	On Earth, Bamboo and Other Materials, lecture by Franz Sam
December 2012:	On Climate Design and Acoustics, lecture by Bernhard Sommer
	On Stages and Staging, lecture by Gregor Holzinger
	On Ghana's Central Region, meeting with Chris Nii Naryea Steiner
February 2013:	[a]FA Staging Apam lab I in Ghana
	On the Arts in Ghana, lecture by Kofi Setordji, Nubuke Foundation Accra
	Lab DC and [a]FA on site, workshops by Baerbel Mueller, Petra Kron, Daniel Aschwanden, Othello Johns, Abiodun Odukoya, Kojo Benedict Quaye Aka Mr Black
	Review with Mae-Ling Lokko, Sophie Alice Morley
March 2013:	Staging Space and Staging Stage: [a]FA & Lab DC, exhibition, Nubuke Foundation Accra
March 2013–January 2014:	[a]FA Staging Apam design phase
June 2013:	The Essence 2013, exhibition, Künsterhaus Vienna
June 2013:	Reviews with Andre Gheorghe, Bernhard Sommer, Daniel Aschwanden, Gregor Holzinger, Klaus Bollinger, Petra Gruber, Reiner Zettl, Reinhard Wagner
July 2013:	Presentation and review with Haduwa: Petra Kron, Mr Black in Vienna
August 2013:	Building permit, led by Gideon Djakumah, Accra
September 2013:	Review of structural model with Clemens Preisinger, Arne Hofmann/ Bollinger Grohmann Schneider Ziviltechniker GmbH
October 2013:	Bamboo 1:1, two workshops led by Franz Sam, at Firma Stelzer in Herzogenburg
	Review and lecture by Hannah Le Roux
November 2013:	On Textiles and Textile Architecture, workshop led by Manora Auersperg, Guest lecture by Serge Attukwei Clottey
December 2013:	Bamboo acquisition by Baerbel Mueller and Mr Black, Central Region Ghana
January–April 2014:	Site mobilization and construction supervision by Joseph Hofmarcher
January 2014:	[a]FA Staging Apam exhibition, Galerie Göttlicher, Stein/Krems, Austria
February 2014:	[a]FA Staging Apam lab II in Ghana
	Meetings with Ablade Glover, Serge Attukwei Cottey
	Bamboo workshop led by Jörg Stamm
	Review with Akwasi McLaren
	First arch-lifting led by Jörg Stamm
March 2014:	Performative and narrative interventions by Serge Attukwei Clottey and GoLokal, Daniel Aschwanden, Conny Zenk, Frida Robles

March–July 2014:	Think Global, Build Social!, group exhibition AzW, Vienna Interweaving lab in the Textiles department, led by Manora Auersperg and Baerbel Mueller, consultant Franz Sam [a]FA Staging Apam detailing phase, consultant Franz Sam
May 2014:	Framewalk Apam, led by Petra Kron, Mr Black, Thomas Klein, Abiodun Odukoya, Kyekyeku, Frank Fergusan Laing, Kofie Anthonio, Alfred Elikem Kunutsor, Morad Hassan
June 2014:	The Essence 2013 exhibition and [a]FA bar, Künsterhaus Vienna
July 2014:	On Tarpaulin Roofing, workshop by Christoph Kaltenbrunner
August–December 2014:	[a]FA Staging Apam lab III: construction of the Haduwa Apata
September 2014:	Prelaunch Haduwa
January 2015:	Design Acts, exhibition participation, Galerie Freihausgasse, Villach
February 2015:	Interweaving field lab, with Barbara Putz-Plecko, Baerbel Mueller and Manora Auersperg Kites & Flags, workshop with the Abrekum school, led by tex/[a]FA, hosted by Haduwa
May 2015:	Collective beach cleaning by students and performers Framewalk performance and workshop for locals and students from Apam and Abrekum
June 2015:	Interweaving, body. Space, exhibition curated by Manora Auersperg, Galerie Göttlicher Krems
September 2015:	Ehalakasa Camp Out
September 2015–February 2016:	Monthly workshops in dance, music and theater with Apam/Abrekum Secondary School, led by Jude Kurankyi, Angelika Kankam, Isabella Narh, the 2 idiots, Nan Senti Awere
October 2015:	[a]FA Helmut Richter Award / Gedächtnispreis für Innovation und kritische Neuordnung
February 2016:	Haduwa Dance Workshops Visit and documentation by photographer Julien Lanoo
May 2016:	Official visit by German Minister Franz-Josef Lerch-Mense and delegation, performance by Abrekum/Apam students and Framewalk performers
June 2016:	[a]FA Hands On exhibition participation, TU Vienna [a]FA Energy Globe National Award Ghana
October 2016:	Ehalakasa Festival

Redesigning the staging grounds on a 1:1 scale

Temporary construction of the new outline of the main stage

Discussing potential designs for windbreaking elements

Presenting to Petra Kron

Kofi Setordji and Barbara Putz-Plecko discussing textile art

Meeting with Bernard Akoi-Jackson

Manora experimenting with wind and windbreaking elements

Tanja mounting and testing a wind-breaking textile piece

A forest of poles is installed as a primary structure for textile elements

February 2014, somewhere in Apam

A lunch break on site with Petra and Arne

Abok, Nap, and Christoph—best cook, best driver, best entertainer

Howard Oduro Kojo

A birthday evening

The August 2014 team, with Stephan and Martin

Kwasi

Fuseini Abubakar aka Balumba

Thomas Philip Quasye

Philipp and Antonella

Celebrating getting the last bamboo arch up

Christoph Kaltenbrunner, aka Mr Bumbum

Stephan Guhs, leaving after weeks of work

A first dance

A last beer

Chrili, work done!

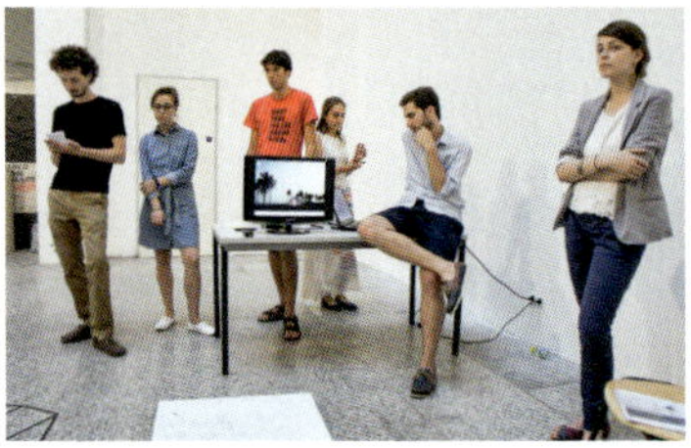

Review with architect Petra Gruber and Petra Kron / Haduwa

Review with architect Gregor Holzinger

Presenting the project to Klaus Bollinger

Opening at Galerie Göttlicher Krems-Stein, January 2014

Exhibition designer Andrea Sachse

The [a]FA bar at The Essence 2014

[a]FA on the facade of AzW

The Essence 2015, [a]FA, IoA,
curated by Studio Hani Rashid

Exhibition participation
"Think Global, Build Social!", AzW

Baerbel Mueller receives the Ars
Docendi State Award for excellence
in teaching, Vienna 2015

Award ceremony Helmut Richter
Gedächtnispreis, Vienna 2015

The proud winners

I spent a couple of months in northern Ghana after my high school graduation, just before I started to study architecture. The experience gave me a new perspective on what's important in life and nearly six years later, I got the opportunity to return to this joyful and energetic country once again as a new chapter of my life was just unfolding.

After our time together in Apam, I had the chance to work on the design of our exhibition at the Nubuke Foundation in Accra. Since I was used to realizing my 3D models and concepts with 3D printers and laser and milling machines, I had to meet whole new challenges, such as bargaining with the taxi driver about transporting 20 bamboo trunks on his roof. This project was not only a great addition to my CV, but also a great selling point in my first job interview. Unfortunately, from that moment on, time and distance made it difficult to continue working on the Haduwa project. Only in January 2014 was I invited to stay in Vienna/Krems for an intense session of designing and realizing the [a]FA exhibition at Galerie Göttlicher, which showed what we had accomplished and what may follow. And now? Dreaming about some Jollof rice on the beach of Apam.

Andrea Sachse
born in Cologne in 1986, studied architecture at the Alanus University of Arts and Social Sciences and at the University of Applied Arts Vienna. Since 2013, she has been working back in her hometown as an architect.

ghana/touching ground

2012—red rusty soil, dirty roads, red dust raised by every step- Ghana, Northern Region, Guabuliga. Researching the architecture of African markets beforehand, our main focus was initially put on roofing systems. By going local with a small interdisciplinary group of students, I was introduced to rural African culture, rich in tradition and rituals. Vernacular techniques in making use of ground with sand, clay, and cement, aroused my personal interest and have been adapted to develop a market stand proposal for the marketplace of the village.

2013—going deeper during a workshop on the potential of local material—clay and bamboo constructions held by specialist Anna Heringer in France.

2014—rich soil merges into poor sand at the beach, grounded by the Atlantic Ocean, Apam, Central Region. Becoming a member of a new [a]FA team, now working on the foundations of the Haduwa Arts and Culture Institute. Concrete foundations supporting a unique symbiosis of a bamboo arch construction roofed with a white membrane.

2015—touching ground again in Apam, a floorscape has been designed to provide a variety of performance situations. Surfaces of concrete, compressed sand, and wooden textures have been shaped. Working with textile experts on textile interventions, a sense for interweaving between roof and ground has been developed.

Implementing projects at full scale within foreign cultures was most enriching for my personal and architectural progress. Working within an interdisciplinary team of landscape designers, environmental experts, performers, and architects influenced by local culture and craft, motivated me to constantly reevaluate habitual thought patterns. I am now capable of critically questioning foreign architectural developments and I am interested in working on spatial interventions on international ground.

Antonella Amesberger
born in Kirchdorf/Upper Austria in 1991, studies architecture at the University of Technology in Vienna, joined [a]FA at University of Applied Arts in 2012. Currently in a joint MA program, she will graduate from the University of Technology Vienna and Tongji University Shanghai.

See page 100
Chrili Car

What I learned in Ghana was an amazing sense of individual action, its very sophisticated layering and improvisation, and flexibility in everyday problem-solving; variations of formal and informal, how elements coexist and feed each other while developing an urban tissue that works so differently from those of Western patterns, which we tend to idealize and refer to. Being part of the [a]FA staging apam lab introduced me to an extremely rich, creative environment and the new design wave emerging on the African

continent. Being fascinated by the way of living, thinking, and creating that I experienced there inspired me and gave me the amazing chance to further develop my interests in Africa. I have visited Ghana twice as a part of the lab, the third time I went there I worked on projects in Ghana and Nigeria for David Adjaye Associates in Accra.

Ewa Lenart
born in Poland in 1991. In 2010, started the Diploma Architecture Program with Wolf D. Prix at the University of Applied Arts Vienna. Graduating in January 2016 under Hani Rashid at the same institution. Studied at the Southern California Institute of Architecture (Sci-Arc) in 2014.

In my working practice as a creative researcher and text-based artist, I focus on the construction of the self, analyzing personal memories and stories. Going to Africa had been a personal dream since I was a child, coming from Mexico, it sometimes felt like a distant one. As part of [a]FA, I went to the Democratic Republic of Congo, and to Ghana.

During both projects, I dedicated myself to the search for local stories and personal takes on water, and on notions of belonging. I enrolled in the course "African Poetry", led by Professor Adams Bodomo at the University of Vienna, as part of a desire to continue understanding this interesting discourse on written and oral language. I am particularly interested in the Négritude movement due to its connections between poetry, politics, and identity.

Frida Robles
born in Mexico City in 1985, studied history and communications (BA) at the Iberoamericana University, and social design (MA) at the University of Applied Arts in Vienna. She recently concluded her first editorial project at Lab for the City, Mexico City's urban lab.

During my studies, I developed an interest in transdisciplinarity and in sustainable materials, which led me to the [a]FA lab. In my two-year-long involvement in the staging apam project, I participated in its research, design, and building phases. This unique, holistic experience broadened my world view of the collective nature of architecture and its power to bridge cultures and people.

Ilias Klis
born in Athens in 1989, studied architecture (BA) at the Bauhaus University Weimar, and received his masters degree from the University of Applied Arts Vienna in the Studio of Greg Lynn.

See page 100
Ioana Petkova

There is something about throwing yourself willingly into an environment that is unfamiliar, meeting other cultures, and feeling their soil under your feel. One of the project's objectives is to challenge the unfamiliar, to assess an intrinsic value in architecture not only from an artistic perspective, but to create a building that corresponds with the context of its surroundings on a very porous and human scale, and that has deep epistemological implications. There is an intimate connection between the stage of Haduwa and everything surrounding it. Unlike art, architecture allows one to in-habit, creates new forms of social engagement, and offers grounds for debate on current production, opening an arena for change in terms of social anticipation. Apart from the technical feasibility of the structure, it was important to understand the holistic conditions of the art made in Africa, where the question of sensibility is connected with the physical experience. What we intended to achieve with our project was to understand the connections between all these senses, the complexities of the human needs, and to create a sort of enchantment that triggers new experiences and has the potential to be re-discovered. We all long for where we have never been.

Joana Lazarova
studied architecture at the Vienna University of Technology and joined [applied] foreign affairs in 2012. She is a fellow at Domaine de Boisbuchet and currently lives and works in Paris.

Through the course of the [a]FA labs, I stayed in Ghana several times; in Guabuliga in 2012, twice in Apam in 2013 and 2014. During these stays, what intrigued me the most in the field of architectural practice were my experiences with developments of details that dealt with material in a state of rapid decay caused by the environmental conditions of the Saharan savanna and the tropical coast of West Africa. It was also a cornerstone in my

experience to be confronted with the academic postcolonial discourse and the realities of West African life, practice, and architecture in situ.

Through the project "Guabuliga—Well by the Thorn Tree" in 2012, I gained ample insight into rural development in northern Ghana. The discourse around our project work questioned rural housing and community setups in a spatial sense. In comparison, I could see and study masterpieces of tropical modernism all over Ghana - buildings of the last century which seemingly function up until today.

Through the design build project "[a]FA staging Apam" in 2013-2014, I got the chance to gain knowledge in bamboo construction, and the implication of a cultural building as an urban satellite in a rural context. Furthermore, I gained experience in working on site with local people and under the extreme climatic conditions there.

In alignment with the "Apam Stage" program, I located my thesis project in Accra and chose a similar topic, only in a larger urban context. As an institute for performing arts with different stages, "The Venue—A Building without Boundaries" had the ambition to be permeable in both a climatic and a public sense.

Travelling between Accra, Apam, and the rural areas of Ghana, I made a lot of friends. All those experiences clearly left traces on my professional and personal life; I'm keeping in touch with Ghana for possible future projects and for a further understanding of the relationship between Africa and the Western world, between Ghana and Europe.

Joseph Hofmarcher born in Austria in 1982, studied architecture (mag.arch.) at Studio Lynn at the University of Applied Arts Vienna. Since the summer of 2013, he has been working as an independent artist and architect in the Eisenstraße region of Lower Austria.

Being an *Obruni* for the first time, which became irrelevant while watching Champions League. The immense satisfaction after lifting an arch, followed by my craving for delicious *Jiboom* sandwiches. The sweet taste of a "club" after a day of work, just like that of a *Kokroko* at the Republic in Osu, Accra. Holding my breath while wading through the lagoon in Apam. Sun screen and dirt mixed on my white skin. Your dazzled faces after still saying "kyena" in Vienna. Junctions buzzing with *trotros* and their mates' hectic calls. Smoothly recovering at Akwasi's paradisiacal escape. The loftiness while surfing my first small wave, or while standing on the bamboo structure, eight meters above the ground. The confusion after the concept of bribery suddenly became something concrete. The slight numbness after scarfing Apok's spicy food. Being given a proper shake in the taxi's trunk while conquering dirt roads. Thunderstruck at the sight of my first cockroach. Waiting in Ghanaian time. Cycling along the beach. Mr. Bum Bum's encouraging cheers. Joyfully anticipating messages from Vienna. The [a]FA gang. So many images, occurrences, and stories I will never forget. When people ask me how it was in Ghana, I simply don't know where to start.

Philipp Reinsberg was educated at the University of Applied Arts Vienna in the Studios of Wolf D. Prix, Fiona Raby, and Hani Rashid. Prior to studying architecture, he was trained as a carpenter in southern Germany.

Through the collaboration between [a]FA and the textile class of the University of Applied Arts, I had the opportunity to travel to Ghana, Apam to do research on local textile materials and techniques. The focus was on what kinds of material are available locally and regionally, and how to potentially include the local population in a designing and/or producing process.

Among many other personal experiences, the most sustainable one for my ongoing work with children/pupils was co-directing a workshop that we did together with two classes from the nearby school in Abrekum. The task for the pupils was to explore the wind on site, which was also something we had focused on during our design process during that particular semester.

I experienced a lot of spontaneous exchanges between myself and the local people, which gave me a better understanding of their situation. I also found myself confronted with postcolonial issues, which allowed me to develop an even greater sensitivity to this topic than I had before. I really appreciate all these exchanges of ideas, interests, and working processes with all the people I worked with throughout this project, including the [a]FA students of architecture as well as local people. I am also grateful that I could get to know

the artists Kojo Benedict Quaye (Mr. Black), Kofi Setordji, and Bernard Akoi-Jackson.

What I take away with me from this journey is how nurturing it is for all participants to enter into a real dialogue and to exchange ideas.

Tanja Happel
born in Vienna, Austria in 1981; studies art education (Textiles and Design, Environment and Architecture) at the University of Applied Arts Vienna.

STAGING APAM

Schedule labs: November 2013 – July 2015

Lab head: Baerbel Mueller

Project partner/client: Haduwa Arts and Culture Institute / Bernhard Akoi-Jackson, Kojo Benedict Quaye aka Sir Black, Petra Kron

Academic partners:
School of Performing Arts, University of Ghana, Legon, Accra, Lab DC / Petra Kron

Institute of Art Sciences Vienna and Art Education, University of Applied Arts / Barbara Putz-Plecko, Daniel Aschwanden, Christoph Kaltenbrunner, Manora Auersperg

[a]FA team design and realization: Christian Car, Ewa Lenart, Ilias Klis, Ioana Petkova, Joana Lazarova, Joseph Hofmarcher, Philipp Reinsberg, with Andrea Sachse, Antonella Amesberger, Frida Robles, Juergen Strohmayer and Stephan Guhs

Lab DC team: Abena Danso Dansoa, Abigail Teiko, Ancilla Avevor, Angelica Kankam, Bella Obiago, Benjamin Nii Amu Solomon, Comfort Chana, Edem Kunkpe, Edwin Brown, Elijah Twum, Elsie Atiase, Emmanuel Bediako, Eric Awere, Frank Baala, Frederick Amoako, Isabella Narh, Jude Kurankye, Kathlyn Addo, Laura Thompson, Michael Ayensu, Nii Quaye Aryee, Vida Kwetso and Wisdom Abutiate

TEX team: Afra Klirchdorfer, Clelia Baumgartner, Julia Galimova, Mave Venturin, Sandra Bamminger, Sarah Steiner and Tanja Happel

Construction team: Christian Oko Adje, Elisha Ehuron, Fuseini Abubakar aka Balumba, Howard Oduro Kojo, Kofi Amissoh, Kwasi aka Tonga, Thomas Philip Quasye with Francis Andoh and Francis Andoh

Workshops: Abiodun Odukoya, Barbara Putz-Plecko, Baerbel Mueller, Christoph Kaltenbrunner, Daniel Aschwanden, Franz Sam, Jörg Stamm, Kojo Benedict Quaye aka Mr Black, Manora Auersperg, Othello Johns, Petra Kron

Lab reviews: Akwasi McLaren, Andre Gheorghe, Bernard Akoi-Jackson, Bernhard Sommer, Gregor Holzinger, Hannah Le Roux, Klaus Bollinger, Mae-Ling Lokko, Petra Gruber, Reiner Zettl, Sophie Alice Morley

Additional lectures and meetings: Arne Hofmann, Ablade Glover, Clemens Preisinger, Chris Nii Naryea Steiner, Kingsley Kwame Safo, Kofi Setordji, Martin C. Hess, Reinhard Wagner, Robert Vierlinger, Serge Attukwei Clottey

Consultant bamboo: Jörg Stamm

Consultant construction: Franz Sam

Consultant structural engineering: Bollinger+Grohmann

Consultant building permit: 3+3 Studio Accra/ Gideon Djakumah

Financial support: Haduwa Arts and Culture Institute; Institute of Architecture, University of Applied Arts Vienna; Engagement Global and the Regional Government of North Rhine Westphalia; German Embassy Accra

Exhibitions: Staging Space and Staging Stage: [a]FA & lab DC, Nubuke Foundation Accra; The Essence 2013, Künstlerhaus Vienna; [a]FA Staging Apam exhibition, Galerie Göttlicher, Stein-Krems, Austria; Think Global, Build Social!, AzW Vienna; The Essence and the essence bar 2014, Künstlerhaus Vienna; Design Acts—exhibition participation, Galerie Freihausgasse, Villach, Austria; Hands On TU Vienna

Conferences: AZA 2016 Conference, Johannesburg 2016

Awards: National Energy Globe Award: Ghana 2015, Helmut Richter Award / Gedächtnispreis für Innovation und kritische Neuordnung

Photos:
Julien Lanoo: 289, 290, 292, 293, 294, 296, 297, 302

Agnes Achleitner: 271
Ars Docendi: 271
Andrea Sachse: 280
Antonella Amesberger: 269
Baerbel Mueller: 170, 171, 172, 173, 206, 207, 228, 235, 236, 237, 239, 240, 241, 243, 245, 246, 247, 248, 250, 251, 252, 255, 257, 258, 259, 260, 261, 262, 263, 266, 267,268, 269, 270, 271, 284
Chrili Car: 196, 198, 236, 243, 244, 251, 253, 259, 262, 263, 270
Christoph Kaltenbrunner: 257, 268, 269
Clelia Baumgartner: 223, 224, 225, 246, 247, 248
Crable Art: 299
Daniel Aschwanden: 170, 171, 172, 173, 178, 179, 180, 181, 221, 236, 238, 239, 240, 241, 242, 249, 252, 253, 255,256, 259, 281, 287
Ewa Lenart: 206, 207, 243
Franz Sam: 244
Gideon Djakumah: 269
Haduwa: 248, 255
Joseph Hofmarcher: 242, 248, 268
Juergen Strohmayer: 235
Manora Auersperg: 235, 256, 267
Markus Krottendorfer: 229
Martin C. Hess: 248, 259, 262, 263, 284, 285, 269, 270, 271
Philipp Reinsberg: 160, 171, 173, 215, 238, 239, 240, 241, 268, 269

Special thanks to: Arne Flekstad, Barbara Putz-Plecko, Chief Nana Edu Effrim X, Dr Awo Mana Asiedu, Ehalakasa Festival / Sir Black, Framewalk / Petra Kron, Firma Stelzer Herzogenburg, Heurigen Sulzer, Mark Sackeyfio, Michael Owu aka Nab, Mildred Abokuma, Moses Denyo, Nii Owure, Prince Amoabeng, Wild Gecko / Kingsley Safo, Poem van Landewijk

STAGING APAM, NUBUKE FOUNDATION, ACCRA

February 2013

This exhibition presented the outcome of the transdisciplinary workshop of [a]FA and the Lab DC on staging in the broadest sense: being on stage and working on stage, staging a space and designing a stage.

"A frame: communicates between inside and outside. Demarcates the creation from its surroundings. Communicates between the spectator and the framed piece."

This five-part exhibition looked at the different STAGES that were investigated, imagined, and outlined during the lab. From LEGON/culture, which was our starting point and reference stage, to TERRAIN/environment, BEACH/body, APAM/urban space, to the FUTURE/vision. It presented individual projects along with documentations of the work process such as films, interviews, and statements about the overall topic of staging.

By walking around the exhibition, you were translocated to the Haduwa site, standing in front of the 8 x 4.5 m frame that was set up there, now filled with the team's experiences, observing the terrain in the back and the beach in front, listening to the soundscapes of the site. Towards the far northeast was the city of Apam along with the horizon. Eventually, the exhibition became a stage itself, not only for our work but also for the performed songs and spoken words that were created on site by our artist collaborators, the Lab DC, expressing the desire and need for a stage in Apam.

Exhibition concept and design: Andrea Sachse
Curators: Daniel Aschwanden, Baerbel Mueller
Participants: [a]FA and Lab DC

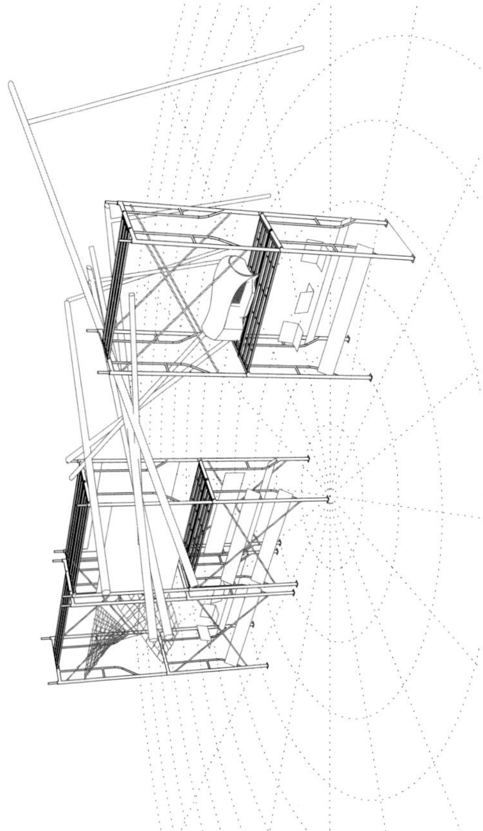

Top view and perspective of the exhibition design
and its positioning

0° 10° 20° 30°

40° 50° 60° 70°

80° 90° 100° 110°

STAGING APAM, GALERIE GÖTTLICHER

Krems-Stein, January 2014

Shortly after the bamboo harvest was commissioned locally, while foundation works were just beginning on site, and two weeks before the remaining team was about for leave to Ghana again, their work in progress was exhibited at Galerie Göttlicher in Krems-Stein.

The exhibition focused on ongoing investigations of structure, material, and program, and how these architectonic elements could be manipulated in order to redefine stage design. In exploring the symbolic language of staging as well, the exhibition contemplated the work in progress visually and formally. Recorded conversations, documented workshops, and construction drawings were shown on several clusters of screens. Physical models of the bamboo dome were staged in the exhibition space.

The gallery itself was transformed into an extensive installation. The geometry of the bamboo dome was inscribed into it on a 1:2 scale, thereby allowing the void spaces of the bamboo grid-shell to materialize.

Installation concept and exhibition design: Andrea Sachse
Curatorial team: Ewa Lenart, Baerbel Mueller,
Joana Lazarova, Ioana Petkova
Opening speeches: Barbara Putz-Plecko, Helga Göttlicher,
Baerbel Mueller, Franz Sam

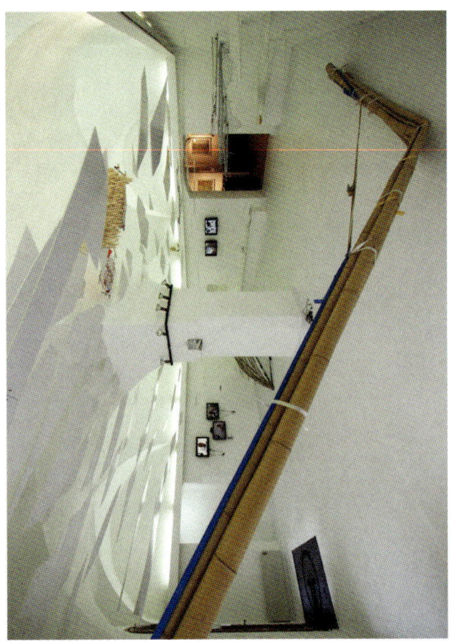

PRELAUNCH OF THE HADUWA STAGE

September 26, 2014

HADUWA ARTS & CULTURE INSTITUTE is a meeting ground for artists and cultural practitioners in Africa and Europe to support excellence and diversity in and through the arts. Haduwa promotes understanding and enhances active local and international collaborations.

The [a]FA LAB of the Institute of Architecture at the University of Applied Arts Vienna, together with the Lab DC, Accra, have been investigating stages and stagings. The aim has been to conceptualize and design a stage for the future initiatives of *Haduwa*. A unique bamboo structure, which serves as shared space, landmark and stage has been built by the [a]FA team, together with international and local experts and workers.

Opening speeches: Petra Kron, Nana Effrim X, Baerbel Mueller
MCs: Dr So and General Nta Tea
Performing artists: Bella Narh and Bella Obiago, GoLokals with Daniel Aschwanden and Conny Zenk, Jude Kurankyi Company, Kyekyeku, Rainers, Nana Senti Awere, Nana Tshito, Reginald Dodoo, Ronaldo Ernest Opoku

APAM APATA: THE DANCING BAMBOO THEATRE

Kwasi Ohene-Ayeh

Walk through Apam Mpoano, past the exhibition of brightly colored, immobile canoes uniquely identified with tall flags and phrases written large on either sides—phrases addressing philosophy, politics, and God, as well as a cosmopolitan aesthetic of national and European football team flags—and see in the distance, about a kilometer and a half away, the iconic bamboo structure through the busy cluster of coconut trees lining the shore of that portion of the Atlantic Ocean.

The structure, appropriating the form of a seashell, is defined by an arch with three open sides that sit firmly in concrete. Bamboo members loop to form its outer 'radial ribs'. The roof is a rhythmic crisscross of bamboo logs fastened and held firmly together with bamboo nails and rope. White tarpaulin is used as the protective membrane on top of the bamboo members, offering the only form of closure to the structure.

This minimalist architectural landmark provides an intimate dialogue with the Atlantic Ocean and will be a space where cultural moments are produced, moments made meaningful by the space's multifunctional intent. Not only will there be psychic meaning-making occurring through conversations, negotiations, and collaborations, but the physical relational element will also deepen the exchanges taking place within this space. The interactions between producer, performer, space, audience, and immediate environment will infuse the structure with life—certainly what a performance arena needs. The iconic structure acts as a symbolic connection between Apam, Abrekum, and the rest of Ghana. More externally, it beams with the potential of becoming a hub for intercultural creative exchanges.

How would contemporary visual artists engage this arena with its inherent possibilities? Conceptually, what it offers is a fervently active space that is always in the process of making or being made. It is the environment and the artwork; the space and the event. It also fosters collaboration between artists practicing within various disciplines and creates a location within which to constantly (re-)think and question existing ways of making. Artists interested in optimizing its potentiality can engage the aforementioned as entry points into a critique of practice, exploration, and discovery, and channel them into the production of new ideas.

KWASI OHENE-AYEH lives and works in Ghana. He received his BFA degree in painting from Kwame Nkrumah University of Science and Technology Ghana in 2009. Using installation, performance, and site-specific and socially engaged projects, Ohene-Ayeh explores ambiguities in Accra's urban contemporary identity.

0244270319
NYAME
NTSI

DANCING THE APATA

Jude Arnold Kuranky
September 2015

The experience I have as a contemporary dance artist with a site, and in relation to the [a]FA project, is really interesting; it opens my mind up to a wider scope of the performance arts. It makes my creativity less narrow than before. You have a direct feeling of a building that has connection to the art that you do. For me it's amazing that, for instance, if you look at the pattern of the whole Haduwa building and the kind of energy and beauty that it gives to you, you really feel that it gives you nothing but beauty. You need to do something beautiful to complement the building, the building would not let you give you something not up to par, you know. It gives you positive energy, it gives you the good vibes to be able to create something good. So, I think the work that Baerbel did with the [a]FA students has actually brought me to a different level of my artistic vision. And I think that was really good.

As a performing artist, a contemporary dance artist, who now has a site to do workshops, I think that is a very good thing for me. Usually you would have the art, you have the creativity, you have things to do, but the venue where you have to do it is a problem. Where to do it is a problem. So getting a site of my own gives me the opportunity to create much more. It gives me the opportunity to collaborate with other people, to bring lots of people here. It really gives me a very good vibe. And this place is also like home.

In Ghanaian language we call it *Apata*. *Apata* is a place where people stay underneath, relax and eat and drink and sing, and talk to each other and play, do stuff. This place actually gives me all the avenues to creating! Creating traditionally, creating contemporary, creating modern stuff. I must say I am fortunate; not all artists have a place of their own. You can do anything here: music, drama, dance, place, chat with friends, you get the breeze from the ocean. So it is really magical for me. I think that this place is like nowhere else, I can't compare it to anywhere else. It makes you complete. You feel good, you feel safe, you feel secure, you feel relaxed, and you are able to jump into the ocean anytime you want. So it is really a good thing to have such a place of my own.

One thing is very important: this particular place combines the two villages, because it is situated right in the middle of them. It is giving them the positive energy that they had lost for a long time, because young artists from Apam and Abrekum have the opportunity to come and do stuff here. And for me, subconsciously, it's building their bond with each other, it makes them forget that they had an ancient conflict, it's building them up together. And that is good for the future, to let them forget their ancestral war, their ancestral conflict. This is a new era. We need unity, we need to come together to build something ahead of us. It brings them together, we will not have two separate villages fighting each other, it brings them together – two strong villages coming together under the roof, under the Apata. It is really a good thing that [a]FA opted to do that for Haduwa. And I love it! A big thank you to Baerbel and to Petra for teaming up. It is really a good thing for me, for the two villages, and for Ghana as a whole.

JUDE ARNOLD KURANKYI, born and bred in Ghana, acquired his education in contemporary dance from the University of Ghana, School of Performing Arts. Participated in dance workshops and festivals such as Framewalk in Germany/Ghana, ImpulsTanz Dance Festival Vienna, MASA International Festival, Lab DC. Collaborations with Kabawil Dusseldorf and Cie Joseph Aka in France.

Dancing the Apata
Jude Arnold Kurankyi: concept, performer
Crable Art: concept, video
Moses Denyo: percussion

MULTI-LAYERED AND NON-LINEAR

A Conversation between
Daniel Aschwanden and Neville Mars

DA: It seems to be a time of a blurring of frontiers between different media, and I tend to choose hybrid formats in order to command situations in the art field as well as in the urban field. Performance and architecture, or performance and urban development are per se areas of blurred boundaries. I feel the city, the urban, is always performing itself. How can performance as an art medium and architecture, or urban development, develop interesting ways of influencing each other?

NM: What's exciting about these times is that everything is urban: the urban condition is all around us and is constantly expanding, so the challenge is to figure out what you can do with that new urban space. It's getting crowded, it's getting complex and dense and challenging for people living in a city. What performers can do is explore these new conditions, these new spatial conditions, and reveal how you can experience these spaces, interact with these spaces, how you can appropriate them, how these new and not always streamlined environments can offer new qualities, offer opportunities, provide a platform for creativity.

DA: The situation is already highly complex in the field of art, but once you put into consideration the site specificity, the location where you produce art, suddenly there is a queerness of formats which escapes many ways of linear thinking. In a certain way, it is asking for non-linearity in terms of relating to things and trying to put things together in another way.

NM: Yes, art tries to explore boundaries. It can reveal how space changes over time simply by the presence of an artist, by interacting with new media, by engaging with communities, by having local communities engage with their environment in an entirely new way. You call it multi-layered?

DA: Multi-layered and non-linear.

NM: We like to think in the same way when we design. It is not about the static end result, it's about the process. It's about the very first moment of conception up to the point of realization and beyond, how you can have a life cycle in a project, have a lasting impact on a place and on a community. I think good examples of artists revealing this non-linear and multi-layered dimension are few. The most obvious are performances that engage with new media. More exciting is when things happen in different places at the same time, maybe a performance appears at the same time in Beijing and Shanghai or in London and Brazil and there is some sort of correlation. Or more complex is when performances leave a trace, so they occur over a longer period of time, simply by changing the environment and leaving a lasting impact.

DA: Performance is set up to be ephemeral. And that's one way it's different from architecture. Performance leaves a trace mainly in people's memories and not in three-dimensional space/time as something that you can touch, that you can walk on, or that you can go in.

NM: Maybe the next step is really where art becomes proactive in forcing architecture to be less static, maybe the buildings we can do are truly dynamic. You cannot just alter them, but you can influence them in a more profound way—how they are used, how they are perceived. So the artist has an influence that I guess architects are looking for and are increasingly losing.

DA: What would you call a radical position in art and in architecture or urbanism? There is always a striving for a radical and clear position, but it has often become just a pose.

NM: I think nowadays radical seems to be more understated, more under the radar, more localized. The world is being infiltrated by big art in big venues in festivals and biennials. The more radical projects seem to be the ones that sort of dig deep into local communities and engage with locals on a much more personal level.

DA: There is a new relation between locality and globality which is actually very challenging. What does it mean to live up to these networked societies we are living in—based on data-fication, on digital connections—and to the very local viewpoints of people, to local sides of life and also of art. How to integrate, also keeping in mind that the frame work of urbanization has a global scale.

NM: I agree it is a global issue, maybe not so much in a way that we like to think of. Urbanization is following similar trends across the globe, which means that we should consider solutions that could be discovered anywhere on the planet and try them elsewhere as a sort of a recycling of innovation, a recycling of knowledge which is not happening because there is this weird angst that we have to be local, we have to be localized in the sense that you can't copy solutions that work in Brazil and apply them to Beijing. The truth is, you definitely can't copy them one to one. But you can probably copy the logic behind them, and adapt it to local conditions and apply it elsewhere and see what happens. So I am actually trying to be a bit more flexible in this whole local-global debate. I try to cross-read, mix and match. It is this superposition, juxtapositions that seem to prove and reveal most of the local condition. It's through the contrast that you can see what is locally valid and valuable.

DA: There is quite a booming buzzword that comes from the design area: "social design". It links to what you said before, the social and design. You did projects in Mumbai which are for me part of an attitude towards finding location-based solutions, but still I feel a bit uneasy about this buzz. What could be the criteria?

NM: It is difficult. If you take the Mumbai example, one of the challenges we had there was that I was invited to come up with a community-oriented urban solution for slums and other sort of fringe communities. But it was funded by exactly the opposite kind of society, mainly the fine arts, big money from that sort of ivory-tower art scene. These two worlds do not mix and match. They are colliding at best. Most likely they are not even touching, which is exactly what happened. The curators involved weren't too keen on entering the communities I was dealing with. So I spent nine months in Mumbai and a lot of time in the local slums, but the people who were supposed to okay the project were not interested.

DA: Looking at this project in Ghana, have you got impressions about that? There were students of architecture design and it was using local resources for materials as well as human resources, and it was creating a certain queerness in the design process. It wouldn't go this straightforward way of, let's just use natural materials, the shell, the cover was made from PVC, it would be actually a very rough constellation of natural bamboo and this plastic. And it would be an example of trying to make a transition or to fuse a certain way of dealing with space, dealing with a situation, dealing with a certain type of knowledge—with local knowledge.

NM: That is exactly the important point. How do you combine a larger macro-perspective of global knowledge, of global experience, and infuse that with local knowledge? That's a very challenging process. On the one hand, it could go wrong because you are not willing or able to adapt quickly enough, you are basically too used to local practices, which often are extremely well-informed about the challenges and the tools they have available, about the way to do things cheaply and efficiently and with a local aesthetic. And sometimes you have a good solution that you know can solve a local problem, but local practices simply don't allow for any new intervention. It can be extremely challenging. But this is where I believe real opportunities lie. This cross-breeding, mixing and matching of different cultural visions and ecologies of solutions.

DANIEL ASCHWANDEN is a Vienna-based performer, choreographer, and curator who creates hybrid interventions in urban contexts. He teaches at the University of Applied Arts Vienna.

NEVILLE MARS is the principal of MARS Architects in Shanghai, a sustainable planning and architecture studio. Mars is also the director of the Dynamic City Foundation, an interdisciplinary research platform that is investigating rapid urbanization in China.

FINDING A PLACE IN THE SUN

A Conversation between
Mae-ling Lokko and Akwasi McLaren

ML: I just finished rereading *A Place in the Sun* by the Indian architect Charles Correa. He begins by asking architects in India to take a chance on their imagination by "lifting themselves out of the freezing European weather into a faraway climate, into another state of mind and ambiance where warm and languid breezes blow". For me, occupying *A Place in the Sun* has been about growth through internalizing what is of value around us in the present. In conversation with clients and architects here in Ghana, one gets the feeling that their minds are elsewhere, in another climate and context. Does that type of frame of mind resonate with you, especially as you began to build Escape-3points?[1]

AM: *A Place in the Su*n has been my preferred circumstance for design since the beginning. Escape3points has been a great opportunity to explore how to create comfortable shelter while facing the harshest conditions from the sun and the wind, but also opening everything up to welcome nature in. It's a continual experiential study in which you are playing with balancing the raw primal elements of nature in indoor and outdoor spaces.

ML: I find that, in the tropics, our understanding of indoor and outdoor space isn't so much a harsh delineation between indoor and outdoor boundaries, but a series of spaces that gradually temper the inhabitant in unique ways that allow one's body to adjust to one's harsh climate. In Ghana, the socialization of this can be seen in the way we spend various quantities of time in verandahs and peri-envelope spaces whether they are outdoor cooking or compound spaces. I feel that that sensibility of 'space-tempering', which is so tightly woven with our social practices, is often lost in what we are building today and consequently, our new spaces are setting up new types of social dynamics and valuation of our appreciation for our natural environment.

AM: Yes, unfortunately, it seems that those intermediate spaces had been lost for some time when meeting places under trees or compound houses were replaced by English-style houses that were not designed for the tropics. As the reasons for this 'space-tempering' were not understood, reviving ancient knowledge back into modern design without bringing the idea that we are stepping backwards into 'village style' is necessary. In this way, these valuable spaces can be appreciated with a Sankofa[2] sentiment.

ML: I guess the 'freedom' to build creatively is as much a deeply psychological one as it is an economical one. Do you think that the cultural trappings of what the Ghanaians have been educated to desire have become the major barrier to the emergence of local innovation, or is it really the harsh economic barriers that exist today?

AK: The limitations on the freedom to build here can in some ways be attributed to economic barriers in terms of the fact that those designing must be able to sustain themselves and therefore, more often than not, they follow conventional design. Clients are not well-informed about alternative methods of construction. So it is also a matter of lack of exposure. We also face negative stigmas that claim that local materials are not modern but inferior, as they are the same materials our forefathers used.

ML: The issue of the stigma around local or low-tech material technologies like bamboo and natural fibers is one I am grappling with in my work that involves upcycling coconut husks. We have spent the past few years developing some high-performance systems made from locally available agricultural waste, but the biggest hurdle is essentially a cultural value system that frowns upon some aspects of it. On the surface, one may say this is a matter of taste and due to a propensity for Ghanaians to want something 'modern'. But dissecting this further has led us to believe that the historic role of local, natural material systems are deeply entrenched in a culture of maintenance and vulnerability, and that, more importantly, occupants' expectations of performance have drastically changed. We want to experience comfort instantly, whether it is thermal, acoustic, or olfactory, and we want it delivered spatially. I think there are ways that culturally situated design, a term coined by my mentor Ron Eglash, can usher in a new

value system. For instance, due to our largely import-based building economy, the building owner in Ghana is not used to technologies made for him/her as the target consumer. I don't mean that in a literal sense, that no one is listening to the wants and desires of the Ghanaian building owner client, but rather that we are embedded within a material culture and technology market that has not evolved with the developing context in mind. So what we want and imagine ourselves building, from the materials we use down to the air conditioning systems we operate, are very much rooted elsewhere, we have never truly been the subject and designer of our own contexts.

AK: I agree completely. The use of local materials has many issues in terms of lacking durability and requiring more maintenance, but that's exactly where the design aspect comes in. A synergy must be formed, combining local and imported 'ideas' to solve these issues. Simply importing quick-fix solutions only creates a new, different set of problems to overcome. We should have faith in locally made products.

ML: Does the lack of creativity and innovation we see in the materials market prevent us from realizing economic potential?

AK: I think our creativity is directly limited by requests for materials that are thought to be good because they have built examples. By building well-designed examples with other materials, people can better understand their options for using different materials that could be more economically viable as well as less detrimental to the environment.

ML: I think that with the ability of Ghanaians to travel more freely, the exposure to other places is changing our ideas of how and what to build, for better or worse. I found some really inspiring examples from tropical modernism—but not because of the rationalism that was justified by the environmental principles of design, since those are incredibly exemplary in that regard. For me, buildings like the old National Science Museum building in Accra, which is lying dormant and being allowed to deteriorate, symbolize a period of experimentation in which someone was looking at us with a keen interest, figuring out what was appropriate and acceptable here. I'm not saying that they didn't impose modern design principles, but they did not divorce themselves from the context—whether it was social, historical, or environmental. That's the beauty of what happened with Modernist architecture in West Africa. And when we see young African architects engage with world-renowned architects from Europe in that era, we see their ability to bring a fresh and innovative approach to design, rooted in ideas of beauty and function that are uniquely original. For you, what projects really get to the heart of material experimentation?

AM: Jörg Stamm's bamboo bridges in Colombia, which traverse huge spans for pedestrians and even cars and that would normally be built from steel, ignites something within me. His way of sharing knowledge instead of withholding the tricks of how to work with bamboo allows others to continue to push the limits in order to discover even more ways of using it. Others, including the Ibuku team and Elora Hardy in the Green Village in Bali, show that the limits of bamboo are only those of your own imagination.

ML: Those are great examples. Somewhere closer to home is the work of Koffi and Diabaté in Ivory Coast and Kengo Kuma in Japan, which has always been an inspiration to me. The language with which they deploy materials instills an unparalleled sense of integrity that is both local and universal. What has the ability to work with and experiment with local materials meant for you?

AK: Being able to work with local materials continues to inspire me to learn more about examples that can be found around the world. I am inspired to build more and share my knowledge so that others can realize the potential of what we already have at hand, if used wisely.

ML: If we were to characterize the challenges faced today by young architects like us, what would they be?

AK: Young architects here in Ghana are often limited when entering the market as the pressure to follow conventional design is high. There aren't many projects available that offer the chance to explore design. Financial pressure for a young architect adds to the challenge of simply sustaining themselves. But there is a light at the end of the tunnel. Lately, I have been learning about various interesting projects throughout the country, many are happening but those doing the projects are still unaware of others doing similar things. If a network is created to share knowledge and

experiences, more energy and support will be breathed into the creative vibe here, opening up the potential architectural possibilities.

ML: It really is exciting. I think the challenge is being able to look within ourselves in both an individual and collective sense, in order to self-determine our own standards and capacity to produce responsibly for the contexts that we live in. I think the platform of sharing is a great place to begin. But the harder part will be agreeing to develop and share common methods and standards that can cumulatively stimulate local knowledge economies for material innovation, technical expertise, and cultural experimentation.

1 Escape3Points is an ecolodge located in Cape Three Points, Ghana, championing sustainable design and alternative low-cost building methods, renewable energy, and alternatives to sanitation.

2 *Sankofa* is a word from the Akan language of Ghana that translates into "reach back and get it" (*san*—to return; *ko*—to go; *fa*—to fetch, to seek and take) and also refers to the Asante Adinkra symbol represented either by a bird with its head turned backwards taking an egg off its back, or as a stylized heart shape.

MAE-LING LOKKO is a Ghanaian-Filipino doctoral student at CASE at the Rensselaer Polytechnic Institute, from which she also holds a Masters in Architectural Science. Her work focuses on the upcycling of agricultural waste by-products into high-performance, building-integrated material systems.

AKWASI MCLAREN is a University of Waterloo Architecture graduate and owner of the Escape3points Ecolodge. He has been designing and building in Ghana since 2003 with an eco-friendly approach that utilizes recycled and local materials.

LUBUNGAMODE
KISANGANI, DR CONGO

ON OTHER ARTISTIC RESEARCH

UNE AUTRE APPROCHE ARTISTIQUE

LUBUNGAMODE / KISANGANI, DR CONGO
ON OTHER ARTISTIC RESEARCH

[A]FA LUBUNGAMODE / KISANGANI, RDC / UNE AUTRE APPROCHE ARTISTIQUE

AFRICA / DRC / KISANGANI / LUBUNGA /
AFRIQUE / RDC / KISANGANI / LUBUNGAMODE

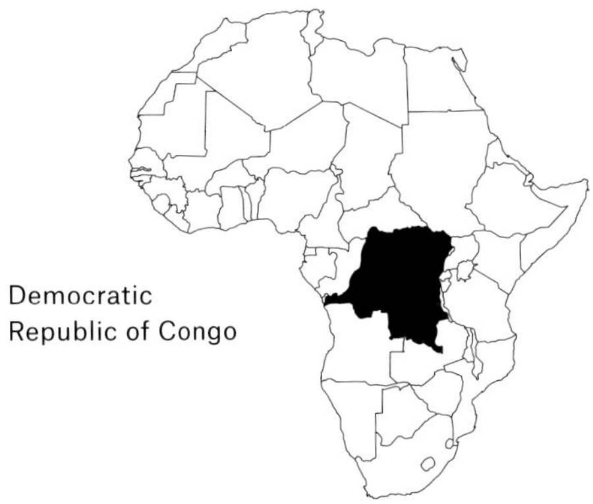

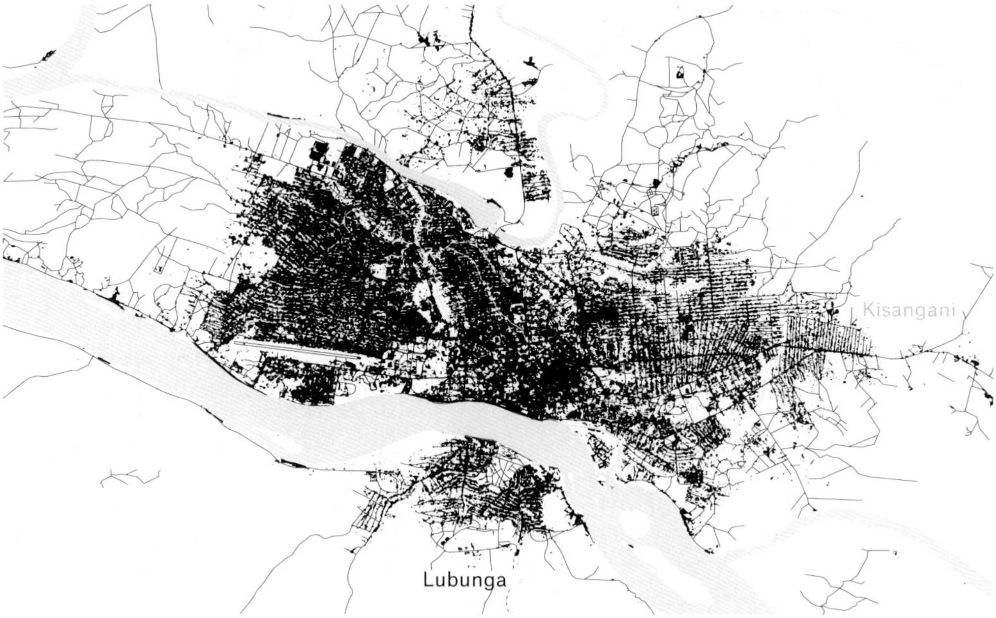

CONGO RIVER / LE FLEUVE CONGO

Length / Longueur : 4,700 km
Basin / Bassin : 4,014,500 km^2
Average discharge / Débit moyen : 41,000 m^3/s

Farthest navigable town upstream (ca. 2,090 km from the Atlantic Ocean) / par navigation (a peu pres a 2,090 km de l'océan Atlantique) : Kisangani

KISANGANI

Coordinates / Coordonnées :
0° 31' 0" N 25° 12' 0" E

Population / Population :
935,977 (2012)
Population density / Densité démographique :
229 habitants/km^2
Population growth / Croissance de la population :
39 % (2003 – 2012)
Main languages / Langues principales :
Lingala, Swahili, (French / français)

Average temperature / Température moyenne :
25.3 °C
Average humidity / Taux d'humidité moyen :
86 %
Average precipitation / Précipitations moyennes :
1,620 mm p. a.
Vegetation type / Type de végétation :
Tropical rain forest / Forêt tropicale

Access to safe drinking water in urban areas of DRC / Accès à l'eau potable en zone urbaine en RDC :
68 % (1990)*, 38 % (2008)*

Reported water-borne diseases / Maladies hydriques signalées :
Cholera, other bacterial and protozoal diarrhea, hepatitis A, typhoid fever / Choléra, diarrhées causées par des agents bactériens ou protozoaires, hépatite A, fièvre typhoïde

* for the population / pour les populations

LUBUNGA

Population / Population :
182,498 (2004)

Google Earth 2004

FROM THE BEND IN THE RIVER

Dorine Mokha

On this set, there are no actors, only people playing their roles in real life. The stakes are not only high, but also vital. The canoe boat drivers and their apprentices are engaged in endless, lively discussions, while street vendors court passersby and passengers who are about to embark or disembark. 'Tolekistes', bicycle taxi drivers, and motorcycle taxis remain vigilant with their hands on the handlebars. Dozens of them can be counted along the road spanning the river. Here, anything can be bought—cigarettes, fuel, goats, clothes, sachet water. Nearby, I can see several public booths one after the other, built with recycled wood or standing under a parasol. There are also some of the famous 'Malewa'—makeshift Congolese restaurants. The setting is perfect, while the décor is the result of complete abandonment. The lighting is natural, with the stage simply set around a big mess that is, in itself, an organized orderliness. It is noisy, with a radio blaring somewhere and an argument taking place elsewhere, as curses from one merge with the laughter of the other. Even the motor boats and row boats bash against each other with the movement of the waves. For all, the only driving force—empty stomachs and pockets—provides enough adrenaline to seek those extra 200 or 500 Congolese Francs. Each person has his or her own strategy. 'Uniformed men' use threats, Malewa 'dadas' their charm, street hawkers their bargaining; parking for commercial bicycles and motorcycles, the click and clack music of 'manicure boys' and biblical predictions by 'men of God', including cheating and theft, as well as smiles and winks. The casting is perfect. I suddenly notice the youngest of the Tolekistes, with neither makeup nor masks, their faces show the difficult struggle for survival and their hardened calves the mileage on the meter.

But today, there is an extraordinary actor: the mayor of the city. A ceremonial arrival of big cars, bodyguards, the media. He is there to inspect some major road construction that only he sees, since nothing seems to have been done on this dilapidated street. Dressed in suit, tie, and Ray Ban UV sunglasses, this rising star in local politics, with an assured but unsatisfied gait, picks up a hoe to show his bureaucrat muscle while the cameras of the national television zoom in on all his actions and gestures. "Cut. We must film the last shot again. A little smile, your Honor, the whole country will be watching you on the evening news!" Yes, they will see him if they have electricity, at least. While they are preparing to re-film the said last shot, I overhear a lady asking her son: "Djo nani tena ule ?", Who is this man? Oh yes, because without electricity and direct contact between the rulers and the ruled, the mayor is, for many, just a name, a faceless voice. And this is why, like everyone present, I don't pay him much attention. Indeed, people should pay less attention to politicians, who have the luxury to re-film the unsuccessful

DE LA COURBE DU FLEUVE

Dorine Mokha

Sur ce plateau, aucun personnage, juste des personnes qui jouent leurs propres rôles, dans la vraie vie : les enjeux ne sont pas simplement importants, mais vitaux. Les conducteurs de pirogues et leurs assistants s'agitent et n'arrêtent pas de parler, les vendeurs ambulants courtisent les passants et les passagers qui s'apprêtent à embarquer ou à débarquer, les tolékistes, ces conducteurs de taxi vélos, et les taxi motards sont en alerte, les mains non loin des guidons de leurs motos et vélos qu'on peut compter par dizaines le long de la route qui longe le fleuve. Ici tout se vend : cigarettes, essence, « cabri », vêtements, eau en sachets… J'aperçois à côté plusieurs cabines publiques en bois recyclé, les unes à côté des autres ou placées sous un parasol, mais aussi plusieurs de ces fameux « Malewa », ces restaurants de fortune à la congolaise. La scénographie est au point, le décor est le fruit de l'abandon. La lumière est naturelle et la mise en scène organiquement construite autour d'un grand désordre qui en constitue même l'ordre établi : le vacarme est au rendez-vous, une radio amplifiée par-ci, une dispute par-là, les râlements des uns face aux rires des autres, même les pirogues à moteur et à pagaies qui se préparent à aller et revenir s'entrechoquent au gré de vagues. Seule motivation pour tous : l'estomac et les poches vides, produisant assez d'adrénaline pour la recherche d'un 200 ou 500 francs congolais de plus. Et pour ça, à chacun sa stratégie : la menace pour les « hommes en uniformes », le charme pour les « dadas » de Malewa, la négociation pour les vendeurs ambulants, le stationnement pour les taxis vélos et motos, la musique clic clac pour les « garçons à vernis », la prédication biblique pour les « hommes de Dieu », mais aussi la ruse et le vol, le sourire et les clins d'œil. Le casting est parfait. Mon regard est frappé par les plus jeunes des tolékistes, sans fard ni masque, leurs visages racontent leur dur combat pour la survie et les mollets endurcis indiquent leur kilométrage au compteur.

Mais aujourd'hui, il y a un acteur exceptionnel : le maire de la ville. Arrivée protocolaire, grosses bagnoles, gardes du corps, presse. Il est là pour inspecter d'importants travaux de voirie que lui seul voit, puisque rien ne semble avoir commencé sur cette rue très délabrée. En costard cravate, lunettes UV Ray Ban, l'étoile montante de la politique locale, d'un pas décidé et insatisfait, récupère une bêche et met en œuvre ses muscles de bureaucrate pendant que la caméra de la chaîne nationale zoome sur chacun de ses faits et gestes. « Coupez, on doit refaire la dernière prise ! Souriez un peu, M. le maire, toute la population vous verra au journal du soir ! » Oui, elle le verra si du moins elle a de l'électricité. Pendant qu'ils s'apprêtent à reprendre ladite prise, j'entends une dame demander à son fils : « Djo nani tena ule ? ». C'est encore qui cet homme-là ? Eh oui, faute d'électricité et de lien direct entre l'administration et

shots of their life in office and concentrate on their daily lives. But this does not prevent the odor of 'disenchantment' from spreading through the air. I have been here for an hour, an observed observer, solitary, with an evasive look and a wandering mind. The Palm Beach Hotel is to my right and to my left is the Kisangani Cathedral, with its 17 steps towering over the statue of a white-robed Jesus with widespread hands who seems, almost, to be saying: "Karibu apa Kisangani." Welcome to Kisangani!

You are all welcome to my Kisangani, the only city where a sign at the entry point says "Welcome to Kisangani" on both sides! Here you are welcome on arrival and departure. I'm looking at the river and the river looks back, reminding me of why I came here. In my right hand, a letter to be sent to a great writer of the 20th century, "a traveler and observer of the Third World, a critic of uncompleted societies created through colonization." And in my left hand, the weight of the over 320 pages of the French version of his book, "A Bend in the River". However, this letter seems heavier. Maybe a last reading at the bend in the River Congo in Kisangani could lighten its weight... *Toleka*. Here I go.

Dear Naipaul,

We don't know each other but I have read your book, so in return I am writing what I think. I know you will understand my state of mind as an exiled person and a vagabond.

After all, we are all authors with different capabilities and from different generations, races, nationalities, ages—different in almost every way. If you are wondering if this is a game, I would say that it is. Writing is already a game, though one of the most risky. It is risky to write about a society while juggling truth and fiction, as we are the only ones capable of gauging the distance we create between the two. Based on their geographical location, some readers read our work the other way round, while others read it literally or do not understand the message behind the traps created by the plays on words. I have a question: Do you think your novel will be your 'personal' observation of a city in the heart of Africa through the eyes of Salim, the main character, or can we, like many experts, consider it an image of the whole continent of Africa? At times, I get the impression that for some people, Africa is one big country of Blacks, with Africans as inhabitants, speaking one language—African. This is sad. Truth be told, Africa has its problems, but the realities are different, as everything needs to be put into context. I believe, even in Lubumbashi, Kinshasa, or Kisangani, three cities in the same country with three different facets, among many others, of the Congolese reality. What do I have the right to say about a work crowned with success, honor, and a Nobel Prize in literature? I, an unknown descendant of free natives, sold into slavery, colonized, formerly colonized, independent, almost free; a Congolese citizen for a while, then a Zaire citizen for 32 years under the regime of someone called 'the Big Man.'

I became Congolese after the coup d'état by a rebel chief, who became president and then a hero after his assassination. He was succeeded by his son, who came from nowhere. He became president based on the nostalgia of his father's death. He became the president with the first mandate after the first supposedly free,

les administrés, le maire est pour beaucoup juste un nom, une voix sans visage. Raison de plus pour que, comme tout le monde autour, je m'occupe moins de lui. Les gens devraient d'ailleurs prêter moins d'attention au luxe qu'ont les politiques de refaire certaines prises ratées de leur long métrage au pouvoir pour mieux se concentrer sur leur vie. Mais cela n'empêche pas cette odeur de « Y en a marre » de circuler dans l'air. Je suis là depuis une heure déjà, observateur observé, ovni, solitaire au regard évasif et à l'esprit vagabond. A ma droite, la façade de l'hôtel Palm Beach et à ma gauche, la cathédrale de Kisangani avec son escalier à dix-sept marches que surplombe une statue de Jésus aux bras grandement ouverts, tout vêtu de blanc, disant presque : « Karibu apa Kisangani ! ». Bienvenue à Kisangani !

Soyez tous les bienvenus dans ma Kisangani, la seule ville où on trouve un panneau à l'entrée sur lequel est écrit « Bienvenue à Kisangani », autant au recto qu'au verso ! Comprenez donc que vous êtes les bienvenus ici, autant en arrivant qu'en partant... Je regarde le fleuve et lui aussi fait de même et cela me rappelle pourquoi j'étais venu là, avec, dans ma main droite, une lettre à envoyer à un grand auteur de ce siècle, « voyageur, observateur du tiers-monde, contempteur de sociétés inachevées nées de la colonisation ». Et dans la gauche, le poids de plus de 320 pages de son livre en sa version française : « A la courbe du fleuve ».

Pourtant cette lettre me semble plus lourde. Peut-être une dernière lecture à la courbe du fleuve Congo à Kisangani pourrait l'alléger... *Toleka*. Je me lance.

Cher Naipaul.

Nous ne nous connaissons pas mais je t'ai lu, alors en retour, je t'écris ce que je pense, je sais que tu pourras comprendre mon esprit d'exilé et de vagabond.

Après tout, nous sommes tous des auteurs, de calibres différents, de générations différentes, de races différentes, de nationalités, d'âges différents, presque différents en tous points. Si tu te demandes si c'est un jeu, je te répondrais oui. Ecrire en est déjà un, mais un des plus dangereux. Dangereux de peindre une société en jonglant entre vérité et fiction, et nous seuls savons estimer la distance que nous prenons entre les deux. Juste en raison de leur position géographique, certains lecteurs nous lisent à l'envers, d'autres prennent tout à la lettre ou bien ne saisissent pas le message derrière les pièges des jeux de mots. Une question : penses-tu que ton roman soit ta « propre » observation d'une ville au cœur de l'Afrique à travers Salim, son personnage principal, ou doit-on comme beaucoup de ces experts le considérer comme une peinture de tout un continent : l'Afrique ? Parfois, j'ai l'impression que pour certains, l'Afrique est un grand pays de Noirs, avec des Africains comme habitants, parlant une seule langue, l'Africain. C'est moche ça. L'Afrique a ses problèmes certes, mais les réalités sont différentes, toutes à contextualiser je pense, même à Lubumbashi, Kinshasa ou Kisangani, trois villes d'un seul pays, trois facettes parmi tant d'autres de la réalité congolaise. Mais suis-je autorisé à dire tout ceci à une plume auréolée de succès, d'honneurs, du prix Nobel de littérature ? Moi, un simple petit descendant des indigènes libres, devenus esclaves, puis colonisés, ex-colonisés, indépendants, presque libres,

fair, and democratic elections since independence and then got a second and last mandate that will end in November 2016 unless he manages, by any means, to get a third one... As you know, decisions by the powers-that-be in Kinshasa influence, greatly, each inhabitant's life in the city of Zabeth and also my future, as was also the case for Salim. You know, like Salim, I am seeking to become someone so as not to be a nobody. To achieve this, there are two ways to go: either get into the system or work against it. And you know your choice for Salim.

Coming back to the anonymous town where your A Bend in the River is set, Kisangani. Yes, this city does have a name. Indeed, it has several names: Kisangani, Boyoma, Singa Mwambe, Martyr Town, Town of Hope, Bicycle Town, the list goes on. You could have even named it whatever you fancy, don't you think so? For me, this city is my adoptive mother. It has been seven years now since I arrived here, unhappy, lost, full of doubts and mistrust, confused, and armed with a collection of clichés from Wikipedia, Google, blogs, and old national and international newspaper clippings that I should have never read. Goodbye Lubumbashi. Goodbye to your tender and boring everyday life. Welcome to Kisangani, where things happen. Things are happening, time is passing, and politicians are hitting out at themselves, citizens are slogging it out while I dance to the rhythm of my wristwatch's ticking needle.

Naipaul. I am in love with a city in ruins. In this city, I am experiencing hardship and not complaining because my small battle with survival draws inspiration from it. You know, Salim is a very interesting character, being neither African nor European. However, I would have loved for him to see through my eyes. The eyes of a Congolese who, since his arrival in Kisangani, feels he has entered another world and has finally obtained the Congolese nationality through experiencing the real problems many Congolese encounter, while facing hardship and feeling the biting economic crisis in this country of 2,345,409 km^2 from a small empty pocket of barely 15 centimeters. And since November 18, 2008, I have been feeling the pinch. Yet, being 19 at that time, I had almost 1,000 US dollars in my pocket, I think, for my funeral. Just some money, received from my dear ones. They had knowing looks on their faces. "Adieu Dorine, take this money, we are not sure if we will see you again... In Kisangani, the war is still ongoing and there are many epidemics." The war and epidemics? Yes, there are. Before my very eyes, they are there, on the two banks at the bend of the river. Seated on the last step of the Kisangani Cathedral, I see the war and the epidemics paralyze the people: this mental war and its psychological epidemics injecting their 'waiting virus.' The perpetual waiting for a bright future, promised long ago in endless political speeches, in unimaginable biblical predictions, and even in our wildest dreams.

Perpetual waiting for everything. Compulsory waiting for a long time. waiting for the long-expected development of an educational system that is worthy of the 21st century, for the hope that has, once again, been dashed, and for the liberty of our dreams that have been tortured by politics and the media, for the realization of Kabila's five projects (Education, Health, Water, Electricity, and Infrastructure), which have since passed over five paths, five shortcuts that all ended in dead ends... Waiting for a revolution through the

congolais un court instant, citoyens zaïrois pendant 32 ans sous le règne de l'homme que tu appelles le « Big Man ».

Je suis devenu à mon tour congolais après le coup d'état d'un chef rebelle devenu président, puis héros après son assassinat, remplacé par son fils sorti de l'ombre, devenu président par nostalgie du décès du père. Il devint président après les premières élections dites libres, transparentes et démocratiques depuis l'Indépendance, puis obtint un second et dernier mandat qui prendra d'ailleurs fin en novembre, à moins qu'il se débrouille pour rester un troisième... Comme tu sais, les décisions dictées par le pouvoir central à Kinshasa influent beaucoup sur la vie de chaque habitant de la ville de Zabeth, donc aussi sur mon avenir, comme cela a aussi été le cas pour Salim. Tu sais, comme lui, je cherche à devenir quelqu'un pour ne pas être rien. Et pour ça, il y a deux voies : entrer dans le système ou nager à contre-courant. Et tu connais le choix que tu as fait pour Salim.

Parlons un peu de cette ville anonyme où ton « A la courbe du fleuve » a planté son décor, Kisangani. Oui, cette ville a bel et bien un nom. D'ailleurs elle en a plusieurs : Kisangani, Boyoma, Singa Mwambe, ville Martyre, Ville d'Espoir, Ville à Vélos et la liste n'est pas exhaustive. Tu aurais bien pu la nommer comme bon t'aurait semblé, non ? Pour moi, elle est ma mère adoptive. Cela fait sept ans maintenant que j'y suis arrivé, triste, perdu, plein de doutes et de méfiance, confus et la tête pleine de clichés ramassés sur Wikipedia, Google, dans des blogs et des anciens tirages de journaux nationaux comme internationaux que je n'aurais jamais dû lire. Au revoir Lubumbashi. Au revoir ton train-train tendre et ennuyeux... Bienvenue à Kisangani, ici ça bouge ! Ça bouge, le temps passe, les politiques s'emmerdent, la population se démerde et moi, je danse sur le tempo des aiguilles de ma montre.

Naipaul. Je suis amoureux d'une ville en ruine. Grâce à elle, je flirte avec la galère et je ne m'en plains pas, car ma petite lutte pour la survie en est nourrie. Tu sais, Salim est un personnage très intéressant car ni africain ni européen. Pourtant, j'aurais aimé lui prêter mes yeux. Les yeux d'un Congolais qui, depuis son arrivée à Kisangani, a l'impression d'être entré dans un autre pays et a finalement obtenu la nationalité congolaise en goûtant aux vrais problèmes de la majorité des Congolais, en goûtant à la galère, en sentant la crise économique que traverse ce grand pays de 2,345,409 km^2 dans une petite poche d'à peine 15 centimètres de profondeur. Et depuis ce 18 novembre 2008, je continue à ressentir cela. Pourtant à cette époque, âgé de 19 ans, j'avais près de 1000 dollars américains dans la poche, je crois que c'était pour mes funérailles. Juste de l'argent triste, reçu de mes proches. Dans leurs regards, tout était clair : « Adieu Dorine, prends cet argent car on ne sait pas si on te reverra... A Kisangani, la guerre continue et il y a plein d'épidémies. » La guerre et les épidémies ? Oui, il y en a. Elles sont juste là en face de moi, sur les deux rives à la courbe du fleuve. Assis sur la dernière marche de l'escalier de la cathédrale de Kisangani, je les vois paralyser la population : cette guerre et ces épidémies mentales inoculant leur « virus de l'attente ». Eternelle attente d'un futur radieux, longtemps promis par de longs discours politiques, de dingues prédications bibliques, et même par nos rêves les plus fous.

Éternelle attente de tout. Faudra attendre longtemps. Attendre pour le développement tant attendu d'une éducation digne

arts and the masses' rebellions, for a decent salary and a profitable banking system for all, for electricity every night, and for drinking water for all… Yes, we must wait. So, I am waiting while looking at the river. And while the masses continue to wait, many Salims have left their cherished India or their home countries to make money in what you call a city that had almost seized to exist. Oh yes! On the ruins, money has already learnt to grow like mushrooms. Americans and Europeans had already understood this, joined now by the Chinese who are leading in this rally of "who will grow more money out of the ruins of cities abandoned by their colonizers?" The Chinese impress me because no sector is spared, not even retail trading, which is normally left to locals.

So Naipaul, do you think that Kisangani should have remained under colonialists in order to be the best or just better? Do you know that Kisangani is called the Martyr Town? And that politicians rebaptized it the Town of Hope in order to make it attractive once again? And it seems like it has worked. But back to your book. You know, I have read Naipaul, "the painter of unfinished societies created from colonization", but I would like to read Naipaul, "the painter of ancient African societies that have existed before the supposed discovery of Africa, destroyed, torn, injured, forever shaken up by colonization, its ambitions and excesses." A utopia? Some will tell me it's a blasphemy. Because your novel has become one of the greatest books dedicated to the African continent. For this, bravo. I duff my hat to you my dear, given that no other book of this kind, written by an African, could command more attention than yours. It seems! This is even so because of the crushing exactness and your keen eye as an outsider, as well as your sense of observation and detail, the star quality of your pen, and your appetite for adventure.

Finally, I would like to let you know that since I arrived in this city, I have not stopped searching for my place, just like everyone here. I am searching for my road through the piles of ruins, inherited from conflicts that have left almost indelible marks on the walls of the city and on the faces of Boyomais, Kisangani's inhabitants, even more strangely on the faces of those born after the last war… Only being able to relive everything in the eyes of others, that's hard. But I stay because I believe joy and happiness are possible, be it in Kinshasa, New Delhi, or London. Even while facing this abandonment, the joy of living can be created. My only daily battle is to grab my right to dream and to live my dreams, and this means going against the system. The most important thing is what I feel for this city and the battle that it presents me—a noble battle. I will stop here but I will write again, once I am sure of having been read.

Yours sincerely.
Kisangani, December 19, 2015.

I needed a minute's silence to realize that time had passed very quickly. "So, hours that I have been here." Mosquitoes warn me that they are ready to dine while several singing insects join toads for a recital. Kisangani's nightlife has started. Slowly, the sky is covered with its beautiful starry coat, while Kisangani divides into two, as is the case every night; partial electricity for right bank Kisangani and its five districts and total blackout for left bank Kisangani and its sole district, Lubunga. And not forgetting that the

d'un pays du XXIe siècle, pour l'espoir encore traîné dans la boue et pour la liberté de nos rêves torturés par la politique et les médias, pour la réalisation des cinq chantiers de Kabila (Education, Santé, Eau, Electricité et Infrastructures) depuis passés par cinq sentiers, cinq raccourcis qui ont fini en impasses... Attendre pour la révolution par l'art et la révolte du peuple, pour un salaire décent et une bancarisation qui profite à tous, pour des ampoules allumées chaque soir et pour une eau potable pour tous... Oui, il faudra attendre. Alors je continue à attendre en regardant le fleuve. Et alors que le petit peuple continue à attendre, beaucoup de Salim ont quitté leur Inde chérie ou leur terre natale pour faire fortune dans ce que tu appelles une ville qui avait presque cessé d'exister. Et oui, sur les ruines, la fortune a déjà appris à pousser comme des champignons. Les Américains et les Européens l'avaient bien compris, rejoints aujourd'hui par les Chinois désormais en tête de ce rallye de « Qui fera pousser le plus d'arbres à dollars sur les décombres des villes abandonnées par leurs colonisateurs ? » Ces derniers m'impressionnent car aucun secteur ne leur échappe, même pas la vente au détail, pourtant habituellement réservée aux nationaux.

Alors Naipaul, penses-tu que Kisangani aurait dû rester sous le joug de la colonisation pour être meilleure ou juste mieux ? Saistu que Kisangani s'est fait appeler ville martyre ? Et que ce sont les politiques qui l'ont rebaptisée ville d'espoir pour la rendre à nouveau attirante. Et on dirait que ça a marché. Mais revenons à ton roman. Tu sais, j'ai lu le Naipaul « peintre de sociétés inachevées nées de la colonisation » mais je serais intéressé de lire le Naipaul « peintre des anciennes sociétés africaines existantes bien avant ladite découverte de l'Afrique, anéanties, démantelées, meurtries, irrémédiablement ébranlées par la colonisation, sa prétention et ses excès. Une utopie ? Blasphème, me diront certains. Car ton roman est devenu l'un de plus grands livres jamais consacrés au continent africain. Alors là, bravo, coup de chapeau mon cher, vu qu'aucun livre du genre, écrit par un Africain, ne pourrait faire le poids face au tien. Paraît-il ! Il apparaît même que c'est en raison de ton impitoyable exactitude, ton regard acéré d'outsider, ton sens de l'observation et du détail, ta plume vedette, ton goût de l'aventure.

Pour finir, j'aimerais te faire savoir que depuis que je suis arrivé dans cette ville, je ne cesse de chercher ma place, un peu comme tout le monde ici. Je cherche ma route à travers un tas de ruines, héritées des conflits qui ont laissé des marques presque indélébiles sur les murs de la ville et des rides sur les visages des Boyomais, même étrangement sur ceux nés après la dernière guerre... Ne pouvoir revivre tout cela que dans les yeux des autres. C'est dur. Mais je reste car je pense que la joie et le bonheur y sont possibles autant qu'à Kinshasa, New Delhi ou Londres. Même face à cet abandon, le bonheur de vivre se crée. Mon seul combat quotidien est d'arracher mon droit de rêver et de vivre mes rêves, et cela signifie nager à contre-courant. Le plus important est ce que je ressens pour cette ville et la lutte qu'elle m'offre : une lutte noble. Je vais m'arrêter là mais je t'écrirai à nouveau dès que j'aurai la certitude d'avoir été lu.

Bien à toi.

Kisangani le 19 décembre 2015.

river with its volume could provide enough power for all of Africa. But where is the Honorable Mayor to hear this? Gone, like all the actors who were enlivening this place a while ago on this bank, where it is time to check proceeds and make inventories, with the last bicycles and motorcycles taxis driving back clients. Passersby are fewer and the last canoe boats are leaving for the day. Luckily, on this side, some bulbs and projectors are already lighting up on some buildings. Contrary to the opposite bank, where Lubunga is already plunged in a dangerous darkness that paralyzes life on this side of the city, forgotten for decades. Everything is in the dark, nothing is spared from it, not even a glimmer of hope. A few hours was all that was needed for Lubunga to go from neglected to abandoned and from abandoned to forgotten and from forgotten to nonexistent! "We are already black, see how they are plunging us into darkness," the wind whispers. I dare not imagine what my friends on the other side see while looking over at the bank where I am. Isaac, Dorcas, Agha, Alain... What do you see? Paradise? A type of Boyomese Paris? Happiness? President Joseph Kabila's ongoing five projects? The gains of colonization? Or colonial negligence, which royally ignored geographical and cultural factors in the division of this big cake? Injustice? The forgetfulness of politicians? Or you just tell yourselves you also deserve it. That you also deserve some electricity and drinking water.

I would love to write another letter through your eyes, a letter to the people responsible for the abandonment inflicted on this part of the city. That would be another story... Right now, I am ashamed to be under the cathedral's projector while children on the other side fear that the darkness will steal their dreams. Yet these dreams are all they have left. Right now, I must return to my house on the 10th Avenue of Tshopo town, not far from the Tshopo dam. All I have left is sadness to accompany me on the 20-minute walk home, as I wonder if I will also find electricity there.

DORINE MOKHA, dancer / choreographer / writer, born in 1989 in Lubumbashi, DRC, degrees in literature from the College Imara (2008) and law from the University of Kisangani (2013). Associate artist at the Studios Kabako and co-artistic director of ART'gument Project; collaborations with artists such as Faustin Linyekula and Desire Davids.

Il m'a fallu une minute de silence pour me rendre compte que le temps avait très vite avancé. « Des heures donc que je suis là. Les moustiques me préviennent qu'ils sont prêts à passer à table pendant que plusieurs bestioles choristes rejoignent les crapauds pour un récital. La vie nocturne de Kisangani commence. Le ciel enfile lentement son beau manteau étoilé tandis que Kisangani se scinde en deux, comme chaque soir : l'éclairage partiel pour Kisangani rive droite et ses cinq communes et l'obscurité totale pour Kisangani rive gauche et son unique commune, Lubunga. Et dire que le fleuve et sa puissance pourraient éclairer toute l'Afrique. Mais où est M. le maire pour entendre ça ? Parti, comme tous les acteurs qui animaient ce lieu il y a peu, sur cette rive où l'heure est aux comptes et aux inventaires. Les derniers taxis vélos et motos ramènent les derniers clients, les passants se font rares et les dernières pirogues partent pour ne plus revenir. Par chance, de ce côté, quelques ampoules et projecteurs s'allument déjà sur les bâtiments. Ce n'est pas le cas sur la rive opposée, Lubunga est déjà plongée dans un noir venin qui paralyse la vie de ce coin de la ville délaissé depuis des décennies. Tout est dans le noir, plus rien ne reste d'elle, même plus l'ombre de l'espoir. Quelques heures ont suffi à Lubunga pour passer de la délaissée à l'abandonnée, de l'abandonnée à l'oubliée, de l'oubliée à l'inexistante ! « Nous sommes déjà des Noirs, voilà qu'on nous plonge encore dans le noir », me souffle le vent. Je n'ose pas imaginer ce que mes amis de l'autre côté voient en regardant la rive où je me trouve. Isaac, Dorcas, Agha, Alain... Que voyez-vous ? Le paradis ? Une sorte de Paris à la Boyomaise ? Le bonheur ? Les cinq chantiers du Président Joseph Kabila en marche ? Les bienfaits de la colonisation ? Ou la négligence coloniale qui ignora royalement les facteurs géographiques et culturels dans le découpage de son grand gâteau ? L'injustice ? L'oubli des politiques ? Ou vous vous dites simplement que vous le méritez aussi. Que vous méritez aussi un peu de lumière et d'eau potable.

J'aurais aimé avoir vos yeux pour écrire une autre lettre, une lettre aux responsables de cet abandon infligé à cette partie de la ville. Ce serait une autre histoire... Sur le coup, j'ai honte d'être sous le projecteur de la cathédrale pendant que des enfants, de l'autre côté, craignent que le noir ne leur vole leurs rêves, pourtant c'est tout ce qui leur reste. A présent, je dois rentrer chez moi sur la 10e avenue bis de la commune Tshopo, non loin du barrage Tshopo. Il me reste donc juste du chagrin à traîner pendant 20 minutes de marche, avant d'y être, me demandant si je trouverai aussi de l'électricité.

DORINE MOKHA, danseur / chorégraphe / écrivain. Né en 1989 à Lubumbashi, RDC, baccalauréat littéraire au Collège Imara (2008) et diplômé en droit de l'Université de Kisangani (2013). Artiste associé des Studios Kabako et co-directeur artistique de ART'gument Project. Collaborations artistiques avec des artistes tels que Faustin Linyekula ou Désiré Davids.

ON LUBUNGA

Faustin Linyekula and
Baerbel Mueller
Kisangani, April 2013

BM: Could you describe Lubunga?

FL: Okay, right now we are sitting by the Congo River on the right bank in Kisangani. Across the river on the left bank is Lubunga. We are not exactly in the city center so we cannot see the urban life, but when you are in the city center and look across, especially at night, you wouldn't imagine that it's actually one of the most populated areas in the city because it's really dark. It never used to be that dark.

Growing up in Lubunga—part of the time, there were years when my base would be in Lubunga—I would always come to school on this side of the river because the best schools were on this side. It was like that already in the '80s. When I was sitting on the right bank and looked across the river, I would see cranes at the port at the train station that still worked, meaning there was still electricity. And around the train station you had beautiful colonial villas that are still there today. These villas belonged to the railway company. And then you had some private houses around the station, mainly colonial houses, beautiful constructions that had electricity. As you went down the river you'd see a long street, actually the only tarmacked one, and this is still the only tarmacked street in Lubunga. It's a small street, not more than 6 meters wide, but we call it Boulevard. Boulevard Hassan II. It was named after Morocco's king Hassan II and you even had street lights on Hassan II. Outside these two areas, the train station and the Boulevard, it was mainly dark. There was no electricity.

The main difference today is that even these islands where there used to be electricity have disappeared. So at night it's dark. You can hardly imagine that there are so many people living there. Maybe 20 percent of Kisangani's population lives there, maybe less, but definitely a big part of the people live there. I grew up in parts there because my mother's family comes from there. My grandmother still lives there. I am particularly attached to this part of the city because it says something about how we deal with periphery in this country. You concentrate on whatever is immediately visible, whatever is immediately accessible, and whatever can serve immediately as a facade. You put all your energy there and everything around can stay in the dark, it's not a big deal really. Life has always been organized like that: You have a few facades that you really take care of, that you try and make shine as much as you can—even though those facades became difficult to maintain throughout the years—and just forget about the periphery. But the politicians around the elections, because they know that maybe 20 percent of the population lives there, they go there and try and get the votes. And once they have the votes, they are gone and they disappear.

So when I look at Lubunga and this black hole that it is, somehow I see a position that I feel I can operate from as a citizen, as an artist. And my being a citizen informs my being an artist and vice versa. In that I don't feel that I can side with the powerful. I don't identify myself with them, I identify myself with this fragile territory trying to remain alive and to propose other ways of getting through the days. I see Studios Kabako as a project trying to speak of whatever is forgotten, from that place of what's forgotten.

BM: From your description, Lubunga seems somehow isolated. How is it lived in by the people living there? Is life centered in Lubunga or is there a lot of transition to the other side?

FL: Kisangani is made up of six districts. Five are on the right bank and only one is on the left, that's Lubunga. And between Lubunga and the city you have this huge, powerful river and there is no bridge. So even physically it is isolated. All manufactured goods have to come from here and go to Lubunga. So yes it is isolated. People's lives are really built around what they can get from this side of the river. And one of the things that you can only get from this side of the river is electricity. Electricity is produced on the right bank, then it has to go across the river a bit further east where you have the Wagenia Falls. If there is rationing of electricity by the electricity company, Lubunga is one of the first places that they cut. It's not the heaviest district on the electricity grid, but they cut there first.

So there are many people I know who would speak of coming to the right bank of the

AUTOUR DE LUBUNGA

Faustin Linyekula et
Baerbel Mueller
Kisangani, avril 2013

BM : Pourrais-tu décrire Lubunga ?

FL : D'accord, nous sommes actuellement assis sur les berges du fleuve Congo, sur la rive droite de Kisangani. De l'autre côté du fleuve, sur la rive gauche, s'étend Lubunga. Comme nous ne sommes pas exactement centre-ville, il nous est difficile de voir la vie urbaine de l'autre côté. Mais même lorsqu'on se trouve au centre-ville et qu'on regarde de l'autre côté, surtout la nuit, jamais on ne pourrait imaginer que c'est l'un des quartiers les plus peuplés de la ville parce qu'il est plongé dans le noir. Et il n'a jamais été aussi noir...

Ayant grandi en partie à Lubunga – j'y ai habité pendant plusieurs années –, je venais toujours à l'école de ce côté-ci du fleuve, parce que les meilleures écoles se trouvent sur la rive droite. C'était déjà comme ça dans les années 80. Pourtant, lorsque je m'asseyais sur la rive droite et regardais de l'autre côté, je pouvais voir les grues s'activer entre la gare et le port, car il y avait encore de l'électricité. Autour de la gare, il y avait de très belles villas de style colonial qui sont toujours là aujourd'hui. Ces villas appartenaient à la compagnie ferroviaire. Il y avait également des maisons privées, principalement des maisons coloniales, de très belles bâtisses dotées d'électricité. En cheminant de la gare au fleuve, on arrive au bas d'une longue rue, la seule rue asphaltée à l'époque, et toujours la seule asphaltée aujourd'hui. C'est une petite rue, pas plus de six mètres de large, mais nous l'appelons Boulevard. Le Boulevard Hassan II, nommé ainsi en l'honneur du roi du Maroc Hassan II. Il y avait même des feux de circulation sur Hassan II. En dehors de ces deux quartiers, il faisait noir. Il n'y avait pas d'électricité.

Aujourd'hui, la principale différence est que même ces îlots urbains où il y avait de l'électricité ont disparu. Il fait donc noir la nuit. Et il est difficile d'imaginer qu'il y a autant de gens qui habitent là. Probablement 20 pour cent de la population de Kisangani vit là, peut-être un peu moins. J'y ai grandi en partie parce que ma mère vient de là et ma grand-mère y habite toujours. Je suis particulièrement attaché à cette partie de la ville parce qu'elle reflète bien la manière dont nous traitons la périphérie dans ce pays. On se concentre seulement sur ce qui est visible, sur ce qui est immédiatement accessible, et sur tout ce qui peut servir de façade. On y met toute notre énergie, et le reste peut bien rester dans le noir, ça n'a pas vraiment d'importance. La vie s'est toujours organisée de cette manière : il y a ces façades dont on s'occupe, qu'on cherche à faire briller autant que possible – même si, au fil des ans, elles sont de plus en plus difficiles à entretenir – et on oublie tout simplement la périphérie. Et c'est seulement lors des périodes électorales que les politiciens s'y rendent pour tenter de gagner des voix, se rappelant soudain que 20 pour cent des gens vivent là-bas. Une fois élus, ils disparaissent et ne reviennent plus jusqu'à la prochaine élection.

Donc lorsque je regarde ce trou noir qu'est Lubunga, cela me renvoie d'une certaine manière, à ma position de citoyen, je suis artiste mais je suis citoyen. Et être un citoyen nourrit ma pratique artistique et vice-versa. Je ne m'identifie pas aux gens au pouvoir. Non, je ne m'identifie pas à eux, mais plutôt à ce territoire fragile qui essaie de survivre et de trouver les moyens de finir la journée. Je vois les Studios Kabako ainsi, comme un projet visant à donner la parole à ce qui est tombé dans l'oubli, à parler depuis cet endroit oublié.

BM : Quand on t'écoute, Lubunga semble d'une certaine manière isolé. Comment se sentent les gens qui vivent là-bas ? La vie est-elle centrée sur Lubunga ou y a-t-il beaucoup d'allers et retours avec l'autre rive ?

FL : Kisangani est constitué de six communes. Cinq se trouvent sur la rive droite et une seule sur la rive gauche, Lubunga. Et entre Lubunga et la ville, il y a cet énorme et puissant fleuve que ne traverse aucun pont. C'est donc une isolation physique. Tous les biens manufacturés passent par ici avant d'arriver à Lubunga. Donc, oui, c'est isolé. La vie des gens s'articule véritablement autour de ce qu'ils peuvent trouver de ce côté-ci du fleuve. Et l'une des choses que l'on peut seulement trouver de ce côté-ci du fleuve, c'est l'électricité. L'électricité est produite sur la rive droite et doit traverser le fleuve un peu plus loin à l'est où se trouvent les chutes Wagenia. Quand la compagnie d'électricité doit rationner l'électricité,

river as a social progression. The best schools in the city are on this side, none of them are over there, really. There is still some faith left in the schools, otherwise people wouldn't be killing themselves to send their children to get some education, even though in reality it's worth nothing really. But people know that if they want to give the best to their children they have to send them to the right bank. At least there is still a hospital in Lubunga that more or less works. But there is no running water because there is no electricity and so people also know that if you want better medical attention, you have to come here. If I lived in Lubunga, at least in the way the city is organized today, unless I build an autonomous infrastructure around me, I need quite a lot from this side.

BM: So you are talking about basic infrastructure on the one hand and about education and urban life on the other hand.

FL: Even just the little entertainment that there still is, which is going to a bar when you can afford it and having a beer or two. You can count maybe five places with loud music in Lubunga, if you are lucky. So people, if they want to have some fun, those who can afford it would come to this side of the city. I remember as a teenager I would stay on this side of the river until 11 or midnight simply because I wanted to see a show. It was never in Lubunga, it was always here. The only thing we had in Lubunga was TV. On my street there were two TVs, two families that had television and one of them would take it outside. They would take the small 14-inch black and white TV outside, so the whole neighborhood would gather there and watch some telenovela, or Dallas. Or a football game. So if you wanted more than telenovelas with 20 other people around you shouting and commenting and no one listening, if you wanted more than that you had to come to this side. Or you had to know someone who lived in some of the better houses around the river, around the railway station, who could invite you over to watch TV. Lubunga, it's a black hole in the city, really.

BM: If I lived in Lubunga, what would I live on? What would people do who don't commute to the other side?

FL: You can work at the railway station, but the railway company is moribund. You have a train going from Lubunga to Ubundu, 100 kilometers south. That was really like the elite. You could be a policeman or a policewoman. You could be a soldier or an officer, because one of the main barracks in the city is over there, the Lukusa camp. You'd be in the military staying at Camp Lukusa. You could be a teacher. You could work on the river taking people across the river. If you are lucky you would be doing that on a motorized pirogue, otherwise it would be a rowing one. Or you could be farming, but not inside Lubunga, you have to get out of Lubunga. There are two main roads out of Lubunga; the railway and also a road going south all the way to Ubundu. And then you have another road going west and then south. That's the road that used to go all the way to Kinshasa until the early '60s, it goes through Kasai and then west all the way to Kinshasa. But now it's been over 40 years since the roads just disappeared because they were not tarmacked, so the forest grew back and took over everything. Along those two roads there are people farming. They grow cassava or plantains and some fruits like pineapples and bananas, corn, maybe rice. Everyone else would be surviving on selling a couple of soap bars outside their house. If you were young, what would you do in the evening? You would go to the church, you would be involved in some activity at your church. Girls become pregnant quite early over there, so boys as well get married early. What would you do in Lubunga? If you are ambitious I think you would dream of leaving Lubunga.

BM: What are the potentials you see in Lubunga in the long term?

FL: I once read something very interesting. It's by Sony Labou Tansi, who is a writer from Congo who died many years ago. Sony wrote in some book: "Everything had fallen to the ground, even the earth had fallen to the ground", but the people were still there. Of course that's very optimistic to say that the people are still there and you have youth. Maybe it's even blindly optimistic in that for those people and for that youth to be an asset, we need to invest today. I don't know of anything that is being done in that sense. We need to invest in their physical and mental health so that those people in the long term really become a generation with assets. So that's what I see and maybe that's the whole idea. What kind of space can we set up that takes into account the fact that the people are still here and what role can I play to turn that potential into an asset? How can I play my part? It will definitely be working on

Lubunga est l'un des premiers endroits où ils coupent. Ce n'est pas, loin de là, la commune qui consomme le plus, mais c'est là où ils coupent en premier.

C'est pour cela que pour certaines personnes que je connais, s'établir sur la rive droite, c'est comme monter dans l'échelle sociale. Les meilleures écoles sont sur cette rive, aucune ne se trouve de l'autre côté. Et les gens ont encore foi dans les écoles, sinon ils ne se tueraient pas au travail pour y envoyer leurs enfants, même si ça n'a pratiquement plus aucune valeur aujourd'hui. Et les gens savent que s'ils veulent donner de meilleures chances de réussite à leurs enfants, ils doivent les envoyer sur la rive droite. Au moins, il y a encore un hôpital à Lubunga, même s'il fonctionne plus ou moins bien. Mais il n'y a pas d'eau courante parce qu'il n'y a pas d'électricité et donc les gens savent que s'ils désirent recevoir de meilleurs soins, ils doivent traverser. Si je vivais à Lubunga, à la manière dont la ville est organisée de nos jours, j'aurais besoin de beaucoup de choses de ce côté-ci du fleuve, à moins de réussir à bâtir une infrastructure autonome autour de moi.

BM : Donc, d'un côté, une infrastructure de base et de l'autre, une éducation générale et une vie urbaine organisée.

FL : Prenons le plus simple divertissement, soit aller dans un bar et boire une bière ou deux si on peut se le permettre... Avec de la chance, on peut compter peut-être cinq endroits où il y a de la musique forte à Lubunga. Donc les gens qui désirent se distraire, ceux qui peuvent se le permettre du moins, viennent de ce côté-ci de la ville. Je me souviens lorsque j'étais adolescent, je restais de ce côté du fleuve jusqu'à 11 heures ou minuit simplement parce que j'avais envie de voir un spectacle. Ce n'était jamais à Lubunga, c'était toujours ici. La seule chose que nous avions à Lubunga, c'était la télévision. Dans ma rue, il y avait deux téléviseurs, deux familles avaient une télévision et l'une d'elles la sortait dans la rue. Ils emmenaient leur petit téléviseur noir et blanc à écran 35 cm dehors et tout le voisinage se rassemblait pour regarder des Telenovelas, Dallas ou un match de foot. Donc si on voulait faire autre chose que regarder une série avec autour une vingtaine de personnes en train de crier, commenter, sans pouvoir rien écouter, si on voulait davantage, il fallait venir de ce côté-ci. Ou bien il fallait connaître une personne qui demeurait dans l'une des belles maisons sur les berges du fleuve ou aux alentours de la gare, une personne qui pouvait vous inviter à regarder la télévision... Lubunga, c'est vraiment un trou noir dans la ville.

BM : Si je demeurais à Lubunga, de quoi je vivrais ? Que font les gens qui ne font pas la navette entre leur domicile et l'autre côté ?

FL : Tu pourrais travailler à la gare, mais la compagnie ferroviaire est aujourd'hui moribonde. Il y a un train de Lubunga à Ubundu, à 100 kilomètres au sud – mais ces emplois, c'était vraiment pour l'élite. Tu pourrais être un policier ou une policière. Tu pourrais être un soldat ou un officier, parce que l'un des principaux camps se trouve là-bas, le Camp Lukusa. Tu serais un militaire demeurant au Camp Lukusa. Tu pourrais être un enseignant. Tu pourrais travailler sur le fleuve pour transporter les gens de l'autre côté. Si tu as de la chance, tu pourrais le faire avec une pirogue motorisée, sinon avec une pirogue à rames. Ou tu pourrais être fermier, mais pas à Lubunga, là tu dois sortir de Lubunga. Il y a deux routes principales pour quitter Lubunga ; le chemin de fer et une route vers le sud en direction de Ubundu. Et il y a une autre route vers l'ouest et puis le sud. C'est par cette route qu'autrefois, tu pouvais te rendre à Kinshasa, jusque dans les années 60. Elle traversait le Kasai, puis obliquait vers l'ouest en direction de Kinshasa. Mais il y a maintenant plus de 40 ans que cette route a disparu parce qu'elle n'était pas asphaltée, donc la forêt a repoussé et tout recouvert sur son passage. Au bord de ces deux routes, il y a des gens qui cultivent. Ils font pousser du manioc, des bananes plantain, quelques fruits comme des ananas ou des bananes, du maïs, et quelquefois du riz. Tous les autres gens survivent en vendant quelques barres de savon devant leur maison. Si tu étais jeune, que ferais-tu le soir ? Tu irais à l'église, tu serais impliquée dans une quelconque activité à ton église. Les filles tombent enceintes assez jeunes par là-bas, donc les garçons se marient aussi jeunes. Que ferais-tu si tu vivais à Lubunga ? Si tu étais ambitieuse, je crois que tu rêverais de quitter Lubunga.

BM : Que vois-tu comme potentiel à Lubunga sur le long terme ?

FL : J'ai lu un jour quelque chose de très intéressant. C'est de Sony Labou Tansi, un écrivain du Congo décédé il y a plusieurs années. Sony a écrit dans l'un de ses livres : « Tout était

a very small scale. But at least I can start something there so that I'm not only waiting for god knows what to come. I should go in there and just play my part. But hey, everything is on the ground, even the earth has fallen to the ground. But you are still here. We are still here. So what is it that we can start imagining, now. We know that demographically we represent 20 percent of Kisangani but concerning political, economic investment we count for what? 0.1 percent? Good, but what can we invest in ourselves. Green power, imagination, and maybe then when we start speaking from that perspective, it's like the city speaking from its weakest or rather most fragile territory. Suddenly. We go here and say okay fine it's a black hole, but we are still here. Maybe we have a matchbox and we start lighting a fire. And maybe it will get big enough to be noticed.

I was reading this by Aimé Cesaire, a Caribbean writer, thinker, political figure, it's an introduction to a poetry collection. "The unequal struggle between life and death, between enthusiasm and lucidity, even if it's only the lucidity of desperation but also the strength to always look forward to tomorrow."

So again yes, it goes back to the people, to individuals, to those who can be lucid about the situation but who would be stubborn enough to look forward to tomorrow. That's the potential that I see there.

BM: You intend to start on the individual level.

FL: Yes, that's where it starts. I can only start from there. Especially in a country where there has never been any space for individuals. The history of this country is that of turning individuals into just a herd, a mass, statistics. So if we can imagine a project where we begin to think from the individual point of view, not to cut off the sense of community, no, but actually not to take the community as a given but rather as something that needs to be constructed—and it can only be constructed by individuals who feel responsible for that sense of community—then there is hope for something. Otherwise no one will ever be responsible for anything. So it should be all about articulating this strengthening of an individual voice with a larger sense of belonging to a greater picture. Maybe that's why as an artist I insist quite a lot on this idea of names. When I talk of my work as an attempt to remember my name, it is that with the name, of course you are at the level of an individual, you are identified as an individual. But if you are serious about the name, you can never afford a collapse into yourself, because the name opens up a world of relationships: relationships to place, to history, to families, to other people and that's what's really interesting. It's focusing on individuals and trying to see how they can be able to say their names and to say, "my name is, and I live in Lubunga, and if I live in Lubunga I know what it means. I have dreams!"

BM: The consequence would be to start investigating Lubunga or working in Lubunga on Lubunga, doing something there on an individual and small scale?

FL: It's about building an infrastructure where people can come together, a small group of people at first. Because you need to build trust for anything to happen and you cannot build trust with a mass immediately. So a small group of people who can believe in this madness. It's crazy really to imagine a project there, especially if you are not a politician seeking people's votes. In fact I am sure that at first people would think: what does he want? What's going on in his head? What's the hidden agenda? So it's about building a small group of people who trust each other and who begin to look at what's going on around them, reflect on that amongst themselves. Then, if you have let's say ten individuals who were brought together there, you can be sure that there are at least ten families that are beginning to get involved indirectly. Through this you begin to actually have an indirect impact on a slightly larger circle. It's about setting up a process. A process that will take time, it will take years, but at least some people, mainly young people can come together and begin to analyze what is going on around them and begin to think about what it is that we can do. And then as an organization like Studios Kabako, we can provide a platform for that to happen and also creative ways of sharing that with others. And then this can become like a platform where that group of people really work around questions of water in Lubunga. They go around, talk to people and they document that and come up with a film, go and see the authorities, the district chief, the major of the city of Kisangani or the governor of the province and say: this is what is happening. They give it a shape that can exist even in the media here. I hope it would have more impact than just once every five years during the election campaigns politicians going there and then people saying:

par terre, même la terre était par terre. » Bien entendu, c'est très optimiste de penser que les gens sont encore là et qu'il y a la jeunesse. C'est peut-être un optimisme aveugle, car pour que ces gens et ces jeunes deviennent un atout, il faut investir maintenant. Je ne suis au courant d'aucune initiative de ce genre. Nous devons investir dans la santé physique et intellectuelle des gens de cette génération pour qu'ils puissent devenir de véritables atouts. C'est ce que je perçois et c'est l'idée. Quel genre d'espace pouvons-nous créer, en tenant compte du fait que les gens sont là, et quel rôle puis-je jouer pour transformer ce potentiel en un atout ? Que puis-je apporter ? Cela se fera définitivement à une petite échelle. Mais au moins, je peux commencer quelque chose là-bas sans attendre que je ne sais quoi d'autre arrive. Je devrais aller là-bas et simplement jouer mon rôle. Mais bon, tout est par terre, même la terre est par terre. Mais tu es encore ici. Nous sommes encore ici. Donc que pouvons-nous imaginer maintenant ? Nous savons que démographiquement, nous représentons 20 pour cent de Kisangani mais en ce qui concerne la politique, l'investissement économique, quel est notre poids ? 0,1 pour cent ? Très bien, mais que pouvons-nous investir de nous-mêmes ? L'énergie verte, l'imagination... peut-être s'agit-il de changer de perspective. Comme si la ville s'exprimait à travers son territoire le plus faible ou plutôt le plus fragile. Nous venons ici et clairement c'est un trou noir, mais nous sommes toujours ici. Peut-être avons-nous une boîte d'allumettes et pouvons-nous allumer un feu. Un feu qui deviendra suffisamment grand pour être remarqué.

J'ai lu ceci d'Aimé Césaire, un auteur des Caraïbes, un penseur, une figure politique. C'est l'introduction d'une collection de poèmes : "L'inégale lutte de la vie et de la mort, de la ferveur et de la lucidité, fusse celle du désespoir et de la retombée. La force aussi toujours de regarder demain." Donc, encore une fois, cela dépend des gens, des individus qui demeurent lucides à propos de la situation mais qui sont tout de même assez têtus pour regarder devant, vers l'avenir. C'est le potentiel que je vois ici.

BM : Tu as l'intention de commencer à un niveau individuel.

FL : Oui, c'est là où tout commence. Je ne peux que commencer par là. Particulièrement dans un pays où il n'y a jamais eu de place pour les individus. L'histoire de ce pays est ainsi faite que les individus sont considérés comme faisant partie d'un troupeau, de la masse, d'une statistique. Donc si nous pouvons imaginer un projet axé sur le point de vue de l'individu, sans éliminer pour autant le sentiment d'appartenance à la communauté, mais en ne prenant pas la communauté comme étant acquise mais plutôt comme quelque chose qui doit être bâti, et qui peut seulement être bâti par des individus qui se sentent responsables d'elle, alors il y aura de l'espoir. Autrement personne ne se sentira jamais responsable de rien. Tout devrait être dans cette articulation entre le besoin de donner plus de pouvoir à l'expression des individus et un sentiment encore plus fort d'appartenance à quelque chose de plus grand. C'est peut-être pourquoi en tant qu'artiste, j'insiste beaucoup sur la notion de nom. Quand je parle de mon travail comme étant une façon de me rappeler mon nom, c'est ce que je veux dire. Bien évidemment, quand on parle du nom, on parle de l'individu, il y a une identification individuelle. Mais si on considère son nom sérieusement, on ne peut dès lors plus se permettre de se replier sur soi, parce qu'un nom ouvre un monde de relations : relations à l'endroit, à l'histoire, aux familles, aux autres gens et c'est ce qui est intéressant, se concentrer sur les individus et essayer de voir s'ils sont capables de dire leur nom. De dire : Mon nom est... Je vis à Lubunga. Et si je vis à Lubunga, je sais ce que ça veut dire. J'ai des rêves !

BM : Faut-il débuter une enquête sur Lubunga ou bien travailler à Lubunga sur Lubunga et faire quelque chose là-bas, sur une base individuelle et à une petite échelle ?

FL : Il s'agit de bâtir une infrastructure dans laquelle les gens puissent se rassembler, un petit groupe de gens au début. Parce qu'il faut gagner la confiance pour qu'il puisse se passer quelque chose et on ne peut pas gagner la confiance de la masse immédiatement. Donc un petit groupe de personnes capables de croire dans cette folie. C'est vraiment fou d'imaginer un projet là-bas, surtout si on n'est pas un politicien qui cherche à se faire des voix. En fait, je suis certain que c'est ce que les gens vont penser : que veut-il ? Qu'est-ce qui lui passe par la tête ? Quel est le but caché derrière tout cela ? Il faut donc rassembler un petit groupe de personnes qui ont confiance les unes dans les autres et qui commencent à observer ce qui se passe autour d'elles, à réfléchir à ça et à en discuter entre elles. Ensuite, si on a, disons, dix individus qui sont rassemblés là-bas, c'est

"Baba, hatuna ta maji uku", because we call politicians baba—father. Father we don't have water here. And then yes, we don't have water, do something for us! And then what? But if you go there and say: If we had ten pumps distributed like this, it would serve that and that population. We would concretely begin to propose solutions for our own things. Maybe a dialogue. Such a project cannot replace a government initiative. That's not the idea. It's about trying to get voices channeled. While doing that, and because I still believe in the power of the arts, may be some artistic voices could begin to come up, artistic voices that could be supported and nurtured through the Studios Kabako.

BM: So is it about articulating needs and desires?

FL: Even remembering that we have needs. It's in Lubunga but it's also the situation of the people in this country in general. We've grown so accustomed to not having anything that we have even forgotten that we have any desires and needs and rights. Already if we can just remember that we have that, that's a first step. Maybe it's a dangerous one, to remind someone who was born to believe that being hungry is the normal state of being that actually it's not, maybe it's like throwing a bomb in someone's head. There is always something to remind me of how hungry we are as a people and maybe I do what I do because I acknowledge that we are hungry. And I don't want to be alone in that journey, it's like trying to infect others around me and Lubunga being so dear to me, it's important for me that the people around me in Lubunga begin to share a bit more my world as well. Otherwise the only way to share my world will be when I give them a hundred dollars every now and then, because a family needs the money to pay the children's school fees. But is there a way of sharing my world at a deeper level? Of course it's necessary, it's important to give the one-hundred-dollar bill, but can I share something with them? So is the answer yes? Do I want yes? So make the space for that to happen.

FAUSTIN LINYEKULA is a choreographer, dancer, and storyteller. He founded Studios Kabako based in Kinshasa in 2001, before moving back to his hometown Kisangani in 2006. With over fifteen creations, Faustin has performed around the world. He was an Associate Artist of the city of Lisbon in 2016.

aussi au moins dix familles qui seront impliquées indirectement. De cette manière, on commence à avoir un impact indirect sur un cercle de gens un peu plus grand. Le but est d'enclencher un processus. Un processus qui prendra du temps, ça va prendre des années, mais qu'au moins quelques personnes, surtout des jeunes, puissent se rassembler et commencer à analyser ce qui se passe autour d'elles et se mettent à penser à ce que nous pouvons faire. Et ensuite à travers l'organisation des Studios Kabako, nous pouvons fournir un soutien pour faire avancer le processus et aussi trouver des façons créatives de partager ce processus avec d'autres. Un groupe qui pourra devenir une véritable plateforme pour développer des réflexions sur la question de l'eau à Lubunga. Imaginons des jeunes qui se promènent, parlent aux gens, documentent leurs discussions et font un film, puis vont voir les autorités, le bourgmestre de la commune, le maire de la ville de Kisangani ou le gouverneur de la province, pour dire : voici ce qui se passe. Ils donnent forme à un projet qui existerait même dans les médias ici. Avec l'espoir que cela ait plus d'impact que les campagnes électorales, une fois tous les cinq ans. Lorsque les politiciens se rendent là-bas et que les gens disent : « Baba, hatuna ta maji uku », parce que nous appelons les politiciens baba – papa. « Papa, nous n'avons pas d'eau ici. » Oui, nous n'avons pas d'eau, fais quelque chose pour nous ! Et puis quoi ensuite ? Mais si on va là-bas en disant : si nous avions dix pompes réparties de cette façon, nous aurions de l'eau pour cette population. Concrètement, nous commencerions à proposer des solutions pour résoudre nos propres problèmes. Peut-être un dialogue. Un projet comme celui-là ne peut pas remplacer une initiative du gouvernement. Ce n'est pas l'idée. C'est plutôt d'essayer de canaliser les voix des gens pour qu'elles soient entendues. En faisant ça, et parce que je crois encore au pouvoir des arts, pourraient peut-être émerger des voix artistiques que nous pourrions accompagner et nourrir à travers les Studios Kabako.

BM : Donc le but est d'articuler besoins et désirs ?

FL : Simplement se rappeler que nous avons des besoins. C'est Lubunga, mais c'est aussi la situation de ce pays en général. Nous sommes devenus tellement habitués à ne rien avoir que nous avons même oublié que nous avons des désirs, des besoins et des droits. Si nous pouvions seulement nous en rappeler, ce serait déjà un premier pas. Peut-être un premier pas dangereux, car rappeler à quelqu'un que d'avoir faim n'est pas un état normal n'est jamais anodin. C'est un peu lancer une bombe à la tête de quelqu'un. Il y a toujours quelque chose pour me rappeler combien notre peuple a faim et peut-être que je fais ce que je fais justement parce que je sais combien nous avons faim. Et je ne veux pas être seul dans cette aventure, alors j'essaie de contaminer les autres autour de moi. Et Lubunga m'est si chère, c'est important pour moi que les gens autour, à Lubunga, commencent à partager un peu de mon monde aussi. Que cela ne se résume pas juste à un cent dollars, donné de temps en temps, parce qu'une famille a besoin d'argent pour payer les frais d'école des enfants. Mais y a-t-il une façon de partager mon monde à un niveau plus profond ? Evidemment, c'est important de donner cent dollars, mais est-ce que je peux partager quelque chose d'autre avec eux ? La réponse est-elle oui ? Est-ce que je le veux ? Il faut créer l'espace pour que cela puisse arriver.

Chorégraphe, danseur, raconteur d'histoires, FAUSTIN LINYEKULA fonde les Studios Kabako à Kinshasa en 2001, avant de les déplacer à Kisangani, la ville où il a grandi, en 2006. Avec plus d'une quinzaine de créations, Faustin s'est produit dans le monde entier, il est artiste associé de la ville de Lisbonne en 2016.

LUBUNGAMODE: ON OTHER ARTISTIC RESEARCH

Baerbel Mueller

I met Faustin Linyekula in 2006, after having seen his latest piece performed on one of Vienna's theater stages. We discussed his perception of space, the time-space relations in his work, as well as the meanings of spatial concepts in Swahili, his mother tongue, and in Lingala, another language spoken in Congo.

He also talked about his vision of creating a network of cultural centers in Kisangani. A few years beforehand, I had imagined a project for Kumasi in Ghana, based on the idea of creating communal spaces that are spread throughout the city like acupuncture points, related to each other through invisible traces. When we identified our mutual interest in the conception of decentralized, dispersed spaces for art and urban culture, Faustin invited me to visit Kisangani and to collaborate on 'acupuncturing' it.

In addition to Makiso and Simisimi[1], Lubunga had been on the agenda from the very beginning. The question was how to relate with and encounter this marginalized part of the city: "How can we get close to the people; how can we be close to what really matters to them?" (Faustin) We found that, instead of any immediate artistic or architectural intervening, the essential topic of water provision could serve as a starting point for setting up a dialogue with the community.

In 2013, [a]FA and Studios Kabako established the collaborative and transdisciplinary lab named Lubungamode. We set the goal to investigate Lubunga's water situation from diverse perspectives—a more precise project brief was not defined. This topical but open strategy of encountering Lubunga allowed us to test the potentials of artistic and applied research as a starting point for communicating to inhabitants on a larger scale and building up personal networks at the same time. What does it mean to artistically produce from and for a specific territory? What does it mean to generate knowledge and a social impact from and for a specific territory? How to address environmental topics and social challenges, privileging the idea that change and development should occur internally? And what is the shared space of artistic research, community, and place in this context?

1 Districts of Kisangani

BAERBEL MUELLER, architect, head of the [applied] Foreign Affairs lab at the Institute of Architecture, University of Applied Arts Vienna, founder of nav_s baerbel mueller (navigations in the field of architecture and urban research within diverse cultural contexts), projects located on the African continent since 2002, recipient of the Ars Docendi State Award for excellence in teaching (2015).

LUBUNGAMODE : UNE AUTRE APPROCHE ARTISTIQUE

Baerbel Mueller

J'ai rencontré Faustin Linyekula en 2006 après avoir vu sa dernière pièce présentée sur l'une des scènes de Vienne. Nous avions alors discuté de sa perception de l'espace, de sa relation au temps dans ses créations, de la signification de différents concepts spatiaux dans sa langue natale, le swahili, et en lingala, une autre langue du Congo, mais aussi de sa vision d'un réseau de plusieurs centres culturels à Kisangani. Quelques années avant, j'avais imaginé un projet pour Kumasi au Ghana autour de l'idée de créer des espaces communaux disséminés dans la ville tels des points d'acupuncture, reliés les uns aux autres par des traces invisibles. Et c'est sur cet intérêt partagé pour la conception d'espaces pour les arts et la culture qui seraient dispersés, disséminés, que Faustin m'a invitée à Kisangani à mettre en œuvre avec lui cette « acupuncture » urbaine...

En plus des projets de Makiso et de Simisimi[1], Lubunga était présent dès le départ. Comment se relier à et aller à la rencontre de cette partie marginalisée de la ville : « Comment être proche des gens et surtout de ce qui compte vraiment pour eux ? » pour reprendre les mots de Faustin. D'où cette idée, non d'une intervention artistique ou architecturale immédiate, mais de partir de la question essentielle de l'approvisionnement en eau pour établir un dialogue avec la communauté.

En 2013, [a]FA et les Studios Kabako ont mis en oeuvre Lubungamode, un laboratoire transdisciplinaire et collaboratif afin d'examiner la situation de l'eau à Lubunga sous différentes perspectives : un programme plus précis fut défini. Cette stratégie thématique mais ouverte pour aller à la rencontre de Lubunga nous a permis d'explorer les potentialités d'une recherche appliquée et d'une démarche artistique comme point de départ pour communiquer avec les habitants sur une plus grande échelle, tout en participant à la construction de réseaux de personnes relais. Que signifie produire artistiquement, générer du savoir et avoir un impact social à partir de et pour un territoire donné ? Comment relever les défis environnementaux et sociaux en privilégiant l'idée que le changement doit venir de l'intérieur ? Et quel est cet espace qui pourrait être partagé entre une recherche artistique, une communauté et un lieu dans ce contexte ?

1 Quartiers de Kisangani

BAERBEL MULLER, architecte, dirige le laboratoire [applied] Foreign Affairs à l'Université des arts appliqués de Vienne. Fondatrice du nav_s baerbel Mueller (navigation dans les champs de l'architecture et de l'urbanisme au sein de différents contextes culturels). Projets situés depuis 2002 sur le continent africain. Elle a reçu en 2015 le prix national Ars Docendi, distinction récompensant l'excellence dans l'enseignement.

MISSION STATEMENT / MISSION

To understand the complexity of Lubunga's water situation, we focused on five geographic areas that are representative of the district as a whole. The chosen focal points have different degrees of urban density and include various scenarios of the local water situation. The areas are described by varying radii on a map. There are three main parameters to distinguish between the five circles, these are urban density, location, and water typology.

The team used three methods to approach these scenarios: spatial, scientific, and narrative. The spatial scenarios were mapped using descriptive drawings, collages, and plans. The scientific approach analyzed the water chain in terms of source, supply, consumption, and disposal. The narrative view was based on personal interviews and a one-question survey of children in Lubunga.

Afin de bien saisir la complexité de la situation de l'eau à Lubunga, l'équipe s'est concentrée sur cinq zones géographiques représentatives de l'ensemble de l'arrondissement. Les endroits ciblés possèdent différents degrés de densité urbaine et représentent divers scénarios de la situation locale de l'eau. Les zones sont détaillées sur une carte à l'aide de rayons variables. Trois paramètres principaux, à savoir la densité urbaine, l'emplacement et la typologie de l'eau, permettent de distinguer les cinq cercles.

Pour exposer ces scénarios, l'équipe s'est servie de trois méthodes : spatiale, scientifique et narrative. Le scénario spatial se schématise à l'aide de dessins descriptifs, de collages et de plans. L'approche scientifique consiste à analyser la chaîne d'eau en fonction de la source, de l'alimentation, de la consommation et de l'évacuation. Le point de vue narratif s'appuie sur des entrevues individuelles ainsi qu'un sondage à question unique réalisé auprès d'enfants de Lubunga.

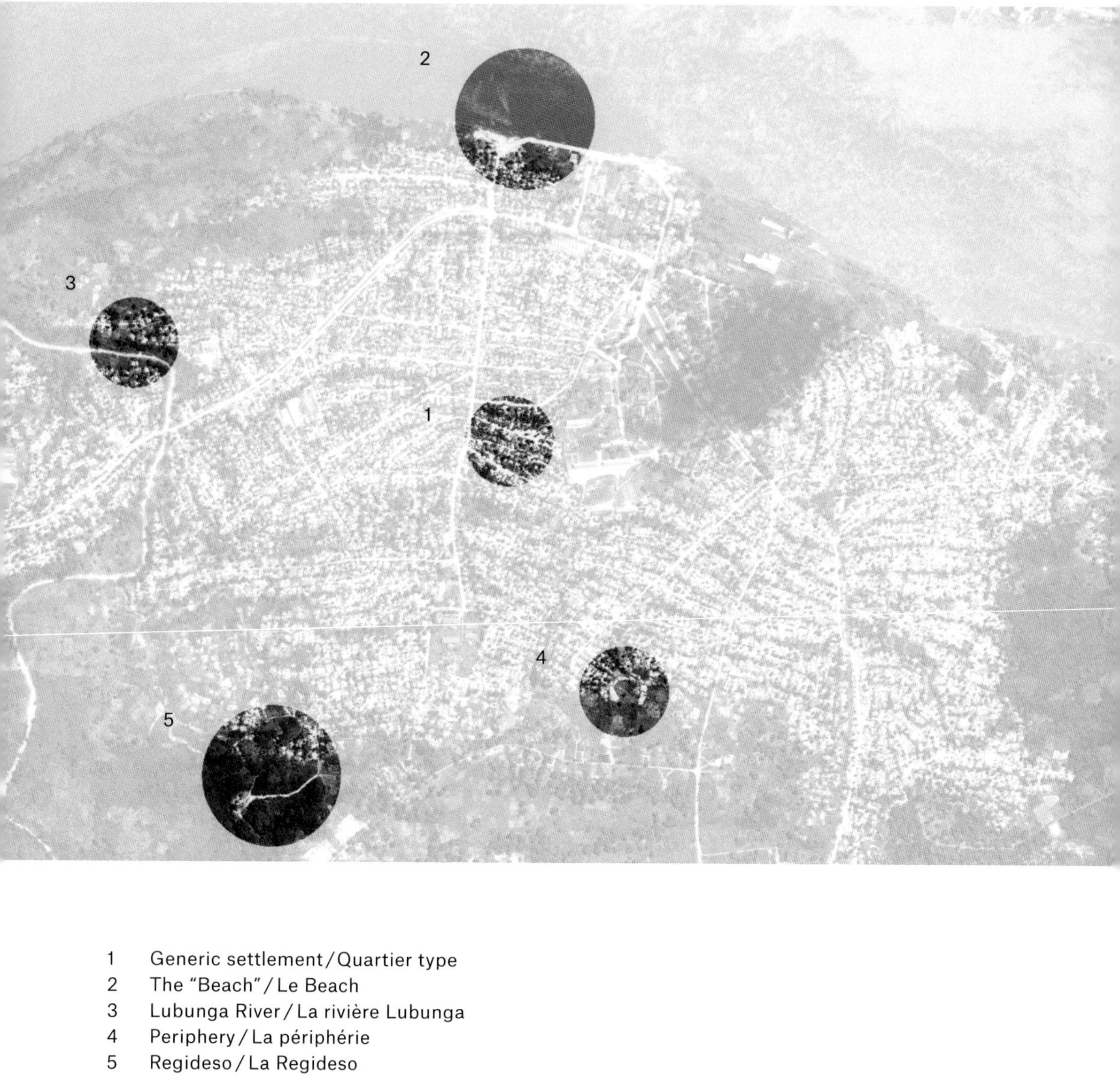

1 Generic settlement / Quartier type
2 The "Beach" / Le Beach
3 Lubunga River / La rivière Lubunga
4 Periphery / La périphérie
5 Regideso / La Regideso

SPATIAL MAPPING

Juergen Strohmayer,
Stefanie Theuretzbacher
September 2013

The spatial manifestations of water in Lubunga are found in the spaces between buildings. The urban paradox of Lubunga is its large area and population which contrasts with its quasi-rural character. Water defines all aspects of life. It is present everywhere and in all scales, from the vast hydrodynamic force of the Congo River and its tributary streams, to natural springs and wells that are dug between houses. Water is right below the ground.

We set ourselves the task of visualizing these manifestations of water, both man-made and natural, in order to provide a descriptive documentation. The five zoom-in circles defined by the group were chosen because of the representative characteristics of water they contained. In the spatial mapping, these were taken literally and created the focus points for the research. Each area was mapped, drawn as panoramic perspectives, and characterized with a table of observations. These three formats focus on interstitial spatial scenarios such as shared backyards that incorporate toilets, bathing spots, cooking areas, gardens, and places of business. Many of these places have a multifaceted character, such as the bathing and cleaning spots along the Lubunga River that are also important places for woman to socialize outside of their homes.

Water was chosen by Studios Kabako as the central topic to begin their exchange with Lubunga because it is the single most important topic of concern for its residents. It was our goal to create a project that would document this but also engage. The panorama drawings are not only illustrations of the current water situation in Lubunga, they also help to raise awareness of the importance of water there in an artistic format. In September 2014, one of the panoramas was printed as a banner and hung on an unused pylon in Lubunga.

Collaborators:
Benjamin Lokele, Jean Amisi Lipame

CARTOGRAPHIE SPATIALE

Juergen Strohmayer,
Stefanie Theuretzbacher
Septembre 2013

Les manifestations spatiales de l'eau à Lubunga se révèlent dans les espaces interstitiels entre les bâtiments. Le paradoxe de Lubunga tient à sa grande superficie doublée d'une forte population qui contrastent avec le caractère quasi rural de son implantation. L'eau définit tous les aspects de la vie. Elle est présente partout, à différentes échelles, du puissant fleuve Congo et ses affluents aux plus modestes sources naturelles et aux puits creusés entre les maisons. L'eau est là, juste sous les pieds de ses habitants.

Notre but était de visualiser ces manifestations de l'eau, qu'elles soient artificielles ou naturelles, afin de fournir une documentation descriptive. Les cinq cercles ciblés par le groupe ont été choisis en raison du caractère représentatif de la situation de l'eau sur leur territoire spécifique. Utilisés tels quels dans la cartographie spatiale, ces cercles ont délimité des zones prioritaires pour la recherche. Chacun a été cartographié, dessiné selon une perspective panoramique et accompagné d'un tableau d'observations. Ces trois analyses se sont spécialement attachées aux espaces interstitiels, tels que les cours communes qui regroupent les toilettes, l'espace pour se laver, l'espace pour cuisiner, des plantations et parfois un lieu pour faire du petit commerce. Beaucoup de ces espaces présentent de multiples facettes et caractéristiques, ainsi les bords de la rivière Lubunga qui servent aux bains et à la lessive sont aussi un lieu important de sociabilisation pour les femmes de Lubunga.

Si les Studios Kabako ont choisi l'eau comme thème central pour leurs échanges avec Lubunga, c'est que l'eau représente l'une des principales préoccupations de ses habitants. Notre objectif était donc de pouvoir documenter ce thème, tout en nous engageant. Ainsi, les dessins panoramiques que nous avons réalisés sont à la fois des illustrations précieuses de la situation actuelle, mais aussi un support artistique pour sensibiliser la population à l'importance de l'eau.

En septembre 2014, l'un des dessins panoramiques a été imprimé sur une bâche de 6 mètres de long et fixé sur un ancien panneau au Beach de Lubunga.

Collaborateurs :
Benjamin Lokele, Jean Amisi Lipame

1 Generic settlement / Quartier type

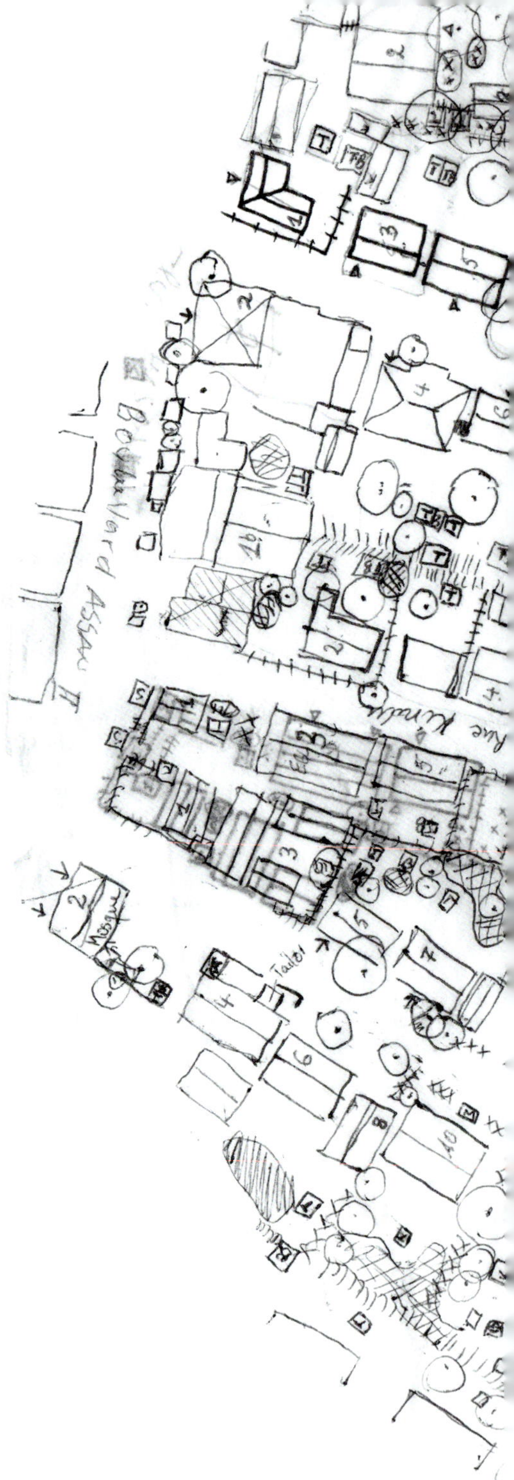

SCRAP
YARD
Hotel

1 Generic settlement / Quartier type

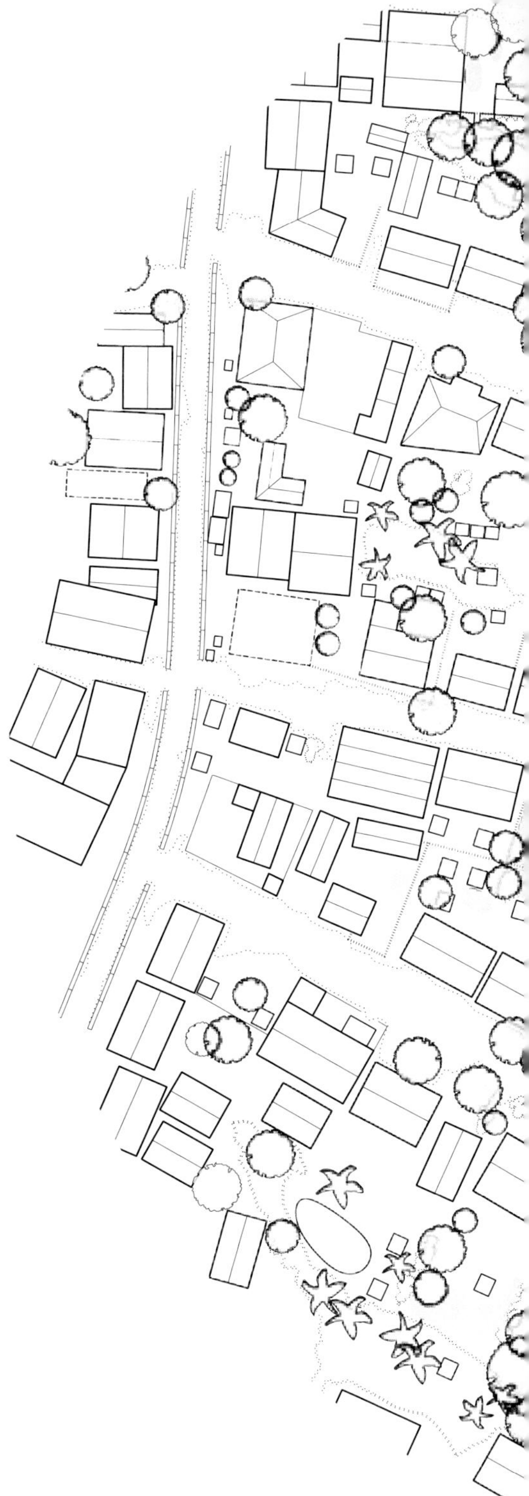

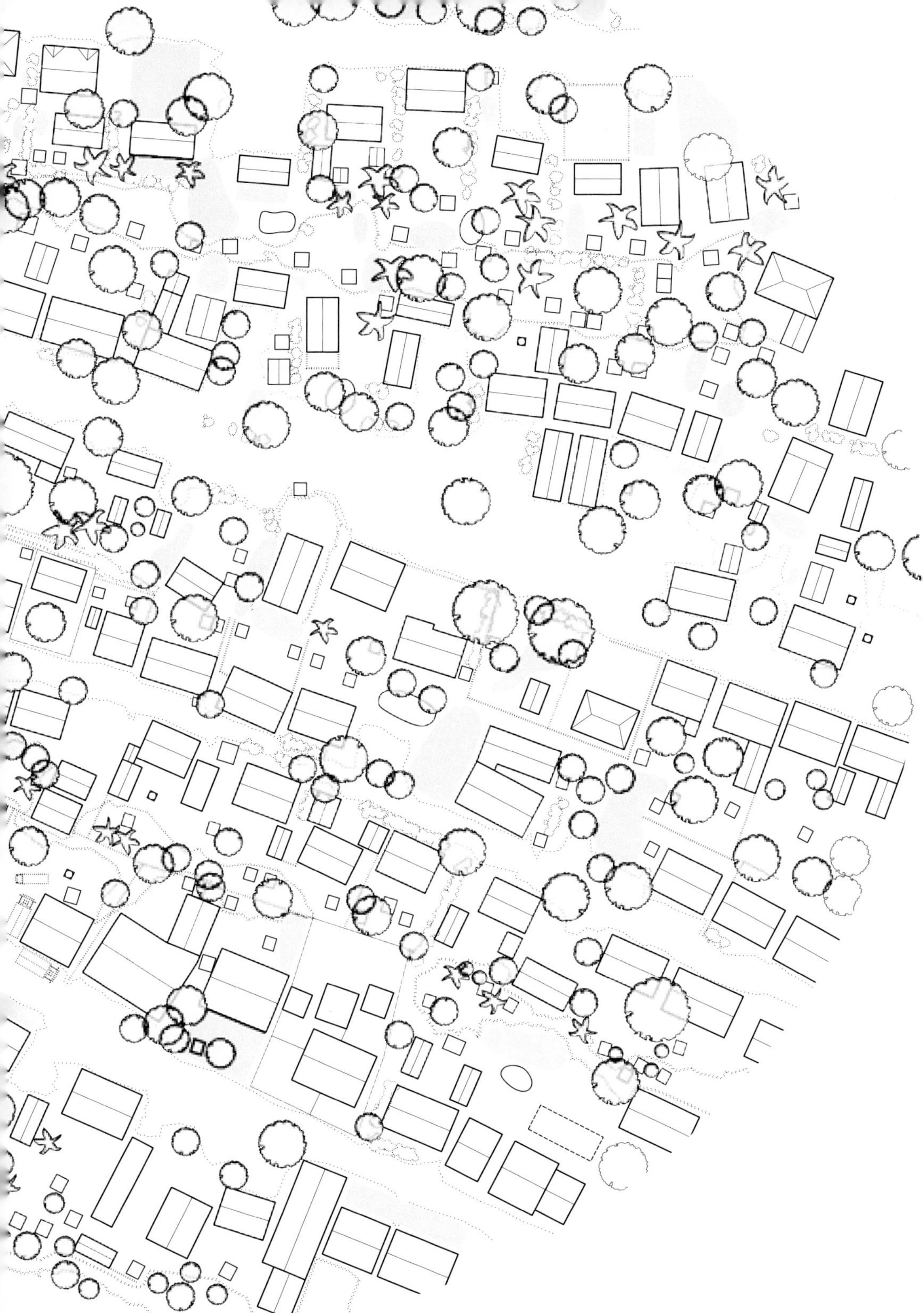

2 The "Beach"/Le Beach

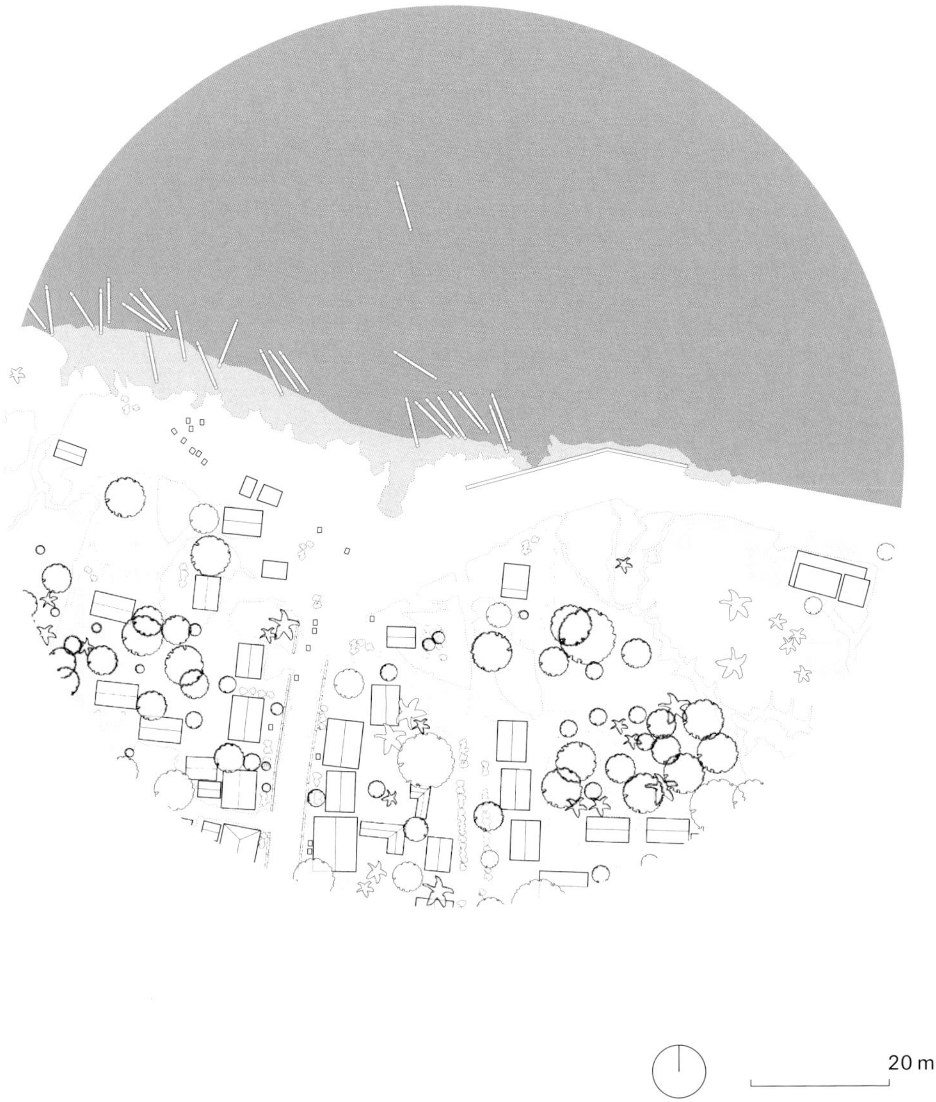

3 Lubunga River / La rivière Lubunga

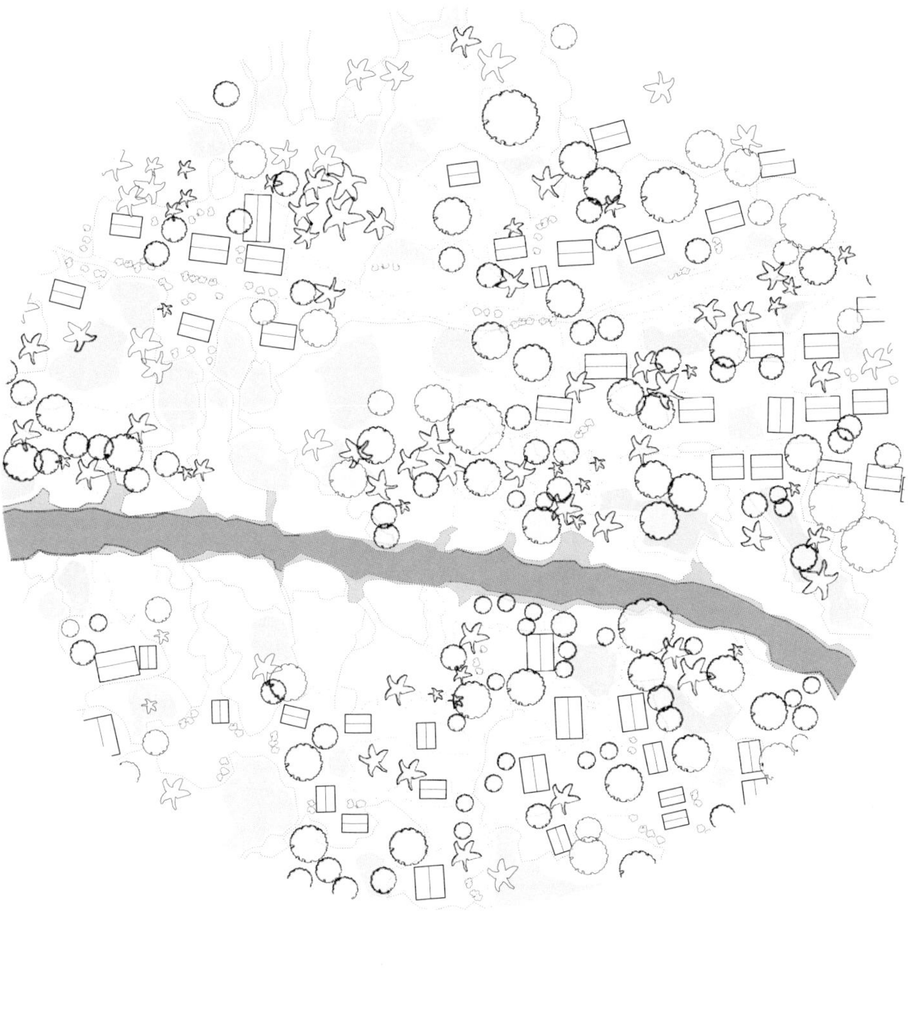

4 Periphery / La périphérie

5 Regideso / La Regideso

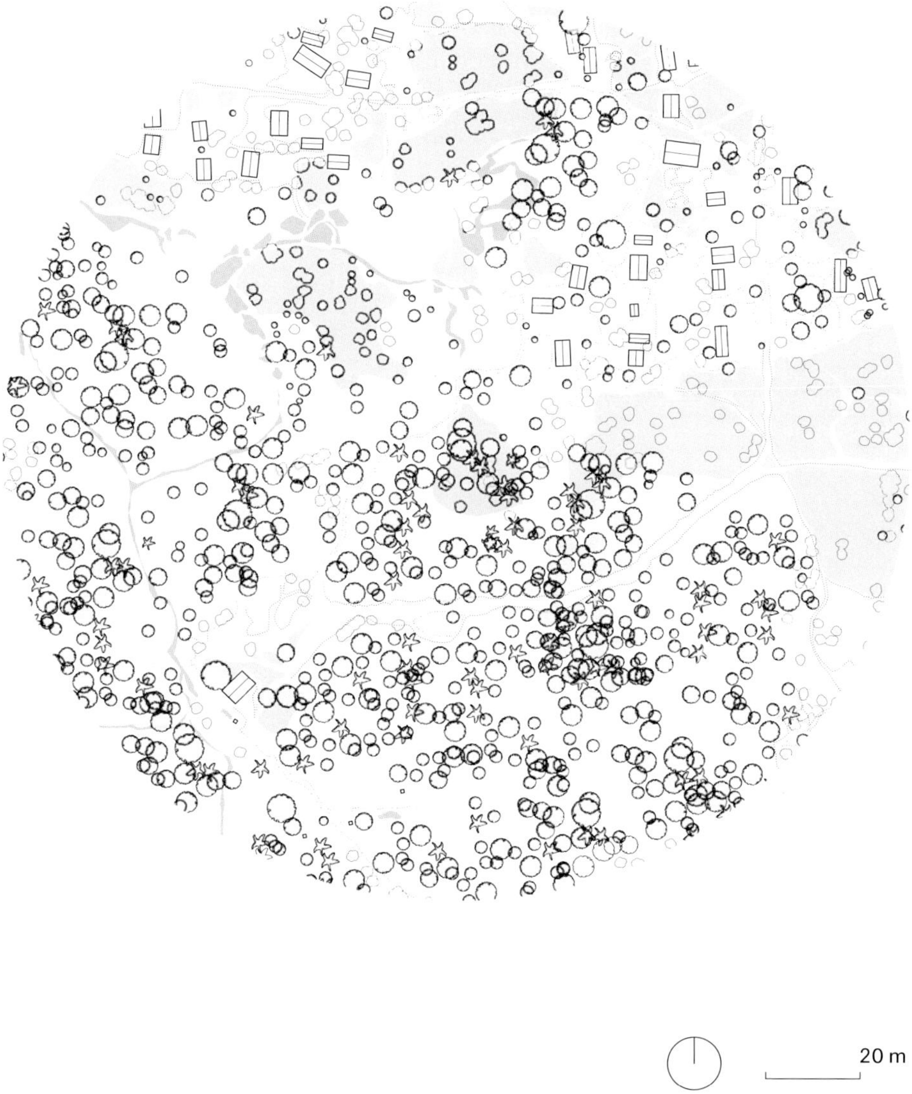

360° Panorama Photos /
Photographies panoramiques : 360°

Five representative spots were selected by the team, one in each circle, that were to be mapped as 360° photos. These dome-like pictures capture scenarios taking place in the different types of spaces in Lubunga highlighting the diverse manifestations of water—its sourcing, consumption, and disposal.

Trois points représentatifs ont été choisis par l'équipe pour faire l'objet d'une prise de vue panoramique à 360 degrés : un point dans chaque cercle. Ces photographies en forme de dôme illustrent différents scénarios dans différents types d'espace à Lubunga, mettant en lumière les diverses activités liées à l'eau : l'approvisionnement, la consommation et l'évacuation.

Generic settlement / Quartier type

The "Beach" / Le Beach

River / La rivière
steep path towards river / sentiers escarpés vers la rivière
accessible river spot / point d'accès à la rivière
gardens / jardins

connected ponds used for fish farming / étangs connectés pour la pisciculture, étangs à poissons, eaux stagnantes

Regideso / La Regideso
water container / bidon d'eau
domestic water fetching (girls) / collecte de l'eau à usage domestique (filles)
colonial water tank (non-functional) / citerne à eau coloniale (hors d'usage)
natural spring / source naturelle
water transport business (boys) / activités de transport d'eau (garçons)
historical water pump (broken) / ancienne pompe à eau (cassée)

Regideso / La Regideso

The "Beach" / Le Beach

	LUBUNGA RIVER / LA RIVIÈRE LUBUNGA	GENERIC SETTLEMENT / QUARTIER TYPE
Water access / Accès à l'eau :	fast flowing stream / courant rapide	taps, potable wells, secondary wells, rain water, standing waste water, transported water / robinets, puits à eau potable, puits secondaires, eau de pluie, eaux usées stagnantes, eau amenée
Water use / Utilisation de l'eau :	bathing, washing dishes, laundry, fetching domestic water, transport, playground / toilette, lessive, vaisselle, usages domestiques, transport, terrain de jeu	domestic water, drinking water, body hygiene / eau à usage domestique, eau potable, hygiène corporelle
Physical / Caractéristiques physiques :	rock plate formations, valley situation, visual privacy, small gardens, steep paths, river bank / formations de roches plates, situation encaissée, protégé des regards, petits jardins, chemins raides, berges de la rivière	backyards, well structures, gardens, toilets, kitchens, stables / arrière-cours, aménagement des puits, jardins, toilettes, cuisines, étables
Social / Environnement social :	gendered space, informal meeting point, domestic education, cleaning habits / espace sexué, point de rencontre informel, éducation domestique, habitudes liées au lavage et à la toilette	backyard-as-living-room, invis-ible borders, communal use of private wells, queuing for water / arrière-cours comme lieu de convivialité, frontières invisibles, usage collectif des puits privés, files d'attente pour l'eau

THE "BEACH"/ LE BEACH	PERIPHERY/ LA PÉRIPHÉRIE	REGIDESO/ LA REGIDESO
Congo River, the "Beach"/ le fleuve Congo, le "Beach"	standing water, ponds, springs/ eaux stagnantes, étangs, sources	springs, water pump/ sources, pompes à eau
transport, fishing, waste water disposal, washing dishes, laundry, bathing, playground, toilet, fetching domestic water/transport, pêche, rejet des eaux usées, lessive, vaisselle, bains, terrain de jeu, toilettes, collecte de l'eau à usage domestique	bathing, washing dishes, laundry, fish hydroculture, fetching domestic water/ toilette, vaisselle, lessive, pisciculture, collecte de l'eau à usage domestique	fetching domestic water, fetching drinking water, potential tap water source/ collecte de l'eau à usage domestique, collecte de l'eau potable, source potentiellement utilisable pour la mise en place d'un réseau d'eau courante
the "Beach", natural river bank, artificial embankments, pirogue boat station, moto taxi station, slaughterhouses, churches, harbour industry, fish traps, sellers/le Beach rives du fleuve non-aménagées, berges aménagées, point de départ/arrivée des pirogues, stationnement des taxis motos, abattoirs, églises, activités portuaires, filets de pêche, vendeurs	marshland, gardens, settle-ments, military barracks/ zones marécageuses, jardins, implantations, casernes militaires	forest, underground springs, abandoned infrastructure, ruins/forêt, sources souterraines, équipements à l'abandon, ruines
commercial interaction, business associations, commuters, social border, communication between between left and right riverbanks/activités commerciales, échanges et affaires, personnes faisant la navette, frontière sociale, communication entre la Rive gauche et la Rive droite	shared wash spaces, supplementary income, army proximity/espaces de lavage/ toilette partagés, revenus complémentaires, proximité militaire	village-scale water source, informal meeting point, water fetching business, expectations, historical relevance, role of the government/source d'eau à l'échelle d'un village, point de rencontre informel, services de livraison d'eau, attentes, pertinence historique, rôle des pouvoirs publics

DRAWING IS.

Nikolaus Gansterer

Travelling means moving through space. Moving offers new modes of experiencing and perceiving space. But how are these dynamic spaces inscribed into our bodily perception and thus constitute inner landscapes and, inversely, how do these inner spaces organize and get inscribed again into shared (public) spaces? If we assume choreography to be the fundamental organization and inscription of movements in time and space—how are maps of these forces which make matter (bodies, objects, etc.) move? What language, alphabet, and sign system have to be developed in order to articulate these elusive and situational in-between spaces?

How can our experiences be distilled into detailed body-mind maps, which are notations of what I would call psychoreographic mindscapes, blurring the boundaries between ego-graphy and geo-graphy? What happens when the map as the representation of space becomes a representative of its own? Where is here?

Rather than writing about drawing, I propose drawing on drawing as a specific practice of sense-making—to practise thinking with our hands. Thinking drawing. Drawing beyond. Drawing conclusions. To follow the lines of thought to the point where thought becomes matter and starts to matter. Here, finding not-(yet)-known modes of manoeuvering through space. Here, performing figures of searching and re-searching. Again and again. Drawing as a space shuttle. As a vehicle to ride. As a machine to question. As an organ to communicate with. Becoming space. Now!

Artist NIKOLAUS GANSTERER (1974) is cofounder of the Institute for Transacoustic Research and currently visiting professor at the Center Research Focus at the University of Applied Arts in Vienna, Austria. He is internationally active in performances, exhibitions, and lectures tracing the speculative potential of diagrams, scores, and maps.

DESSINER.

Nikolaus Gansterer

Voyager signifie se déplacer à travers l'espace. Se déplacer offre de nouvelles modalités d'expérimentation et de perception de l'espace. Mais comment ces espaces dynamiques sont-ils inscrits dans notre perception physique, dessinant ainsi des espaces intérieurs – et inversement, comment ces espaces intérieurs s'organisent et s'inscrivent-ils dans des espaces partagés (publics) ? Si nous partons du principe que la chorégraphie représente fondamentalement l'organisation et l'inscription du mouvement dans le temps et l'espace, comment peut-on représenter ces forces qui font bouger la matière (corps, objets...) ? Quel langage, quel alphabet, quel système de signes peut-on développer pour rendre compte de ces espaces intermédiaires, insaisissables, conjoncturels?

Comment nos expériences peuvent-elles irriguer ces cartes du corps et de l'esprit, tels des systèmes de notation de ce que j'appellerais des paysages mentaux psychoréographiques, brouillant les frontières entre égo et géographie ? Que se passe-t-il lorsque les cartes comme représentations de l'espace deviennent des représentations en soi ? Où est ici ?

Plutôt que d'écrire sur le dessin, je propose de dessiner sur les dessins, le dessin comme une pratique spécifique faisant sens ou comment pratiquer la pensée avec nos mains ?

Penser le fait de dessiner. Dessiner au-delà. Dessiner des conclusions. Suivre les lignes de la pensée jusqu'au point où cette pensée devient matière et commence à importer.

Trouver ici des modalités encore inconnues de manoeuvrer à travers l'espace. Ici, figures de représentation de l'acte de chercher et de re-chercher. Encore et toujours. Le dessin comme une navette spatiale. Comme un véhicule à conduire. Comme une machine à questionner. Comme un organe pour communiquer. Devenir l'espace. Maintenant !

NIKOLAUS GANSTERER (1974) co-fonde l'Institut de Recherche Transacoustique (IFTAF) et est professeur invité au Centre Research Focus à l'université des arts appliqués de Vienne en Autriche. Il est reconnu sur le plan international pour ses performances, expositions et conférences sur le potentiel spéculatif des diagrammes, cartes et autres notations.

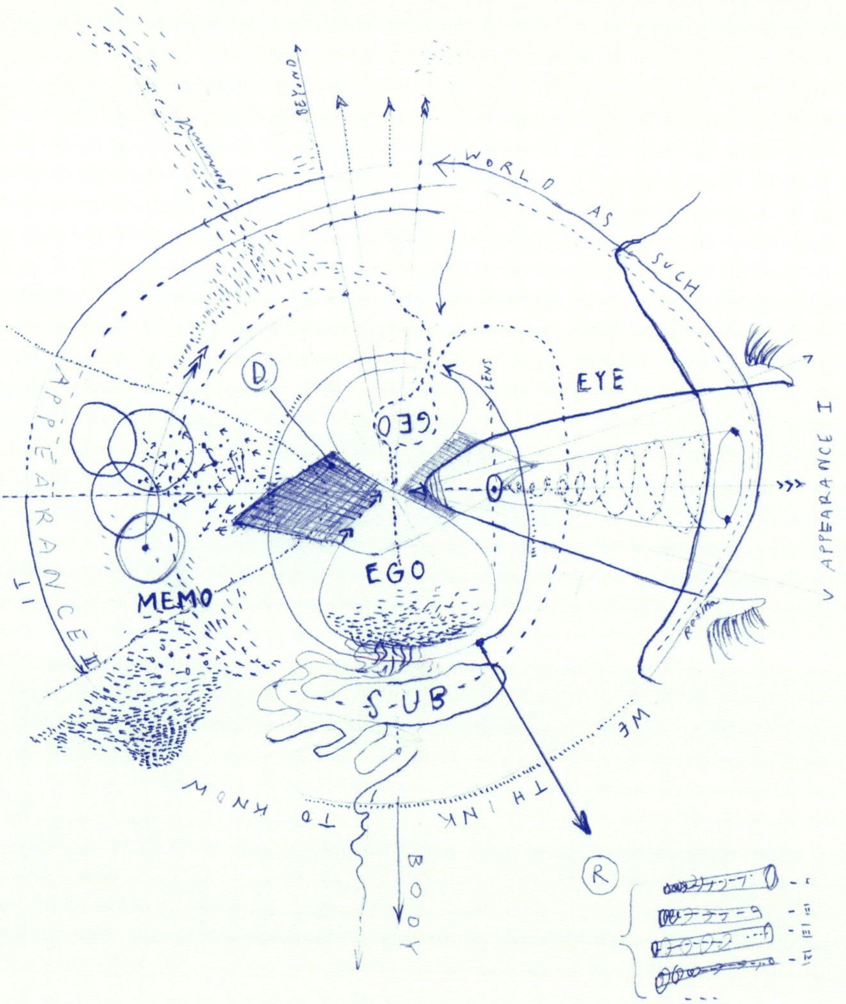
BEYOND
WORLD AS SUCH
EYE
LENS
GEO
D
EGO
MEMO
S-UB
APPEARANCE II
APPEARANCE I
Retina
WE THINK TO KNOW
BODY
R

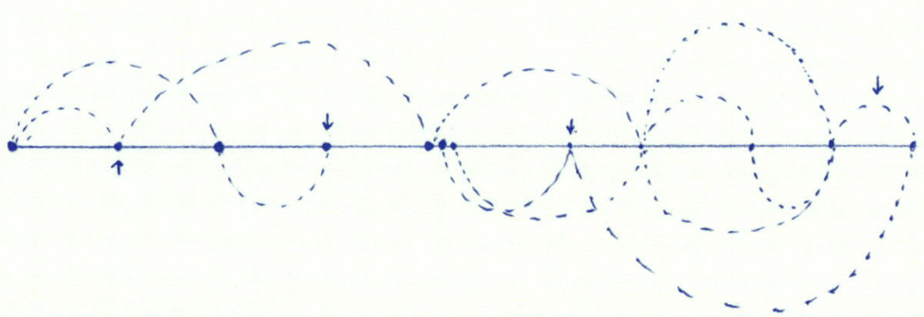

Figures of re-searching / Figurer l'acte de re-chercher

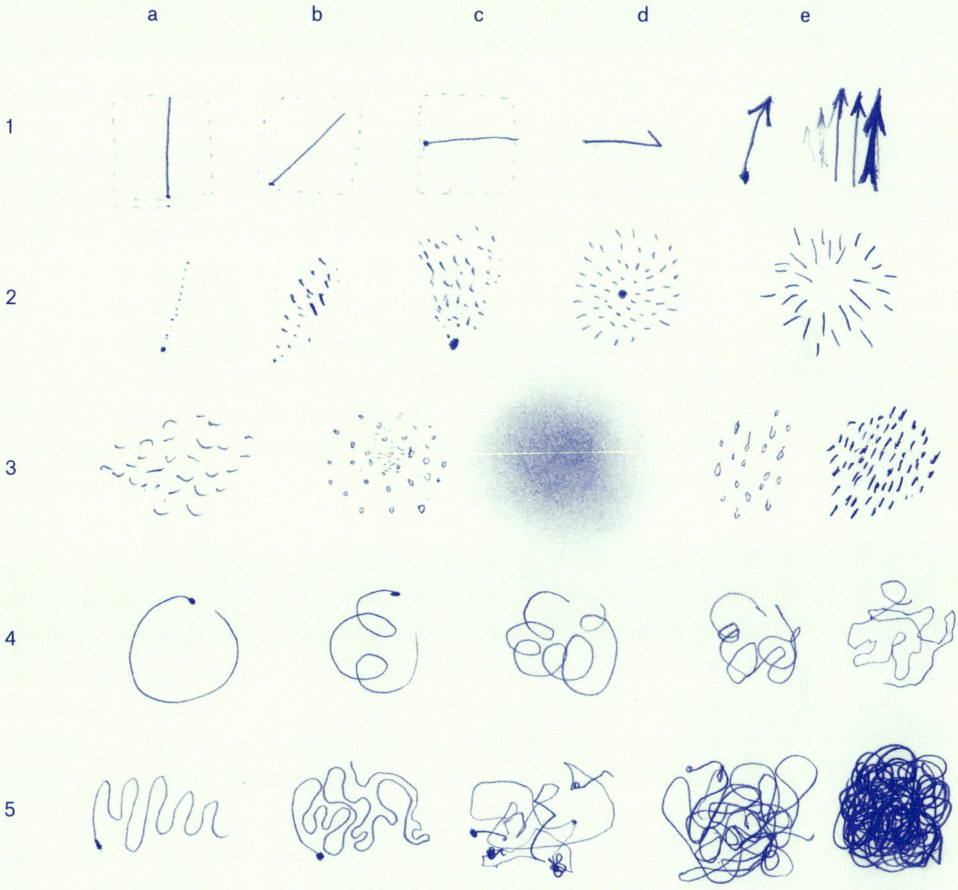

1a) straight / droite, 1b) afférent / afférente, 1c) linear / linéaire, 1d) directed / orientée, 1e) reinforcing / renforcée, 2a) tentative / ébauchée, 2b) attentive / vigilante, 2c) swarming / grouillante, 2d) radiant / rayonnante, 2e) explosive / explosive, 3a) cloudy / nuageuse, 3b) abeyant / en attente, 3c) foggy / brumeuse, 3d) trickling / goutte à goutte, 3e) pouring / à verse, 4a) circling / circulaire, 4b) circulating / circulante, 4c) spinning / tournoyante, 4d) swaying / balancée, 4e) spooky / lugubre, 5a) meandering / sinueuse, 5b) winding / enroulée, 5c) twisted / vrillée, 5d) weird / étrange, 5e) tangled / enchevêtrée

Figures of re-searching / Figurer l'acte de re-chercher

1a) serrated / dentelée, 1b) zigzag / en zigzag, 1c) toothed / dentée, 1d) starry / étoilée, 2a) systematic / systématique, 2b) squared / au carré, 2c) indexical / indexée, 2d) meticulous / méticuleuse, 3a) crescive / croissante, 3b) dendritic / dendritique, 3c) reticulate / réticulée, 3d) rhizomatic / rhizomatique, 4a) dynamic / dynamique, 4b) rotating / rotative, 4c) turbulent / turbulente, 4d) cellular / cellulaire, 5a) spiraling / en spirale, 5b) concentric / concentrique, 5c) twirling towards / tournoyante vers, 5d) cyclonic / cyclonique

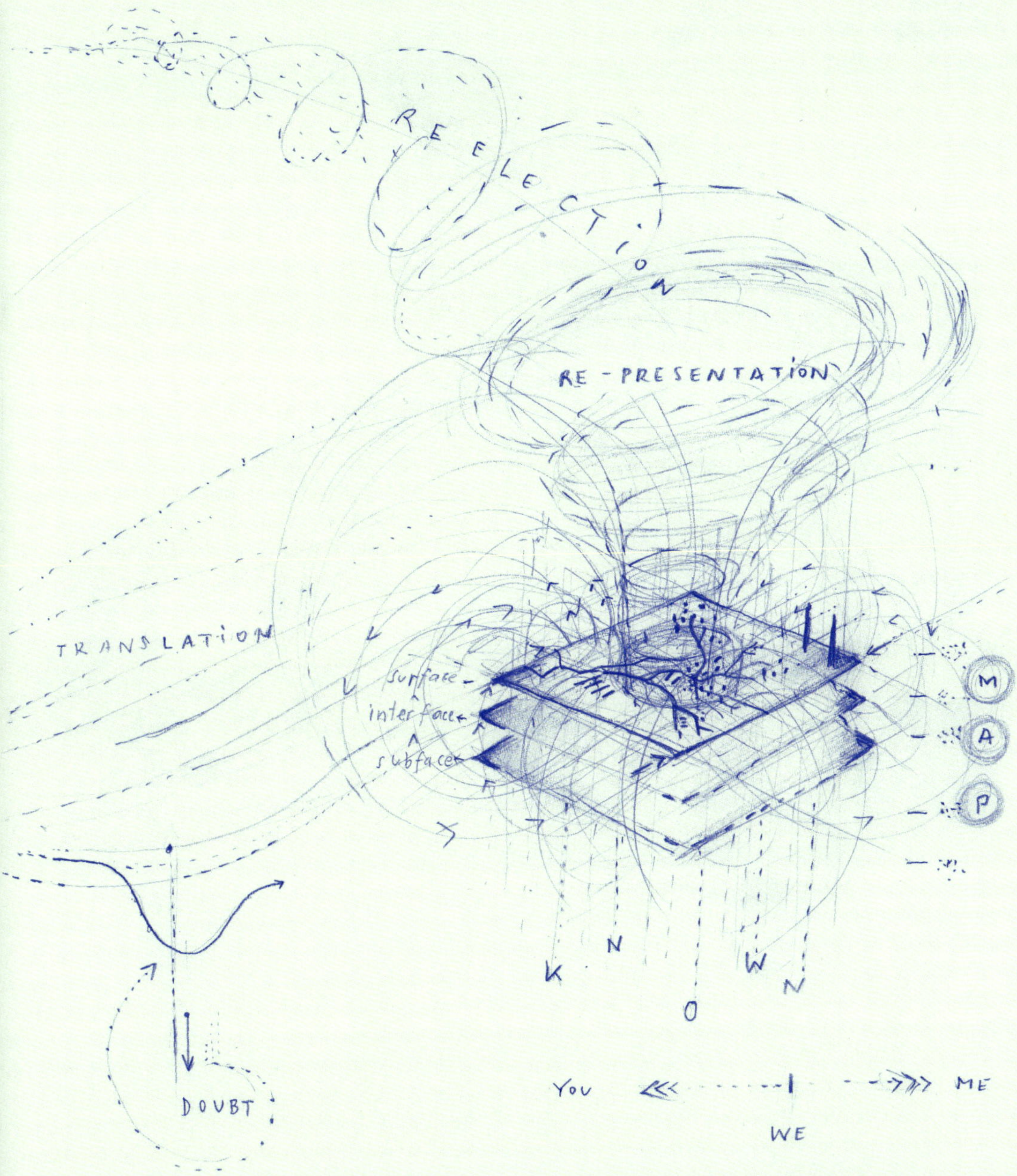
REFLECTION
RE-PRESENTATION
TRANSLATION
surface
interface
subface
M
A
P
K N O W N
DOUBT
YOU
ME
WE

Billboard Intervention /
Intervention sur un panneau d'affichage

Lubunga, September 2014 /
Septembre 2014

With the aim of bringing the project back to Lubunga and sharing it in a public space, a 12 x 3 m canvas print of the colored panorama drawing of the "Beach" was hung on the empty billboard at that location. Billboard skeletons are part of the visual landscape of Lubunga, with the one at the "Beach" being the most prominent, widely visible from across the river and signposting this busy arrival point in Lubunga. The location was the motif for the drawing, creating a mirroring effect—subjects and viewers looking at each other and making the transient, ephemeral space of the "Beach" visible for a moment.

Afin de ramener le projet à Lubunga et de le partager dans un espace public, une bâche de 12 mètres par 3 représentant un dessin panoramique et en couleurs du Le Beach a été accrochée à un panneau vide sur le lieu-même. Les squelettes d'anciens panneaux font partie du paysage visuel de Lubunga, celui du Le Beach, situé au point d'arrivée à Lubunga, toujours effervescent, est le plus imposant, visible même depuis l'autre côté du fleuve. L'emplacement a constitué l'objet du dessin, créant ainsi un effet miroir – les sujets dessinés et les spectateurs se regardant les uns les autres, rendant pour un moment visible l'espace éphémère du « Beach ».

[a]FA
Les Studios Kabako

NARRATIVE MAPPING

Frida Robles, Isaac Yenga
September 2013

Taking into account that narration helps defining the distribution of spaces, times and forms of activity and that stories are used to construct diverse realities, it felt necessary to undertake a narrative quest in order to get a broader understanding of the water situation in Lubunga. Therefore, a handful of personal interviews were conducted with some of Lubunga's inhabitants. The interviews dealt with their personal relationships with water and their place of residence. The interest of conducting these interviews was to engage the inhabitants on an emotional and individual level with their stories. The collected answers shed light on topics such as feelings of belonging, local government structures, family networks, and, of course, the current water situation. In this regard, we got a common answer when asking for the best solution for water in Lubunga. We repeatedly heard "the restoration of the water distribution center in Lubunga [the Regideso]" mentioned. This water distribution center was built during colonial times and supported only a portion of the population. Furthermore, this infrastructure has not received proper maintenance due to political, social, and economic unrest. Practically speaking, it wouldn't be enough to just restore the Regideso in order to provide water to the whole of Lubunga's population. However, this structure is still narrated as a space of hope. It is suggested that in order to establish a more organic and socially-based structure for a water solution in Lubunga, there needs to be a narrative shift.

These are the basic theoretical premises upon which the narrative approach is based, most of them originated upon the reading of philosopher Jacques Ranciere*:

- Space is practiced in narrative ways.
- Urban spaces are marked by memories. Some can be considered scars in the spatial and social tissue.
- The configurations of spaces are intrinsically related to political and social configurations.
- These configurations are part of the distribution of the sensible, politics of the aesthetic.
- Every demarcation in space is political.
- Artistic spatial actions could deal with the dismantlement of inoperative distributions of the sensible.
- A new narrative of space creates new social and political configurations.

* Jacques Ranciere, The Politics of Aesthetics: The Distribution of the Sensible (2000)

CARTOGRAPHIE NARRATIVE

Frida Robles, Isaac Yenga
Septembre 2013

Partant du principe que la narration aide à définir le « partage des espaces, des temps et des formes d'activité » * et que les récits servent à la construction de diverses réalités, il semblait nécessaire d'entreprendre une recherche narrative afin de mieux comprendre la situation de l'eau à Lubunga. C'est pourquoi une série d'entretiens individuels ont été menés avec des habitants de Lubunga autour de leurs relations à l'eau et à leur quartier. L'objectif de ces entretiens était d'encourager les habitants à livrer leurs visions personnelles et leurs ressentis. Les réponses recueillies apportent des éléments sur le sentiment d'appartenance, les structures de décision et de gestion locales, les réseaux familiaux, et, bien entendu, la situation de l'eau aujourd'hui. A la question « Quelle serait la meilleure solution pour l'eau à Lubunga ? » s'est fait jour un réponse commune : « La restauration du centre de distribution d'eau à Lubunga, la Regideso. » Ce centre de distribution d'eau, construit durant la période coloniale, desservait seulement une partie de la population. En outre, cette infrastructure n'a pas reçu un entretien adéquat en raison des troubles politiques, sociaux et économiques. Ainsi, d'un point de vue pratique, restaurer la Regideso ne suffirait pas à fournir de l'eau à l'ensemble de la population de Lubunga. Pourtant, nombreux sont ceux qui mettent tous leurs espoirs dans cette structure. Une solution au problème de l'eau à Lubunga basée sur une structure plus organique et socialement acceptable ne pourra donc faire l'économie d'un changement de perspective.

L'approche narrative repose sur un certain nombre de prémices théoriques de base, empruntés notamment au philosophe français Jacques Rancière* :

- L'espace s'exprime de manière narrative.
- Les espaces urbains sont marqués par la mémoire et certains souvenirs sont autant de cicatrices sur le tissu spatial et social.
- Ces configurations spatiales sont intrinsèquement liées aux configurations sociales et politiques.
- Ces configurations font partie du « partage du sensible » et des « politiques de l'esthétique ».
- Chaque démarcation de l'espace est politique.
- Les actions artistiques spatiales pourraient traiter du démantèlement du partage du sensible inopérant.
- Un nouveau récit de l'espace crée de nouvelles configurations sociales et politiques.

* Jacques Rancière, Le Partage du sensible : esthétique et politique (2000).

ISAAC

That is to say, if you are an enemy of water, you don't exist.

C'est-à-dire que si tu es ennemi de l'eau, tu n'existes pas.

PAPA MODI

I really love this job [water management] because it allows me to live better.

J'aime beaucoup ce métier [l'eau] parce qu'il me permet de mieux vivre.

PAPA IGNACE

For me, the water problem is, let's say... what can I say... a disaster... because it is never... you see...

Pour moi, l'eau représente, disons... qu'est-ce que je vais dire... une catastrophe... parce que c'est jamais... voyez...

GRAND-MÈRE

Our Lubunga River is very dangerous because children have drowned there while bathing. The water is worm-infested and dangerous.

Notre rivière Lubunga est très dangereuse parce qu'elle emporte des enfants quand ils viennent se laver et ils meurent. L'eau de cette rivière est pleine de vers intestinaux et elle est mauvaise.

HENRIETTE

Water is colorless, but this river water is murky, while other sources are clear, which is why we drink from them instead of the river.

L'eau n'a pas de couleur, sauf que l'eau du fleuve contient des poussières, tandis que d'autres (sources) sont claires et c'est pourquoi nous les buvons.

JEAN

There is a water source in Wagenia that is somehow located close to the people who have been using it. As it is in the open, this source is responsible for the outbreak of many epidemics.

Il y a une source à Wagenia qui est un peu tout près des gens et qu'ils ont l'habitude d'utiliser, c'est par cette source-là qu'il y a beaucoup d'épidémies qui naissent, parce que c'est à l'air libre.

TRAVAILLEUR À LA REGIDESO

Poverty is widespread here, and there is no cash flow.

Il y a vraiment une pauvreté géante ici, l'argent ne circule pas.

PAPA AMISI

In Lubunga we are, traditionally, farmers; that's our strength. When you can't offer services anymore, you return to cultivating the land.

A Lubunga, nous sommes vraiment des cultivateurs, ça c'est notre force. Quand vous n'avez rien à faire, vous allez en brousse et vous cultivez.

GORETTE

We paid the Regideso. We don't have water at the moment. I think we haven't had water for six or five years, if I am not mistaken.

On payait la Regideso. Pour le moment, on n'a pas d'eau. Il y a de cela je crois six ou cinq ans, si je ne me trompe pas, que l'eau n'arrive plus.

DOCTEUR

The hospital water supply came from the Regideso, but it has been quite a while since it has been able to supply us with water here: 26 February 2013 was the last day. It was 81 m^3. For electricity, it is 81.

L'hôpital était approvisionné en eau à partir de la Regideso, mais il y a un bon moment qu'elle n'est plus en mesure de nous fournir de l'eau ici : le dernier jour, c'était le 26 février 2013. C'était 81 m^3. Pour l'électricité, c'est 1981.

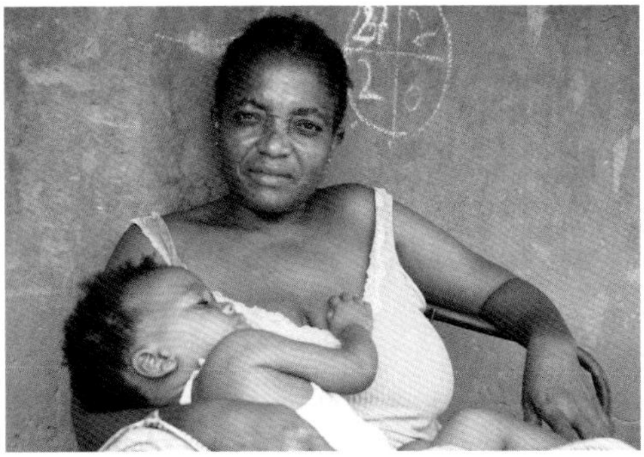

MAYAZA

Presently, there's no way to be happy. The only thing is that at sunrise, you praise the Lord.

Présentement, il n'y a pas moyen d'être heureuse. L'unique chose est quand le jour se lève, tu rends grâce à Dieu.

PAPA BALOMBA

When I return to Lubunga after work, I first go home to rest. After that, if I have something, I can take a walk along the river. After that, I go straight back home and stay there.

Quand j'arrive à Lubunga après le travail : d'abord je me repose chez moi à la maison. Après cela, si j'ai quelque chose, je peux me promener aux abords du fleuve. Après, je retourne directement à la maison pour y rester.

BI ATOSHA

A fable teaches us about how to be.

Une fable nous instruit sur la manière d'être.

PAPA ASSANI

During World War I, Lubunga didn't really exist... I can say that around 1910, we could already start talking about Lubunga, but as far as everything else is concerned, it all came after World War II.

Pendant la Première Guerre Mondiale, Lubunga n'existait pas vraiment... Je peux dire, vers 1910, on pouvait cependant déjà parler de Lubunga, mais le reste, c'est venu après la Deuxième Guerre Mondiale.

REGINE

It is quiet here compared to the other side, over there, it's rather noisy, there are a lot of people. Here it is quiet, it feels like... we are at home, we are home.

C'est calme ici par rapport à l'autre côté, là-bas, il y a un peu de bruit, il y a beaucoup de gens. Ici c'est calme, on a comme l'impression que... , on est chez nous, on est à la maison.

MAURICE

Beauty is, above all, nature.

La beauté, c'est avant tout la nature.

MAURICE

How long have you been working with Regideso?

I have been here for a long time now; let's say for several years...

What was it like working here before?

Before, the work was interesting because there was a reliable power suppply. Everything was functioning; even the water supply centers were maintained.

And today?

Today, we are only seven because power is almost never available. The water no longer flows as before. This is why the authorities had to retrench workers.

How was water distribution in Lubunga carried out when Regideso was still in operation?

When the water fountain was regularly filled up, everyone in the avenue or neighborhood went there to get drinking water and people were able to pay. When the water supply became irregular, people came less and less. And then one day, when the water fountain system stopped working, Regideso contacted those who had wells on their plots and suggested to them that they put these wells to use and pay their own bills. That is why, today, these people have wells.

In your opinion, what is the best solution for water distribution in Lubunga?

Regideso can manage everything. It has technicians, nurses, maintenance technicians. It has everything and it does not need outsiders to come and help.

Can you describe the Lubunga of your childhood?

At home, we had water taps. Our father had water connected up to the bathroom. Everyone on the avenue came to bathe there. But in recent times, we use a bucket with water to bathe. Before, we woke up in the morning and had water for our bath. After school, lunch was ready. We could also easily do laundry.

What does this neighborhood mean to you?

Lubunga is beautiful, much better than the other side of the river. Here, there is water everywhere. So even if the taps are dry, people are not worried, but on the other side, if there is no water, people become very worried. Here, you can always go to Regideso for water or get it from the wells. Lubunga is also nice because there is no famine in this county; the air is clean because there are trees everywhere. It is neither noisy nor messy here.

What do you like most in Lubunga?

People in Lubunga are hospitable. For example, when you arrived, the children asked you to take their pictures; they were following you around saying, "Madam, Madam..." This is the mentality of our people in Lubunga, there is no animosity against anyone. On the contrary, people are still expected to lend a helping hand.

What is beauty to you?

Beauty is, above all, nature. You, you came with your camera and you looked at the sun and moved from place to place to find a vantage point. This

MAURICE

Depuis quand travaillez-vous à la Regideso ?

J'ai déjà fait longtemps ici, disons plusieurs années...

Comment c'était de travailler ici auparavant ?

Quand je suis arrivé, le travail était magnifique car il y avait de l'électricité en permanence, tout marchait, même les sources étaient entretenues.

Et aujourd'hui ?

Aujourd'hui, nous ne sommes plus que sept parce qu'il n'y a presque plus d'électricité, l'eau ne coule plus comme avant. C'est pourquoi les autorités ont dû diminuer le nombre d'ouvriers.

Comment s'effectuait la distribution de l'eau à Lubunga quand la Regideso fonctionnait encore ?

Quand la borne-fontaine était régulièrement alimentée, c'était toute l'avenue ou tout le quartier qui partait là pour s'approvisionner en eau potable et les gens pouvaient payer sans problème. A partir du moment où l'eau a commencé à ne plus arriver en continu, les gens venaient de moins en moins. Et puis un jour, voyant que le système borne-fontaine ne fonctionnait plus, la Regideso a contacté toutes les personnes qui avaient une borne dans leur parcelle pour leur proposer de s'approprier ces bornes et de payer elles-mêmes leur facture. C'est pourquoi aujourd'hui ces gens-là possèdent des bornes-fontaines.

Quelle serait, selon vous, la meilleure solution pour la distribution de l'eau à Lubunga ?

La Regideso peut tout gérer. Elle a des techniciens, des infirmiers, des gens pour la maintenance. Elle a tout et elle n'a pas besoin de personnes extérieures pour venir l'aider.

Pouvez-vous nous décrire le Lubunga de votre enfance ?

Chez moi, nous avions des robinets. Notre père avait fait mettre l'eau jusqu'à la douche. Toute l'avenue venait s'y laver. Mais ces derniers temps, pour nous laver, nous utilisons un seau. Avant de partir à l'école, tu te réveillais le matin, tu trouvais de l'eau et tu prenais ton bain. Au retour, tu trouvais à manger. On pouvait aussi facilement faire la lessive.

Qu'est-ce que ce quartier signifie pour vous ?

Lubunga, c'est magnifique, bien mieux que de l'autre côté du fleuve. Ici, il y a de l'eau partout. Donc même s'il n'y a pas d'eau aux robinets, les gens ne s'inquiètent pas, mais de l'autre côté, s'il n'y a pas d'eau, les gens vont beaucoup s'inquiéter. Ici, tu peux toujours venir à la Regideso pour prendre de l'eau ou tu peux en chercher aux puits. Lubunga, c'est bien aussi car il n'y a pas la famine dans cette commune, l'air est pur parce qu'il y a des arbres partout, il n'y a pas trop de bruit et de désordre.

Qu'est-ce que vous aimez le plus à Lubunga ?

La population de Lubunga est hospitalière. Par exemple, quand tu es arrivée, tous les enfants t'ont demandé de les prendre en photo, ils te suivaient partout en disant : « Madame, Madame...». C'est la mentalité de notre population à Lubunga, il n'y a pas d'animosité, contre personne, par contre, les gens attendent toujours qu'on vienne à leur secours.

Qu'est-ce que c'est la beauté pour vous ?

La beauté, c'est avant tout la nature. Toi, tu es venue avec ta caméra et tu as regardé le soleil et tu t'es déplacée de lieu en lieu afin de chercher une bonne place. C'est ainsi que la nature t'aide à mieux réaliser ton travail. Tu voulais te mettre par terre, mais nous t'avons offert une chaise. Si c'était ailleurs, peut-être que cela n'aurait pas été le cas car les gens auraient pu se dire que tu travaillais pour ton intérêt personnel.

Avez-vous eu une vie heureuse ?

Rien... J'ai un diplôme, mais pas de travail. J'ai cinq enfants et j'ai du mal à les scolariser. Pour survivre, il nous faut faire des acrobaties. Comment peux-t-on travailler alors qu'il n'y a pas d'électricité ? Pour recevoir son salaire, on attend parfois deux ou trois mois. La Regideso dit ne pas avoir

is how nature helps you to do your work better. You wanted to sit on the floor, but we offered you a chair. If it were somewhere else, maybe it would not have been possible because people might have thought you were only working in your personal interest.

Have you had a happy life?

Nothing... I have a diploma but no work. I have five children and I am struggling to pay their school fees. We play a juggling game to survive. How can one work without electricity? Sometimes, we wait two to three months to get our salaries. Regideso says it has no money because the Lubunga center is not operating. They ask us to be patient. But in the meantime, I am hungry and the children need to go to school. It is not even possible to buy a pair of shoes.

Can you remember a story about water? Perhaps a story that your grandmother could have told you?

I have a story on water. I have traveled a lot around the Congo. I even left the Congo. I was, for example, in Mbuji-Mayi. There, there was a woman who had gone to the farm with her two small children. While working, the children were thirsty and they started crying. Their mother, in turn, started crying and asked, "Where can I find water for my children?" If you go to Mbuji-Mayi, you will find the Mukamba lake in the form of a human being. Why? Because as the children were looking for water, it sprang from the ground and formed the lake. That is why the town is called Mbuji-Mayi which means: "The children cried and water gushed out."

What do your ancestors mean to you?

Our ancestors are of great importance. There is a proverb that says, "The mouth of an old man smells, but it only speaks the truth." In the village, problems are presented to him as only he is able to provide solutions. He is very intelligent. He watches without talking too much, because he has already done everything we are doing. Dead ancestors are our bearings because we remember them by name. Thus, if we mention an ancestor's name, we remember his/her whole history.

What is one important lesson that you have learnt in your life?

The day I finished my primary education, my grandmother spat on my head. When I think of that, I am convinced that this gesture has helped me to further my education because I have a state diploma. My father took me to a bar to buy a sweet, but my grandmother only gave me her blessing, which, nevertheless, has continued to help me till now. I have a diploma. I can write and speak a little French. I know that in life, there is this and that... But she, my grandmother, could not even write.

What is your hope for your children?

As I'm educated, my children need to be educated. This year, I have to pay a hundred dollars in school fees and so far I have not yet paid anything. I told the school director to be patient because I will pay. I enrolled my children in a private school because there, there is a good quality of teaching. They must continue their studies.

d'argent car l'agence de Lubunga ne produit rien. Elle nous dit de patienter. Mais en attendant, j'ai faim, les enfants doivent aller à école, il n'y a même pas moyen de s'acheter une paire de chaussures.

Pouvez-vous vous souvenir d'une histoire autour de l'eau ? Peut-être une histoire que votre grand-mère vous aurait racontée ?

J'ai une histoire sur l'eau. Moi, j'ai beaucoup parcouru le Congo. Je suis même sorti du Congo. J'ai été par exemple à Mbuji-Mayi. Là, il y avait une mère qui était partie aux champs avec ses deux petits enfants. En travaillant, les enfants avaient soif. Ils commençaient à pleurer. La mère aussi commença à pleurer : où puis-je trouver de l'eau pour mes enfants ? Si tu vas à Mbuji-Mayi, tu trouveras le lac Mukamba qui a la forme d'une personne humaine. Pourquoi ? Parce que comme les enfants cherchaient de l'eau, celle-ci a jailli de terre et a formé le lac. C'est pourquoi la ville s'appelle Mbuji-Mayi qui signifie : « Les enfants ont pleuré et l'eau a jailli ».

Que représentent vos ancêtres pour vous ?

Les ancêtres ont une grande importance. Il y a un adage qui dit : « La bouche d'un vieillard sent, mais ne parle que la vérité. » Dans le village, tout problème lui est soumis car lui seul est capable de trouver la solution. Il est très intelligent. Il observe sans toutefois trop parler, car tout ce que vous faites, il l'a déjà fait. Les aïeux morts sont nos repères, car nous nous souvenons d'eux par leur nom. Ainsi, si on cite le nom d'un ancêtre, on se rappelle toute son histoire.

Quelle est une leçon importante que vous avez apprise dans votre vie ?

Ma grand-mère, le jour où j'ai fini mes études primaires, est venue me jeter de la salive sur ma tête. Quand je pense à ça, je suis convaincu que c'est ce qui m'a permis d'aller plus loin puisque j'ai un diplôme d'Etat. Mon père, lui, m'avait emmené dans un bar pour m'acheter un sucré. Mais ma grand-mère ne m'avait donné que de la salive, qui pourtant continue à m'aider jusqu'à aujourd'hui. J'ai un diplôme, je sais écrire, je parle un peu français, je sais que dans la vie, il y a ceci et cela... Elle, elle ne savait même pas écrire.

Qu'espérez-vous pour vos enfants ?

Comme j'ai étudié, il faut que mes enfants étudient. Cette année, je dois payer cent dollars à l'école pour leur scolarité et jusqu'à présent, je n'ai encore rien payé. J'ai dit au directeur de l'école de patienter car je payerai. Mes enfants, je les fais scolariser dans une école privée parce que là, il y a un enseignement de qualité. Ils doivent poursuivre leurs études.

Regideso is an institution, a building, a location in Lubunga. It is a projection of desire, a machine, an infrastructure. It is a space, a water source, it is a monument of failure. Regideso stands for Régie de Distribution d'Eau de la République Démocratique du Congo, the governmental institution responsible for the water supply in DRC. Lubunga was planned in the early 20th century as a residential area located around a railway station and a harbor with colonial villas. A water pump station was constructed close to natural springs to supply the area with water. The infrastructure of the Regideso was planned to serve a small colonial community. Due to extreme corruption, political instability, and wars that have occurred since the country's independence, the institutions and infrastructure have been severely damaged and abandoned. Throughout the years, Lubunga has also outgrown its infrastructure and a rehabilitation of the water distribution system would not be productive, as it would still not be sufficient for the community.

La Regideso est à la fois une institution, un bâtiment physique, un lieu à Lubunga. La projection d'un désir, une machine, une infrastructure. C'est un espace, une source d'eau, un monument au failli... La Regideso, Régie de Distribution d'Eau de la République Démocratique du Congo, est l'institution publique chargée de la distribution d'eau en RDC. Au début du XXe siècle, Lubunga se construit comme une zone résidentielle, avec des villas coloniales, autour de la gare et du port. Une station de pompage est mise en place, à côté d'une source naturelle, pour l'approvisionnement en eau du quartier. L'infrastructure n'est alors prévue que pour fournir de l'eau à une petite implantation coloniale. Mais les institutions comme les infrastructures ont beaucoup souffert de la mégestion, de l'instabilité politique et des différents conflits que le pays a traversés depuis l'indépendance. Au cours des années, le fort développement de Lubunga a rendu la réhabilitation du système existant de distribution d'eau caduque, car il ne pourrait suffire à approvisionner toute la commune.

DU CONGO
BELGE

THE IMPOSSIBLE IS NOT CONGOLESE: CITY LIFE IN THE DRC

Sammy Baloji and Filip De Boeck
with Dominique Malaquais
Brussels, May 2016

DM: I would like to address the question of levels. You are both interested in looking at the city as a form of polycest and as a layering of utilization, time, and practice. This is not possible from a vertical point of view. And you place the focus on the surface. In Sammy's photographs, there is a strong focus on the surface of the image and on what it might say about the depth of the image.

SB: While working in Kinshasa, we decided to showcase the city, amongst other things, through a portrait of traditional chiefs, highlighting how the city had seized the chiefs´ traditional power by focusing on the insignificance of their personal space, which is representative of their identity. In my photographic approach, I focused less on the face of the person and more on the foreground and the background as two elements that define the city. As a result, I gave preference to the depth of field. For these traditional rulers, all that remains as signs of their power—at least visibly—are their costumes and emblems. Modernization has overtaken the setting surrounding these symbols. With regard to these cities, this is metaphorical, as they have developed on lands previously owned by these rulers. The lands have dwindled, and the chiefs have had to deal with a more diverse population that mainly answers to the state. Symbols are the only things that remain of their power.

FDB: Regarding the layeredness of the horizontal and the vertical, in a previous project on Kinshasa with Marie-Françoise Plissart, I made an effort to plunge into the depths of the city as a mental space, as a kind of imaginary and used photography that acts like a mirror to the unconscious of the city. In my current collaboration with Sammy, we stayed much more on the surface, as you said, and looked at how the city invents itself within its very landscape, topography, buildings, and infrastructure, as well as how the city emerges and connects between one space and the next. Yet there is always a vertical dimension, too. As soon as you cross that landscape horizontally, you are immediately faced with the matter of time, the past, present, and future—with all its utopian imagery—and how these levels of time connect with each other. So every time we select a specific building, field, cemetery, or pothole in the road, and try to approach them ethnographically and photographically, we have tried to create a narration around that spot in order to show how it brings or does not bring people together and how these spaces connect with each other. Once you stick your analytical needle into such a place, it becomes a kind of testing tool that penetrates all these different layers and historical moments that have created that surface. All these histories continue to have a say in terms of the actual surface of the city today, which was of interest to us. It was not just a nostalgic look at history or tradition. A lot of what tradition is in Congo is a very recent invention anyway, an amalgamation of many different times, actors, and logics that come together, there's nothing traditional about it. It's a very modern thing, tradition, in that sense. That's what we wanted to do with that horizontality and with our method of 'urban acupuncture'.

DM: Could you talk about this notion of urban acupuncture and analytical needles?

FDB: I derived the notion of urban acupuncture from a number of sources. First of all, the texts of the architect Baerbel Mueller were a source of inspiration, as was the work of Ariel Osterweis Scott, who has written about the dance practices of Faustin Linyekula as a form of acupuncture, a kind of geo-choreography or acupuncture through his body. Through his dancing, Scott says, Faustin reopens space, he generates alternative ways of creating publics, a public space. Mueller and Scott refer to this as a kind of acupunctural movement. Through his body, Faustin also reowns space and time. And of course, the other influence on this notion of urban acupuncture comes from the "weak architecture" movement, with people like Isola Morales, Jaime Lerner, and Bruno Casagrande, who through very neat, small kinds of architectural interventions in urban landscapes try to "heal" and to make urban life better. We've used that notion to talk about what we have done by choosing specific spots in the city and sticking our needle into these places, in

L'IMPOSSIBLE N'EST PAS CONGOLAIS :
VIE URBAINE EN RDC

Sammy Baloji et Filip De Boeck,
en conversation avec Dominique Malaquais
Bruxelles, mai 2016

DM : Je voudrais commencer par évoquer avec vous deux la notion de niveaux. Vous abordez en effet la ville comme un polyceste, comme une superposition de différentes strates liées aux usages, au temps, aux pratiques, une approche qui n'est pas possible avec un point de vue vertical. Et vous vous intéressez particulièrement à la surface. Dans les photographies de Sammy, l'accent est mis sur la surface de l'image et sur ce que cette surface pourrait révéler de la profondeur de cette image.

SB : Lorsque nous avons commencé à travailler sur les différentes communes de Kinshasa, nous avons décidé de les représenter à travers le portrait de leurs chefs traditionnels : de montrer comment la ville avait envahi le pouvoir traditionnel en se focalisant sur le petit espace intime laissé au chef et représentatif de son identité. Dans mon approche picturale, je me suis moins focalisé sur le visage de la personne que sur l'avant-plan et l'arrière-plan comme deux éléments définissant la ville. De ce fait, j'ai privilégié la profondeur de champ. Tout ce qui reste comme signes de pouvoir à ces chefs traditionnels, du moins visibles dans l'image, sont leurs costumes et emblèmes. La modernisation a envahi le reste du décor. Telle une métaphore de ces villes qui se sont agrandies sur les terres possédées auparavant par ces chefs. Ainsi, les terres du chef se sont rétrécies, il doit faire face à une population de plus en plus variée qui ne rend plus compte qu'à l'Etat. De son pouvoir ne restent que les symboles.

FDB : Je reviens à cette notion de stratification entre horizontal et vertical. Dans un précédent travail avec Marie-France Plissart, j'ai fait l'effort de plonger dans les profondeurs de la ville, la ville comme un espace mental, comme une photographie imaginaire et usée qui renverrait tel un miroir à son inconscient. Dans ce travail avec Sammy, nous sommes davantage restés à la surface comme tu disais et avons observé comment la ville s'invente, non seulement dans son architecture, mais aussi dans son paysage même, dans sa topographie, ses bâtiments, ses infrastructures, comment elle émerge et se connecte, entre un espace et le suivant. Et pourtant, il y a toujours une dimension verticale aussi. Car dès qu'on traverse le paysage horizontalement, surgit immédiatement la notion de temps, le passé, le présent et le futur – avec toutes les imageries utopiques qu'il recèle – et comment ces différentes couches temporelles se relient. Donc à chaque fois que nous avons sélectionné un bâtiment spécifique, un terrain, un cimetière, un nid de poule sur une route, en tentant une approche à la fois ethnographique et photographique pour construire une histoire, chaque fois nous avons essayé de créer une narration et de montrer comment l'élément choisi rassemblait ou ne rassemblait pas les gens autour de lui et comment les espaces se reliaient les uns aux autres. Une fois que tu plantes ton aiguille analytique dans un tel endroit, c'est comme faire un prélèvement des différentes couches et moments de l'histoire qui ont créé cette surface. Ces histoires ont toujours quelque chose à dire sur la surface de la ville telle qu'elle est aujourd'hui, c'est ça qui nous a intéressés. Ce n'est pas juste un regard nostalgique sur l'histoire et la tradition. D'ailleurs, ce que l'on considère comme la tradition au Congo est dans une large mesure une invention très récente, ce sont des amalgames issus de la confrontation de plusieurs temps, de plusieurs facteurs, de logiques différentes, il n'y a rien de traditionnel. En ce sens, c'est quelque chose de très moderne, la tradition. Voilà ce que nous avons voulu faire avec cette horizontalité et cette méthode d'« acupuncture urbaine ».

DM : Pourrais-tu revenir sur cette notion d'acupuncture urbaine et ces aiguilles analytiques ?

FDB : Cette notion d'acupuncture urbaine vient de plusieurs choses. Les textes de l'architecte Baerbel Mueller ont été source d'inspiration, comme l'a été le travail d'Ariel Osterweis Scott qui a relié la démarche chorégraphique de Faustin Linyekula à une forme d'acupuncture, une sorte de géo-chorégraphie ou d'acupuncture à travers son propre corps. Ariel dit qu'à travers sa danse, Faustin rouvre l'espace, il génère d'autres façons de créer des publics, d'installer un espace public. Ce que Baerbel et Ariel traduisent comme une sorte d'acupuncture du mouvement. A travers son corps,

our case, not in order to heal or to intervene or to therapeutically reassemble the city, but as a very delicate way of interacting with the city without too much intervening, without weighing on it too much. It allows us to rethink the city in an alternative way, to reassemble it differently. How can you live, what does living together in a city mean, and how does it come about?

SB: One of the things Filip's writing highlights is the term or concept of *libulu*, which means "trou" in Lingala, "hole", and this also relates to my own work on archives as part of a history that I did not learn anything about at school or at university. The colonial past was hidden and that was intentional. I grew up under Mobutu's dictatorial regime, which totally denied the Belgians' heritage in Congo. Instead, we went through the ideology of "Back to Authenticity". I didn't know anything except that Belgians were bad people, as were Westerners in general. Then the '90s arrived: crisis, the fall of Mobutu, and the beginning of the so-called "democracy". Suddenly, everything fell down. When I was young, I knew the importance of the Gécamines, one of the main mining companies in the Congo. But I never got the opportunity to go inside their mining sites. The Gécamines was in the heart of the country and we were so proud of it. In 2003 or 2004, working as a documentary photographer, I discovered some mining sites. While working there, I found archives from the colonial period: I discovered a story that had never been told to me, and it came as a shock. That's how I started these photo montages, mixing colonial archives with today's landscape of abandoned sites. Combining the present of this mining area with the archives, I have tried to suture, to stitch together, to link the holes. It was also interesting to use this to talk about how the city is growing, about our own way of thinking the city and thinking about us, the Congolese, in the city in our country.

DM: Let's talk about this concept of the hole and the notion of suturing, both of which are so central to the process of your joint work. Knowledge, information, histories, biographies, and people seem to disappear into this black hole, which is, as you have explained, a critical signifier for ways in which people in Kinshasa apprehend the city. Can you tell us more?

FDB: You could say that the postcolonial reality has become that of the hole, the trou, libulu. In Lingala, this concept refers to the physical holes that you find everywhere in the landscape in Kinshasa and throughout Congo: it may refer to the potholes that you find on the streets, or the unmarked holes of anonymous graves that are scattered throughout the city and beyond, all over Congo. Many people have died displaced and we don't even know where their graves are. Libulu may also refer to the holes of artisanal mining sites, which are so common in Katanga and other places in Congo. The hole is almost a generic infrastructure of postcolonial reality. But in local speak, in the local mind, it has also become a kind of meta-concept for thinking about the quality of life itself in that urban setting or in that country at large. Libulu can refer to feelings of being imprisoned by darkness, of informality, of things that don't work. A nightclub in downtown Kinshasa that is very popular these days is called "le grand Libulu", "the big hole". It is so popular that a second one has been opened and in their wake there have been all kinds of bars that have taken on the name "hole", there's even a nightclub in Bobigny, Paris named after a famous hole in one of the main streets of Kinshasa, the Libulu Manzengele. The hole captures the idea of what postcolonial life in the urban setting is. The nightclub offers a specifically Congolese response to the hole: if we have to live in a hole, we may as well dance in it. You could say it's funny. But at the same time, that local concept of the hole should be taken very seriously, and I've therefore linked it to the notion of 'suture'. Of course, suture, stitching together, refers to closing wounds and healing. It's also a psychoanalytical Lacanian concept, though it was not invented by Lacan but by one of his co-fellows, Jacques-Alain Miller, who used that notion of suture to denote a lack. The suture is a zero but a zero that can be redefined as a one. It is an impossibility that can be rethought and reformulated as a possibility.

DM: You show the symbiotic relationship between the countryside and the city, which is of course something that itself gets radically evaluated through the overwhelming fascination with it by anthropologists, art historians, and filmmakers today through this notion of the African city.

FDB: The countryside itself formats the urban. Long before starting to work in the urban field, I spent a number of years in a rural area, a small village community along the border with Angola. A lot of these rural people were involved

Faustin se réapproprie aussi l'espace et le temps. Et puis bien sûr, en évoquant cette acupuncture urbaine, je pense également aux courants liés à « l'architecture fragile ». A des personnes comme Isola Morales, Jaime Lerner ou Bruno Casagrande qui, à travers des gestes architecturaux modestes, délicats, posés dans le paysage urbain, essaient de soulager, de soigner, de rendre la vie urbaine un peu meilleure. Nous avons utilisé cette notion pour parler de notre démarche : choisir dans la ville des points spécifiques pour planter notre aiguille, non dans notre cas pour guérir, non pour agir ou pour essayer d'une manière un peu thérapeutique de recomposer la ville, mais pour interagir de la façon la plus délicate possible avec elle, sans trop intervenir, sans trop peser sur elle. Cela nous a permis de repenser la ville d'une autre manière, de la réassembler différemment. Comment peut-on vivre dans la ville, qu'est-ce que vivre ensemble signifie et comment cela arrive ?

SB : L'un des éléments auquel nous nous sommes attachés est le terme ou le concept de *libulu* qui signifie trou en lingala, un terme qui renvoie aussi aux archives, à cette partie de l'histoire que je n'ai pas apprise à l'école ou à l'université. Le passé colonial a été caché, à dessein. J'ai grandi sous le régime dictatorial de Mobutu, un régime qui a totalement occulté l'héritage laissé par les Belges au Congo. A la place, on nous a servi l'idéologie du « Retour à l'authenticité ». Je ne savais rien des Belges, sauf que c'était de mauvaises personnes, comme tous les Occidentaux en général. Et puis les années 90 sont arrivées, la crise, la chute de Mobutu, les soi-disant débuts démocratiques. Soudain, tout s'est écroulé. Enfant, je connaissais l'importance de la Gécamines, l'une des principales sociétés minières du pays. Mais je n'avais jamais eu l'occasion de me rendre sur l'un de ses sites miniers. La Gécamines était au cœur du pays et nous en étions tellement fiers. En 2003 ou 2004, j'étais alors dans la photographie documentaire, j'ai pu découvrir plusieurs sites miniers. Et alors que je travaillais là-bas, je suis tombé sur des archives de la période coloniale : toute une histoire qui n'avait jamais été dite, c'était un vrai choc ! C'est comme ça que j'ai commencé à faire ces photomontages, superposant des archives coloniales avec les paysages des sites abandonnés aujourd'hui. J'ai mélangé le présent de ces sites miniers avec les archives, comme une tentative pour suturer, pour recoudre les éléments ensemble, pour relier les trous. C'était intéressant de poursuivre cette démarche ici pour montrer comment la ville s'est développée, montrer notre propre façon de penser la ville, de nous projeter, nous Congolais, dans la ville, dans notre pays.

DM : Parlons un peu de ces concepts de trou et de suture, qui tous deux sont au coeur du processus de cette collaboration. La connaissance, l'information, l'histoire au pluriel, les biographies, les gens semblent disparaître dans ce trou noir... Ce qui constitue, comme vous l'avez expliqué, un indicateur critique de la façon dont les gens à Kinshasa appréhendent la ville. Vous pouvez nous en dire plus ?

FDB : On pourrait dire que la réalité postcoloniale s'apparente à celle d'un trou, d'un libulu. Le concept en lingala renvoie aux trous physiques que l'on retrouve partout dans le paysage à Kinshasa et dans tout le Congo : les trous des nids de poule sur les routes, les trous des tombes anonymes qui sont éparpillées à travers la ville et au-delà, dans le pays. Beaucoup de gens sont morts, déplacés, et on ne sait même pas où ils ont été enterrés. Ce sont aussi les trous des mines artisanales que l'on trouve tant au Katanga, mais aussi dans d'autres endroits du Congo. Le trou est presque devenu une infrastructure générique de la réalité postcoloniale. Mais dans les conversations, dans l'entendement courant, c'est une sorte de méta-concept pour parler de la qualité de la vie dans une environnement urbain donné, ou plus largement dans tout le pays. Libulu renvoie alors au fait de se sentir prisonnier de l'obscurité, de l'informel, de toutes ces choses qui ne marchent pas... Un des clubs les plus connus en ville aujourd'hui s'appelle « Le grand Libulu », « le grand trou ». C'était tellement fréquenté qu'un deuxième a ouvert ses portes et que dans la foulée, plein de bars ont pris ce nom, « le trou », il y a même une boîte près de Paris qui a pris le nom d'un grand trou dans l'une des rues principales de Kinshasa, Manzengele. Le trou rend compte de cette réalité de la vie postcoloniale dans un environnement urbain. Le nightclub propose une réponse typiquement congolaise au trou : si on doit vivre dans un trou, autant pouvoir y danser ! Vous pouvez trouver ça drôle. Mais en même temps, ce concept local de trou doit être pris au sérieux, et c'est pourquoi je l'ai relié à la notion de « suture ». Bien sûr, cette idée de suturer, de raccommoder revient à celle de fermer une blessure, de guérir. C'est aussi une concept psychanalytique lacanien, même s'il n'a pas été inventé par Lacan lui-même mais par l'un de ses compagnons, Jacques-Alain

in a trans-border diamond trade and smuggling operations between Angola and Congo. Over time, they slowly worked their way up to secondary towns and major cities such as Kikwit and Kinshasa. I started to follow them. It wasn't a conscious kind of research choice. I've always thought of this as a lucky coincidence that allowed me to discover, see, read, understand, and feel the city in the way that many Congolese do, namely, coming from the village and going to the city. From that perspective and with that kind of rural background and rural network, you can access and read a city in a very different way. It's a totally different story from when you take an airplane from the Brussels airport and arrive in Kinshasa. Accessing a city such as Kinshasa from the other side, you start to notice how much the rural actually constructs and builds the city. We tend to think of the city as a kind of a modernist project that is there, a solid thing, perhaps unfinished at its fringes, where the rural penetrates the urban. But in fact, it's not like that at all. It's quite the opposite, it's the rural that formats, gives form to, enables the urban to take place. And indeed, anthropologists used to be so good at talking about rural worlds and small-scale communities on the village level. Today, we're all working in Kinshasa, Lagos, Nairobi, not too far away from our fridges, our cold beers, our bars, it's easy, it's trendy, it's hip. And in a country like the DRC, everyone is in Kinshasa or Lubumbashi, no one really knows what's going on in the countryside anymore, but that's where the country and the city are being made, in a way. I think it is necessary to take that into account in order to understand the urban world we live in.

SB: Yes, and I think that the city and the country, Congo, are the result of an invention, of something that has been imposed, and of colonial exploitation. My work "Essay on Urban Planning" portrays the practices of segregation and racial discrimination that are responsible for the planning of cities in Congo. The "cordon sanitaire," a physical and geographical space of 500 meters that separates the whites from the natives, is still present in most cities like Lubumbashi. This racial violence and system of exploitation of natural and human resources, which has ultimately resulted in a totally inequitable distribution of resources, persists today under a postcolonial socio-political system that has accommodated the gangrene inherited from colonization.

With reference to the current socio-political and cultural system, I'm seeking, through my artistic work, to tap into pre-colonial knowledge and perception, not for the sake of restoring "tradition as a fundamental value of our societies", but rather to link the past with the present while making a critical analysis of the colonial era.

Suturing the City, Living Together in Congo's Urban Worlds
(Filip De Boeck & Sammy Baloji, 2016)

SAMMY BALOJI is a visual artist based in Brussels and Lubumbashi. He is the co-founder of the PICHA Encounters at the Lubumbashi Biennale. His work has been exhibited in prestigious venues and featured in numerous catalogues and books.

FILIP DE BOECK is an urban anthropologist working in the DRC. He published "Kinshasa: Tales of the Invisible City" with photographer Marie-Françoise Plissart in 2004 and curated the exhibition "Kinshasa: The Imaginary City" for the 9th International Architecture Biennale in Venice, awarded the Golden Lion (best installation).

Miller qui a utilisé cette notion de suture pour rendre compte d'un manque. La suture est un zéro, mais un zéro qui peut se redéfinir comme un un. C'est une impossibilité qui peut être repensée et reformulée comme une possibilité.

DM : Vous montrez la relation symbiotique entre la campagne et la ville, une position qui n'est pas anodine face à l'intense fascination qu'exerce aujourd'hui la notion de ville africaine sur les anthropologues, les historiens de l'art ou les réalisateurs...

FDB : Le rural formate l'urbain. Bien avant de travailler sur le champ urbain, j'ai passé de nombreuses années dans une zone rurale, un petit village à la frontière avec l'Angola. Beaucoup d'habitants de cette zone étaient impliqués dans un trafic transfrontalier de diamants et dans des opérations de contrebande entre l'Angola et le Congo. Avec le temps, ils ont peu à peu rejoint des villes secondaires ou des grandes villes comme Kikwit ou Kinshasa. Je me suis mis à les suivre. Ce n'était pas un choix conscient de recherche. J'ai toujours considéré cela comme une coïncidence heureuse qui m'a permis de découvrir, de voir, de lire la ville, de la ressentir et de la comprendre comme beaucoup de Congolais l'ont fait, c'est-à-dire en quittant leur village pour rejoindre la ville. Avec cette perspective, avec en toile de fond le monde rural et ses connexions, vous pouvez vous saisir de la ville, la lire d'une façon très différente. Une histoire qui n'a rien à voir avec celle que vous pourriez avoir si vous preniez juste votre avion à Bruxelles pour atterrir à Kinshasa. Abordant la ville par l'autre côté, on commence à remarquer combien le rural façonne et construit la ville. On a tendance à voir la ville comme une sorte de projet moderniste qui serait là, un objet solide, peut-être pas tout à fait fini à la marge, là où le rural entre en contact. Mais en fait, ce n'est pas comme ça du tout. C'est le contraire, c'est le rural qui formate, qui modèle, qui permet à la ville de devenir. Les anthropologues étaient avant connus pour parler du monde rural et des petites communautés au niveau d'un village. Aujourd'hui, on se retrouve tous à travailler à Kinshasa, Lagos ou Nairobi, pas trop loin de nos frigidaires, de nos bières fraîches, de nos bars, c'est facile, c'est à la mode, c'est là où il faut être. Et dans un pays comme la RDC, tout le monde est à Kinshasa ou à Lubumbashi, mais personne ne sait plus vraiment ce qui se passe en brousse, pourtant c'est là que le pays, que la ville se font en un sens. Je crois qu'il est nécessaire de prendre ça en compte pour bien comprendre le monde dans lequel nous vivons.

SB : Oui, et je crois que la ville, le pays-même, le Congo, sont la conséquence d'une invention, de quelque chose qui a été imposé, de l'exploitation coloniale. Mon travail « Essay on Urban Planning » rend compte de la ségrégation et de la discrimination raciales à l'origine de la planification urbaine des villes au Congo. Le « cordon sanitaire », espace physique et géographique de 500 mètres qui séparait les Blancs de Indigènes, reste encore visible de nos jours dans la plupart des villes comme à Lubumbashi. Cette violence raciale, ce système d'exploitation des ressources naturelles et humaines avec à la fin une répartition totalement inéquitable des bénéfices perdurent de nos jours sous un système socio-politique postcolonial qui s'est accommodé de la gangrène héritée de la colonisation.

Evoquant le système socio-politique et culturel actuel, je cherche dans mon travail artistique à puiser dans les connaissances et les savoirs précoloniaux, non par souci de restaurer la « tradition comme valeur fondamentale de nos sociétés », mais plutôt afin de jeter un pont entre ce passé et le présent, tout en posant une analyse critique sur la période coloniale.

SAMMY BALOJI est un artiste plasticien vivant entre Bruxelles et Lubumbashi. Il a co-fondé les Rencontres Picha, Biennale de Lubumbashi. Le travail de Sammy Baloji a été montré dans des lieux prestigieux et publié dans plusieurs ouvrages et catalogues.

Anthropologue, FILIP DE BOECK questionne les contextes urbains et a travaillé en RDC. Il a publié en 2004 « Kinshasa : Récits de la ville invisible » avec la photographe Marie-Françoise Plissart et a assuré le commissariat de l'exposition « Kinshasa: The Imaginary City » à la 9e Biennale internationale d'architecture de Venise, pour laquelle il reçu le Lion d'or pour la meilleure installation.

Threefold Choreography: On Beauty, Community and Water / Un triptyque chorégraphique : De la beauté, la communauté et l'eau

Character: Dancer (Yves Mwamba), Narrator (male voice in French and Swahili). Stage: There is no back or front, the representation is conceived from a circular perspective, no fixed borders. The representation takes place outdoors, on wet soil. Props: There is a metallic bowl as a symbol of the world, the world as a reflection, the world as a container, the world as a community. A white, light fabric represents water and community.

Beauty
What is beauty?
Silence

Beauty can be found with a flashlight. Beauty is there, waiting for us to see it.

Dancer's solo begins; on the notion of beauty. Beauty is nature. It is the kindness of the people. Beauty lives in the confines of Lubunga.

Community
The world is in our gaze.
The world is the force with which we live.
Dancer's solo begins; on the notion of community.

Water
Choreographic representation of the history of Lake Mukamba, formed by the tears of a mother.

I was once in Mbuji-Mayi. There, there was a mother who went to the fields with her two small children. While working, the children became thirsty. They began to cry. The mother also began to cry: "Where can I find water for my children?" Today you will find Lake Mukamba in the shape of a human person because, as the children were seeking water and the mother was crying, the water arose from the earth and this is the water we now call the lake. That is why Mbuji-Mayi means "the children cried for water and water arose".

Where is the water?
In the same place where beauty lies, in strength.
End.

Personnage : un danseur (Yves Mwamba), un narrateur (une voix masculine en français et swahili). La scène : pas de représentation frontale, mais un point de vue circulaire, sans frontières fixes. La représentation se tiendra en extérieur, sur un sol humide. Accessoires : un globe métallique comme symbole du monde, le monde comme réflexion, le monde comme contenant, le monde comme communauté. Un tissu blanc, léger symbolise l'eau et la communauté.

La Beauté
Qu'est-ce que la beauté ?
Silence

La beauté ne se voit que dans la lumière d'une lampe de poche. La beauté est là tapie, attendant qu'on la voit.

Le solo du danseur commence, autour de la beauté. La beauté est dans la nature, dans la gentillesse des gens, jusque dans les confins de Lubunga.

La Communauté
Le monde réside dans notre regard.
Le monde réside dans la force qui nous fait vivre.
Le solo du danseur commence, autour de la notion de communauté.

L'Eau
Représentation chorégraphique de l'histoire du lac Mukamba, né des larmes d'une mère.

J'ai été une fois à Mbuji-Mayi. Là-bas, on raconte l'histoire de cette mère qui était aux champs avec ses deux jeunes enfants. En travaillant, les enfants commencèrent à avoir soif. Ils se mirent à pleurer. La mère aussi se mit à pleurer : « Où puis-je trouver de l'eau pour mes enfants »? Aujourd'hui, on trouve le lac Mukamba qui a la forme d'une personne humaine, car alors que les enfants cherchaient de l'eau et que la mère pleurait, l'eau jaillit du sol et c'est cette eau qui forma le lac. C'est pourquoi Mbuji-Mayi signifie « les enfants ont pleuré et l'eau a jailli ».

Où se trouve l'eau ?
Là où la beauté se cache, dans la force.
Fin.

SCIENTIFIC MAPPING

Theresa Theuretzbacher
September 2013

The scientific approach complements the holistic approach towards understanding the water situation in Lubunga by providing a methodology for determining water sources, supply, consumption, and disposal, and their interaction.

The geographic location of water- and waste water-related sites like water-fetching points, open water sources, or washing places were located and recorded via GPS devices. In individual interviews with district representatives, health care institutions, households, and operators of boreholes, the current water and waste water situation was analyzed, ideas for improvements were shared, and a water-use pattern was identified. Three water samples from selected sources were analyzed by the Laboratoire d'analyse d'eau at the University of Kisangani.

A map of Lubunga was created showing all water-related places of activity and a water-related description of each district. This mapping can be used to identify areas with a need for improvement and different methods towards achieving this.

Case studies and projects for household water treatment, water supply, and corresponding sanitation solutions implemented in countries such as India and Kenya were analyzed and introduced in a scientific report.

Partners: Papa Assani, Ignace Yenga

CARTOGRAPHIE SCIENTIFIQUE

Theresa Theuretzbacher
Septembre 2013

Afin de comprendre la situation de l'eau à Lubunga, toujours dans une approche holistique, l'étude scientifique a proposé une méthodologie pour identifier et analyser les points d'eau, l'approvisionnement, la consommation, l'évacuation et les différentes interactions à l'oeuvre entre ces éléments.

Les sites liés à l'eau et au rejet des eaux usées, parmi lesquels les points d'approvisionnement, les sources d'eau ouvertes ou les lieux pour faire la lessive, ont été localisés et enregistrés avec des appareils GPS. Des entretiens individuels des représentants de la commune et des centres de santé, des ménages et des propriétaires de puits ont permis d'appréhender la situation actuelle de l'eau courante et des eaux usées, de dégager des idées sur les améliorations à apporter et d'identifier un modèle type de consommation d'eau. Des échantillons d'eau provenant de trois sources sélectionnées ont été analysés par le laboratoire de l'Université de Kisangani.

La réalisation d'une carte a permis de situer l'ensemble des endroits liés aux ressources hydriques et de dresser un portrait de chaque quartier en fonction de la situation de l'eau. Cette cartographie identifie les zones nécessitant des améliorations et les différentes méthodes possibles pour ce faire.

Le rapport scientifique comprend aussi des études de cas d'approvisionnement en eau, de traitement des eaux usées et des exemples de solutions sanitaires mises en œuvre dans des pays tels que l'Inde et le Kenya et qui nous semblent pertinents pour Lubunga.

Partenaires : Papa Assani, Ignace Yenga

Map and Catalogue of Water Sources/
Carte et liste des sources d'eau

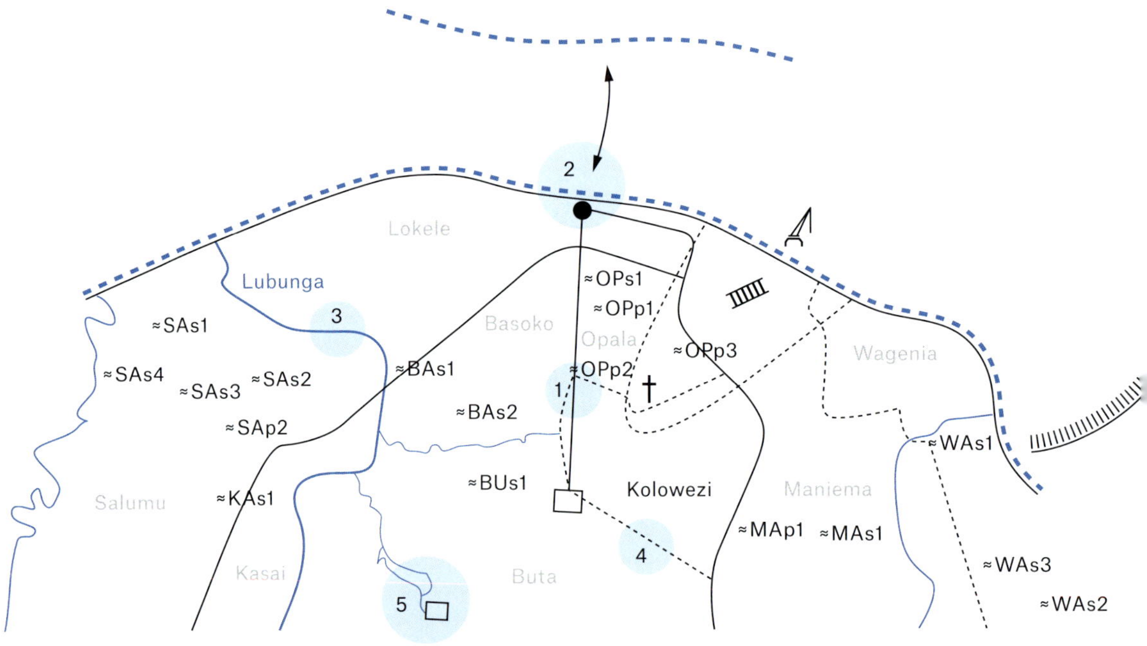

1 Generic settlement/Quartier type
2 The "Beach"/Le Beach
3 Lubunga River/La rivière Lubunga
4 Periphery/La périphérie
5 Regideso/La Regideso

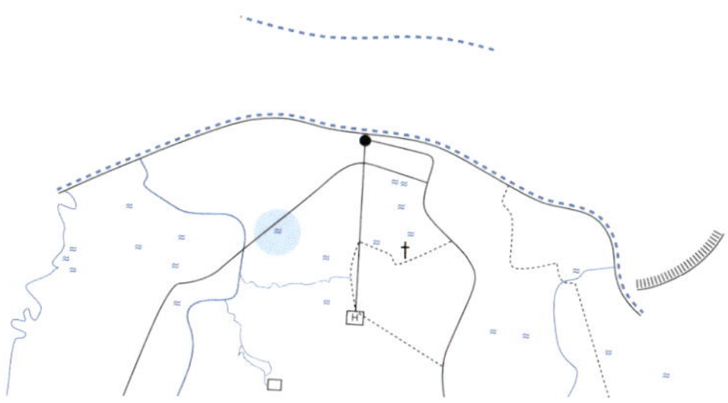

Bosoko - BAs1

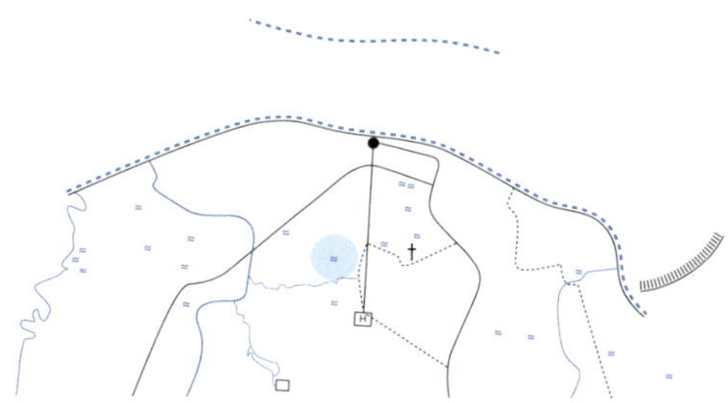

Bosoko - BAs2

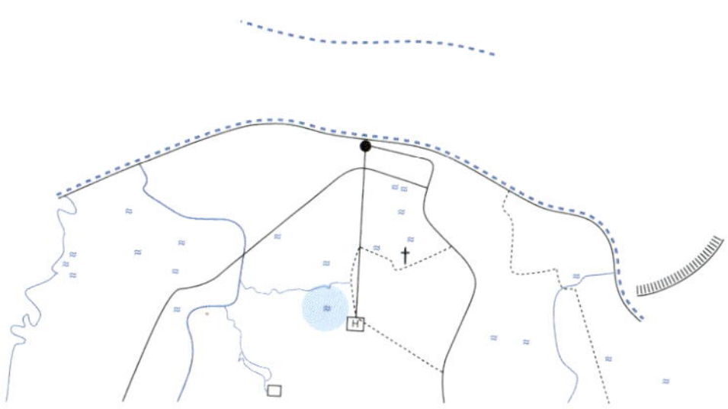

Buta - BUs1

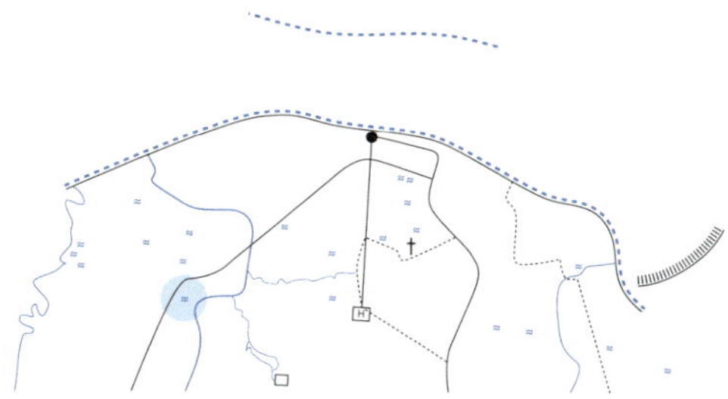

Buta - Regideso

Salumu - Litale

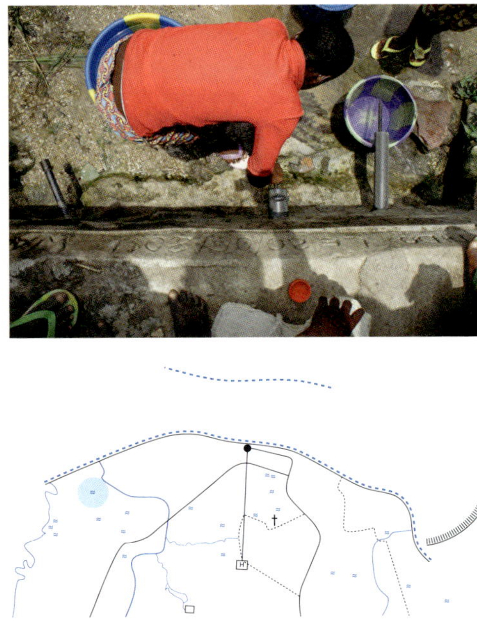

Salumu - SAs1

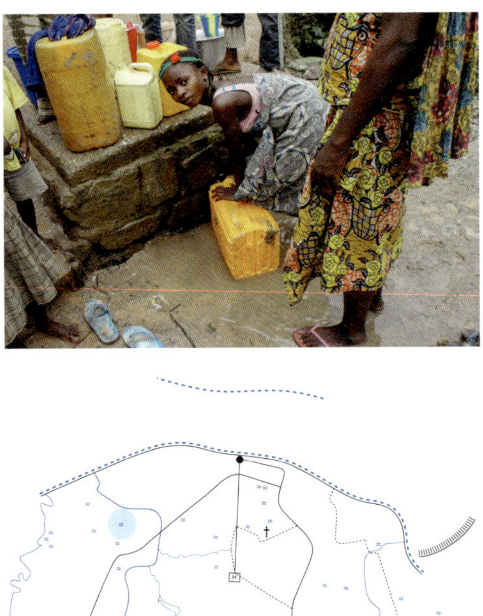

Salumu - SAs2

Salumu - SAs3

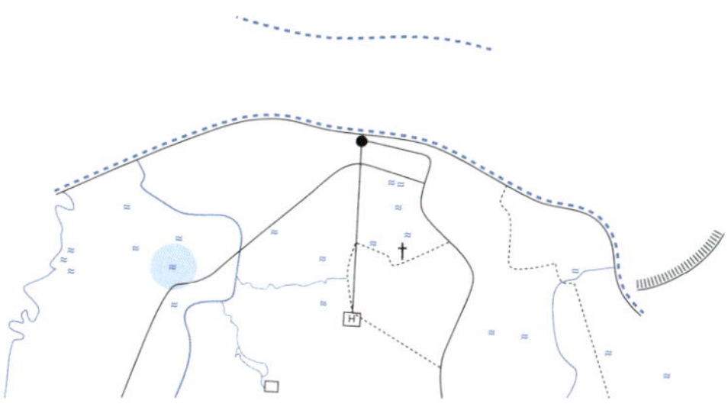

Salumu - SAp1

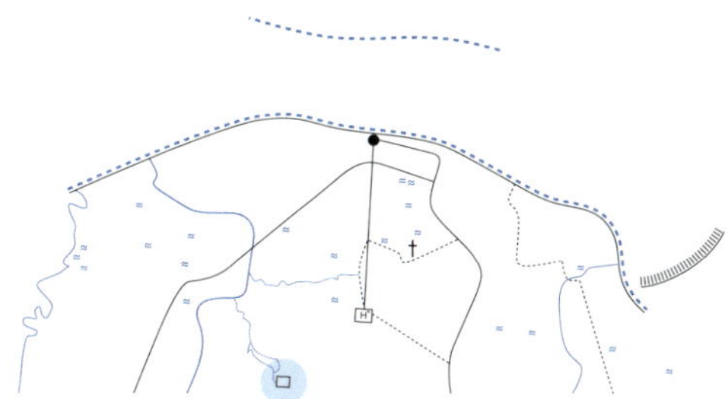

Kasai - KAs1

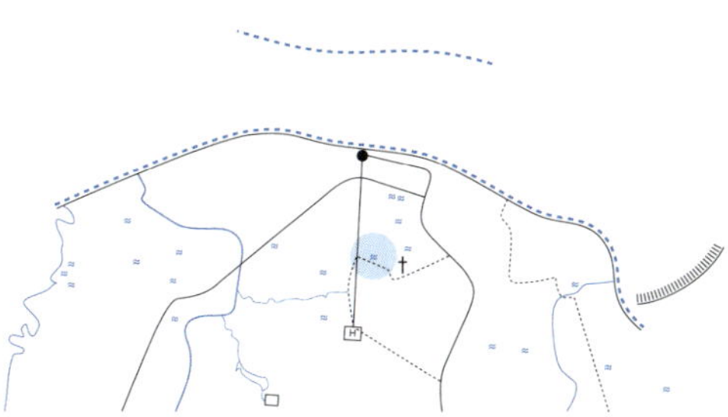

Opala - OPp2

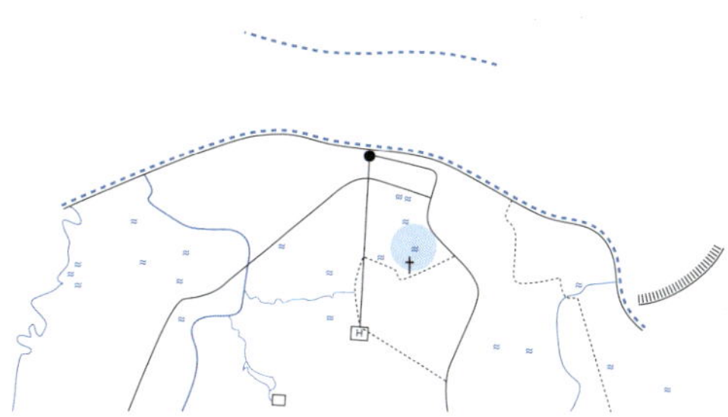

Opala - OPp3

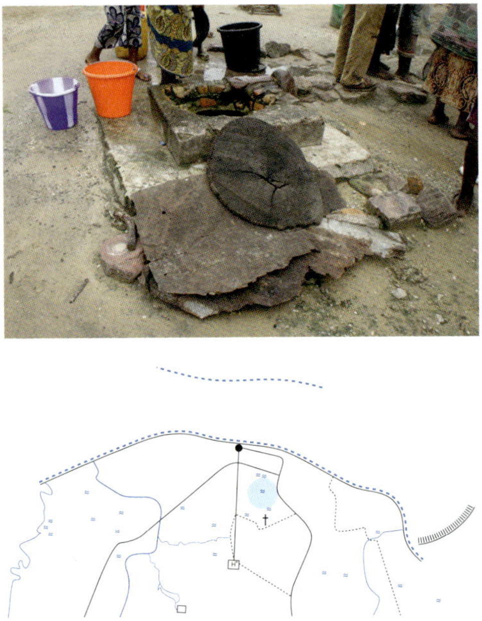

Opala - OPp1

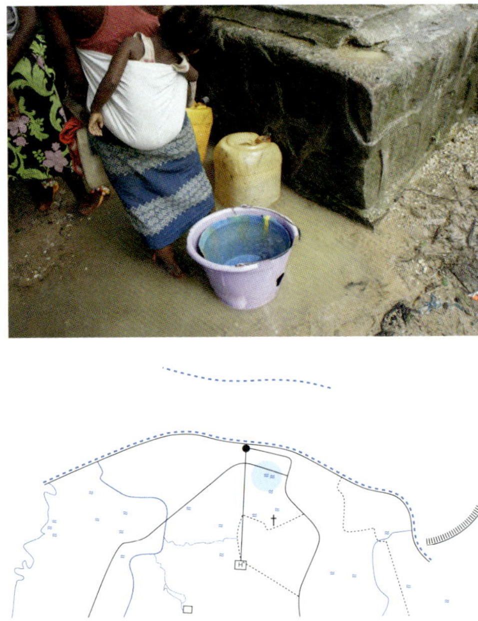

Opala - OPs1

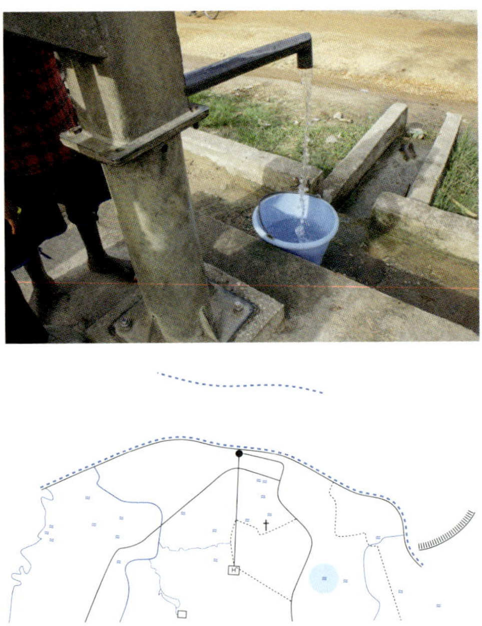

Maniema - MAp1

Maniema - MAs1

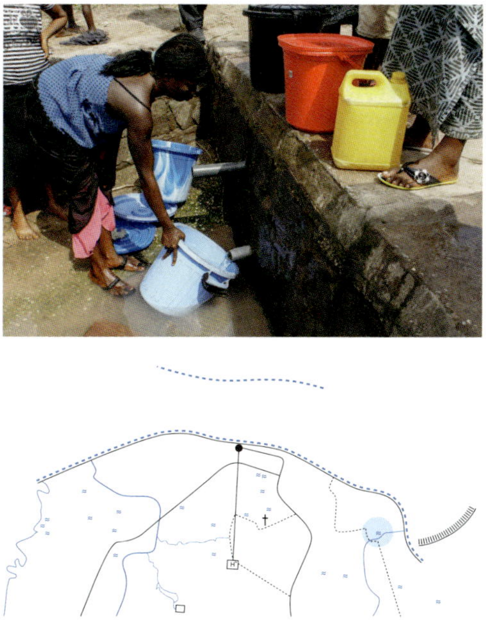

Wagenia - WAs1

Wagenia - WAs2

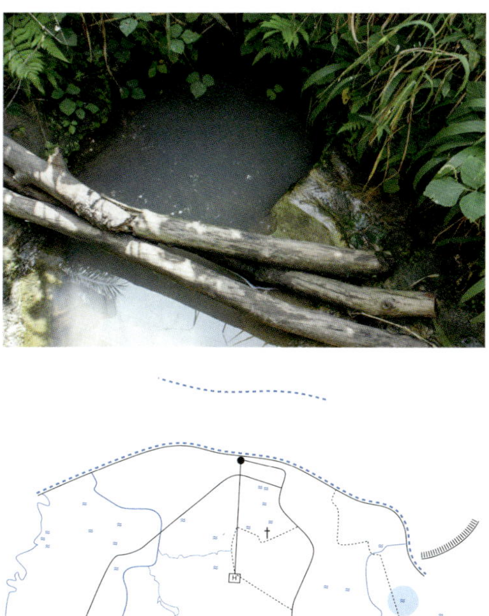

Wagenia - WAs3

Quotes from the Wells

Women often prefer rain water as then they don't have to carry water over a long distance.

Latrines and homes get temporarily flooded by the Congo and contaminate the river.

For an average family size of 12 people, a 20 liter container of drinking water is used per day.

Drinking water is generally not treated before consumption.

The geology in Wagenia consists of a rocky underground, which makes it nearly impossible to dig latrines by hand.

The last cholera outbreak occurred in 2011 and claimed 40 lives.

Regideso has a potential water supply from 25 different underground springs.

The last time the Regideso offered water was on February 26, 2013, only for a few hours.

The results of the bacteriological analysis showed that all tested drinking water sources are contaminated with coliforms and E. coli, an indicator of fecal contamination.

The inadequate and inconsistent operation and maintenance of water sources is a major problem in Lubunga.

Large, expensive spare parts are not necessarily available in Kisangani and need to be ordered, which can take several weeks.

Water kiosks serve as an appropriate solution for underserviced suburbs of larger cities.

Setting up water kiosks should come along with effective education programs, promotional techniques, and locally adapted billing schemes that facilitate regular purchases of treated water.

The water from informal water vendors is much more expensive than the water supplied through regulated service provision by formal water providers.

The technology has to be chosen with consideration for low costs, efficiency, and environmental sustainability.

Echanges autour du puits

Les femmes préfèrent souvent (recueillir) l'eau de pluie pour ne pas avoir à transporter l'eau sur de longues distances.

Parfois, les latrines et les maisons, inondées par le Congo, contaminent la rivière.

Une famille moyenne de 12 personnes utilise un bidon de 20 litres d'eau potable par jour.

L'eau à boire n'est généralement pas traitée avant consommation.

La géologie au niveau de Wagenia se caractérise par un sous-sol rocheux qui rend presque impossible le fait de creuser des latrines à la main.

La dernière épidémie de choléra s'est produite en 2011 et a fait 40 victimes.

La Regideso a potentiellement accès pour l'alimentation en eau à 25 sources souterraines.

Le 26 février 2013, la Regideso a distribué l'eau pour la dernière fois, et seulement pendant quelques heures.

Les résultats de l'analyse bactériologique ont montré que toutes les sources d'eau potable testées sont contaminées par des coliformes et E. coli, deux indicateurs de contamination fécale.

L'utilisation et la maintenance inadéquates des sources d'eau sont un problème majeur pour Lubunga.

Des pièces de rechange, volumineuses et coûteuses, ne sont pas nécessairement disponibles à Kisangani et doivent être commandées, ce qui peut prendre plusieurs semaines.

Les kiosques à eau sont une solution appropriée pour les périphéries mal desservies des grandes villes.

La mise en service des bornes-fontaines devrait s'accompagner de programmes éducatifs efficaces, de techniques de communication appropriées et de systèmes de facturation adaptés au contexte local pour favoriser l'achat régulier d'eau traitée.

L'eau auprès des vendeurs informels est beaucoup plus chère que l'eau fournie par les distributeurs officiels d'eau.

Le choix de la technologie doit tenir compte des coûts, de l'efficacité et de la durabilité environnementale.

The results of the bacteriological analysis of the drinking water in Lubunga show that all tested water sources are contaminated with coliforms and E. coli, both indicators of fecal contamination. Water samples were sourced from a house well, a spring from the governmental Regideso water supply company, and a spring with a built spring intake.

Although E. coli is part of the natural fecal flora, some strains of this bacterium can cause gastrointestinal illness, along with other, more serious health problems. If the indicator is isolated from the water supply, this infers that other serious pathogenic organisms could be present and indicates that the water is unfit for human consumption.

Based on the findings of this analysis, it is most likely that the high percentage of bacterial contamination in the well OPp1, as an example, comes from human and animal feces adjacent to the water source. The groundwater table in Lubunga is very high, 1.5 m, which contributes to the underground flow of microorganisms. While the WHO recommends a distance of about at least 40 m between wells and latrines, some only have 10 m between them. Based on the results of the bacteriological analysis, the hazardous conditions of sources of drinking water is alarming and does not conform with WHO guidelines.

The whole area of Lubunga lacks access to safe drinking water. Therefore, a holistic concept in accordance with regional and governmental decisionmakers is essential. Bottom-up business models are no replacement for the need for an organized water network, and local authorities should be included in the development process in order to assure a long-term, sustainable operation of water services in Lubunga.

Les résultats de l'analyse bactériologique de l'eau potable démontrent que toutes les sources d'eau potable testées sont contaminées par des coliformes et E. Coli, deux indicateurs de contamination fécale. Les échantillons ont été prélevés respectivement sur un puits d'une maison d'habitation, à la source utilisée par la compagnie nationale de distribution d'eau Regideso, et à une source d'eau aménagée.

Même si le E. coli fait partie de la flore intestinale naturelle, certaines souches de cette bactérie sont à l'origine de nombreuses maladies gastro-intestinales, mais aussi d'affections plus sérieuses. Cet indicateur, isolé à partir des échantillons d'eau, témoigne aussi d'une possible présence d'autres agents pathogènes et prouve que l'eau est dans tous les cas impropre à la consommation.

Les résultats des analyses laissent supposer que la forte contamination bactérienne du puits OPp1 provient essentiellement de la présence d'excréments d'origine humaine ou animale à proximité de la source d'eau. La nappe phréatique à Lubunga est proche de la surface, à 1,5 mètre environ, ce qui favorise le déplacement souterrain de micro-organismes. L'OMS recommande une distance d'au moins 40 mètres entre un puits et des latrines, alors que dans plusieurs cas à Lubunga, seule une dizaine de mètres les séparent. L'analyse bactériologique montre une situation alarmante pour les sources d'eau potable à Lubunga, très loin des normes préconisées par l'OMS.

Ce manque d'accès à l'eau potable caractérise toute la commune de Lubunga. C'est pourquoi une approche holistique en lien avec les autorités locales et nationales est essentielle. Les modèles de petites entreprises à approche ascendante ne sauraient donc se substituer à une nécessaire réorganisation du réseau de distribution et les autorités locales doivent être associées afin de garantir sur le long terme un service de distribution d'eau durable.

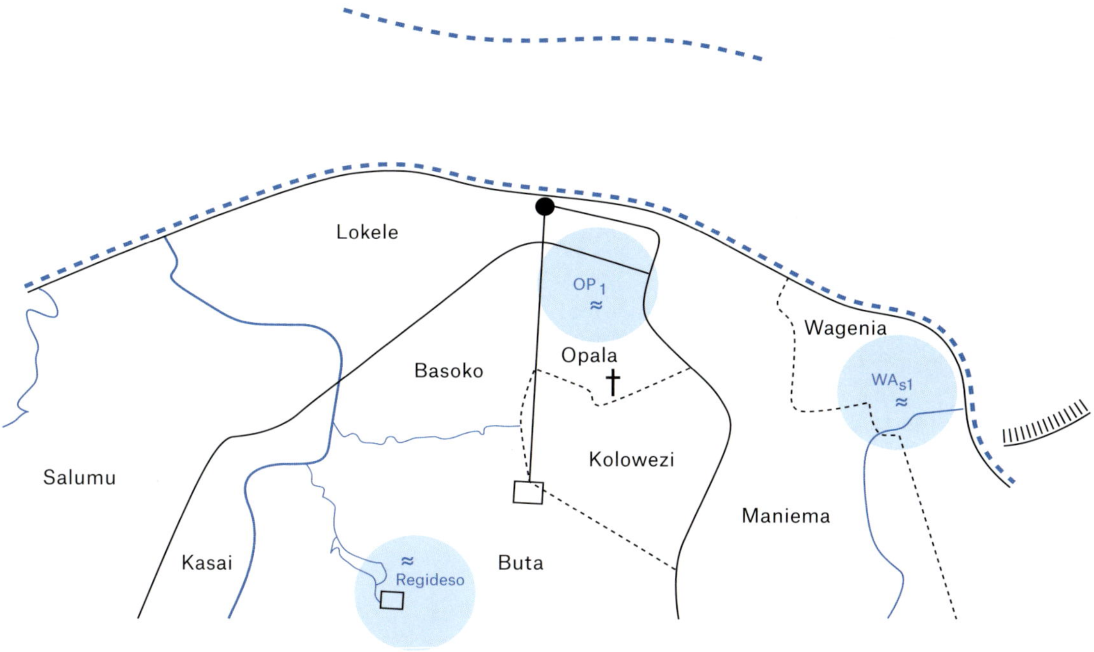

	E. coli per 100 ml
WHO guidelines	0
Lubunga data	
OP1	17
WAs1	19
Regideso	9

		Escherichia Coli	Coliformes Fecaux	Salmonelles
Directives OMS	CFU/100ml	0	0	0
Sur le terrain à Lubunga				
	OP1	17	139	12
	WAs1	19	143	18
	Regideso	9	68	2

... ANYTHING ELSE IS JUST A BUILDING

A conversation between
Wolf Prix und Baerbel Mueller
Vienna, July 2016

BM: I'd like to start with the topic of water, the project "COOP Himmelblau Havana 1995", and your interest in this topic as an architect. Water has become amazingly important in all the [a]FA projects and it was the main theme at Lubungamode: a project with the task of spatially, narratively, and scientifically mapping the local water situation. Therefore, I also introduced your Havana project to the team. Here, the idea was to contribute something that was related to urban development and the response was infrastructural but also very urban.

WP: Architectural! We were in Havana often and I was not so much inspired by the romanticization of Cuban life as I was interested in Havana as a city. I have said that "Learing from Las Vegas" is stupid because it's so one-dimensional, in a very American way. Learning from Havana would in fact be a more interesting topic because there, a multifunctional city can already be seen in its layout, so there are places, like the one for the army "Placa del Armas", places for the market, places for the church, cultural places, and they are interwoven through arcade houses. In other words, there is an urban idea there which is influenced by European cities, but nowhere in Spain or Europe have I seen a similar density or similarly clear starting point for urban development. When we were asked to develop a project that had to have an architectural signal effect for Havana—without the content being exactly defined—I thought to myself, the old Havana has a densely interwoven history and the *Habana Nueva* is a modern metropolis, one would have to actually combine both in order to be able to take the next step. I then realized that the city lacked infrastructure, especially in terms of water. The old infrastructure was totally decayed, as there was no money for repairs, and the ground was unbelievably bogged down in water. That was the starting point of this project. Without infrastructure, you can't build any city. The soft infrastructure is included here, such as, for example, education, without this infrastructure, one cannot deal with cities architecturally. I think urban space is one of the most important paradigms that the city can still produce today, if you lose the urban space, you lose the body of the city.

On the topic of water itself: I think that architects must begin to understand global contexts in order to be able to detect the causes of the problems that we have early on. And one serious problem is certainly the lack of water. We know that water will be the most precious resource in the future. It would be good if one deals with water as a resource and a potential, but also as a threat. Why are architects now limited, as we can currently see, to designing small boxes for refugees or the poorer classes in South America while it would be a lot more important to find solutions for protecting the cities in Asia that are threatened by rising water levels, and to build new floating cities.

BM: The Havana project was somehow revolutionary, or provocative. There were very interesting fellow architects and everybody went wild, but this project went underground and dealt with a resource and an infrastructural problem and was framed as a statement and a manifesto.

WP: Yes, because I was already pretty sad that architects—without knowing the point of what they're building and what the contexts are—just go ahead and design away unseriously. That still makes me sceptical.

BM: The project is 21 years old, however. It would have been very suitable for the 2016 Venice Biennale and would probably still have been "from the front". At the time, architects did not deal with infrastructure in this way and it was a real statement. Now many do that, but in a more down-to-earth way, or with new technologies and innovative systems. Engineers and climate designers actually can do this quite well, too.

WP: I think we can deal with all issues, with social issues and infrastucture issues, as well as research. One should never forget however that architecture will be created from this and that these things must be implemented three-dimensionally. The best research has missed the point if a boring building arises from it, which we've seen happen a thousand times. When I think about how a town or a campus, or a home for refugees should

SINON, C'EST JUSTE UN BÂTIMENT !

Une conversation entre
Wolf Prix et Baerbel Mueller
Vienne, juillet 2016

BM : J'aimerais commencer avec la thématique de l'eau : le projet Coop Himmelblau Havana 1995 et ton intérêt en tant qu'architecte. L'eau est devenue un élément incroyablement important dans tous les projets [a]FA, c'était au cœur du projet Lubungamode, une cartographie narrative, spatiale et scientifique de la situation de l'eau à Lubunga. Dans cette perspective, j'avais parlé du projet Havana à mon équipe. Havana devait contribuer à quelque chose de l'ordre du développement urbain, avec une réponse structurelle, mais aussi très urbaine.

WP : Architecturale ! Nous avons souvent été à La Havane et j'ai toujours été moins inspiré par la vision romantique de la vie cubaine que par La Havane en tant que ville. J'ai dit combien je trouvais « Learning from Las Vegas » (L'enseignement de Las Vegas) stupide parce que tout y est qu'à une seule dimension, et tellement à l'américaine. L'enseignement de la Havane serait beaucoup plus intéressant parce qu'ici, il s'agit d'une ville multi-fonctionnelle, qui se révèle dans ses couches successives, ainsi il y a différents types de places, certaines pour l'armée comme la « Placa del Armas », d'autres pour le marché, des places pour l'église, des places culturelles, tout cela imbriqué entre des maisons à arcades. En d'autres mots, il y a bien là une idée autour de l'urbanisme, qui est certes influencée par l'Europe, mais nulle part en Espagne ou en Europe, j'ai pu voir une telle densité ou un point de départ aussi clair pour un développement urbain. Lorsqu'on nous a demandé de développer un projet qui devait agir comme un signal architectural pour La Havane, sans que le contenu n'en soit précisément défini, j'ai pensé : le vieux Havane a une histoire dense et entremêlée, tandis que le *Habana Nueva* est une métropole moderne, il faudrait pouvoir combiner les deux... J'ai ensuite réalisé combien la ville manquait d'infrastructures, notamment au niveau de l'eau. Les installations anciennes étaient totalement délabrées, faute de moyens pour les réparer et le sol était devenu un incroyable bourbier à cause de l'eau. Ce fut le point de départ du projet. Sans infrastructure, une ville ne peut être bâtie. J'inclue ici les infrastructures immatérielles, comme par exemple l'éducation, sans ce type d'infrastructure, il est impossible d'appréhender une ville architecturalement. Je crois que l'espace urbain est l'un des paradigmes les plus importants que la ville puisse produire aujourd'hui, perdre l'espace urbain, c'est perdre le corps même de la ville.

Pour revenir à la thématique de l'eau, je crois que les architectes doivent commencer à comprendre le contexte global pour déceler au plus tôt les causes des problèmes qui vont surgir. Et l'un des problèmes sérieux est à n'en pas douter le manque d'eau. Nous savons que l'eau sera la ressource la plus précieuse dans le futur : une ressource, un potentiel, mais aussi une menace. Pourquoi les architectes se limitent-ils, comme on le voit aujourd'hui, à concevoir de petites boîtes pour les réfugiés ou les classes les plus défavorisées en Amérique du Sud, alors qu'il est bien plus important de trouver des solutions pour protéger les villes en Asie de la montée du niveau des eaux ou construire de nouvelles villes flottantes ?

BM : Havana a été un projet révolutionnaire, voire provocateur. Ce projet, qui s'est développé sous terre, en se focalisant sur une ressource et un problème structurel, fut présenté comme une déclaration de principes, un manifeste.

WP : Oui, parce que j'étais déjà assez triste de la façon dont les architectes, sans connaître ni le pourquoi ni le contexte se lançaient dans la conception. Cela me rend encore aujourd'hui perplexe.

BM : Le projet s'est passé il y a 21 ans et pourtant il aurait très bien pu s'intégrer à la Biennale de Venise 2016 et aurait probablement été toujours à l'avant-scène... Mais à cette époque, les architectes n'abordaient pas les infrastructures de cette façon et c'était une vraie profession de foi. Aujourd'hui, beaucoup le font, mais d'une manière plus pragmatique, ou avec des nouvelles technologies et des systèmes innovants. Les ingénieurs et les spécialistes en design énergétique font cela aussi très bien.

WP : Je crois que nous pouvons nous confronter à tous les sujets, le social, le structurel, sans laisser de côté le processus de recherche.

look, then of course I have to do some research—cultural research. But it must also be a sign—a welcome sign, if you like. Otherwise, one creates barracks, where only function has priority. In addition, architecture must materialize as a symbol of the subject that is being dealt with.

This is the task of our architectural culture: that architecture is a three-dimensional expression of a society on a meta-level, because anything else is just a building. As I have said many times before, the message of salvation behind this is ridiculous, the architects are concerned with themselves. I think that a strategic approach to problems is important, especially if it is to become a design. Of course, I distinguish between form and *Gestalt: Gestalt* is more than form; form and content as synthesis intertwine with the meta-level of timeliness, then it becomes architecture! By the way, we already said in 1983: timely architecture is social. And we have dealt with this topic on countless projects. The idea was that self-determined architecture is intended to promote the self-determination of its inhabitants.

BM: I'd like to talk about the topic of scale in order to defend, so to speak, operating on a small scale. For some time now, I have been interested in the idea of urban acupuncture, that something on an urban scale can be triggered by small, isolated, networked interventions, which work in the same way that acupuncture does, which has a certain radiance and effect. What I sometimes find annoying in connection with Africa—or India—is this claim that it's totally acceptable to operate here in Austria and Europe on a small scale, to convert attics or plan single-family homes based on a kind of legitimacy of the aim, to change the lives of a handful of people for the better using quite a few resources and through considerable effort—possibly even with the meta-claim of making a statement in the history of architecture,because we do believe in our architecture, don't we? But if I do this in Ghana, the DRC, or Mumbai, there is the claim, especially by those who do not operate in these contexts, that these must always be the big solutions for the masses.

WP: I find the acupuncture methods totally correct. They also work on a large scale. In Los Angeles, investors have built museums in intervals, so that between each museum project, the land prices go up. Paris has planned a second city center in order to leave the old city in peace, as well as to create a field of tension between the two, and since then every large project has emerged along this field of tension. This is a legitimate urban strategy that could work well on a small scale if the network is expanded, and the interventions are combined with each other, in order to define points that mean something and from which meaning can be gleaned. But, if the Mexican Palapa was investigated as an ideal roof in 36.2° heat, I think it's bullshit, or annoying know-it-all-ness.

BM: We're actually in the middle of the architectural scale here, so in the [a]FA context the bamboo roof, which was developed as a stage area and has many parallels to the roof in Mexico, namely the claim that it creates a community space that will achieve an iconic status, around which something that is less expressive is located. In the preface to the *Mexico Revisited* book you wrote: "It is only through experience that information becomes knowledge."

What I found liberating was that you credited the 2003 project in Mexico as experimental architecture rather than an aid project. In my own projects and in the [a]FA context, it became clear that the space for radical experiments lies in art, and that I feel slightly uncomfortable in the NGO context, in which the call to help indeed lies. In the following projects, I have therefore tried to work with artists.

WP: I think that is a radically good approach.

BM: In a lecture at the Bartlett, Lesley Lokko recently pointed out that in the African context, it's always about participation and not the issue of risk in a productive sense. Which was also your approach in Mexico: you're experimenting now, and that is a risk, so then it's a failure or success—an experimental aspiration, not a participatory one.

The idea of closed systems always did seem to alienate you, you represent the idea of open systems, in your teaching and architecture. I found it interesting that you said beforehand, why not merge an augmented reality from Greg Lynn with a mud-cocoon from Anna Heringer and see what emerges? That was also your criticism of many universities that go to South Africa or Mexico and represent a regionalism that they then upgrade with a tendency towards building construction and structural engineering. The digital

On ne doit jamais cependant oublier que l'architecture sera conçue à partir de ces matières mêmes qui devront être « retranscrites » en trois dimensions. La meilleure recherche aura échoué si c'est un bâtiment ennuyeux qui sort de là. Lorsque je réfléchis à ce à quoi une ville, un campus, une maison pour les réfugiés devrait ressembler, il est évident que je dois faire certaines recherches, sur le contexte culturel. Mais le résultat doit être aussi un signe, un signe de bienvenue. Sinon on crée des baraquements où seul prime le fonctionnel. De surcroît, l'architecture doit matérialiser symboliquement le sujet que l'on adresse.

C'est le rôle de notre culture architecturale : l'architecture doit être une expression en trois dimensions d'une société à un méta-niveau parce que sinon, c'est juste un bâtiment. Mais comme je l'ai dit plusieurs fois avant, le côté salvateur derrière tout ça est ridicule, les architectes se préoccupent d'eux-mêmes. Je crois qu'une approche stratégique face aux problèmes est importante. Bien sûr, je distingue la forme du *Gestalt* : le *Gestalt* dépasse la forme, c'est la forme et le contenu, comme une synthèse imbriquée au méta-niveau d'un temps qui serait exact, juste, alors là, cela devient de l'architecture ! D'ailleurs, nous avions déjà dit en 1983 qu'une architecture ancrée dans son temps est nécessairement sociale. Et nous avons abordé ce sujet dans tant de projets. L'idée était qu'une architecture auto-déterminée a pour fonction de promouvoir l'autodétermination de ses habitants.

BM : J'aimerais aborder aussi la question de l'échelle, le fait d'oeuvrer à une petite échelle. Depuis un certain temps, je suis très intéressée par l'idée d'une acupuncture urbaine, c'est-à-dire que quelque chose au niveau urbain puisse être mis en mouvement par de petites interventions, isolées, mais mises en réseau, qui agiraient sur le même principe que l'acupuncture. Mais il y a quelque chose qui me questionne, en lien avec l'Afrique ou l'Inde. Il y a en Europe un consensus sur le fait qu'œuvrer à une petite échelle est totalement légitime : transformer un grenier ou dessiner une maison pour une seule famille, avec peut-être cet espoir sous-jacent d'apporter sa pierre à l'histoire de l'architecture – et ce sur fondement d'une certaine légitimité liée à l'intention, changer pour le mieux la vie d'une poignée de personnes avec peu de ressources et beaucoup d'énergie, je dis cela car nous croyons tous à notre architecture, non ? Mais lorsqu'il s'agit du Ghana, de la RDC ou de Bombay, il y a cette idée, surtout venant de ceux qui ne travaillent pas dans de tels contextes, que toute intervention doit être massive et pour le plus grand nombre.

WP : Je trouve ces méthodes d'acupuncture tout à fait pertinentes. Elles s'appliquent d'ailleurs à plus grande échelle aussi. A Los Angeles, des investisseurs ont bâti des musées par intervalle, afin qu'entre chaque projet de musée, le foncier prenne de la valeur. Paris a planifié un deuxième centre urbain pour laisser le cœur historique en paix et créer de la tension entre les deux et depuis, tous les grands projets ont émergé sur cette ligne de tension. C'est une stratégie urbaine légitime qui pourrait aussi marcher à petite échelle si le réseau est élargi et si les interventions se combinent les unes aux autres pour définir des points significatifs et susceptibles de créer du sens. Mais si le Palapa mexicain n'est compris que comme le toit idéal sous 36.2° de chaleur, alors, là c'est du baratin, ou un ennuyeux je-sais-tout-qui-ne-sait-rien...

BM : Nous sommes en fait ici en plein dans la question de l'échelle architecturale, ainsi dans la perspective [a]FA, le toit en bambou qui a été développé comme un espace scénique renvoie à plusieurs égards au toit mexicain, par exemple dans cette conviction qu'il crée un espace communautaire qui pourra atteindre un statut emblématique, autour duquel quelque chose de moins central et de moins expressif peut se loger. Dans la préface de ton livre *Mexico Revisited*, tu écris : « C'est seulement à travers l'expérience que l'information devient savoir. »

J'ai trouvé vraiment libérateur le fait que tu présentes le projet de 2003 à Mexico non comme un projet d'aide au développement mais bien comme un projet d'architecture expérimentale. Que ce soit dans mes propres projets ou dans le contexte [a]FA, j'ai réalisé combien l'espace pour des expérimentations radicales est lié à l'art, je ne suis plus très à l'aise avec le contexte des ONG qui repose justement sur cet appel à aider. Dans les projets suivants, j'ai ainsi essayé de travailler avec des artistes.

WP : Je pense que c'est radicalement une bonne approche.

BM : A une conférence au Bartlett, Lesley Lokko a fait remarquer combien, dans le contexte africain, le « participatif » primait sur la notion de risque dans une logique de production. Cette notion de risque était au cœur de ton approche au

and manual, low-tech and high-tech have always interested you concurrently.

WP: I think augmented reality would be a great step forward, if one could plan cities in Africa in that direction. I think it is ridiculous to go to places that you don't know—this applies also to African colleagues in the diaspora—and patronizingly build a school, that is not enough, the people could do that themselves if they wanted!

So your approach is that the residents could build the houses themselves. A mapping that identifies opportunities and scenarios is done, but then it is left up to the people in which direction they go. If you did this on a larger scale, you would probably have more popularity than the concrete jungles that the Chinese set up there so that they can then in turn buy the land and implement their interests. It surprises me that in these exhibitions where the social impact is in the foreground the dangers that exist already are not shown. That is then a one-dimensional statement: "My God, they built a nice camp, they built some nice social housing"—with six houses, and next to it there's a six-lane concrete highway. This should be approached with differentiated strategies.

BM: Perhaps to conclude, another glimpse into the future. You have mentioned that you are now working on a project in Mumbai.

WP: Yes, where to start.

I just came from Mumbai, where the rehabilitation of slums by an investor who has invited us to work there is going well, because capitalism is combined with a social approach in an excellent way. I've never seen or heard of this kind of slum rehabilitation, even though I know it from Rio.

Mumbai has the problem that it no longer has any land left for growth, yet it's growing rapidly. The slums are the only large areas that can still be used. I don't have this romanticized view that the slums are something great. They are well-organized and there's also work there, but the infrastructure is horrible. The investor says the following: If you provide me the land, I will build you high density lowrise buildings for you, which comply with your needs for clean water, plumbing, and cooking facilities—if I can build three towers there, in order to get my money back, and of course to make some money. So the combination of social thinking and economic strategies: the residents can live there for 10 years without having to pay for rent. There are also shopping streets and workshops, the structure is transferred to clean buildings with basic infrastructure. I have seen two of the renovated slums and wouldn't have realized that they were previously slums. I only think that we can better define the urban space, so it has brought us to the environment. This will be a long way.

To free themselves from the sense of architecture lacking any meaningful future, architecture schools must do their part by revisiting experimentation and turning the constraints upside down in order to develop new strategic, political, and conceptual ideas of how we can deal with the future of the city—not only in Europe.

WOLF D. PRIX is CEO of COOP HIMMELB(L)AU. He has taught at the Harvard Graduate School of Design, Columbia University, SCI-Arc , UCLA, and the Yale School of Architecture, From 1990–2011 he taught at the University of Applied Arts Vienna , where he was also Vice Rector and Head of the Institute of Architecture from 2003 to 2012.

WOLF D. PRIX est Président Directeur Général de COOP HIMMELB(L)AU. Il a enseigné à la Graduate School of Design de l'Université de Harvard, à l'Université de Columbia, SCI-Arc, UCLA et à l'Ecole d'Architecture de Yale. De 1990 à 2011, il a enseigné à l'Université des arts appliqués de Vienne où il a été aussi vice-recteur, puis directeur de 2003 à 2012.

Mexique : tu expérimentes quelque chose maintenant, ce qui implique un risque, ça peut marcher ou pas – il y a donc là une aspiration expérimentale et pas un désir de participation.

L'idée d'un système fermé m'a toujours semblé aliénant pour toi qui, tant dans ton enseignement que dans ton architecture, incarnes l'idée de systèmes ouverts. Cela m'a semblé intéressant que tu dises avant : pourquoi ne pas croiser la réalité augmentée telle qu'utilisée par Greg Lynn avec les cocons d'argile d'Anna Heringer et voir ce qui pourrait bien en sortir ? Cela renvoie aussi à tes critiques face à ces universités qui vont en Afrique du Sud ou au Mexique pour appliquer un régionalisme qu'elles élèvent en principe pour la construction de bâtiments ou l'ingénierie structurelle. Le digital et le manuel, les hautes technologies mais aussi des technicités plus rudimentaires t'ont toujours intéressé à parts égales.

WP : Je crois que la réalité augmentée serait un grand pas en avant si on pouvait l'appliquer dans la planification des villes en Afrique. Je crois qu'il est ridicule d'aller dans des endroits que vous ne connaissez pas – cela s'applique aussi aux collègues africains de la diaspora – pour simplement y construire, avec un certain paternalisme, une école, ce n'est pas assez, les gens pourraient le faire eux-mêmes s'ils le désiraient.

Donc ton approche, c'est que les habitants pourraient construire leurs maisons eux-mêmes. Une cartographie qui identifie les opportunités et les scénarios est dressée, mais ensuite c'est aux gens de décider dans quelle direction ils veulent aller. Si tu appliquais ce principe à une grande échelle, ce serait probablement plus populaire que les jungles de béton construites par les Chinois là-bas et qui leur permettent en retour d'acheter la terre et d'œuvrer pour leurs intérêts. Cela me surprend toujours que dans des expositions qui mettent l'impact social au premier plan, les dangers qui existent déjà ne sont pas abordés. Il y a juste ce constat unidimensionnel : « Mon dieu, ils construisent un beau camp, de jolis logements sociaux » – soit six maisons et à côté une autoroute en béton à six voies. Tout cela devrait faire l'objet de stratégies différenciées.

BM : Pour conclure, pouvons-nous évoquer rapidement le futur. Tu as mentionné que tu travaillais actuellement sur un projet à Bombay.

WP : Je reviens juste de Bombay où un investisseur nous a invité à intervenir sur la réhabilitation d'un bidonville. Tout se passe bien car l'approche capitaliste est combinée à une approche sociale, et ce d'une excellente manière. Je n'avais jusqu'ici jamais vu ou entendu parler d'une telle réhabilitation là-bas, même si je connais cela à Rio.

Bombay a ce problème qu'il n'y a plus d'espace pour l'expansion de la ville, en effet très rapide. Les bidonvilles sont les seuls grands espaces restants qui peuvent encore être utilisés. Je n'ai pas ces idées romantiques sur les bidonvilles. Ils sont certes bien organisés, mais les infrastructures sont horribles. L'investisseur a dit : si vous mettez à ma disposition le terrain, je construirai pour vous des habitations de faible hauteur à haute densité et qui répondent à vos besoins en eau propre, plomberie et équipements de cuisine, en contrepartie vous me laissez construire trois tours pour récupérer mon investissement et bien sûr faire de l'argent. Il y a donc cette convergence d'une pensée sociale et de stratégies économiques : les résidents pourront vivre là dix ans sans avoir à payer de loyer. Il y aussi des rues marchandes, des ateliers, la structure actuelle est transférée dans des bâtiments propres avec des infrastructures de base. J'ai vu deux projets de rénovation et ne pouvais pas me douter que c'était avant des bidonvilles. Je crois que nous pouvons mieux définir l'espace urbain, ce qui nous amènera à l'environnement. Mais ce sera un long chemin.

Pour se défaire d'un sens de l'architecture qui ne prendrait pas en compte un futur qui ferait sens, les écoles d'architecture doivent faire leur part pour revisiter le processus expérimental et utiliser les contraintes pour développer de nouvelles idées stratégiques, politiques, conceptuelles sur comment nous pouvons envisager le futur de la ville, et pas seulement en Europe.

Approaching Lubunga/
A l'approche de Lubunga

The project team/L'équipe du projet

Avenue Hassan II

Regideso/La Regideso

Navigating Lubunga / Se déplacer à Lubunga

Lubunga River / La rivière Lubunga

The abandoned Lubunga harbor / Le port abandonné de Lubunga

Mapping Lubunga /
Une cartographie de Lubunga

Lubunga River /
La rivière Lubunga

Regideso / La Regideso

Spatial mapping /
Cartographie spatiale

A house well /
Un puits domestique

Sanitary situation in the generic settlement / Bilan sanitaire dans le quartier type

Rotten Belgian-colonial infrastructure / Infrastructure Belge-Coloniale rouillée

Isaac and Frida / Isaac et Frida

Papa Assani in Wagenia /
Papa Assani au quartier Wagenia

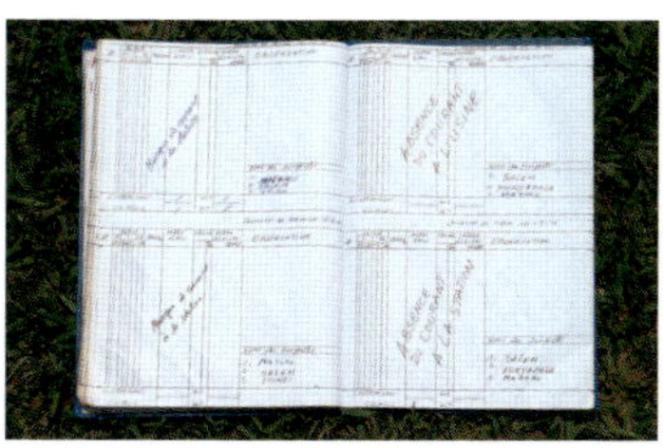

Theresa and Ignace /
Theresa et Ignace

Quotes from the wells /
Echanges autour du puits

A work day at the Lubunga Catholic parish / Une journée de travail à la paroisse catholique de Lubunga

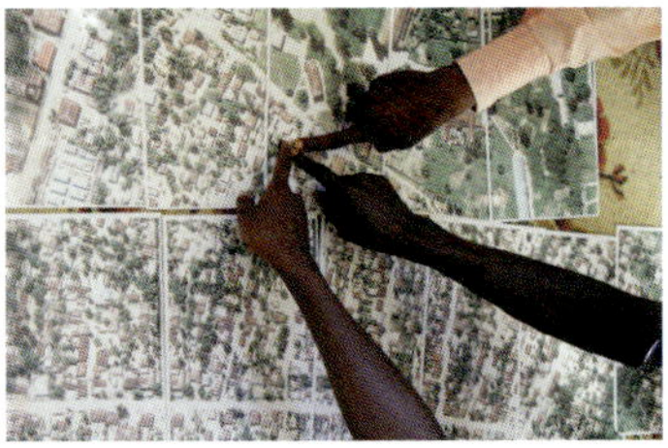

Lunch time invitation / Invitation à déjeuner

Presentation with Faustin / Présentation avec Faustin

Review with Virginie / Vérification avec Virginie

Final discussion in Lubunga / Discussion finale à Lubunga

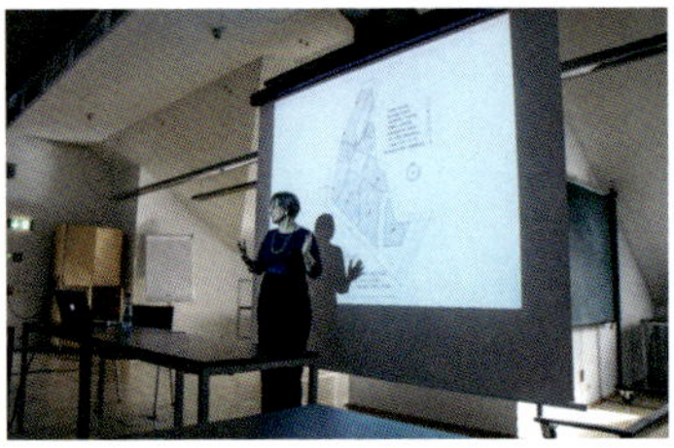

Review and lecture by Hannah le Roux / Vérification et lecture avec Hannah Le Roux

A workday in Kinshasa / Une journée de travail à Kinshasa

Vienna review with Faustin Linyekula / Analyse à Vienne avec Faustin Linyekula

Stefan Gruber, Andrea Börner, Günther Langergraber

Setting up the exhibition at Alliance Kisangani / Montage de l'exposition à l'Alliance française de Kisangani

Virginie Dupray at the exhibition venue / Virginie Dupray à l'exposition

Stefanie Theuretzbacher, Antonella Amesberger

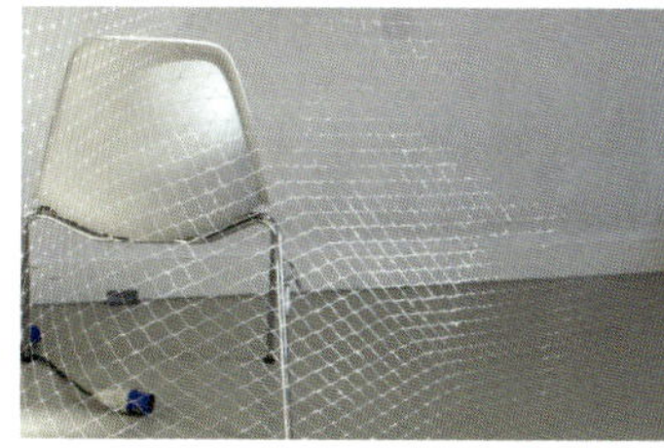

KVS Brussels, exhibition set-up / Montage de l'exposition au KVS Bruxelles

Studios Kabako video workshop / Atelier vidéo organisé par les Studios Kabako à Lubunga

Faustin Linyekula and the Curry Stone Award Jury / Faustin Linyekula et le jury du prix Curry Stone

The [a]FA trio with Peter Sellars / Le trio [a]FA avec Peter Sellars

Studios Kabako's future site in Lubunga / Le futur site des Studios Kabako à Lubunga

STATEMENTS/
TÉMOIGNAGES

English version page 110, 300

Ma pratique de recherche, toujours ouverte à la créativité, et mon travail artistique basé sur le texte s'attachent tous deux à la construction de soi, à travers les mémoires et les histoires personnelles. Aller en Afrique, c'était un rêve depuis l'enfance, un rêve que je sentais parfois un peu inaccessible, vu du Mexique d'où je viens. Dans le cadre du programme [a]FA, je suis allée en République démocratique du Congo et au Ghana.

Lors de ces deux expériences, je me suis consacrée à la recherche d'histoires et de témoignages personnels autour de la question de l'eau, mais aussi autour des notions de propriété. A l'université de Vienne, j'ai suivi les cours sur la poésie africaine du professeur Adams Bodomo, avec le désir de poursuivre cette conversation passionnante entre langage écrit et langage parlé. Je m'intéresse tout particulièrement au mouvement de la Négritude en ce qu'il croise poésie, politique et identité.

Née à Mexico en 1985, Frida Robles est licenciée en histoire et communication (BA) à l'Université Iberoamericana et a obtenu un master en design social à l'Université des arts appliqués de Vienne (MA). Elle vient de terminer son premier projet éditorial au Laboratorio para la Ciudad (Laboratoire pour la ville), une expérience urbaine dans la ville de Mexico.

Je comprends mon travail d'architecte comme celui d'un praticien de la culture, ce qui demande de prendre en compte une multitude de contextes. Collaborer sur des projets au Ghana ou au Congo n'a pas seulement apporté des directions thématiques à mon travail, mais m'a obligé à prendre position au sein de ces contextes particuliers.

Mes recherches aujourd'hui explorent les environnements urbains dynamiques et l'architecture kinétique à la lumière des avalanches de données et de la robotique. Pour moi, les villes en mutation permanente d'Afrique subsaharienne, assimilant si rapidement les nouvelles technologies, offrent un vrai potentiel à cette direction du design architectural. Au sein des laboratoires [a]FA, mon travail s'est souvent attardé sur les incongruités et les paradoxes des espaces confrontés aux technologies. Dans mon travail »Will you come back tomorrow?« (Vas-tu revenir demain ?), la photographie et des performances participatives mettent en lumière l'étrangeté d'une soirée dans un village au nord du Ghana, étrangeté qui pourrait facilement être romancée. L'un des projets sur lesquels je travaille actuellement est une série de designs architecturaux spéculatifs au Ghana qui suggèrent d'autres futurs possibles pour les villes en Afrique. Avec ce travail, j'essaie d'interroger certains postulats au sujet de l'architecture sur le continent africain.

Dans le cadre de ses études à l'Université des arts appliqués de Vienne conclues par un diplôme du Studio Greg Lynn en janvier 2015, Juergen Strohmayer a participé à l'ensemble des laboratoires [a]FA. Il vit aujourd'hui à Addis Abeba en Ethiopie où il est chargé de cours invité à l'Institut éthiopien pour l'architecture, le bâtiment et le développement urbain (EiABC).

Aujourd'hui, je vis à Lagos. Je suis amoureuse de Lagos, je m'y sens à la maison. Une maison en mouvement à travers cet immense Moloch urbain, au bord de l'eau, ce désert de béton, cette marée stagnante et visqueuse de véhicules, d'hommes et de biens. Lagos, c'est le glamour, la richesse, le champagne, le pétrole et les clubs nautiques. Lagos, c'est aussi l'obscurité la plus complète, la pauvreté, les pénuries de carburant, les bidonvilles sur l'eau. Des gratte-ciel illuminés au canon d'un policier pointé sur vous au prochain croisement, dans une rue la nuit.

Le rythme des tambours m'a menée au Mali, le pays du Blues du désert et de l'architecture en terre des Dogons. Vivre dans des habitations en pisé m'attirait et m'a aidée à comprendre comment culture et croyances pouvaient se manifester dans les constructions. Un an plus tard était fondé [a]FA et j'ai pu poursuivre mes recherches dans le nord du Ghana.

La collaboration avec les Studios Kabako et Faustin Linyekula à Kisangani a aussi changé ma perception de

l'espace. Le pouvoir de l'eau et le pouvoir du dessin dans le paysage urbain. Le pouvoir de la performance et comment le corps peut définir l'espace à travers le mouvement. Le pouvoir d'une exposition quand l'Etat a baissé les bras. Le voyage seul vaut toute une histoire.

Lagos, maintenant, et la cadence de la ville qui me suit jusque dans mes rêves. Le bruit profond et crépitant des générateurs et des ventilateurs qui soulagent de la chaleur, l'appel du Muezzin suivi par les tambours des églises et le son à fond des films Nollywood depuis l'appartement de mes voisins. Le motif polyrythmique des klaxons, le Shoki et Fela Kuti. Le claquement d'une pluie tropicale sur les toits en tôle.

Née à Vienne, Stefanie Theuretzbacher travaille comme architecte depuis son diplôme à l'Université des arts appliqués de Vienne. Son intérêt professionnel s'attache pour le moment au continent africain.

Plusieurs laboratoires [a]FA en zone rurale au Ghana, en République démocratique du Congo et en Alaska m'ont permis d'accroître mon expérience dans la recherche de solutions d'approvisionnement, d'assainissement et de traitement des déchets au niveau local. Dans tous les cas, mes recherches prenaient pour cadre le trajet de l'eau dans un village ou un quartier donné, de la source à l'approvisionnement, la consommation jusqu'à l'évacuation.

L'implication à Guabuliga au Ghana a permis une collaboration avec l'ONG Braveaurora pour la mise en place d'un système solaire d'approvisionnement en eau à l'échelle du village. A partir de ce travail, j'ai proposé, dans le cadre de la 9e édition des Journées anthropologiques de Vienne, un atelier sur les « Aspects socio-économiques de la maintenance des infrastructures techniques en architecture et pour la gestion de l'eau ».

Avec mes partenaires en Alaska, nous avons reçu le North American Partnership on Environmental Community Action Grant (bourse du partenariat nord-américain pour des actions communautaires environnementales) pour l'amélioration du traitement communautaire des déchets organiques humains (CSFWT) en zone arctique d'Amérique du Nord. En 2014, nous avons remporté le Alaska Water and Sewer Challenge (Défi de l'eau et du traitement des eaux en Alaska) pour développer un système innovatif et accessible de traitement des eaux usées pour les habitations en zone rurale en Alaska. Cela m'a poussée à terminer ma thèse autour de la « Conception d'un système d'assainissement Biochar à Kivalina, Alaska », prenant conscience ainsi que les défis à relever pour la mise en place de systèmes d'approvisionnement et d'assainissement en eau sont similaires à travers le monde.

Ingénieur d'Université, Theresa Theuretzbacher a étudié la gestion de l'eau et l'ingénierie environnementale à l'Université des ressources naturelles et des sciences de la vie (BOKU) à Vienne. Elle vit aujourd'hui en Norvège où elle travaille pour la Fondation du climat comme ingénieur environnemental en charge du traitement des déchets humains. Elle suit des projets en Alaska et en Inde.

Tackling the problem of citizens being deprived of tap water (and drinking water) in an area where there is no actual lack of water is just one of the absurdities of Lubunga. The water problem is disturbing because it demonstrates the hopelessness and suffering of the inhabitants of the town. Abandoned, they have adopted a new set of criteria by which, if the water is clear, then it is considered potable, and if it is not clear, then it will be used for other things. It is as simple and dangerous as that...

People have long stopped counting the number of deaths that have resulted from water-borne diseases. In fact, are the causes of deaths even known? This town is particularly vulnerable to water-borne epidemics. So, we have, bitterly, witnessed the deaths of our parents, uncles, aunts, sisters, cousins, nephews, and other relatives. This situation discourages sugar-coated speeches regarding the water problem.

Several projects have been carried out, especially by international or national non-governmental organizations, in order to proffer solutions—temporary solutions which only respond to epidemiological emergencies. Once the epidemic is contained, the project disappears, thereby creating mistrust and even disgust among citizens regarding any project tackling the water problem. The mapping exercise

I participated in was a new experience for the people, and created an impact. I feel like people are ready to invest, even with their limited resources, in order to ensure the sustainability of the project. The inhabitants are indeed ready to invest in buying "drinking water" (which is not even potable) provided by Regideso. As Regideso is now unable to distribute water through their domestic network, unemployed youths collect water from the water station to sell in jerry cans to households in town, and this practice has met the needs of the people, but perhaps way too much? The selling of water was finally banned by the Regideso authorities.

There are, therefore, great expectations from the people. The particularity and originality of this project emerge through the consideration given to the locals during the investigative period and during subsequent periods. This is enough reason to be hopeful...

The acquisition in December of a plot of land by Studios Kabako raises this hope. People are saying that "a serious project by white people takes time, though it is the sustainability that is most desired." However, in this particular case, it concerns the project and dreams of one of the neighbourhood's sons, Faustin Linyekula.

Evoquer la question de l'eau dans un endroit si riche en eau mais dont la population est privée d'eau courante (et donc d'eau potable) n'est pas le moindre des paradoxes de Lubunga. La question de l'eau inquiète car elle renvoie aux désespoirs et angoisses des habitants de la commune. Laissés pour compte, ils ont instauré un nouveau critère. Si l'eau est limpide, elle est potable, dans le cas contraire, elle sera réservée à d'autres usages. Aussi simple et dangereux que cela...

On ne compte plus depuis longtemps le nombre de pertes humaines causées par des maladies hydriques, sait-on d'ailleurs de quoi l'on meurt ? Cette commune est particulièrement vulnérable face aux épidémies hydriques. Ainsi, amèrement, nous avons vu mourir nos parents, oncles, tantes, sœurs, cousins, neveux, les nôtres. Cette situation ne laisse plus d'espace aux discours démagogiques en matière d'eau.

Plusieurs projets ont été réalisés, surtout par des organisations non-gouvernementales, internationales ou nationales, pour proposer des solutions. Mais des solutions éphémères, ne répondant qu'à des urgences épidémiologiques. Une fois l'épidémie calmée, le projet disparaît. D'où la méfiance voire le mépris de la population à l'égard de tout projet sur la question de l'eau.

Le mapping auquel j'ai pris part était une expérience nouvelle pour la population marquant ainsi les esprits. Il me semble que les gens sont prêts à s'investir avec leurs petits moyens pour assurer la pérennité du projet. Les habitants sont en effet prêts à dépenser de l'argent pour acheter de l'« eau potable » (qui ne l'est en fait pas) produite par la Regideso mais qui est désormais incapable de la distribuer dans son réseau domestique. Alors les jeunes désœuvrés amenaient de l'eau depuis la station pour la vendre en ville par bidons auprès des ménages, une pratique qui a rencontré les besoins de la population, trop peut-être ? La vente a finalement été interdite par la hiérarchie de la Regideso.

Il y a donc une forte attente de la population. La singularité et l'originalité du projet viennent de la place accordée à la population locale pendant la phase de diagnostic et les phases qui ont suivi. Il y a là une raison de croire...

L'acquisition en décembre d'une parcelle par les Studios Kabako encourage l'espoir. Les gens ne cessent de répéter que « la chose sérieuse d'un Blanc prend du temps, mais c'est la durabilité qui est à tout prix recherchée. » Même si dans ce cas, il s'agit bien du projet et des rêves d'un enfant du quartier, Faustin Linyekula.

Isaac Yenga Lomami was born and raised in Kisangani, right in Lubunga. After his secondary school education in general teaching studies, he left his hometown for the Great Seminary of Redemptoris-Mater in Goma. He returned to Kisangani later, where he studied philosophy and obtained his bachelor's degree in 2015. Since September 2013, he has been coordinating all of Studios Kabako's activities in Lubunga.

Isaac Yenga Lomami naît et a grandi à Kisangani, précisément à Lubunga. Après des études secondaires en pédagogie générale, il part au Grand Séminaire Redemptoris-Mater à Goma, puis

revient à Kisangani pour suivre des études en philosophie, il obtient son diplôme de licence en 2015. Depuis septembre 2013, il coordonne les activités des Studios Kabako à Lubunga.

I remember in May or June 2013, we received the information and on September 28, we celebrated the end of the first phase of the mapping.

Presently it is the drought period and people are suffering trying to get water—especially drinking water. On Lokandu Avenue, we are besieged each day from 5:30am to 12:30pm because of our regulation and we are often reminded of Studios Kabako's project. However, the song "Bilengi ya Mayi" encourages people to believe that the project is still dear to Studios Kabako.

In our daily conversations in the house and in town, we are hopeful that Studios Kabako will provide, if possible, two wells over the course of the year.

The youth, particularly those involved in the Community Coordination of Sociocultural Activities, are pleased to have the project on Baraka Avenue, where they hope to have a cultural center built for them.

We often reflect on what will be, firstly, the government's, and secondly, the project beneficiaries' contributions, respectively. In addition, we could, if possible, set up a "think tank" committee for this purpose here in Lubunga.

Je me souviens qu'en mai ou juin 2013, l'information nous avait été transmise et que le 28 septembre, nous avions célébré la fin de la première phase du mapping.

Actuellement, nous sommes en période de sécheresse et les gens souffrent pour trouver de l'eau. Encore pire de l'eau à boire. Sur l'avenue Lokandu, nous sommes envahis chaque jour de 5h30 à 12h30, conformément à notre règlementation et on nous rappelle souvent le projet Kabako. La chanson « Bilengi ya Mayi » encourage cependant la population à croire que Kabako tient encore à ce projet. Dans nos conversations chaque matin, ici à la maison et à la cité, les gens souhaitent que les Studios Kabako arrangent, si possible au courant de cette année, deux puits. Les jeunes, particulièrement au travers de la Coordination Communale des Activités Socio-Culturelles, se réjouissent du projet sur l'avenue Baraka de leur monter un center culturel.

Nous nous posons souvent la question de savoir quelle sera la contribution d'abord de l'Etat et ensuite de la population bénéficiaire du projet ? Et pourquoi pas monter un « Groupe de réflexion » dans ce sens ici à Lubunga...

Papa Assani Ga-Losomia was born in Yanonghe but has been living in Lubunga since 1958. He is a father of eight children and works in the primary school section of the inspectorate in charge of national education. His house on Lokandu Avenue has a well that is highly frequented by locals living nearby who consider its water drinkable. Papa Assani is involved in many associations involving mainly young people.

Papa Assani Ga-Losomia est né à Yanonghe mais vit à Lubunga depuis 1958. Père de huit enfants, il travaille dans l'Inspection pour l'éducation nationale - école primaire. Sa parcelle, avenue Lokandu, comprend un puits très utilisé par les habitants autour, considéré comme potable. Papa Assani est impliqué dans de multiples associations, pour les jeunes notamment.

Since our seven-day on-the-ground visit to see the water distribution points for Lubunga inhabitants, and following our observation that the water used by the inhabitants was impure, all of our interviewees are hopeful that the situation will soon improve.

Many people are inquiring about the follow-up to the mapping. Sometimes, I don't have any answers, but my main answer is that, hopefully, one day, this project will be carried out. Recently, because of the drought, the water level in some wells is low while others are completely dried out, thereby requiring long trips made in search of water. Regideso, the company in charge of water distribution to the district, forbids anyone from fetching water from the Dalma station in the military cantonment. This has created a very difficult situation.

The exhibition by [a]FA at the Alliance Francaise in Kisangani is a signal that is as clear as the signboard at the Beach moteur[1] on the left side of the river. It was a very

important gesture for the people. The discussions with school children last year, and in particular, the song "Mayi ya Lubunga", by the primary school pupils, is today a sign of hope. People are convinced after watching this clip that the project will, eventually, be carried out.

I wish everybody at Studios Kabako good luck as the people await the implementation, someday, of this project.

Depuis que nous avons effectué une descente sur le terrain, pendant sept jours pour voir toutes les sources qui alimentent la population de Lubunga en eau à boire et après avoir constaté que l'eau que consomment les gens est impropre, toutes les personnes que nous avons interviewées avaient l'espoir que la situation serait rapidement améliorée.

Beaucoup de gens me demandent la suite de ce mapping. Parfois, je manque de réponse, mais l'espoir est qu'un jour le projet sera réalisé, voici ma principale réponse. Ces derniers temps, en raison de la sécheresse, certains puits manquent d'eau, d'autres sont à sec. Il faut alors faire des kilomètres pour se procurer d'eau. La Regideso, la société qui devrait fournir l'eau à la cité, interdit à toute personne de puiser l'eau à la source Dalma qui se trouve dans le camp militaire. Ceci rend la situation catastrophique.

L'exposition à l'Alliance française de Kisangani réalisée par [a]FA était un signe fort, comme le grand panneau, au Beach moteur rive gauche, il était très important pour la population. Le dialogue avec les élèves l'année dernière et surtout la chanson des élèves des écoles primaires « Mayi ya Lubunga » est aujourd'hui un signe d'espoir. La population est convaincue, en voyant ce clip, que le projet sera mis en place un jour.

Je souhaite une bonne réussite aux Studios Kabako car la population attend un jour que ce projet se réalise.

Ignace Franklin Yenga was born in Lubunga, where he still lives. He is a tailor by profession and father to eight children. He is a catechist of the Neocathechumenate Way at the Catholic parish of Lubunga.

Ignace Franklin Yenga est né et vit depuis à Lubunga. Père de huit enfants et tailleur de métier, il est aussi catéchiste du chemin néo-cathéchuménat à la paroisse catholique de Lubunga.

[1] Arrival and departure points of motorized canoes used for crossing the river / [1] Point de départ/d'arrivée des pirogues à moteur pour traverser le fleuve

LUBUNGAMODE

Schedule / Périodes :
September 2013 – September 2014

Lab head / Direction du Lab :
Baerbel Mueller, Faustin Linyekula

[a]FA team / Equipe [a]FA :
Frida Robles, Juergen Strohmayer,
Stefanie Theuretzbacher,
Theresa Theuretzbacher

Lubunga team / Equipe de Lubunga :
Papa Assani, Ignace Yenga, Isaac Yenga,
Jean Amisi Lipame, Benjamin Lokele,
Yves Mwamba

Project partner / Organisation partenaire :
Faustin Linyekula, Virginie Dupray /
Studios Kabako Kisangani

Lab review guests / Collaborateurs extérieurs :
Hannah Le Roux, Andrea Börner,
Stefan Gruber, Günter Langergraber

Financial support / Soutien financier :
Institute of Architecture, University of
Applied Arts Vienna, Studios Kabako,
Bundeskanzleramt Sektion II: Kunst and Kultur

Exhibitions / Expositions :
Lubunga en Rés(eau), Alliance française,
Kisangani; KVS Brussels; Think Global,
Build Social!, AzW Vienna

Exhibition graphics / Graphisme exposition :
Nataša Sienčnik

Exhibition support / Partenaires exposition :
Alliance française Kisangani,
KVS Brussels, Curry Stone Foundation,
Albert Schiessling Plotservice

Photos:
Baerbel Mueller:
395, 396, 397, 398, 399, 410, 411, 412,
413, 414, 415, 416, 417, 429, 430, 431
Frida Robles:
374, 375, 376, 377, 378
Juergen Strohmayer:
326, 336, 410, 411, 412, 413, 414, 415,
Stefanie Theuretzbacher:
371, 391, 411, 416, 426, 427
Studios Kabako:
410, 416, 417, 425, 439, 440, 442

Founded in 2001 in Kinshasa by Faustin Linyekula, STUDIOS KABAKO is a platform for training, research, and creation for dance, visual theater, music, and film: "a workplace where one is constantly on a personal quest that sometimes one reaches. It is a place of much questioning but where, on some evenings, certainty becomes obvious. A place where the notions of elegance will often override those of efficiency and profitability..."

Fondés en 2001 à Kinshasa par Faustin Linyekula, LES STUDIOS KABAKO sont un espace de formation, de recherche et de création autour de la danse, du théâtre visuel, de la musique et la vidéo : « un lieu où l'on travaille, où toujours on se cherche et où parfois on trouve. Un lieu où l'on doute beaucoup, mais où certains soirs, s'impose une certitude. Un lieu où souvent les notions d'élégance priment sur celles d'efficacité et de rentabilité... »

LUBUNGA EN RES[EAU], ALLIANCE FRANÇAISE, KISANGANI

September / Septembre 2014

Coming back to Kisangani one year after [a]FA's first residency allowed us to share the elaborated mappings of Lubungamode, both in Lubunga itself, and in Kisangani town; in public and in institutional spaces with diverse audiences.

An exhibition was conceptualized and designed to be shown at the Alliance Française, located in Kisangani's central district of Makiso. The idea was to network the three different mapping approaches—spatial, narrative, and scientific—and to create one overall field of visual and textual information and narrations.

To emphasize the fragmented and incomplete character of the investigations and encounters with Lubunga, A4 sheets of paper were hung in a fishing net creating a sea of pixels. This illuminated net appropriated the exhibition space, creating a light and uneven background, which shimmered like water.

The exhibition opening allowed Studios Kabako to communicate to politicians regarding Lubunga and its challenges. Two provincial ministers, the Minister of Culture and the Minister of Planning, as well as the Governor's Chief of Staff were in attendance. The local press was also present resulting in coverage on local radio and TV channels.

Revenir à Kisangani un an plus tard nous a permis de partager cette cartographie complexe dressée lors de Lubungamode, à la fois avec Lubunga, mais aussi avec la ville de Kisangani : dans des espaces publics ou institutionnels, avec des publics variés.

Une exposition a été conçue et réalisée pour l'Alliance française située à Makiso, la commune la plus centrale. L'idée était de relier les trois approches cartographique, spatiale, narrative et scientifique, et de créer un champ global d'informations visuelles et textuelles et de narrations. Témoignant du caractère incomplet et fragmenté de nos recherches et de nos rencontres à Lubunga, une mer de feuillets A4 était suspendue – tels des pixels – à un filet de pêche. Un filet lumineux à même de s'approprier l'espace d'exposition, créant un fond délicat et mouvant qui scintillait presque, comme l'eau.

Le vernissage de l'exposition a permis aux Studios Kabako de sensibiliser les autorités politiques sur la situation de la commune de Lubunga et sur les défis à relever. Etaient présents deux ministres provinciaux : la Ministre de la Culture et des Arts et le Ministre du Plan, ainsi que le Directeur de Cabinet du gouverneur. La presse locale était aussi au rendez-vous avec une belle couverture auprès des radios et télévisions locales.

Curatorial team / Commissariat :
Baerbel Mueller, Frida Robles, Juergen Strohmayer, Stefanie Theuretzbacher
Graphic design / Graphisme : Nataša Sienčnik

LUBUNGA
EN RÉS(EAU)

LUBUNGA EN RES[EAU], KVS, BRUSSEL / BRUXELLES

October / Octobre 2014

"Réseau" means network, a structure in which all the elements participating are interconnected. A net is also a tool, a tool for fishermen to catch their prey of the day. Lubunga en Rés(eau) is an exhibition that tries to capture Lubunga from three different angles (spatial, narrative, and scientific); it is the flowing presentation of an ongoing research project on water. It is a net to continue capturing impressions, beauties, desires, and stories of this place. The installation consists of portraits, maps, drawings, stories, statistics, and scientific findings, among other elements. The elements are displayed as clouds—a metaphor for the urban density in Lubunga. It is an abstract mapping of the reflections on Lubunga.

Lubunga en Rés(eau) est une structure dans laquelle tous les éléments participants sont interconnectés. Un réseau - du latin *retiolus*, diminutif de *retis* qui signifie filet - est également un outil, un outil pour le pêcheur qui saisit sa proie dans son filet. Lubunga en Rés(eau) est une exposition qui cherche à saisir Lubunga sous trois angles différents (spatial, narratif et scientifique). C'est la représentation fluide d'un projet de recherche en cours sur l'eau. Un filet pour attraper les impressions, beautés, désirs et histoires de cette commune, ponctué de portraits, cartes, dessins, histoires, statistiques et analyses scientifiques... Les éléments sont présentés comme des nuages de condensation - une métaphore de la densité urbaine de Lubunga. Lubunga en Rés(eau) se veut une cartographie abstraite de notre regard et de nos réflexions sur Lubunga.

Curatorial team / Commissariat: Baerbel Mueller, Frida Robles, Juergen Strohmayer, Stefanie Theuretzbacher
Exhibition design / Scénographie : Stefanie Theuretzbacher

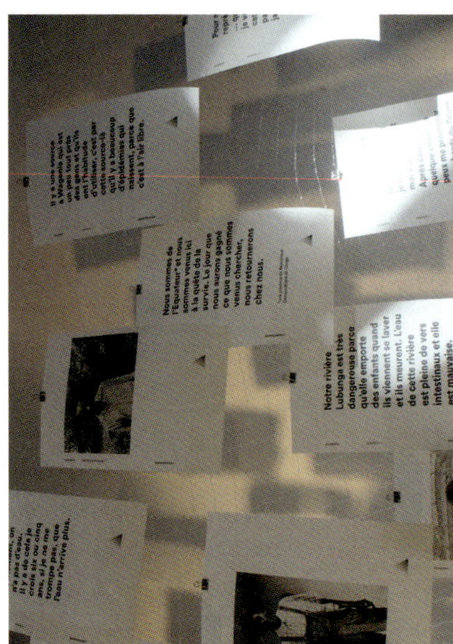

2829 NORTH AMERICAN STREET, PHILADELPHIA

Virginie Dupray

"I do not live by bread alone
In the early morning cold
I soaked up in the river
A piece of clear sky..."

Varlam Shalamov

North American Street runs through the town over several kilometers with its neighborhoods changing radically as one goes up north. The American Dream dissipates, slowly, starting from Fairmount and finally goes up in flames at Girard Avenue. The North American Dream indeed or what remains of it. There are several courtyards, crumbling walls, piles of bricks, barrels, scrap metal piled up here and there, with only the deep blue sky for a roof, a majestic red brick smoke stack cutting into the heavens. For three weeks, we occupied one of those numerous unused industrial spaces—"vacant" spaces that have become ubiquitous from Baltimore to Detroit and in a city that lost 75% of its industrial fabric between 1940 and 1980. Under the Re-PLACE-ing Philadelphia project, Faustin Linyekula chose to work in this former factory—on the American Dream Street in the Puerto Rican neighborhood, where Spanish holds sway—in order to read the city and its emblematic history, though not through its monuments, museums and statues, but through its vulnerability, through crumbling, vacillating, squeaking, and scratchy things, all things that are also living and evolving every day. Or finding a way to talk to the city from its most fragile part? "But time. Time has stopped. The sky, the earth, things, everything / Completely grounded," wrote Sony Labou Tansi. In fact, on North American "Dream" Street, everything is somehow grounded; even the "world-famous" strip club across the street had to close its doors. But people are still there—Carmen, Celina, Daniel and the young artists he accompanies, and Julio, the guarding angel of the building who came, long ago, from Nicaragua and with whom we awaited nightfall drinking Coronas and listening to salsa from his car radio.

In Lubunga, thousands of kilometers away to the east, beyond the ocean and forests (or what remains of it), people are, also, still there, even though at this hour, everyone is already long asleep; Isaac, Uncle Ignace, Jacob and Bi Atosha who is guarding her house from above. In Lubunga, everything is equally grounded and only old people could remember that there was, once, tap water and electricity in, at least, the Belgian neighborhood, close to the station where the trains (with first, second and third class coaches) ran daily, but

2829 NORTH AMERICAN STREET, PHILADELPHIE

Virginie Dupray

« Je ne vis pas seulement de pain
Dans le froid du petit matin
J'ai trempé dans la rivière
Un morceau de ciel clair... »

Varlam Chalamov

North American Street, l'une de ces rues qui traversent la ville sur plusieurs kilomètres et qui voit ses quartiers radicalement changer au fur et à mesure que l'on monte vers le Nord... *L'American Dream* s'essouffle un peu à partir de Fairmount, pour définitivement partir en fumée à Girard Avenue. North American Dream donc, ou ce qu'il en reste... Plusieurs cours, des murs qui s'effritent, des tas de briques, bidons, ferrailles entassés ici et là, l'azur comme toit, une cheminée majestueuse rouge brique tranche le bleu pétant du ciel. Nous avons investi pour trois semaines l'un de ces si nombreux espaces industriels désaffectés, ces espaces « vacant », devenus omniprésents de Baltimore à Détroit, dans cette ville qui a perdu 75% de son tissu industriel entre 1940 et 1980. Dans le cadre du projet *Re-PLACE-ing Philadelphia*, Faustin Linyekula a choisi de travailler dans cette ancienne fabrique, rue du rêve américain, dans ce quartier portoricain où l'espagnol est de mise, pour tenter de lire la ville et son histoire si emblématique non à travers ses monuments, ses musées et ses statues, mais à l'aune de sa vulnérabilité, du côté de ce qui s'effrite, de ce qui vacille, de ce qui grince, de ce qui gratte, mais aussi de ce qui vit et se transforme au quotidien. Ou comment parler à la ville de sa partie la plus fragile ? « Mais le temps. Le temps est par terre. Le ciel, la terre, les choses, tout./Complètement par terre, » a écrit Sony Labou Tansi. Oui, à North American « Dream » Street, tout est un peu par terre, même le « world-famous » club de strip en face a dû fermer ses portes. Mais les hommes sont toujours là, Carmen, Daniel et les jeunes artistes qu'il accompagne, Celina ou Julio, le (ange)gardien du bâtiment venu il y a bien longtemps du Nicaragua et avec qui on laisse le soir venir en buvant des Coronas et en écoutant de la salsa sur son autoradio.

A Lubunga, des milliers de kilomètres à l'est, par-delà océan et forêts (ou ce qu'il en reste), les hommes aussi sont toujours là, plus que jamais, même si à cette heure-ci, tout le monde dort depuis longtemps. Isaac, Oncle Ignace, Jacob et Bi Atosha qui veille sur sa maison de tout en haut. A Lubunga, tout est aussi par terre et seuls les vieux se souviennent qu'il y eut un jour de l'eau courante et de l'électricité, dans le quartier des Belges du moins, près de la gare où les trains partaient chaque jour, avec des premières, secondes

these old people are becoming rare. Those who like Faustin are in their 40s remember the free ferries crossing, hourly, the Congo River. But, the young ones, they just remember that everything has always been grounded. In Lubunga, the sky is rarely startling blue and "vacant" spaces do not exist. There is always a church or a family to occupy them. As for piles of bricks or scrap metal, they will not last for long. Here, everything can be made useful again, items have a long lifespan, from empty bottles to rusty sheet metal. In Lubunga, the city seems to only know, by heart, one day or maybe two days of the week, (weekdays and Sundays included), as invariably the days are all similar though always different because nothing is guaranteed, especially not the meal for dinner. Each person displays an overwhelming inventiveness in creating something out of nothing—a wonderful improvisation. The Congolese are wizards at getting by each day, from popular Kinshasa neighborhoods to mud houses in Lubunga.

Since 2010, Studios Kabako have gradually been making forays into Lubunga, little by little, first with concerts and performances, at the station on a stage built upon a carriage, in the Catholic parish, and at the motor boat beach. Using the inhabitants' imaginative inputs and some scientific analyses, Studios Kabako and [a]FA carried out the mapping and drawing of a profile of the town to resolve the water issue—from its collection to utilization and disposal. Additionally, Studios Kabako and [a]FA did an exhibition, and last year, Studios Kabako provided training to school children and high school students on sounds and images.

Why Lubunga? Why has Lubunga emerged as a testing ground, demanding Studios Kabako's presence? For so many reasons: Because Faustin grew up there; because situated off Avenue Hassan II is Avenue Kindu, where Faustin's dear grandmother, the mischievous-looking Bi Atosha, lived; because there is no bridge over the Congo River and because artists are born to build bridges; because Lubunga is, precisely, situated on the outskirts, facing the five districts on the other side of the river and the outskirts have always been of interest to Faustin, who frames his creations to get a better look of the fringes. On the outskirts is Kisangani facing voracious Kinshasa, on the outskirts are the northern neighborhoods of Philadelphia. Decentralization has always been at the heart of Studios Kabako's projects; because Lubunga has this unknown beauty with its entire walkway bordering the river and providing a contemplative view, from the opposite side, of the "real" city. Lubunga with its rivers, luxuriousness, and almost 200,000 inhabitants (in a country where numbers have become unimportant a long time ago), as well as its abandoned train station, big market, magnificent church, rammed earth houses and dirt avenues, is, timidly, caught up trying to be either a village or a city, a rural or urban location. Lubunga, because there is water everywhere though this water makes people fall sick and die and because we realized that something could, perhaps, be done; since according to Sony our companion, artists do not produce engaged art but art produces engagements.

"When pious people say: 'It is,' and sad people say: 'It was,' the artist says with a smile: 'It will be.'", wrote Rainer Maria Rilke. What will Lubunga, then, become? We have thousands of dreams, we have never lacked dreams. To hold onto these dreams, we chose

et troisièmes classes, mais les vieux se font plutôt rares. Ceux qui comme Faustin sont dans leur quarantaine se souviennent des bacs gratuits qui traversaient chaque heure le fleuve Congo. Les jeunes, eh bien, ils se souviennent juste que tout a toujours été par terre. A Lubunga, le ciel est rarement bleu pétant et les « vacant » n'existent pas. Il y a toujours une église ou une famille pour s'y installer, quant aux tas de briques ou de ferrailles, ils ne feraient pas long feu... Ici, tout retrouve usage, les objets ont longue vie, des bouteilles vides aux bouts de tôles rouillées. A Lubunga, la ville ne semble avoir appris par cœur qu'un seul jour, ou peut-être deux, les jours de la semaine et le dimanche, invariablement les mêmes, et toujours différents car rien n'est acquis, surtout pas ce que l'on aura dans son assiette le soir. Chacun déploie des trésors d'inventivité pour créer un peu avec du rien, la débrouille magnifique : les Congolais sont des magiciens du quotidien, des quartiers populaires de Kinshasa aux maisons en terre de Lubunga.

Depuis 2010, les Studios Kabako investissent Lubunga, petit à petit, d'abord des concerts et des performances, à la gare avec une scène montée sur un wagon, à la Paroisse catholique, au Beach moteur, puis un mapping ou comment dresser un portrait de la commune autour des questions de l'eau, de la collecte à la consommation et à l'évacuation, des histoires, de l'imaginaire des habitants aux analyses scientifiques, puis une exposition, et enfin l'année dernière, une formation pour des écoliers et lycéens autour du son et de l'image.

Alors pourquoi Lubunga ? Pourquoi Lubunga s'est-elle imposée comme un terrain d'expérimentation, une présence nécessaire ? Pourquoi et tant de réponses. Parce que Faustin y a grandi. Parce que de l'avenue Hassan II part l'avenue Kindu où vivait sa chère grand-mère, Bi Atosha, aux yeux malicieux. Parce qu'aucun pont ne traverse le Congo et que les artistes sont nés pour construire des ponts. Parce que Lubunga est définitivement à la périphérie face aux cinq autres communes de l'autre côté du fleuve et que la périphérie a toujours intéressé Faustin qui met des cadres dans ses créations pour mieux regarder à côté. A la périphérie, Kisangani face à la vorace Kinshasa, à la périphérie, les quartiers nord de Philadelphie. La décentralisation a toujours été au cœur de la démarche des Studios Kabako. Parce que Lubunga a cette beauté qui s'ignore, avec sa promenade longeant le fleuve d'où l'on peut contempler de l'autre côté la « vraie » ville, avec ses rivières, sa luxuriance, hésitant encore avec ses presque 200,000 habitants (dans un pays où l'on ne compte plus depuis longtemps), avec sa gare à l'abandon, son grand marché, sa magnifique église, ses maisons en pisé et ses avenues de terre, entre village et ville, entre rural et urbain. Lubunga, parce qu'il y a de l'eau partout mais que cette eau rend malade et tue les gens et qu'on se dit un jour qu'il y aurait peut-être quelque chose à faire : comme dit notre compagnon Sony, on ne produit pas de l'art engagé mais c'est l'art qui produit des engagements.

« Et lorsque les gens pieux disent : ‹ Il est ›, et que les gens tristes disent : ‹ Il fut ›, l'artiste dit dans un sourire : ‹ Il sera. ›», a écrit Rainer Maria Rilke. Que sera Lubunga, donc ? Nous avons des milliers de rêves, nous n'en avons jamais manqué. Et pour abriter ces milliers de rêve, nous avons choisi avenue Baraka la bien-nommée, avenue de la chance, une parcelle acquise en décembre dernier.

Baraka Avenue, aptly named Avenue of Luck, by acquiring a plot of land last December. Baraka Avenue will, therefore, be home to a pilot water treatment plant that will supply water, daily, to 10,000 persons; a beginning that will hopefully incite the authorities. This is not about replacing Regideso; no pipe dreams on our part. But if Lubunga inhabitants are already making daily trips on foot, motorbike or bicycle to wells for water that is allegedly potable, then they could go to Baraka Avenue, making similar efforts at similar costs, to fetch potable water. Baraka Avenue will also be a neighborhood cultural center, where one can see a movie, listen to a concert, and watch a performance. A room will be provided for students and pupils, who will revise their school work using electricity and access data on computers, put at their disposal—an iota of light in a town often plunged in darkness. Baraka Avenue will be a training venue for the continuation of the workshop instituted last May-June involving about 60 primary and secondary school pupils. Training in writing, sound and image that is not necessarily geared toward creating artistic vocations (but better still if artists are born!), but proposed to awaken the senses, generate perspectives on the environment (that will necessarily be the better for it), to stimulate these children, these young adults and young citizens into developing opinions, taking part, shouldering their responsibility in a country which must become if it does not want to disappear. Indeed, our Baraka Avenue house should have the beauty of the clear water-soaked sky, because it is in such places where life is so difficult that beauty ceases to be a luxury to become a necessity.

Indeed, there should be more Baraka Avenues, providing ideas and inspirations so that other neighborhood cultural centers, potable water outlets, solution-providing dream factories can grow like some rapidly increasing weeds, in Lubunga and in other districts like Tshopo or Mangobo[1], and in small towns around Kisangani, Ubundu and Yangambi[2].

1 Other districts of Kisangani
2 Small cities around Kisangani

VIRGINIE DUPRAY studied European economics (HEC Paris) and art history. She worked for the French Institute in London and was in charge of communication at the National Center of Dance in Pantin. She has managed many artists, among them Nacera Belaza. She has been managing Studios Kabako since 2003. Virginie writes, occasionally, for various cultural magazines.

Avenue Baraka abritera donc une unité pilote de traitement d'eau qui pourra approvisionner chaque jour 10,000 personnes, un début qui nous l'espérons, donnera des idées aux autorités. Il ne s'agit pas de remplacer la Regideso, nulle tuyauterie dans nos rêves, mais si les habitants de Lubunga font déjà chaque jour des trajets à pied, en moto ou en vélo vers les puits jugés potables, alors ils pourront venir avenue Baraka et obtenir pour le même effort et le même coût de l'eau réellement potable. Avenue Baraka sera aussi un centre culturel de quartier : on pourra venir voir un film, écouter un concert, assister à une performance, une salle sera réservée à l'accueil des étudiants et des écoliers qui pourront réviser et avoir accès à des banques de données sur des ordinateurs mis à leur disposition, un îlot de lumière dans une commune le plus souvent plongée dans le noir. Avenue Baraka sera un lieu de formation dans la continuité de l'atelier mis en place en mai-juin dernier auprès d'une soixantaine d'élèves du primaire et du secondaire. Formation à l'écriture, au son et à l'image, non nécessairement pour créer des vocations artistiques (et tant mieux si des artistes émergent !), mais pour éveiller les regards, générer des points de vue sur l'environnement qui s'en trouvera nécessairement revalorisé, pour pousser ces enfants, ces jeunes adultes et ces jeunes citoyens, à prendre position, à s'engager, à prendre leurs responsabilités dans un pays qui doit devenir s'il ne veut pas disparaître. Enfin, notre maison avenue Baraka devra avoir la beauté de ce ciel clair trempé de rivière, car c'est bien dans les endroits où la vie est si difficile que la beauté cesse d'être un luxe pour devenir une nécessité.

Avenue Baraka devra essaimer, donner des idées, inspirer pour que d'autres-centres-culturels-de-quartier-fabriques-à-eau potable-à solutions-et-à-rêves puissent pousser comme des herbes un peu folles, à Lubunga, à la Tshopo ou à Mangobo[1], à Ubundu ou à Yangambi[2]...

1 Autres communes de Kisangani
2 Petites villes autour de Kisangani

Formée en économie européenne (HEC Paris) et en histoire de l'art, VIRGINIE DUPRAY travaille pour l'Institut français à Londres, puis dirige la communication au Centre national de la danse à Pantin. Elle accompagne ensuite différents artistes dont Nacera Belaza et est administratrice des Studios Kabako depuis 2003. Virginie écrit ponctuellement pour différentes revues culturelles.

LUBUNGA IN PICTURES / LUBUNGA EN IMAGES

An audiovisual workshop for children and adolescents in Lubunga by Studios Kabako / Un atelier audiovisuel des Studios Kabako pour des enfants et adolescents de Lubunga

How can views on the environment be changed among Lubunga's young adolescents and children? How can these future leaders be coerced into taking a stand and getting involved in a society where everything must be rebuilt? How can they be helped to have viewpoints, to be critical about their daily life, their world and their communities?

How can one, ultimately, re-infuse life into an often forgotten and depreciated town, while igniting collective thinking? Perhaps by providing tools to help its citizens tell their stories and create their own representations of words, pictures, and sounds using video materials, microphones, and softwares.

For five weeks in May/June 2015, about sixty school children and adolescents from three schools in Lubunga were introduced to video and audio production and also writing.

These pictures are some of the outcomes from this workshop: *Nadia* is a short film written, acted and directed by students of Salongo Institute and *Mayi ya Lubunga* is a song written and performed by primary school pupils of Lualaba and Mufaume on the question of water.

Comment changer le regard de jeunes adolescents et d'enfants de Lubunga sur leur environnement, comment amener ces futurs citoyens à prendre position et à interagir dans une société où tout est à reconstruire ? Comment créer des points de vue, un regard critique, sur leur quotidien, leur monde, leurs communautés ?

Comment enfin revaloriser une commune le plus souvent oubliée, parfois dépréciée, et accompagner des réflexions collectives ? Peut-être en proposant des outils pour raconter leurs histoires et créer leurs propres représentations : des mots, des images, des sons, des boîtiers vidéo, des micros, des logiciels...

Pendant cinq semaines, en mai–juin 2015, une soixantaine d'enfants et adolescents de trois écoles de Lubunga ont été initiés à la prise d'images et de sons, mais aussi à l'écriture.

Ces photos sont extraites du résultat de cet atelier : *Nadia*, un court métrage écrit, joué et réalisé par des lycéens de l'Institut Salongo, et *Mayi ya Lubunga*, une chanson écrite et interprétée par des élèves des écoles primaires Lualaba et Mufaume autour de la question de l'eau à Lubunga.

Artistic director / Directeur artistique : Faustin Linyekula
Team / Equipe : Jean Fundi, journalist / journaliste : Franck Moka
Guest artist / artiste invité : Dorine Mokha
With the support of DuckDuck, Vienna /
Avec le soutien de DuckDuck, Vienne

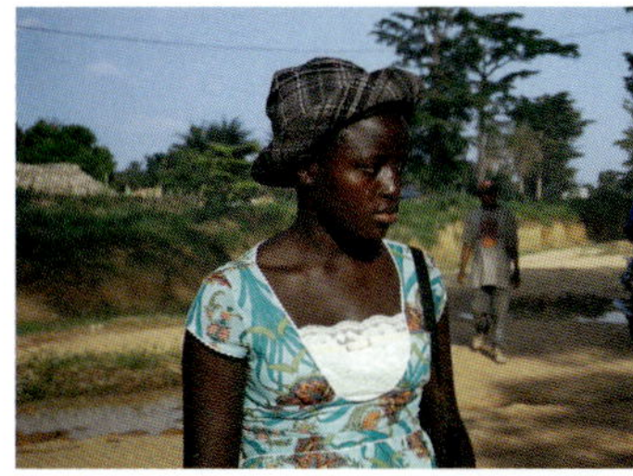

Nadia, Video, 06:01 min

Bilengi ya mayi, Video, 05:03 min

Timeline: Studios Kabako and [a]FA in Lubunga

2001:	Creation of Studios Kabako by Faustin Linyekula in Kinshasa
October 2006:	Establishment of Studios Kabako in Kisangani
July 2008:	Concert by Pasnas + Alesh + Deep, at Saint Marthe Catholic Parish Chapel
June 2010:	*3 jours pour 50 ans !*, Concert by Alesh + Pasnas, at the Lubunga Train Station
September 2013:	Lubungamode led by Faustin Linyekula and Baerbel Mueller
September 2014:	*Lubunga en Rés(eau)*, an exhibition at the Alliance Française, Kisangani, produced and designed by [a]FA, coordinated by Stefanie Theuretzbacher
September 2014:	Lubungamode, a weekend of performances and concerts in Lubunga with Yves Mwamba, Trésor Mawese and his group
October 2014:	*Lubunga en rés(eau)*, an exhibition produced by [a]FA at the KVS-Brussels on the occasion of the presentation of the Curry Stone Prize for the work done by Faustin Linyekula and Studios Kabako in Kisangani
May–June 2015:	*Lubungaschool*, an audio-visual workshop for 60 Lubunga primary and secondary school pupils
December 2015:	Acquisition by Studios Kabako of a plot of land on Baraka Avenue, in Lubunga

Agenda : Les Studios Kabako et [a]FA à Lubunga

2001 :	Création des Studios Kabako par Faustin Linyekula à Kinshasa
Octobre 2006 :	Installation des Studios Kabako à Kisangani
Juillet 2008 :	Concert de Pasnas + Alesh + Deep, chapelle paroisse catholique Ste Marthe
Juin 2010 :	*3 jours pour 50 ans !*, concert d'Alesh + Pasnas, gare de Lubunga
Septembre 2013 :	Lubungamode sous la direction de Faustin Linyekula et Baerbel Mueller
Septembre 2014 :	*Lubunga en Rés(eau)*, exposition à l'Alliance française de Kisangani, produite et mise en oeuvre par [a]FA, coordonnée par Stefanie Theuretzbacher
Septembre 2014 :	Lubungamode, un week-end performance et concert à Lubunga, avec Yves Mwamba et Trésor Mawese et son groupe
Octobre 2014 :	*Lubunga en rés(eau)*, exposition produite par [a]FA au KVS à Bruxelles à l'occasion de la remise du prix Currystone pour le travail effectué par Faustin Linyekula et les Studios Kabako à Kisangani
Mai–juin 2015 :	*Lubungaschool*, un atelier audiovisuel pour 60 élèves du primaire et du secondaire de Lubunga
Décembre 2015 :	Acquisition par les Studios Kabako d'une parcelle à Lubunga, avenue Baraka

A PLACE FROM WHICH TO SPEAK TO THE WORLD.

A Conversation between
Faustin Linyekula and Peter Sellars
Lisbon, May 2016

PS: One of the most important things in my life was meeting Faustin Linyekula, and feeling a completely new sense of possibility from the work being generated out of Kisangani and the idea that Kisangani is a place from which to speak to the world. What theater actually does is speak from a place and move history across time and space. I was so moved by Faustin's early work because it was not about elaborate resources, but rather about the infinite capacity of a human being. The total resources were actually inside the skin and they include ancestors, both old and recent, and unborn children, and everything we are actually carrying with us as we move our bodies through time and space, in this world we are living in now where we can be in China tomorrow. But what goes to China when we go to China? And what from China touches us or doesn't? What's the same wherever you go? And also, what is truly different wherever you go? The beautiful thing about the human being is that we are not things, we are not objects. We are beings, so we are changing all the time. What about you changes when the landscape changes? What about you changes when the government changes? What about you changes when history moves? Are we moving through history? And how is history moving through us?

I think theater is the place to carry these histories. And one of the most important things in my life was the discovery of dance as a carrier of history. History is in motion and therefore, many cultures chose dance as a way to embody history and history is danced rather than written. This man on my left took history that was impossible to describe with words, where words would not suffice. What overwhelmed me about his work was this idea that the only possible testimony comes from his body and that our habit of wanting to reduce history to words, when actually history is not reducible. The body is actually insisting on the full dimensionality of history as experience.

FL: There is this word that exists in Lingala, which is *lobi*, we use exactly the same word to say yesterday or tomorrow, so if someone says *lobi* it could mean yesterday but it could also mean tomorrow. I find that fascinating, that the ancient could invent that relationship with time, where the ancient and the unborn are kind of intertwined, so maybe the context can tell you that they are talking about the future or the past, but actually it is just one big cycle, *lobi*, which shifts the relationship to time from the timeline, where actually antiquity is part of tomorrow and tomorrow isn't antiquity. I was born in the 70s, so books were part of the culture I was born into, and having a father who is a school teacher, writing and reading was part of my life. And yet, when I started becoming aware of the world I was living in and trying to make sense of it, I realized that maybe words are not enough, or at least written words. Somehow spoken words are another physical manifestation. I could take more risks with spoken words than written ones because the spoken words are like a breath, they acknowledge the passage of time and they are meant to disappear, only leaving an echo of something. So how then would this notion of time, which is bounding together the past and the future through the present, with this acknowledgement that it is always changing like the body itself, how then can this manage to capture something of our place and our time?

PS: Actually, if you look into the eyes of that little girl, you'll see your great-grandmother's eyes, your body is made from and belongs to all these other people. This is what I think eternal life means. Literally, not just as a metaphysical idea, but actually a physical idea. For me, the sheer physicality of what is passed on is really powerful. So, our friend Guillermo Gómez Peña, who is a Mexican performance artist, always likes to say that when he sits in a cafe in Mexico City and writes in his notebook and sips his cappuccino, he has to think of twenty generations in his family, who were in the fields before dawn and worked till after dusk, so he could sip his cappuccino. And that is why we are here on earth, to do something our parents couldn't do, our grandparents couldn´t do. Here we are. What can we do? And you can feel not just the weight of that but also the joy of it. The planet has been waiting for what we are going to do next. And it creates a different kind of energy, of weight and power and beauty in the gestures we make.

UN ENDROIT D'OÙ PARLER AU MONDE…

Une conversation entre
Faustin Linyekula et Peter Sellars
Lisbonne, mai 2016

PS : Ma rencontre avec Faustin a été l'un des moments les plus importants dans ma vie, ouvrant un nouvel espace de possibles autour de ce travail né à Kisangani, de l'idée d'une ville, Kisangani, à partir de laquelle on pourrait parler au monde… C'est ce que fait le théâtre, parler depuis un endroit pour mettre en mouvement l'histoire à travers l'espace et le temps… Je me souviens de mon émotion devant ce premier travail de Faustin, cela ne tenait pas à des moyens ou des savoir-faire sophistiqués, mais plutôt aux possibilités infinies de l'être humain. Tout était là, sous la peau : les ancêtres, certains très anciens, d'autres plus proches, les enfants à naître, et tout ce que nous transportons en nous lorsque nous déplaçons nos corps à travers le temps et l'espace, dans ce monde dans lequel nous vivons aujourd'hui et dans lequel nous pouvons être en Chine demain. Mais qu'est-ce qui se déplace en Chine lorsque nous allons en Chine ? Et qu'est-ce qui nous touche de la Chine ou ne nous touche pas ? Qu'est-ce qui est toujours semblable où que nous allions ? Et inversement, qu'est-ce qui est vraiment différent où que nous allions ? Ce qui est beau dans l'être humain, c'est que nous ne sommes pas des choses, nous ne sommes pas des objets. Nous sommes des êtres, donc nous changeons à chaque instant. Qu'est-ce qui change en vous lorsque le paysage change ? Qu'est-ce qui change en vous lorsque le gouvernement change ? Qu'est-ce qui change en vous lorsque l'histoire se met en mouvement ? Est-ce que nous nous mettons en mouvement à travers l'histoire ? Et comment l'histoire se déplace-t-elle à travers nous ?

Je crois que le théâtre est cet espace à même de porter ces histoires. Et l'une des choses les plus importantes dans ma vie fut la découverte de la danse comme vecteur pour porter l'histoire. L'histoire est en mouvement, c'est pourquoi de nombreuses cultures ont choisi la danse pour incarner l'histoire, et l'histoire n'est pas écrite, mais dansée. Cet homme à ma gauche s'est saisi de de cette histoire impossible à raconter avec des mots, parce que les mots seuls ne peuvent suffire. Ce qui m'a bouleversé dans ce travail, est cette idée que le seul témoignage possible vient du corps, et non de notre habitude à vouloir réduire l'histoire à des mots, quand justement l'histoire ne saurait se réduire. Le corps témoigne de la pleine dimension de l'histoire comme expérience.

FL : Il y a ce mot en lingala, *lobi*, et nous utilisons ce même mot pour dire hier et demain, donc si quelqu'un dit *lobi*, cela peut vouloir dire hier, et tout aussi bien demain. Je trouve cela fascinant, cette relation que les anciens ont inventé avec le temps, où les ancêtres se mêlent à ceux qui ne sont pas encore nés… Le contexte pourra peut-être vous indiquer s'il s'agit du futur ou du passé, mais en fait c'est juste un grand cycle, *lobi*, qui déplace la relation au temps, qui délaisse le temps chronologique, l'antiquité fait partie de demain, et demain n'est pourtant pas l'antiquité. Je suis né dans les années 70, donc les livres ont fait partie de ma culture, d'autant que mon père était instituteur, écrire et lire faisaient donc partie de ma vie. Et pourtant lorsque j'ai pris conscience du monde dans lequel je vivais, lorsque j'ai essayé de lui donner un sens, j'ai compris que les mots n'étaient peut-être pas assez, du moins les mots écrits. Car d'une certaine façon, les mots parlés constituent une manifestation physique. Je pourrais prendre plus de risques avec les mots parlés qu'avec l'écrit, car les mots parlés sont comme une respiration, ils témoignent du temps qui passent, ils sont voués à disparaître, laissant seulement derrière eux l'écho de quelque chose. Comment cette notion du temps qui lie passé et futur à travers le présent, sachant que tout se transforme toujours comme le corps lui-même, comment cette notion peut-elle dire quelque chose de notre temps et du lieu où l'on est ?

PS : En fait, si vous regardez dans les yeux de votre petite-fille, vous verrez le regard de votre arrière-grand-mère… Notre corps appartient à et est fait de tous ces gens. C'est cela la vie éternelle. Littéralement, ce n'est pas juste une notion métaphysique, mais au contraire une notion très physique. Pour moi, la pure physicalité de ce qui n'est plus est tellement puissante. Je pense à Guillermo Gómez Peña, un ami artiste performeur, qui raconte toujours que lorsqu'il s'assoit dans un café de Mexico pour siroter un capuccino et prendre des notes dans son cahier, il se doit de penser aux

The reason we get most things wrong in this life is because we don't know what the context of most things we are looking at is. To take an obvious stupid example, Europe after Brussels and the Paris bombings, it has joined the war on terror: "your freedom fighter is my terrorist". It is the same gesture. But two different sets of people read the same gesture in a completely opposite way because of the context. And so, theater is the art of creating a context so that a gesture has resonance. Resonance for me is this thing that has not only to do with how something speaks across generations and time, but also how it resonates in place. Because place is not actually about what it looks like, a place is about sound; place is about echo. And it is about deep listening, it is finding the point where truth resonates. Where you are actually achieving an interaction with the landscape, the place, and the place is answering back to you. And it is all about being able to go to a place, anywhere, and sit there and listen, and know everything that ever happened at that place. And realizing that every place is speaking.

FL: We dream of poetry, we hope that the work that we are doing is somewhat poetic, but what does poetry mean outside of a context? What does theater as a poetic act mean? At least I'm clear about one thing, that art cannot save Kisangani; but maybe no one is asking art to do that anyway. But what does it mean to come up with a poetic theatrical gesture in a context? In this scary America that is coming; the context of permanent violence between one and the other, the context of the commodification of human beings and lives and dreams, the commodification of beauty, what does it mean to make a theatrical gesture in a context like that one?

PS: I think one of the most beautiful parts of being alive in this period is that we can visit each other. We are travelers. And this idea of how deeply you travel and how deeply you look and how places in the world and histories relate to each other in your own body and in your own experience is a really important thing, and I just want to emphasize how important one part of the world is to another part of the world, that is to say, I can do something in America because I'm thinking about Faustin in Kisangani. And when I visit Kisangani and say, "This is what Faustin is dealing with," I go back to Los Angeles and see Los Angeles totally differently and I can tell my students in Los Angeles, "Do you realize what is happening in Kisangani?" And that changes what people in Los Angeles think they can do. We are only permissioned from somewhere else to do something we wouldn't dare to. It is acts of courage in distant locations that actually inspire people's imagination to transform their own situations. We all need some China of the imagination. We all need some place where a courageous act is possible in order to bring that home into our own reality and create a courageous act.

And so it is that resonance where you can actually imagine that you are not alone. For me, this idea of not being alone is crucial to theater. In fact, theater was invented to gather people, to say we are not alone. Theater gets us out of the "single great man" theory—nobody achieved anything on their own, and gets us into the idea that it is a community that is moving at any given time. There is not a historical fact, there is a dynamic. And at any given moment in history, the question is not, what are the facts?, the question is, what is the dynamic that makes certain things possible or not possible? Can we understand what the spark is? How things are moving or not moving? This is why theater was invented, to acknowledge and create a space to recognize a dynamic among people. And then the project of theater is the project of understanding equality and how can we create structures that demonstrate equality. When the whole world is given back to a mirror that shows unequality. And all these things are determined by where we stand. The question is where do you stand? Which side are you on? Those are literal questions in geography, in a landscape, and in a city. It is important to be standing somewhere in order to be able to say something. And if you are not standing there, keep your mouth shut. The nightmare is people that don't live somewhere speaking for the people who do live there. What does it mean to actually be in a deeper solidarity? By being part of and in a certain community? As opposed to being a tourist and artistic tourist, political tourist, and opportunist? Where is the omni-ground humility?

Standing in the real place makes you humble. It is easy to talk about the LAPD and the prison system until you are in it and then you realize it is not so easy to talk about it. And all the opinions of the world from outside the system will never move anything and will never have any impact in terms of changing the system, it is only the people that testify from within who are actually going to create change, so this gesture of rootedness, which is all about, where are your roots? I tell my

vingt générations qui l'ont précédé, travaillant dans les champs avant même l'aube et jusqu'après la tombée du jour pour qu'il puisse, lui, être assis là à siroter son capuccino. Et c'est pour cela que nous sommes sur cette terre, pour faire quelque chose que nos parents et nos grands-parents n'ont pas pu faire. Nous voici là, que pouvons-nous faire ? Et nous pouvons sentir non seulement le poids de cela, mais aussi la joie que cela procure. La planète a attendu pour ce que nous allons réaliser demain. Et de cela émane une autre sorte d'énergie, il y a certes la charge, mais aussi le pouvoir et la beauté dans les gestes que nous faisons.

La raison pour laquelle on se trompe sur la plupart des choses dans cette vie est parce que nous ignorons le contexte des choses que nous côtoyons. Il suffit de prendre un exemple évident et stupide, l'Europe qui, après Bruxelles et les attaques à Paris, a rejoint la guerre contre la terreur... « Ton combattant pour la liberté est mon terroriste » : il s'agit du même geste et pourtant deux groupes de personnes lisent ce même geste d'une façon totalement opposée et ceci en raison du contexte. Et pour moi, le théâtre est l'art de créer un contexte pour qu'un geste ait une résonance. La résonance est cette chose qui non seulement se rapporte à comment quelque chose fait son chemin à travers les générations et le temps, mais aussi comment cela résonne dans des lieux. Car le lieu n'est pas ce à quoi il ressemble, le lieu est dans le son, il se lit dans l'écho, dans cette écoute profonde, à la recherche de ce point où la vérité résonne, où vous réussissez à interagir avec ce qui vous entoure, avec le lieu et le lieu vous répond. Et il s'agit d'être capable d'aller dans un endroit, n'importe où, de s'asseoir et d'écouter et d'entendre tout ce qui s'est passé dans cet endroit. Et de prendre conscience que chaque endroit parle.

FL : On rêve de poésie, on espère que le travail que nous faisons recèle quelque part cette poésie, mais que signifie la poésie en dehors d'un contexte ? Que signifie le théâtre comme acte poétique ? Au moins, une chose est claire pour moi, le théâtre ne sauvera pas Kisangani, et peut-être que personne ne demande cela à l'art de toute façon. Mais qu'est-ce que cela signifie d'amener un geste théâtral poétique dans un contexte ? Dans cette Amérique qui va venir et qui fait tellement peur... Dans ce contexte de violence incessante des uns contre les autres, de marchandisation des êtres humains, des existences, des rêves, de marchandisation de la beauté, qu'est-ce que cela veut dire de produire un geste théâtral dans un tel contexte ?

PS : Et c'est ça qui est si beau dans le fait de vivre à notre époque, au moins nous pouvons nous rendre visite. Nous sommes des voyageurs... Et cette idée de la profondeur avec laquelle on voyage, de la profondeur avec laquelle on regarde et de comment les endroits du monde et les histoires sont liés les uns aux autres dans ton propre corps, dans ta propre expérience, cette idée-là est vraiment essentielle. Je voudrais juste insister sur l'importance qu'une partie du monde a pour une autre partie du monde, c'est-à-dire que je peux mettre en œuvre quelque chose en Amérique parce que je pense à ce que Faustin fait à Kisangani. Et lorsque je viens à Kisangani et découvre ce avec quoi Faustin négocie chaque jour, je reviens à Los Angeles et voit Los Angeles d'une façon totalement différente et je peux dire à mes étudiants à Los Angeles : « Vous vous rendez compte de ce qui se passe à Kisangani ? ». Et cela change ce que les gens à Los Angeles pensent qu'ils peuvent faire. Et c'est cet ailleurs qui nous donne la permission de faire ce qu'autrement nous n'oserions faire. Et ce sont ces actes de courage à l'œuvre dans des pays éloignés qui inspirent les gens et les poussent à transformer leur propre situation. Donc nous avons tous besoin d'une Chine de l'imagination, nous avons tous besoin d'un endroit où un acte courageux est possible pour le ramener chez nous, dans notre propre réalité, et poser à notre tour un acte courageux. Et c'est cette résonance qui permet de réaliser que nous ne sommes pas seuls. Et cette idée de ne pas être seul est au centre du théâtre. Le théâtre a en effet été inventé pour rassembler des gens, pour dire que nous ne sommes pas seuls.

Le théâtre nous a libéré de la théorie du Grand Homme Unique – personne, jamais, n'a réussi quoi que ce soit seul –, il nous montre comment, à chaque moment, c'est la communauté qui crée le mouvement. Il n'y a pas de faits historiques, il y a des dynamiques. Et à n'importe quel moment donné de l'histoire, la question n'a jamais été de savoir quels sont les faits, mais plutôt quelle est la dynamique qui a permis à certaines choses d'être possibles et d'autres pas ? Quelle fut l'étincelle ? Comment les choses ont-elles bougé ou pas ? C'est pourquoi on a inventé le théâtre, pour créer et affirmer un espace de reconnaissance des dynamiques à l'œuvre entre les gens. Et alors le projet du théâtre est aussi de comprendre l'égalité et de trouver comment construire des structures

students: what stories do you have the right to tell and what stories do you not have the right to tell? What stories are simply not your stories, so just shut up and get out of the way. Recognize, look in your own body, look in your own eyes, recognize what stories you are empowered to tell and recognize which stories you are absolutely not empowered to tell and respect that. Create the conditions for the people who should be telling the story. What you can do is deepen the resonance of their voices. But the idea of where you are standing, that's the heart and soul of it.

FL: Listening to you now, I remembered something I was reading by Fred Moten, who is an African American poet and thinker. He says we cannot represent ourselves, so we cannot be represented.

If theater is a space where we can negotiate the possibilities, the possibility of a circle, what goes always comes back and you could say that is the world as it should be, but we all know that we live in a world that is not like that. But how much are we ready to take responsibility? To give that circle a chance to exist? Even for a minute. Being responsible for your own life, but taking responsibility for your position in this circle, knowing that you can only represent yourself; but maybe you could create a space where it becomes possible for the person next to you to also represent themselves.

PS: We have created every architecture to actually cover that up, but in fact the circle is the reality, the ecosystem is the reality, the acknowledgment of the ecosystem. The question of the 21st century is going to be shared space. How do we share the air? How do we share the water? How do we actually recognize every single thing we do and have it shared? And so, the circle is actually the reality. Not the metaphor. And again this project of theater is the record of shared space.

You are not yourself, you are all the people that shape your life. You are all the people you imagined. You are all the people you are thinking about, who are not with you. You are carrying them with you all the time, every single day. There is no such thing as you. The more you look, you are everyone else in your life. It is just recognizing the you that turns out to be Faustin's circle.

Excerpts from a conversation at the Teatro Maria Matos Lisbon, as part of the Biennale Artista Na Cidade, with the support of EGEAC.

PETER SELLARS is an internationally renowned American theater director, noted for his unique stagings of classical and contemporary operas and plays. Sellars is a professor in the Department of World Arts and Cultures at UCLA and recipient of several fellowships and prizes, including the MacArthur Fellowship and the Erasmus Prize.

à même de fonder cette égalité. Et ce alors que le monde entier recule devant un miroir qui renvoie à toutes les inégalités.

Et toutes ces choses sont déterminées par l'endroit où nous nous tenons, l'espace est au cœur de ce que nous sommes, de la façon dont nous nous conduisons, de ce que nous voyons ou ne voyons pas. La question est donc quelle est notre position ? De quel côté nous tenons-nous ? Il est essentiel de se tenir quelque part pour dire quelque chose sur un endroit. Et si l'on n'est pas là, il vaut mieux se taire. Le cauchemar, ce sont ces gens qui ne vivent pas quelque part et qui parlent pour les gens qui y vivent. Que signifie être profondément solidaire ? N'est-ce pas faire partie et être dans une vraie communauté ? A l'inverse de la position du touriste, du touriste culturel, du touriste politique, de l'opportuniste… Comment retrouver une humilité tout terrain ? Etre au bon endroit force l'humilité. Il est facile de parler de la police de Los Angeles ou du système carcéral tant que l'on n'y a pas été, et c'est lorsqu'on y est qu'on mesure combien il est difficile d'en parler. Et toutes les opinions du monde venant de l'extérieur ne feront rien bouger et n'auront aucun impact sur le changement du système, seuls ceux qui témoignent de l'intérieur contribueront vraiment au changement, d'où cette action de s'ancrer… Tout est là, où sont nos racines ? Je dis toujours à mes étudiants : quelles histoires avez-vous le droit de raconter ou pas ? Quelles sont celles qui tout simplement ne sont pas vos histoires, donc taisez-vous et passez votre chemin. Il faut le reconnaître, il suffit de regarder dans son propre corps, dans ses propres yeux et reconnaître quelles histoires vous êtes en droit de raconter et quelles histoires ne vous appartiennent pas. Et respecter cela. Et créer les conditions pour que les gens qui devraient dire ces histoires puissent le faire. Tout ce que pouvez faire, c'est donner une plus grande résonance à leurs paroles. De fait, l'idée de savoir où l'on se tient, c'est le cœur et l'âme de tout cela.

FL : En t'écoutant maintenant m'est revenu quelque chose que j'ai lu de Fred Moten, ce poète et penseur afro-américain. Il disait que nous ne pouvions pas nous représenter nous-mêmes et donc que nous ne pouvions pas être représentés.

Donc si le théâtre est cet espace où l'on pourrait négocier la possibilité d'un cercle, cette figure où tout ce qui part revient toujours, et se dire que cela pourrait être le monde tel qu'il devrait être, même si nous savons tous que nous ne vivons pas dans un tel monde… Mais dans quelle mesure sommes-nous prêts à prendre nos responsabilités pour que ce cercle puisse exister ? Même une minute. Etre responsable de sa propre vie, mais aussi de sa position dans ce cercle, ayant conscience que l'on ne représente que soi-même, mais avec l'idée peut-être que l'on pourrait créer un espace où il devient possible pour les personnes à côté de nous de se représenter aussi.

PS : Toute architecture a été créée en effet dans ce but, le cercle est la réalité, l'écosystème est notre réalité, comme la reconnaissance de cet écosystème. Et la grande question du XXIe siècle sera bien celle du partage de l'espace. Comment nous allons partager l'air, comment nous allons partager l'eau… Comment nous allons prendre en compte chaque action que nous faisons pour la partager… C'est pourquoi le cercle est bien réel, ce n'est pas une métaphore. Et l'objet du théâtre qui est de rendre compte de cet espace partagé sera encore plus essentiel que jamais.

Vous n'êtes pas juste vous, vous êtes toutes les personnes qui ont façonné votre vie. Vous êtes toutes les personnes que vous imaginez, toutes les personnes auxquelles vous pensez et qui ne sont pas avec vous. Vous les emportez avec vous à chaque moment, chaque jour. Il ne s'agit pas de vous, mais plus vous y pensez, plus vous voyez que vous êtes fait de toutes ces personnes qui sont dans votre vie. Et vous reconnaissez ce *vous* qui en fait constitue le cercle de Faustin.

Extraits d'une conversation au Théâtre Maria Matos à Lisbonne (mai 2016), dans le cadre de la Biennale Artista Na Cidade, avec le soutien de EGEAC.

PETER SELLARS est un metteur en scène américain de renommée internationale, reconnu pour ses mises en scène uniques de pièces et d'opéras classiques et contemporains. Peter est Professeur au Département des Arts et Cultures à UCLA, il a reçu plusieurs distinctions et prix prestigieux, comme le prix MacArthur ou le prix Erasmus.

Thanks to Alhaji Alhassan, Andrea Börner, Christian Seethaler, Faustin Linyekula, Gideon Djakumah, Joe Osae-Addo, Lesley Lokko, Linus Müller, Mbatakora, Martin C. Hess, Peter Sellars, Reiner Zettl, Vera Kotschral, Virginie Dupray and Wolf Prix.